Maths Progress
Core Textbook

Series editors: Dr Naomi Norman and Katherine Pate

3

P Pearson

Published by Pearson Education Limited, 80 Strand, London, WC2R 0RL.

www.pearsonschoolsandfecolleges.co.uk

Text © Pearson Education Limited 2019
Project managed and edited by Just Content Ltd
Typeset by PDQ Digital Media Solutions Ltd
Original illustrations © Pearson Education Limited 2019
Cover illustration by Robert Samuel Hanson

The rights of Nick Asker, Jack Barraclough, Sharon Bolger, Gwenllian Burns, Greg Byrd, Lynn Byrd, Andrew Edmondson, Bobbie Johns, Catherine Murphy, Naomi Norman, Mary Pardoe, Katherine Pate, Harry Smith and Angela Wheeler to be identified as authors of this work have been asserted by them in accordance with the Copyright, Designs and Patents Act 1988.

First published 2019

22 21 20 19
10 9 8 7 6 5 4 3 2 1

British Library Cataloguing in Publication Data
A catalogue record for this book is available from the British Library.

ISBN 978 1 292 28003 5

Printed in Italy by LEGO S.p.A.

Note from the publisher
Pearson has robust editorial processes, including answer and fact checks, to ensure the accuracy of the content in this publication, and every effort is made to ensure this publication is free of errors. We are, however, only human, and occasionally errors do occur. Pearson is not liable for any misunderstandings that arise as a result of errors in this publication, but it is our priority to ensure that the content is accurate. If you spot an error, please do contact us at resourcescorrections@pearson.com so we can make sure it is corrected.

Contents

Maths Progress Second Edition

Confidence at the heart

Maths Progress Second Edition is built around a unique pedagogy that has been created by leading mathematics educational researchers and Key Stage 3 teachers in the UK. The result is an innovative structure, based around 10 key principles designed to nurture confidence and raise achievement.

Pedagogy – our 10 key principles

- Fluency
- Problem-solving
- Reflection
- Mathematical Reasoning
- Progression
- Linking
- Multiplicative Reasoning
- Modelling
- Concrete - Pictorial - Abstract (CPA)
- Relevance

This edition of Maths Progress has been updated based on feedback from thousands of teachers and students.

The Core Curriculum

Textbooks with tried-and-tested differentiation

Core Textbooks *For your whole cohort*

Based on a single, well-paced curriculum with built-in differentiation, fluency, problem-solving and reasoning so you can use them with your whole class. They follow the unique unit structure that's been shown to boost confidence and support every student's progress.

Support Books
Strengthening skills and knowledge

Provide extra scaffolding and support on key concepts for each lesson in the Core Textbook, giving students the mathematical foundations they need to progress with confidence.

Depth Books
Extending skills and knowledge

Deepen students' understanding of key concepts, and build problem-solving skills for each lesson in the Core Textbook so students can explore key concepts to their fullest.

Welcome to Maths Progress Second Edition Core Textbooks!

Building confidence

Pearson's unique unit structure has been shown to build confidence. Here's how it works.

Master

1 Students are helped to **master** fundamental knowledge and skills over a series of lessons.

Check

2 Before moving on with the rest of the unit, students **check** their understanding in a short formative assessment, and give an indication of their confidence level.

Master

Learn fundamental knowledge and skills over a series of lessons.

Unit opener
Lesson opener outlines lesson objectives, and links to the accompanying online content.

Hints
Guide students to help build problem-solving strategies throughout the course.

Warm up
Lessons begin with accessible questions designed to recap prior knowledge, and develop students' mathematical fluency in the facts and skills they will soon be using.

Challenge
Rich, problem-solving questions to help students apply what they've learned in the lesson and think differently.

Worked examples
Provide guidance around examples of key concepts with images, bar models, and other pictorial representations where needed.

Key point Explain key concepts and definitions where students need them.

Reflect Metacognitive questions that ask students to examine their thinking and understanding.

Check up

At the end of the Master lessons, students check their understanding with a short, formative Check Up test, to help decide whether to Strengthen or Extend their learning.

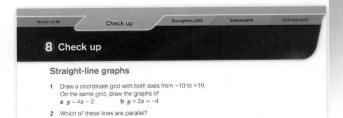

In areas where they have yet to develop a solid understanding or do not feel confident, they can choose to **strengthen** their learning.

3 Students decide on their personalised route through the rest of the unit:

Strengthen

Extend

Test

4 Finally, students do a **test** to determine their progression across the unit.

In areas where they performed well in the assessment and also feel confident, they can choose to **extend** their learning.

Strengthen
Students can choose the topics that they need more practice in. There are lots of hints and supporting questions to help.

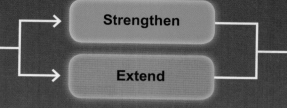

Extend
Students can apply and develop the maths they know in different situations.

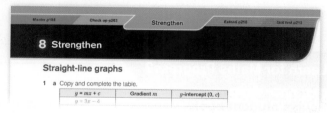

Test
Students can show everything they have learned and check their progress using the end of unit test.

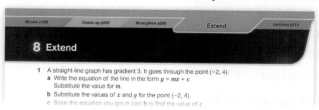

Students can use the Support and Depth Books at any point throughout the unit. They're designed to give the right level of support and additional problem-solving content to help strengthen students' understanding of key concepts.

Progress with confidence!

This innovative Key Stage 3 Mathematics course builds on the first edition KS3 Maths Progress (2014) course, drawing on input from thousands of teachers and students, and a 2-year study into the effectiveness of the course. All of this has come together with the latest cutting-edge approaches to shape Maths Progress Second Edition.

Take a look at the other parts of the series

*Active*Learn Service

The *Active*Learn service enhances the course by bringing together your planning, teaching and assessment tools, as well as giving students access to additional resources to support their learning. Use the interactive Scheme of Work, linked to all the teacher and student resources, to create a personalised learning experience both in and outside the classroom.

What's in ActiveLearn for Maths Progress?

- ☑ **Front-of-class student books** with links to PowerPoints, videos, animations and homework activities

- ☑ **96 new KS3 assessments and online markbooks,** including end-of-unit, end-of-term and end-of-year tests

- ☑ **Over 500 editable and printable homework worksheets** linked to each lesson and differentiated for Support, Core and Depth

- ☑ **Online, auto-marked homework activities**

- ☑ **Interactive Scheme of Work** makes re-ordering the course easy by bringing everything together into one curriculum for all students with links to Core, Support and Depth resources, and teacher guidance

- ☑ **Student access to videos, homework and online textbooks**

ActiveLearn Progress & Assess

The Progress & Assess service is part of the full ActiveLearn service, or can be bought as a separate subscription. It includes assessments that have been designed to ensure all students have the opportunity to show what they have learned through:

- a 2-tier assessment model
- approximately 60% common questions from Core in each tier
- separate calculator and non-calculator sections
- online markbooks for tracking and reporting
- mapped to indicative 9–1 grades

New *Assessment Builder*

Create your own classroom assessments from the bank of Maths Progress assessment questions by selecting questions on the skills and topics you have covered. Map the results of your custom assessments to indicative 9–1 grades using the custom online markbooks. *Assessment Builder* is available to purchase as an add-on to *Active*Learn Service or Progress & Assess subscriptions.

Purposeful Practice Books

Over 3,750 questions using minimal variation that:

- ✓ build in small steps to consolidate knowledge and boost confidence
- ✓ focus on strengthening skills and strategies, such as problem-solving
- ✓ help every student put their learning into practice in different ways
- ✓ give students a strong preparation for progressing to GCSE study.

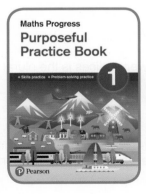
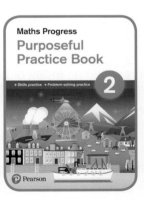

1 Indices and standard form

Master   Check up p15   Strengthen p17   Extend p22   Unit test p24

1.1 Indices

Active Learn
Homework

- Calculate combinations of indices and brackets, including nested brackets
- Use index laws to simplify expressions

Warm up

1 **Fluency** Which of these are raised to a power?
   8^2 64 5^3 625

2 What are the missing numbers?
   a $\frac{2}{2} = \square$ **b** $3^3 = \square$ **c** $5^3 = \square$ **d** $10^3 = \square$

   e $2^\square = 8$ **f** $3^\square = 9$ **g** $3^\square = 27$ **h** $4^\square = 16$

3 Work out
   a 2^4 **b** $3^2 \times 3$ **c** $2 \times 3^2 \times 5$ **d** $3^2 \times 10^3$

4 Work out
   a $(-4)^2$ **b** $(-4)^3$

   > **Q4 hint** $(-4)^2 = -4 \times -4 = \square$
   > $(-4)^3 = -4 \times -4 \times -4 = \square$

5 Use the priority of operations to calculate
   a $3 + 4^3$ **b** 2×3^2 **c** $2(1 + 3^2)$ **d** $(2 \times 5)^2$

6 Work out
   a $6 + (-3)^2$ **b** $6 - 3^2$ **c** $(-5)^2 - 5$
   d $-2 - 2^3$ **e** $(-4)^2 - 4^2$ **f** $5 - (-5)^3$

Key point
A small raised number is called an **index** or **power**. Indices is the plural of index.

7 **a** Use your calculator to work out
   i 2^5 **ii** $2^2 \times 2^3$

   > **Q7a hint** Use the power key on your calculator, $\boxed{y^x}$ or $\boxed{x^\square}$.

   b What do you notice about the answers in part **a**?
   c **Reasoning** What do you notice about the index in part **a i** and the indices in part **a ii**?
   d **Reasoning** Use your answer to part **c** to copy and complete $2^3 \times 2^4 = 2^\square$
      Check your answer to part **d** on your calculator.

8 Copy and complete the multiplication grid of powers of 3.
   Write your answers as powers of 3.
   The first one is done for you.

×	3^4	3^5	3^6
3^2	3^6		
3^3			
3^4			

9   Write each product as a single power.

   a $2^5 \times 2^3$ **b** $4^3 \times 4^3$ **c** 3×3^4

   d $5^3 \times 5^2$ **e** $7^2 \times 7^3 \times 7$ **f** $2^3 \times 2^4 \times 2^2$

   g $(-3)^2 \times (-3)^3$ **h** $-2 \times (-2)^2$ **i** $(-8)^3 \times (-8)^4 \times (-8)$

> **Q9c hint**
> 3 can be written as 3^1 (3 to the power of 1).

10 Write these calculations using powers of a single number.
    Give your answers in index form.

   a $8 \times 2^4 = 2^\square \times 2^4 = 2^\square$ **b** $9 \times 3^3 = 3^\square \times 3^3 = 3^\square$

   c 64×4^2 **d** 3×27

   e 25×125 **f** $16 \times 4 \times 8$

> **Q10 hint** 'Index form' means numbers raised to a power.

11 **Problem-solving**   One byte of computer memory is 8 bits of data.

   a Write 8 as a power of 2.

   b A sector of a disk drive on Petra's computer contains 2^{12} bytes of data.
       Work out the number of bits it contains.
       Write your answer as a power of 2.

   c Write your answer to part **b** as a simple number (not using powers).

12 Brendan works out $\dfrac{3 \times 3 \times 3 \times 3}{3 \times 3}$ by simplifying first, like this:

$$\frac{\cancel{3}^1 \times \cancel{3}^1 \times 3 \times 3}{\cancel{3}_1 \times \cancel{3}_1} = \frac{9}{1} = 9$$

   Use Brendan's method to work out

   a $\dfrac{5 \times 5 \times 5}{5}$ **b** $\dfrac{7 \times 7 \times 7 \times 7}{7 \times 7 \times 7}$ **c** $\dfrac{3 \times 3 \times 3 \times 3 \times 3}{3 \times 3}$

13 **a** Work out $\dfrac{2 \times 2 \times 2 \times 2 \times 2 \times 2 \times 2}{2 \times 2 \times 2 \times 2}$ by simplifying.

   b Write your answer to part **a** as a power of 2.

   c Copy and complete $\dfrac{2 \times 2 \times 2 \times 2 \times 2 \times 2 \times 2}{2 \times 2 \times 2 \times 2} = \dfrac{2^\square}{2^\square} = 2^\square$

   d Copy and complete $2^5 \div 2^3 = \dfrac{2^5}{2^3} = \dfrac{\square \times \square \times \square \times \square \times \square}{\square \times \square \times \square} = 2^\square$

   e **Reasoning**   How can you work out the answers using the indices?

14 Write each division as a single power.

   a $5^5 \div 5^2$ **b** $4^6 \div 4$ **c** $3^{10} \div 3^7$ **d** $2^8 \div 2^7$

   e $5^3 \div 5$ **f** $6^8 \div 6^5$ **g** $(-2)^3 \div -2$ **h** $(-3)^4 \div (-3)^3$

15 Write these calculations using powers of a single number.
    Give your answers in index form.

   a $16 \div 2^2 = 2^\square \div 2^2 = 2^\square$ **b** $32 \div 2^2$ **c** $3^3 \div 9$

16 Problem-solving A memory stick holds up to 2^{28} bytes of data.
Alan's computer hard drive holds up to 2^{40} bytes of data.
How many memory sticks does Alan need if he wants to save all the data on his computer hard drive on memory sticks?

17 Write each calculation as a single power.

Q17 hint Work from left to right.

a $3^2 \times 3^4 \div 3^3$
b $4^5 \div 4^3 \times 4^2$
c $5^2 \times 5^3 \div 5$
d $2^5 \times 2^4 \div 2^3 \div 2$

18 Reasoning Are the brackets necessary in these calculations?

a $2^7 \div (2^2 \times 2^3)$
b $4^8 \div (4^2 \times 4^3)$
c $2^8 \div (2^7 \div 2^5)$
d $(2^8 \div 2^7) \div 2^5$

Q18 hint Work out each calculation with brackets (using the priority of operations) and without brackets (working from left to right). Do you get the same answer?

Key point   Some calculations have nested brackets. This is one set of brackets inside another set of brackets. Sometimes the outer brackets are square brackets [ ] to make them easier to see. Use the priority of operations to work out calculations inside the outer brackets.

Worked example

Work out $[10 - (5 - 2)]^2$.

$10 - (5 - 2) = 10 - 3$ ———— First, work out the calculation inside the square brackets.

$\qquad = 7$

$\qquad 7^2 = 49$ ———— Then complete the calculation.

---

19 Work out these calculations. Check your answers using a calculator.

a $[2 \times (1 + 2)]^2$
b $[(6 + 10) \div 2]^2$
c $[11 - (9 - 3)]^3$
d $[(3 + 5) \times 2]^2$
e $[(3 + 12) \div 5]^2$
f $[12 \div 2 - (8 - 7)]^2$
g $10 - [10 - (10 - 1)^2]$
h $[48 \div (5 - 3)^3 - 4] \div 2$

Q19 hint Input square brackets as round brackets on your calculator.

Challenge

The diagram shows three squares.
Which one of these calculations gives the total area?

A $(3 + 5 + 5)^2$
B $3^2 + (2 \times 5)^2$
C $3^2 + 2 \times 5^2$
D $[3 + (2 \times 5)]^2$

3 cm   5 cm   5 cm

Reflect   For each statement **A**, **B** and **C**, choose a score:

1 – strongly disagree   2 – disagree   3 – agree   4 – strongly agree

A I always try hard in mathematics.

B Doing mathematics never makes me worried.

C I am good at mathematics.

For any statement you scored less than 3, write down two things you could do so that you agree more strongly in future.

1.2 Calculations and estimates

Active Learn
Homework

- Calculate combinations of powers, roots, fractions and brackets
- Estimate answers to calculations

Warm up

1 **Fluency** Round
  a 71 cm to the nearest 10 cm
  b £2.99 to the nearest pound
  c 15 to the nearest square number
  d 65 to the nearest cube number

2 Estimate the cost of 9 tickets at £19.80 each.

3 Use the priority of operations to work out
  a $24 \div 0.1$
  b $(-3)^3$
  c $6 \times \sqrt{81}$
  d $\sqrt[3]{125}$
  e $(\sqrt[3]{125} + 3) \times 6$
  f $\sqrt{1600} = \sqrt{\square \times 100} = \sqrt{\square} \times \sqrt{100}$
  g $\sqrt{4 \times 16} = \sqrt{4} \times \sqrt{16} = \square$
  h $\dfrac{4^2 + 4}{1 + \sqrt{16}}$

> **Q3e hint** Use the priority of operations.

> **Q3h hint** Work out $(4^2 + 4) \div (1 + \sqrt{16})$

4 Work out these calculations. Write each answer in its simplest form.
  a $\dfrac{4}{5} \times \dfrac{4}{5}$
  b $\dfrac{25 \times 8}{5}$
  c $\dfrac{7 \times 27}{9 \times 14}$
  d $\dfrac{16 \times 12}{6 \times 4}$

> **Q4c hint** Simplify first.
> $\dfrac{^1\cancel{7} \times 27^3}{_1\cancel{9} \times \cancel{14}_2}$

5 Work out
  a $\sqrt[3]{-8}$
  b $\sqrt[3]{-27}$
  c $\sqrt[3]{-125}$
  d $\sqrt[3]{-1000}$

> **Q5a hint**
> $-\square \times -\square \times -\square = -8$

> **Key point** To estimate the square root of a number:
> Round to the nearest square number. Then square root $\sqrt{\square}$.
> To estimate the cube root of a number:
> Round to the nearest cube number. Then cube root $\sqrt[3]{\square}$.

6 Estimate
  a $\sqrt{17}$
  b $\sqrt{23.9}$
  c $\sqrt{120}$
  d $\sqrt[3]{8.5}$
  e $\sqrt[3]{-65}$
  f $\sqrt[3]{-0.99}$

> **Key point** An **overestimate** is an estimate that is greater than the accurate answer.
> An **underestimate** is an estimate that is less than the accurate answer.

7 A campsite charges £12.75 per adult and £8.95 per child for one night's camping.
  a Estimate the cost for a group of two adults and three children camping for two nights.
  b **Reasoning** Is your estimate an overestimate or underestimate? Explain.

8 **Problem-solving** A roll of turf is 61 cm wide and 164 cm long. One roll costs £3.99.

Q8a hint Convert metres to centimetres. Sketch a diagram to help you.

  a Estimate the cost of turf required for each of the sizes of lawn.

  i 3 m by 3.2 m   **ii** 2.4 m by 6.4 m   **iii** 4.8 m by 16 m

  b Use a calculator to work out each answer.
  How good were your estimates?

  c Is it better to overestimate or underestimate the amount of turf? Explain.

9 **Problem-solving** A roll of carpet is 4 m wide. It costs £8.98 per square metre. You can buy any length of carpet.

  a Estimate the cost of carpet required for each of these rooms.

  i 3.6 m by 1.2 m

  ii 4.65 m by 3.71 m

  iii 8.15 m by 6.35 m

Q9a hint Think about how many widths of carpet you need for one side of the room.

  b Use a calculator to work out each answer.
  How good were your estimates?

10 a Estimate 34 × 57 by rounding both numbers up.
  b Is your answer to part **a** an overestimate or underestimate?
  c Estimate 34 × 57 by rounding both numbers down.
  d Is your answer to part **c** an overestimate or underestimate?
  e Estimate 34 × 57 by rounding one number up and one number down.
  f Repeat part **e** but rounding the numbers the opposite way.
  g Which estimate do you think is closest to the exact answer?
  Use a calculator to check if you are correct.

11 To estimate a multiplication or addition, Sally says,
  'It is best to round one number up and the other number down.'
  To estimate a division or subtraction, Sally says,
  'It is best to round both numbers up or both numbers down.'
  a For each of these calculations, work out an estimate using Sally's 'rule'.

  i 11.6 × 12.3   **ii** 58.1 ÷ 11.5   **iii** 71.1 − 52.2

  iv 2778 + 1217   **v** $9.5 × 10.85^2$ **vi** 577 ÷ 171

  b Now work out the calculations by rounding the numbers in another way.
  c Which estimate is closer to the accurate answer?
  d What do you think of Sally's rule? Explain.

12 a Use the priority of operations to estimate the answers to these calculations.

  i $(14.8 - \sqrt[3]{124}) \times 2.19$ **ii** $5.03 \times (\sqrt{35} + 3.79)$

  iii $(\sqrt[3]{26} - 1.93) \times 8.1^2$ **iv** $(22.49 + \sqrt[3]{-7.7}) \div 0.09$

  b Use a calculator to work out each answer.
  Give your answers correct to 1 decimal place.

13 **Reasoning** Pam says, 'Another estimate for the calculation in part **a ii** of Q12 is −10.'
  Explain why Pam is wrong.

Q13 hint 35 has a positive and a negative square root. The principal square root of a number is always the positive square root. For example, $\sqrt{4} = 2$

14 a Estimate the answers to these calculations.

i $\dfrac{82.36 - 63.25}{\sqrt{15.4}}$ ii $\dfrac{449 - 9.3}{15.1 + 6.7}$

Q14a ii hint Round the calculation in the numerator and the calculation in the denominator to make it an easy division.

iii $\dfrac{\sqrt{3.9 \times 16.1}}{2.1^2}$ iv $\dfrac{\sqrt{1600}}{\sqrt{24.9} \div 0.98}$

b Use a calculator to work out each answer.
Give your answers correct to 1 decimal place.

15 a Work out

i $\sqrt{\dfrac{64}{4}}$ ii $\dfrac{\sqrt{64}}{\sqrt{4}}$

b What do you notice?

c Work out

i $\sqrt{\dfrac{125}{5}}$ ii $\sqrt{\dfrac{144}{16}}$

d Reasoning Did you use the same or different methods to work out the answers to parts **c i** and **c ii**? Explain.

e Work out

i $\sqrt{\dfrac{1}{9}}$ ii $\sqrt{\dfrac{9}{25}}$

Q15e i hint

$\dfrac{\sqrt{1}}{\sqrt{9}} = \dfrac{\square}{\square}$

The answer is a fraction.

16 a i Work out $\left(\dfrac{2}{3}\right)^2$ as a fraction in its simplest form.

Q16a i hint Work out $\dfrac{2}{3} \times \dfrac{2}{3}$.

ii Work out $\dfrac{2^2}{3^2}$ as a fraction in its simplest form.

iii What do you notice?

b i Work out $\left(\dfrac{2}{3}\right)^3$ as a fraction in its simplest form.

ii Work out $\dfrac{2^3}{3^3}$ as a fraction in its simplest form.

iii What do you notice?

c Reasoning Copy and complete this rule:
To find a power of a fraction, work out _____.

17 a Work out these calculations.
Give your answers as fractions in their simplest form where necessary.

i $\left(\dfrac{3}{5}\right)^2$ ii $\left(\dfrac{7}{9}\right)^2$ iii $\left(\dfrac{4}{5}\right)^3$ iv $\left(\dfrac{3}{4}\right)^3$

b Reasoning   Is the square of a fraction bigger or smaller than the original fraction? What about a cube of a fraction?

18 Work out these calculations. Give your answers as integers or mixed numbers.

a $\left(\dfrac{18}{3}\right)^2$ **b** $\left(\dfrac{7}{2}\right)^2$ **c** $\left(\dfrac{11}{5}\right)^2$

d $\left(1\dfrac{1}{5}\right)^2$ **e** $\left(2\dfrac{1}{3}\right)^2$

Q18d hint Write $1\dfrac{1}{5}$ as an improper fraction.

Work out $\dfrac{(4 \times 5)^2}{5 \times 2^2}$

$$\dfrac{(4 \times 5)^2}{5 \times 2^2} = \dfrac{4^2 \times 5^2}{5 \times 2^2}$$

$$= \dfrac{4 \times 4 \times 5 \times 5}{5 \times 2 \times 2}$$

$$= \dfrac{\cancel{4}^2 \times \cancel{4}^2 \times \cancel{5}^1 \times 5}{\cancel{2}^1 \times \cancel{2}^1 \times \cancel{5}^1}$$

> Cancel the common factors.
> $5 \times 2 \times 2$ is the same as $2 \times 2 \times 5$

$$= 2 \times 2 \times 1 \times 5$$

$$= 20$$

19 Problem-solving Copy and complete these calculations

a $\sqrt{\dfrac{25}{\square}} = \dfrac{\square}{6}$ **b** $\left(\dfrac{1}{\square}\right)^3 = \dfrac{\square}{8}$ **c** $\left(\dfrac{\square}{7}\right)^2 = \dfrac{4}{\square}$

20 Work out

a $\dfrac{3^2 \times 4^2}{2^2}$ **b** $\dfrac{(6 \times 2)^2}{3^2}$ **c** $\dfrac{16 \times 18}{(2 \times 3)^2}$

d $\dfrac{(3 \times 4)^3}{3^2 \times 4^2}$ **e** $\dfrac{6^2 \times 2^3}{2^2 \times 3}$ **f** $\dfrac{(2 \times 5)^3}{5^2 \times 2}$

Challenge   Copy and complete this calculation

$$\dfrac{\sqrt[3]{\square} + 15.8}{\square}$$

so that the estimated answer is
a 2   **b** 3   **c** −5

Reflect   Antony looks back at Q14 part **a** in this lesson. He says, 'For part **ii**, I wanted to divide by a nice number, so first I looked at the calculation in the denominator. I estimated this to be 20.'
What do you think Antony estimated for the numerator? Explain.
What do you think of Antony's method? Explain.
Look back at part **iv** of Q14 part **a**.
What did you do first to estimate this calculation? Why?
Could you have done it a better way? Explain.

1.3 More indices

- Understand numbers written in index form that are raised to a power
- Understand negative and zero indices
- Use powers of 10 and their prefixes

*Active*Learn
Homework

Warm up

1 **Fluency** What is
   a the missing number in $10^4 = \square$
   b 0.01 as a fraction
   c $\frac{1}{1000}$ as a decimal
   d the reciprocal of these numbers? 2   7 $\frac{1}{5}$

2 Write each calculation as a single power.
   a 4×4 **b** $3 \times 3 \times 3 \times 3 \times 3$
   c $5^2 \times 5^2$ **d** 9×9^4
   e $10^3 \times 10^4$ **f** $2^5 \div 2^2$
   g $10^5 \div 1000$ **h** 8×2^2

3 Convert
   a 45 m to kilometres   **b** 250 mm to metres.

4 **Reasoning**
   a Copy and complete the table of equivalent expressions.

Expression	Number in index form raised to a power	Single power
$4^3 \times 4^3$	$(4^3)^\square$	$4^\square$
$7^3 \times 7^3 \times 7^3$	$(7^3)^\square$	$7^\square$
$3^2 \times 3^2 \times 3^2 \times 3^2$	$(3^2)^\square$	$3^\square$

   b What is the rule for writing a number in index form raised to a power as a single power?

   Q4b hint Compare the second and third columns of each row in the table in part **a**.

5 Write each of these as a single power.
   a $(2^3)^4$ **b** $(11^2)^6$
   c $(10^3)^8$ **d** $(2^4)^7$
   e $(6^7)^4$

6 Write
   a 8^4 as a power of 2
   b 16^5 as a power of 4
   c 125^4 as a power of 5.

   Q6a hint
   $8 = 2^\square$
   $8^4 = (2^\square)^4$
   $= 2^\square$

7 a Copy and complete the sequence.
Write your answers as whole numbers or as
decimals or fractions for numbers less than 1.

b Work out 10^{-6} using your calculator.
Add the result to your sequence.

10^5	100 000
10^4	10 000
10^3	
10^2	
10^1	
10^0	
10^{-1}	
10^{-2}	
10^{-3}	
10^{-4}	
10^{-5}	

$\Big\} \div 10$
$\Big\} \div 10$

8 a To write 10^{-2} as a fraction, copy and complete
$$10^{-2} = \frac{1}{10^{\square}}$$

b Copy and complete these statements.

  i $10^{-3} = \frac{1}{10^{\square}}$ **ii** $10^{-1} = \frac{1}{10^{\square}}$

  iii $\frac{1}{10^6} = 10^{\square}$ **iv** $\frac{1}{10^9} = 10^{\square}$

  v The reciprocal of 10^4 is $10^{\square}$.

c Copy and complete the rule: $10^{-n} = \frac{1}{10^{\square}}$

> **Key point** Some powers of 10 have a name called a **prefix**.
> Each prefix is represented by a letter. For example, mega means 10^6 and is represented by
> the letter M, as in MW for megawatt.

9 Copy and complete the table of prefixes.

> **Q9 hint** The prefix micro is
> represented by μ. This is a
> Greek letter, pronounced 'mu'.

Prefix	Letter	Power	Number
tera	T	10^{12}	1 000 000 000 000
giga	G		1 000 000 000
mega	M	10^6	
kilo	k		1000
deci	d	10^{-1}	
centi	c		0.01
milli	m	10^{-3}	
micro	μ		0.000 001
nano	n	10^{-9}	
pico	p		0.000 000 000 001

10 For each number, write its equivalent power of 10 and its prefix, if it has one.

a one million   b $\frac{1}{100}$ c one billion

d $\frac{1}{10}$ e $\frac{1}{10\,000}$ f one trillion

g $\frac{1}{100\,000}$ h one billionth   i $\frac{1}{1000}$

11 Use the table in Q9 to work out these conversions.
Write your answers as powers of 10.

a 1 kilometre (km) = ☐m   b 1 microsecond (µs) = ☐s

c 1 megatonne (Mt) = ☐t   d 1 picogram (pg) = ☐g

e 1 terahertz (THz) = ☐Hz   f 1 nanometre (nm) = ☐m

12 How many

a µg in a gram   b pm in a metre

c dl in a litre   d nanoseconds in a second?

> **Q12a hint** From the prefix table,
> $1\,\mu g = 10^{-6}g = \frac{1}{1\,000\,000}$ g.
> So 1 g = ☐ µg.

13 Convert

a 5 m to µm   b 2.5 g to mg

c 4 GW to watts   d 1.9 s to nanoseconds

e 4.23 g to picograms f 5000 µg to grams.

> **Q13a hint** How many µm are in a metre?

14 **Problem-solving** A nanorobot that can repair scar tissue is 1 µm wide.
How many nanorobots can fit across a scar 2.5 mm wide?

> **Q14 hint** Convert both measurements to the same units first.

15 Copy and complete the sequence.
Write your answers as whole numbers and fractions.

2^5	32
2^4	16
2^3	
2^2	
2^1	
2^0	
2^{-1}	
2^{-2}	
2^{-3}	
2^{-4}	
2^{-5}	

$\Big\} \div 2$
$\Big\} \div 2$

16 **Reasoning** a What do you notice about 10^0 (in Q7) and 2^0 (in Q15)?
b Use your calculator to work out n^0 for other values of n. What do you notice?

17 Reasoning

    a What do you notice about 10 raised to a negative power (in Q7) and 2 raised to a negative power (in Q15)?

    b Use your calculator to work out $n^{-\square}$ for other values of n.
    What do you notice?

18 Write 2^{-3} as a fraction.

19 Copy and complete

    a $2^{-3} = \dfrac{1}{2^{\square}}$ **b** $2^{-4} = \dfrac{1}{2^{\square}}$ **c** $2^{-1} = \dfrac{1}{2^{\square}}$ **d** $\dfrac{1}{2^2} = 2^{\square}$

    e $\dfrac{1}{2^6} = 2^{\square}$ **f** The reciprocal of 2^5 is $2^{\square}$.   **g** $2^{-n} = \dfrac{1}{2^{\square}}$.

20 Evaluate

    a 3^{-2} **b** 5^{-3}

    c 6^{-1} **d** 8^0

> **Q20 hint Evaluate** means 'find the value of'.

21 Write each calculation as a single power.

    a $10^5 \times 10^{-2}$ **b** $4^{-5} \times 4^3$ **c** $2^{-5} \times 2^{-2}$

    d $10^3 \times 10^{-8}$ **e** $10^3 \div 10^5$ **f** $2^{-5} \div 2^{-2}$

    g $5^{-2} \div 5^3$ **h** $3^3 \div 3^{-4}$

> **Q21 hint** Add the indices when multiplying powers. Subtract the indices when dividing powers.

22 Work out these calculations.
    Write each answer as a whole number or a fraction.

    a $2^3 \div 2^5$ **b** $4^3 \times 4^{-4}$ **c** $2^3 \times 2^3 \div 2^7$ **d** $3^5 \div 3^5$

    e $1 \div 2^{-3}$ **f** $\dfrac{3^4 \times 3^2}{3^3}$ **g** $\dfrac{1}{2^3 \times 2^2}$ **h** $\dfrac{4^2 \times 4^6}{4^5}$

Challenge

1   **a** Work out

      i $\left(\dfrac{2}{6}\right)^2$ **ii** $\left(\dfrac{6}{2}\right)^{-2}$ **iii** $\left(\dfrac{10}{5}\right)^2$ **iv** $\left(\dfrac{5}{10}\right)^{-2}$

    b What do you notice?

2 Repeat Q1 using powers of 3 and −3.

3 Copy and complete the rule:
    A negative power of a fraction is the same as _____.

4 Use your calculator to test the rule with other negative powers of fractions.

Reflect   Carla says, 'Mathematics is often about spotting patterns.'
Do you agree with her? Explain.
Why does it help to spot patterns in mathematics? Explain.

> **Hint** Look back at this lesson and the previous lesson. Can you find any questions where you were spotting a pattern? Where else in mathematics have you used pattern spotting?

1.4 Standard form

Active Learn
Homework

- Write large and small numbers using standard form
- Enter and read standard form numbers on a calculator
- Order numbers written in standard form

Warm up

1 **Fluency** How many
   a grams in 1 kg   **b** metres in 5 km   **c** metres in 7 Gm?

> **Q1c hint**
> 1 Gm = 1 000 000 000 m

2 Copy and complete
   a $3 \times 3 \times 3 \times 3 \times 3 = 3^{\square}$ **b** $10^6 = \square$
   c $\frac{1}{1000} = 10^{\square}$ **d** $6000 = 6 \times \square$
   e $25\,000 = 2.5 \times \square$ **f** $31\,000\,000 = 3.1 \times \square$
   g $2\,300\,000 = \square$ million   **h** $8\,440\,000 = \square$ million

3 Work out
   a 2×10^3 **b** 6×10^6 **c** 7.1×10^7 **d** 3.9×10^9

> **Key point** Multiplying by a negative power of 10 is the same as dividing by a positive power of 10.
> For example, $3 \times 10^{-4} = 3 \times \frac{1}{10^4} = \frac{3}{10^4}$
> $\qquad\qquad\qquad = 3 \div 10\,000 = 0.0003.$

4 **a** Work out
   i 7×10^{-2} **ii** 5×10^{-3} **iii** 3.8×10^{-5} **iv** 7.1×10^{-9}
   v 1.2×10^{-4} **vi** 3×10^{-6} **vii** 4×10^{-1} **viii** 1×10^{-9}
   b Does multiplying a number by a negative power of 10 make it bigger or smaller?

> **Key point** A positive number written in **standard form** is a number between 1 and 10 multiplied by 10 to a power.
> Using algebra, standard form is $A \times 10^n$ where $1 \leqslant A < 10$ and n is an integer.

5 Which of these numbers are written in standard form?
   A 9.3×10^5 **B** 25×10^7 **C** 6×10^{-5}
   D $10\,000$ **E** 5.7×2^{10} **F** 0.83×10^{-7}
   G 10×10^6 **H** 7.2 million   **I** 1.09×10^{12}
   J -2.1×10^4 **K** 9.7×10^2 **L** 7.52×10^{-4}

Write each number using standard form.

a 230 000

   $230\,000 = 2.3 \times 10^5$

b 0.000 453

   $0.000\,453 = 4.53 \times 10^{-4}$

> 2.3 lies between 1 and 10.
> Multiply by the power of 10 needed to give the original number.
> 2 3 0 0 0 0

> 4.53 lies between 1 and 10.
> Multiply by the power of 10 needed to give the original number.
> 0 · 0 0 0 4 5 3

6 Write each number using standard form.
   a 4200
   b 9 000 000
   c 27
   d $0.0064 = 6.4 \times 10^{\square}$
   e 0.0219
   f 0.000 000 7
   g 0.3
   h 0.000 000 000 099

7 **Reasoning** Jacqui writes 6.4 billion in standard form as 6.4×10^6
   a What mistake has she made?
   b Write 6.4 billion in standard form.

8 **Problem-solving** Write each scientific quantity using scientific notation (standard form).
   a Quasar SDSS 1044-0125 is one of the furthest known objects in space
      at a distance of 240 000 000 000 000 000 000 000 000 m from Earth.
   b One of the smallest known particles is the neutron of an atom, with an estimated
      diameter of 0.000 000 000 000 0018 m.
   c The temperature of the Sun at its core is 15 million °C.
   d Botulin is the main ingredient of Botox. It is so poisonous that just 0.000 000 075 g is
      enough to kill a person.

9 Write each answer
      i as an ordinary number
      ii using standard form.
   a The mass of the Hubble space telescope is 11 000 kg.
      Convert this to grams.
   b The distance of the Sun from the Earth is 149 600 000 000 m.
      Convert this to kilometres.
   c The diameter of the red supergiant star Betelgeuse is 1350 Gm.
      Convert this to metres.
   d The diameter of a human hair is 25 µm. Convert this to metres.
   e A granule of quartz has a mass of 1.4 mg. Convert this to grams.

> **Q9 hint** Look at the table in lesson 1.3 Q9.

10 These numbers are written in standard form.
    Write them as ordinary numbers.
    a 3.6×10^4
    b 9.27×10^6
    c 1.8×10^{-2}
    d 7.5×10^{-7}
    e 5.4×10^0
    f Write the numbers in parts **a** – **e** in ascending order.

11 **Reasoning** Here are some incorrect answers given by students when asked to write
    numbers in standard form. Rewrite each answer correctly.
    a 55×10^{11}
    b 0.732×10^8
    c 102×10^{-9}
    d 0.045×10^{-15}

12 Reasoning

  a The maximum distance of Pluto from Earth is 7.38×10^{12} m.

   i Is the number 7.38×10^{12} written using standard form?

   ii Write 7.38×10^{12} as an ordinary number.

   iii Enter the number into your calculator and press the = key.
       Compare your calculator display with the standard form number.
       Explain how your calculator displays a number in standard form.

  b Gold leaf is approximately 1.25×10^{-7} m thick.

   i Write 1.25×10^{-7} m as an ordinary number.

   ii Enter the number into your calculator and press the = key.
       Compare your calculator display with the standard form number.

13 Problem-solving Vega is 2.39×10^{17} m from Earth and Pollux is 3.2×10^{17} m from Earth.
Which is closer?

14 Problem-solving The distance of each space object from Earth is shown here. Write the objects in order, from closest to furthest from Earth.

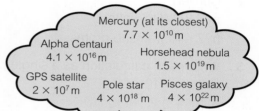

15 Problem-solving An optical microscope can be used to see objects as small as 2×10^{-7} m.

  a Which of these objects can be seen with it?

  b The smallest transistor in a computer chip is 2.6×10^{-7} m. Can this be seen using the microscope?

  c Write the objects in order of size, from smallest to largest.

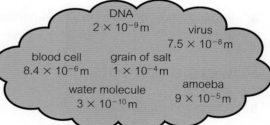

Challenge   A 3D electron microscope magnifies 100 000 times.
The diameter of a molecule of insulin appears to be 0.5 mm when viewed using the microscope. Work out the actual diameter. Give your answer in metres using standard form.

Reflect   Sophie and Jamie discuss how they used the worked example in this lesson.

Sophie says, 'I read the whole worked example before starting Q6. I read each question and its answer. If I wasn't sure how to get the answer, then I read the note box.'

Jamie says, 'I went straight to Q6. Then, I looked back at the questions, answers and note boxes in the worked example to help me when I needed to.'

Write a sentence explaining how you used the worked example in this lesson. How did it help you? Compare with other people in your class.

1 Check up

Indices and powers of 10

1   Write each calculation as a power of a single number.
   a $5^3 \times 5^2$ **b** $3^{10} \div 3^7$
   c $7^4 \times 7 \times 7^3$ **d** $(-6)^4 \div (-6)^3$
   e $4^4 \times 4^3 \div 4^2$ **f** 8×2^7
   g 9×3^7 **h** $(7^3)^5$

2   Convert
   a $3.8\,\text{GW}$ to watts
   b 7 milligrams to grams.

3   Write each calculation as a single power.
   a $10^{-3} \times 10^{-2}$
   b $2^{10} \div 2^{-5}$
   c $3^{-7} \div 3^{-9}$

4   Write each of these as a whole number or a fraction in its simplest form.
   a 5^{-2} **b** 2^0

Powers and roots

5   Which two calculations give the same answer? Show working.
   A $3^2 \times 4^2$ **B** $3^2 \times 4$ **C** $(3 \times 4)^2$ **D** 3×4^2

6   Work out $\sqrt[3]{-64}$.

7   Work out
   a $(-2)^3 + 3$ **b** $10 - (-3)^2$.

8   Work these out as whole numbers or fractions in their simplest form.
   a $\left(\dfrac{3}{5}\right)^2$
   b $\dfrac{2^3 \times 6^2}{2}$
   c $\dfrac{(2 \times 5)^2}{8 \times 50}$

9   Estimate the answers to these calculations.
   a $(\sqrt{69} - 3.5) \times 3.4$
   b $(9.6 - 15.3) \times (8.6 + 9.8)$
   c $\dfrac{56.4 + \sqrt[3]{30}}{7.8 \times 4.12}$

Standard form

10 Write each of these as an ordinary number.

  a 4.5×10^4 **b** 1.2×10^{-3}

11 Which of these numbers are written using standard form?

  A 10×10^4 **B** 5.2×10^{-4} **C** -2.5×10^2 **D** 43×10^{-3}

12 Write each number using standard form.

  a 750 000   **b** 0.000 000 02   **c** 8.3 billion

13 A student is asked to write an answer in standard form.

  The student incorrectly writes $371 \times 10^{-4.}$

  Rewrite the answer correctly, so that it is in standard form.

14 It has been estimated that the Arctic may hold 14 000 000 000 000 litres of oil.

  Write this

  a using a suitable prefix   **b** using standard form.

15 The recommended adult daily intake for vitamin B12 is $2.4 \times 10^{-6}\,\text{g}$ and for iodine is $1.5 \times 10^{-4}\,\text{g}$.

  Which does an adult need most of – B12 or iodine?

Challenge

1 Insert brackets in this calculation to give an answer of 4.

$$\frac{-4^2 + 8 \times 3}{10}$$

2 **a** Copy and complete the pattern.

     $4 + 2^2 = \square$

     $4 + 2^2 + 2^3 = \square$

     $4 + 2^2 + 2^3 + 2^4 = \square$

   b What do you notice about the answers?

   c Write down the answer to

     i $4 + 2^2 + 2^3 + 2^4 + 2^5$ **ii** $2 + 2^2 + 2^3 + 2^4 + 2^5$.

   d Write an algebraic expression that gives the sum of the first n powers of 2.

3 Copy and complete each calculation using powers of a single number and × and ÷ signs.

   a $10^3\,\square\,\square = 10^{-3}$ **b** $2^4 \times \square\,\square\,\square = 2^4$

   c $5^8\,\square\,\square\,\square\,\square\,\square\,\square = 5^{-8}$ **d** $10^5\,\square\,10^6\,\square\,\square\,\square\,10^{-5}\,\square\,\square \div \square = 10^5$

Reflect

How sure are you of your answers? Were you mostly

☹ **Just guessing**   😐 **Feeling doubtful**   🙂 **Confident**

What next? Use your results to decide whether to strengthen or extend your learning.

1 Strengthen

Indices and powers of 10

1   Write each product as a single power.

   a $3^2 \times 3^4 = 3^{\square + \square} = 3^{\square}$

   b $5^2 \times 5^3 = 5^{\square + \square} = 5^{\square}$

   c $2^3 \times 2^3 = 2^{\square}$

   d $7^3 \times 7 = 7^{\square}$

   e $5^2 \times 5^3 \times 5^4 = 5^{\square + \square + \square} = 5^{\square}$

   f $10^4 \times 10 \times 10^3 = 10^{\square}$

> **Q1a hint**
>
> $$3^2 \times 3^4 = \overbrace{3 \times 3}^{2} \times \overbrace{3 \times 3 \times 3 \times 3}^{4}$$
>
> How many 3s are multiplied together?

> **Q1d hint** $7 = 7^1$

2   Write each division as a single power.

   a $6^5 \div 6^2 = 6^{\square - \square} = 6^{\square}$

   b $5^7 \div 5^5 = 5^{\square - \square} = 5^{\square}$

   c $2^7 \div 2^3 = 2^{\square}$

   d $7^3 \div 7 = 7^{\square}$

> **Q2a hint**
>
> $$6^5 \div 6^2 = \frac{6^5}{6^2} = \frac{\overbrace{\cancel{6} \times \cancel{6} \times 6 \times 6 \times 6}^{5}}{\underbrace{\cancel{6} \times \cancel{6}}_{2}}$$
>
> How many 6s are left after simplifying?

3   **a**   To work out $2^4 \times 2^3$, Asifa said, 'Four times three is twelve' and wrote '2^{12}'. Explain why she is wrong.

   b   To work out $10^8 \div 10^2$, Jeremy said, 'Eight divided by two is four' and wrote '10^4'. Explain why he is wrong.

4   Write each product as a single power. Work from left to right.

   a $2^4 \times 2^3 \div 2^5 = 2^{\square + \square - \square} = 2^{\square}$

   b $10^7 \times 10^2 \div 10^4 = 10^{\square + \square - \square} = 10^{\square}$

   c $8^5 \div 8^2 \times 8^3 = 8^{\square}$

   d $4^5 \div 4 \times 4^2 = 4^{\square}$

   e $3^5 \div 3^2 \div 3^2 = 3^{\square}$

5   Copy and complete

   a $6^2 = \square \times \square$ **b** $(6^4)^2 = 6^4 \times 6^4 = 6^{\square}$

   c $6^3 = \square \times \square \times \square$ **d** $(6^4)^3 = 6^4 \times 6^4 \times 6^4 = 6^{\square}$

   e $(7^3)^2 = \square \times \square = \square^{\square}$ **f** $(7^5)^3 = \square \times \square \times \square = \square^{\square}$

> **Key point**
>
> ← To convert bigger units to smaller units, multiply
>
>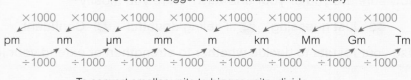
>
> To convert smaller units to bigger units, divide →

6   Convert the units.

   a $0.034\,\text{m}$ to mm   **b** $0.25\,\text{Tm}$ to km   **c** $0.0000008\,\text{mm}$ to nm

> **Q6 hint** How many times do you have to multiply by 1000?

7 Convert the units.

a 4500 mm to m

b 80 000 nm to mm

c 3500 km to Mm

Q7 hint How many times do you have to divide by 1000?

8 Convert the units.

a 0.46 GHz to MHz   **b** 530 µg to mg

c 0.000 007 MW to W   **d** 270 000 litres to ml

Q8 hint Use the key point to decide whether to multiply or divide.

9 a Copy and complete $4^2 \div 4^2 = \dfrac{4^2}{4^2} = \dfrac{\square}{\square} = \square$

b Copy and complete $4^2 \div 4^2 = 4^{\square - \square} = 4^{\square}$

c Use your answers to parts **a** and **b** to find the value of 4^0.

d i Repeat parts **a** and **b** for $5^2 \div 5^2$.

  ii What is the value of 5^0?

e Copy and complete the rule:

When you write a number to the power 0, the answer is _____.

10 a Copy and complete

  i $4^3 \div 4^5 = 4^{\square - \square} = 4^{-\square}$

  ii $4^3 \div 4^5 = \dfrac{4^3}{4^5} = \dfrac{\cancel{4} \times \cancel{4} \times \cancel{4}}{\cancel{4} \times \cancel{4} \times \cancel{4} \times 4 \times 4} = \dfrac{1}{4^{\square}}$

  iii $4^{-2} = \dfrac{1}{4^{\square}}$

b Copy and complete

  i $10^4 \div 10^7 = 10^{\square - \square} = 10^{-\square}$

  ii $10^4 \div 10^7 = \dfrac{10^4}{10^7} = \dfrac{10 \times 10 \times 10 \times 10}{10 \times 10 \times 10 \times 10 \times 10 \times 10 \times 10} = \dfrac{1}{10^{\square}}$

  iii $10^{-3} = \dfrac{1}{10^{\square}}$

c Copy and complete

  i $2^{-3} = \dfrac{1}{2^{\square}}$ **ii** $10^{-4} = \dfrac{1}{10^{\square}}$

  iii $\dfrac{1}{10^2} = 10^{\square}$ **iv** $\dfrac{1}{10} = 10^{\square}$

Q10c iv hint $10 = 10^{\square}$

11 Reasoning Four students each work out 4^{-3} as shown.

Paul $4^{-3} = 4 \times -3 = \ldots$ Terri $4^{-3} = 4 - 3 = \ldots$

Sandhu $4^{-3} = \dfrac{1}{4^3} = \ldots$ Marcia $4^{-3} = -4^3 = \ldots$

Who is correct? Explain.

12 Write each of these as a single power.

a $10^3 \times 10^{-1} = 10^{3 + -1} = 10^{\square}$

b $10^{-2} \times 10^{-4} = 10^{\square + \square} = 10^{\square}$

c 2×2^{-4}

d $10^4 \div 10^7 = 10^{\square - \square} = 10^{\square}$

e $10^{-4} \div 10^2$

f $\dfrac{10^2}{10^6}$

Q12c hint $2 = 2^{\square}$

Q12f hint Work out $10^2 \div 10^6$.

13 a Write 8 as a power of 2.

   b Use your answer to write each product as a single power of 2.

     i $8 \times 2^5 = 2^\square \times 2^5$

     ii $2^6 \times 8$

     iii 8×8

Q13a hint
$8 = 2 \times 2 \times \ldots$
How many 2s are multiplied together to make 8?

Powers and roots

1 Work out

   a $2^2 \times 3^2 = 4 \times \square = \square$ **b** $5^2 \times 4^2 = \square \times \square = \square$ **c** $4^2 \times 10^2 = \square \times \square = \square$

2 Work out

   a $(2 \times 3)^2$

   b $(5 \times 4)^2$

   c $(4 \times 10)^2$

Q2a hint Work out the calculation inside the brackets first.

3 a What do you notice about your answers to Q1 and Q2?

   b Write the calculation $(5 \times 6)^2$ without brackets.

4 **Reasoning**   **a** Use the $\boxed{x^2}$ key on your calculator to work out -4^2 and $(-4)^2$.

   b Explain why you get two different answers.

   c Use your answers to work out

     i $20 + (-4)^2$ **ii** $20 - -4^2$ **iii** $(-4)^2 - 4^2$ **iv** $-4^2 - (-4)^2$

     v $10 - (-3)^2$ **vi** $15 - 2^2$ **vii** $(-5)^2 - 3^2$ **viii** $-5^2 - (-3)^2$

5 Work out

   a $-2 \times -2 \times -2$ **b** $\sqrt[3]{-8}$ **c** $-3 \times -3 \times -3$

   d $\sqrt[3]{-27}$ **e** $\sqrt[3]{-64}$ **f** $\sqrt[3]{-125}$

6 Work out

   a i 2^2 **ii** 7^2 **iii** $\left(\frac{2}{7}\right)^2$

   b i 5^2 **ii** 9^2 **iii** $\left(\frac{5}{9}\right)^2$

Q6a iii hint $\left(\frac{2}{7}\right)^2 = \frac{2}{7} \times \frac{2}{7} = \frac{\square}{\square}$

7 Copy and complete

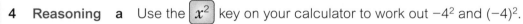

   a $\dfrac{4^2 \times 5^3}{10} = \dfrac{4 \times \square \times 5 \times \square \times 5}{10} = \dfrac{\square}{\square} = \square$ **b** $\dfrac{(4 \times 5)^2}{10} = \dfrac{4 \times 5 \times \square \times \square}{10} = \dfrac{\square}{\square} = \square$

8 a Sally estimates $\dfrac{12.5}{4.2} + 3.9$ like this

     $\dfrac{12}{4} + 4 = 3 + 4 = 7$

   Why did she round 12.5 down and not up?

   b Estimate $\dfrac{18.3}{6.8} - 1.5$

   c Estimate

     i $\sqrt{80}$ **ii** $\sqrt{80} + 30.4$

     iii $\sqrt{50}$ **iv** $\dfrac{\sqrt{50} - 4.9}{1.85}$

Q8c i hint What square number is close to 80?

Q8c iv hint First estimate $\sqrt{50} - 4.9$

Standard form

1 Work out
  a 2.3×10
  b 2.3×10^2
  c 2.3×10^3
  d 1.6×10^2
  e 1.6×10^4
  f 3.9×10^4
  g 3.9×10^5
  h 3.9×10^6

Q1 hint

Th	H	T	O	.	$\frac{1}{10}$
			2	.	3
	2	3	0		
2	3	0	0		

2.3×10^2 means multiply by 10 twice
2.3×10^3 means multiply by 10 three times
and so on.

2 The temperature of the Sun at its core is 1.5×10^7 °C.
Write this as an ordinary number.

3 Work out
  a 1.7×10^{-1}
  b 1.7×10^{-2}
  c 1.7×10^{-3}
  d 8.2×10^{-3}
  e 8.2×10^{-4}
  f 9.4×10^{-4}
  g 9.4×10^{-5}
  h 9.4×10^{-6}

Q3 hint

O	.	$\frac{1}{10}$	$\frac{1}{100}$	$\frac{1}{1000}$
1	.	7		
0	.	1	7	
0	.	0	1	7

1.7×10^{-1} means $\div 10^1$ so divide by 10 once
1.7×10^{-2} means $\div 10^2$ so divide by 10 twice
and so on.

4 A number written using standard form looks like this.

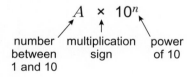

$$A \times 10^n$$

number   multiplication   power
between   sign   of 10
1 and 10

Which one of these numbers is written using standard form?
A 54×10^4 **B** 5.4×10^{-4}
C 0.54×10^{-4} **D** $5.4 \div 10^4$

5 Write each number using standard form.
  a $5300 = 5.3 \times 10^{\square}$
  b $49\,000 = 4.9 \times 10^{\square}$
  c $63\,000\,000 = \square \times 10^{\square}$
  d $700\,000 = 7 \times 10^{\square}$
  e $9\,000\,000 = \square \times 10^{\square}$
  f $56\,000\,000\,000$

Q5a hint 5.3 lies between 1 and 10. How many times do you have to multiply 5.3 by 10 to get 5300?

6 Write each number using standard form.

a $0.0029 = 2.9 \times 10^{-\square}$ b $0.057 = 5.7 \times 10^{-\square}$

c $0.000\,063$ d $0.000\,000\,7$

e $0.000\,000\,009$ f $0.000\,000\,000\,000\,56$

> **Q6a hint** 2.9 lies between 1 and 10. How many times do you have to divide by 10 to get 0.0029?

7 Write each quantity using standard form.

a The circumference of the Earth at the equator is approximately $40\,000\,000$ m.

b A molecule of sugar has a diameter of $0.000\,000\,001\,4$ m.

8 Write each of these sets of standard form numbers in order, from smallest to largest.

> **Q8 hint** Look at the powers of 10 first.

a 2.7×10^{-4} 7.3×10^{2} 4.3×10^{7} 9×10^{-6}

b 7.3×10^{6} 3.5×10^{7} 5×10^{7} 1.2×10^{6}

Challenge

1 a Follow these steps to find out how thick a page of this textbook is.

  i Use a ruler to measure the thickness of the book in mm.
  ii Work out the number of sheets of paper.
  iii Use your calculator to divide the thickness by the number of sheets.
  iv Round your answer to two decimal places.
  v Write your answer in mm using standard form.
  vi Convert your answer to part **v** to μm.

 b Repeat the question for different books or glossy magazines.
  What can you say about the thickness of the paper used?

2 In spreadsheets, these symbols are used to enter calculations.

  / instead of ÷
  * instead of ×
  10^2 instead of 10^2
  SQRT(16) instead of $\sqrt{16}$

Write these calculations using spreadsheet notation.

a $5 \times 2 + 3^2$ b $(5 - 2)^3$ c $\sqrt{4 + 12}$

d $20 \div 2^2$ e $\dfrac{4^2}{\sqrt{16}}$ f $\dfrac{3^2}{2 \times 9}$

> **Q2c hint** Use brackets.

Reflect

Luke says, 'Working with indices, powers and roots is all about adding, subtracting, multiplying and dividing.'

Look back at the questions you answered in this Strengthen lesson. Describe when you had to

- add
- subtract
- multiply
- divide.

Do you agree with Luke's statement?
Give some examples to explain why.

1 Extend

1 **Problem-solving** The Eiffel Tower is 324 m tall.
  a The height was halved repeatedly to make a model around 30 cm tall.
    What power of 2 was the height divided by?
  b A computer-controlled laser was used to engrave the Eiffel Tower onto the head of a pin.
    The laser was programmed to make an engraving 100 times smaller than the model.
    How tall was the engraving?
  c How many times taller is the real Eiffel Tower than the engraving?
    Write your answer using standard form.

2 **Problem-solving / Reasoning** Some 56 cm by 27.5 cm
rectangular stone slabs are used to cover a rectangular courtyard
measuring 12 m by 18 m.
Find the best way to estimate the number of slabs needed.
State whether your answer is an overestimate or an underestimate.

> **Q2 hint** Make some sketches. Why is your way the best?

3 **a** Write each decimal as a fraction in its simplest form and
    then using powers.
    i 0.25
    ii 0.125
    iii 0.015 625
  b Use your answer to part **a iii** to write 2^{-5} as a decimal.

> **Q3a hint**
> $0.25 = \dfrac{1}{\square} = \dfrac{1}{\square^{\square}} = \square^{\square}$

4 A pile driver is a machine that repeatedly drops a heavy ram to drive heavy metal beams
into the ground to support buildings.
This formula gives the load L that a pile can support when it is made from a 3000 lb ram
dropped from 8.5 feet.

$$L = 51.52 \times \frac{3000 \times \sqrt[3]{8.5}}{4}$$

Estimate L.

5 The graph shows the national debt of
the USA between 2000 and 2010.
  a Estimate the US national debt in 2004.
    Write your answer in dollars using
    standard form.
  b Work out the increase in the US national debt
    between 2000 and 2010.
    Give your answer as an ordinary number.
  c Estimate the US national debt in 2009.
    Give your answer in millions of dollars.

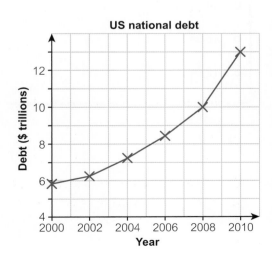

6 The distance of Jupiter from Earth is approximately 9.3×10^8 km.

Use the formula time $= \dfrac{\text{distance}}{\text{speed}}$ to estimate the time it would take a rocket travelling at 10^3 km/h to reach Jupiter.

7 Work out
   a $(2 \times 5)^2$ **b** $2^2 \times 5^2$ **c** $(2 \times 5)^3$ **d** $2^3 \times 5^3$

8 **a** Use your answers to Q7 to write a rule for calculating a power of a product.
   b Check that your rule works for
      i $(2 \times 5)^4$ **ii** $(2 \times 5 \times 3)^2$

> **Q8a hint** Multiplying two numbers together gives their **product**.

9 Work out   **a** $(6 \div 3)^2$ **b** $6^2 \div 3^2$

10 **a** Use your answers to Q9 to write a rule for calculating a power of a division.
   b Check that your rule works for powers higher than 2.

11 The number of intelligent civilisations, N, in the Milky Way galaxy has been estimated using Drake's equation:
   $$N = R \times F \times L \times S \times I \times C \times T$$

Scientists disagree about the values to substitute into the formula. The table shows the ranges of values they have suggested.

R	F	L	S	I	C	T
1 to 7	0.4 to 1	0.2	10^{-11} to 0.13	10^{-9} to 1	0.1 to 0.2	10^9 to 10^{11}

   a Work out the largest possible value of N.
   b **i** Work out the smallest possible value of N.
      ii Does this equation predict that there are other intelligent civilisations in the Milky Way?
   c The Milky Way is just one of 100 billion galaxies in space.
   Does Drake's equation suggest there are other intelligent civilisations in space?

> **Q13 hint** A billion is 10^9.

Challenge   Copy and complete these calculations.

a $\left(1\dfrac{\square}{\square}\right)^2 = 1\dfrac{9}{16}$

b $\left(6\dfrac{\square}{\square}\right)^2 = 44\dfrac{4}{9}$

c $\left(2\dfrac{2}{\square}\right)^2 = \square\dfrac{1}{9}$

1 Unit test

1 Write each calculation as a power of a single number.
   a $10^3 \times 10^4$
   b $4^{10} \div 4^8$

2 Convert
   a 4.3 m to mm
   b 3.16 GW to W

3 Write each calculation as a single power.
   a $2^5 \times 2 \div 2^2$
   b 9×3^4

4 Write each of these as an integer or a fraction in its simplest form.
   a 3^0
   b 5^{-3}

5 Which one of these calculations gives the answer 144? Show working.
   A $4 \times (1 + 2)^2$
   B $4 \times 1 + 2^2$
   C $[4 \times (1 + 2)]^2$
   D $(4 \times 1 + 2)^2$

6 Work out
   a $\sqrt[3]{-1000}$
   b $5^2 - (-2)^3$

7 Estimate the answers to these.
   a $\dfrac{13.7 + \sqrt{119}}{4.9}$

   b $(5.98 - \sqrt[3]{9}) \times 11.8$

8 A roll of wool insulation is 114 cm wide and 5.2 m long. One roll costs £19.65.
   Estimate the cost of wool insulation required for a loft floor that is 4.5 m by 10 m.

9 A power station can produce 3.2 gigawatts (GW) of power.
   a How many watts is this?
   b How many kilowatts (kW) is this?

10 Write each of these as a single power.
   a $5^{-2} \times 5^{-1}$
   b $3^8 \div 3^{-4}$

11 Write each of these as an ordinary number.

    a 2.7×10^5

    b 6×10^{-4}

12 Work out

    a $\left(\dfrac{12}{3}\right)^2$

    b $\dfrac{2^2 \times 2^2}{2}$

    c $\dfrac{18 \times 4}{(2 \times 3)^2}$

13 The distance of the Sun from Earth is approximately $150\,000\,000\,000$ m.
Write this distance

    a using a suitable prefix

    b using standard form.

14 Write $(5^7)^6$ as a single power.

15 Write each number using standard form.

    a $0.000\,000\,047$

    b 12 billion

16 A protein has a width of 5.3×10^{-8} m and a virus has a width of 2.5×10^{-7} m.
Which is bigger?

Challenge

1 Write $\left(\dfrac{2}{3}\right)^{-2}$ as a fraction in its simplest form.

2 **a** Choose any word on this page, for example the word 'page'.
Use the positions of the letters in the alphabet to make a number.

a	b	c	d	e	f	g	h	i	j	k	l	m	n	o	p	q	r	s	t	u	v	w	x	y	z
1	2	3	4	5	6	7	8	9	10	11	12	13	14	15	16	17	18	19	20	21	22	23	24	25	26

The number for the word 'page' is 16 175.

    b Write the number using standard form.

    c Repeat for another nine words.

    d Write the words in order, from the smallest standard form number to the largest.

    e Can you use the length of a word to predict its position in your list from part **d**?
Use the previous sentence to test your prediction.

    f Find a word with a standard form number containing 10^{12}.

Reflect

• Which of the questions in this unit test took the shortest time to answer? Why?
• Which of the questions in this unit test took the longest time to answer? Why?
• Which of the questions in this unit test took the most thought to answer? Why?

2 Expressions and formulae

2.1 Solving equations

- Write and solve equations with fractions
- Write and solve equations with the unknown on both sides

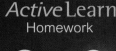

Active Learn
Homework

Warm up

1 Fluency Write down the size of each angle labelled with a letter. Give your reasons.

a

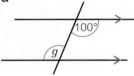
$100°$
g

b

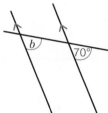
b
$70°$

2 Write an expression for the perimeter of each shape.

a

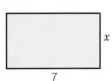
x
7

b

y

3 Solve

a $x - 7 = 15$ **b** $5y = 30$ **c** $\dfrac{z}{3} = 6$ **d** $\dfrac{w}{2} = -4$

e $2a - 5 = 1$ **f** $4b + 16 = 8$ **g** $2c - 5 = 4$ **h** $3(d + 4) = 45$

Key point

In the balancing method you solve equations by doing the same operation to both sides.

4 Solve these equations. The first one is started for you.

a
$$\times 2 \left(\frac{5x}{2} = 15 \right) \times 2$$
$$5x = \square$$
$$\div 5 \left(\right) \div 5$$
$$x = \square$$

b $\dfrac{3x}{2} = 12$

c $\dfrac{2x}{3} = 12$

d $\dfrac{8x}{3} = -16$

5 Solve these equations. Write your solutions as fractions.

    a $5y = 2$ **b** $3y = 7$ **c** $4y + 5 = 8$

    d $3y - 5 = -3$ **e** $6y + 10 = 7$ **f** $4y - 2 = 3$

6 Solve these equations. Write your solutions as decimals.

    a $10x = 9$ **b** $5x = 3$ **c** $4x = -3$

    d $6x + 7 = 10$ **e** $4x - 7 = -1$ **f** $5x + 1 = 9$

Worked example

Solve $\dfrac{x}{3} + 5 = 7$

$$-5 \left(\begin{array}{c} \dfrac{x}{3} + 5 = 7 \\ \dfrac{x}{3} = 2 \end{array} \right) -5$$

Do the same to both sides to get the x term 'on its own'.

$$\times 3 \left(\begin{array}{c} \dfrac{x}{3} = 2 \\ x = 6 \end{array} \right) \times 3$$

Check: $\dfrac{6}{3} + 5 = 2 + 5 = 7$ ✓

---

7 Solve

    a $\dfrac{x}{2} + 7 = 12$ **b** $\dfrac{y}{3} + 11 = 13$ **c** $\dfrac{a}{5} - 2 = 1$

    d $\dfrac{b}{4} + 20 = 18$ **e** $\dfrac{c}{6} - 9 = -3$ **f** $\dfrac{d}{2} + 3 = 3.5$

8 Solve these equations. The first one is started for you.

    a
$$\times 5 \left(\begin{array}{c} \dfrac{x + 2}{5} = 3 \\ x + 2 = \square \end{array} \right) \times 5$$
$$-2 \left(\begin{array}{c} \\ x = \square \end{array} \right) -2$$

    b $\dfrac{x + 2}{3} = 4$

    c $\dfrac{x - 2}{3} = 4$

    d $\dfrac{x + 7}{5} = -2$

9 **Problem-solving** I think of a number, halve it and add 5. The answer is 8. Write an equation and solve it to find my number.

10 **Problem-solving** The mean of these five values is 4.

    x 6   2   4   5

    Write and solve an equation to find the value of x.

Key point When there is an unknown on both sides, use the balancing method to get the unknowns on one side only.

---

11 Copy and complete to solve

    $3x = 2x + 7$

$$-2x \left(\begin{array}{c} 3x = 2x + 7 \\ \square = \square \end{array} \right) -2x$$

12 Solve

   a $2x = x + 4$ **b** $5x = 4x + 7$ **c** $3x - 2 = 4x$

   d $6x = 3x + 6$ **e** $7x = 2x + 50$ **f** $6y + 4 = 5y + 12$

   g $3y + 7 = 4y - 1$ **h** $3y - 2 = 5y + 10$ **i** $5x - 8 = 3x$

13 Problem-solving Work out the sizes of the angles.

   a

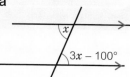

   b

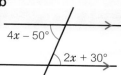

14 Problem-solving I am x years old. My brother is 15 years older than me.
In one year's time my brother will be exactly double my age.
Write and solve an equation to find x.

15 Expand the brackets and solve these equations.

   a $4(d + 1) = d + 10$ **b** $10s - 2 = 4(s + 7)$

   c $5(t + 2) = 3(t + 6)$ **d** $2(x - 1) = 3(x + 1)$

   e $3(2n + 3) = 2n + 21$ **f** $2(3v + 1) = 5(v + 2)$

16 Problem-solving The hexagon and rectangle have the same perimeter.
Work out the value of x.

   a

   b

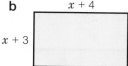

Challenge

This square has the same perimeter as the rectangle.

a Write down an equation using a.

b **i** Solve the equation.
   ii Work out the lengths of the sides of the rectangle.

c Replace 3 and 4 with two other whole numbers. Repeat parts **a** and **b**.
What do you notice about the value of a?

Reflect   Which questions did you answer by writing and solving an equation?
Was there another way of working out the answers? If so, which way was easiest and why?

2.2 Substituting into expressions

Active Learn
Homework

- Use the priority of operations when substituting into algebraic expressions
- Substitute values into expressions involving powers and roots

Warm up

1 **Fluency** Write down the value of
   a 3^2
   b 2^3
   c $\sqrt{16}$
   d $\sqrt[3]{27}$

2 Work out
   a $12 + 3 \times 5$
   b $3 \times 4 + 4 \times 5$
   c 2×3^2
   d $4(9 - 2)$
   e $\dfrac{5 + 7}{6 - 2}$
   f $\dfrac{4^2 + 8}{\sqrt{16}}$

3 Write down the value of each expression when $a = 8$ and $b = 5$.
   a $a + b$
   b $a - b$
   c ab
   d $6ab$
   e $\dfrac{a}{b}$
   f $2a + 3b$
   g $a^2 + b^2$
   h $a^2 - b^2$

4 Work out the value of each expression when $x = 3$ and $y = -5$.
   a $2x + 3$
   b $4y - 5$
   c $8x + 2y$
   d xy
   e x^2
   f y^2
   g $x^2 + y^2$
   h $x^2 - y^2$
   i x^3
   j y^3

5 Work out the value of each expression.
   a x^2 when $x = 0.4$
   b z^2 when $z = -0.6$

6 Work out the value of each expression when $c = 3$ and $d = 2$.
   a $c^2 + 4$
   b $c^2 + 4d$
   c $4c^2$
   d $3d^3$
   e $3d^3 + 5$
   f $3d^3 + c$
   g $3d^3 - 10c$
   h $-5c + 2d^3$

7 Work out the value of each expression when $a = 3$ and $b = 4$.
   a a^2b
   b ab^2
   c $2ab^2$
   d $2a^2b^2$

Key point

The **priority of operations** is

Brackets → Indices (powers) → Division and Multiplication → Addition and Subtraction

Worked example

Work out the value of $a + (2b + c)^2$ when $a = 4$, $b = 2$ and $c = 3$.

$a + (2b + c)^2 = 4 + (2 \times 2 + 3)^2$ ⟶ Substitute the values of a, b and c.

$\qquad = 4 + (4 + 3)^2$ ⟶ Follow the priority of operations: 1) Work out the brackets.

$\qquad = 4 + 7^2$ ⟶ 2) Work out the index (power).

$\qquad = 4 + 49$

$\qquad = 53$ ⟶ 3) Add.

8   Work out the value of each expression when $x = 5$ and $y = 2$.

   a $(5y)^2$ b $(2x)^2$ c $(x + y)^2$

   d $(2x + y)^2$ e $(x + 3y)^2 - 4$ f $(3x - y)^2 + 7$

   g $(-2x + 3y)^2 + 1$ h $(4y - x)^2 + y$ i $(x - 4y)^2 + 2y - 1$

9   The cards show two different expressions that you can use to estimate the weight, in kilograms, of a child aged between 1 and 5, where A is the age of the child in years.

   $2(A + 4)$ $2.5A + 8$

   a Use the two expressions to give two estimates for the weight of a 3-year-old child.

   b Copy and complete this table showing the estimates of the weight of a child, from both expressions.

Age	$2(A + 4)$	$2.5A + 8$
1	10 kg	10.5 kg
2		
3		
4		
5		

   c Write the term-to-term rule for the sequence of numbers generated by each expression.

   d What does the term-to-term rule represent?

10 Substitute the given values to work out the value of each expression.

   a $10(2x + 4y)$ when $x = 6$ and $y = 3$

   b $35 - (b^3 - a)$ when $a = 2$ and $b = 3$

   c $\dfrac{4y - 2}{3}$ when $y = 5$

   d $\dfrac{5a + 2b}{a}$ when $a = 10$ and $b = 7$

   e $\dfrac{ab + cd}{b + c}$ when $a = 6$, $b = 3$, $c = 1$ and $d = 4$

   f $\dfrac{(a - b)^2}{(a + b)^2}$ when $a = 12$ and $b = 8$

> Q10c hint $\dfrac{4y - 2}{3} = (4y - 2) \div 3$

11 Work out the value of each expression.

   a $\sqrt{xy}$ when $x = 2$ and $y = 8$

   b $\sqrt{a + b}$ when $a = 7$ and $b = 18$

   c $\sqrt{c - d}$ when $c = 12$ and $d = 3$

   d $3\sqrt{e}$ when $e = 64$

   e $\sqrt[3]{e}$ when $e = 64$

   f $\sqrt[3]{fg}$ when $f = 4$ and $g = 250$

12 Problem-solving Using the values of the letters in the table, is **A**, **B** or **C** the correct value for each of these expressions?

Letter	a	b	c	d	e	f
Value	2	−1	7	−4	6	16

a $e + (ad)^2$ **A** −58   **B** 38   **C** 70

b $a(c - d)^2$ **A** 18   **B** 78   **C** 242

c $(c + d)^3 - 2f$ **A** −23   **B** −5   **C** 1299

d $e\sqrt{f} - 3bd$ **A** 12   **B** 36   **C** 52

e $\sqrt[3]{4f} - a^3$ **A** −4   **B** −2   **C** 13

13 Work out the value of each expression when $x = 4$, $y = 2$ and $z = -5$

a $3(x^3 + y)$

b $3x(x + z)$

c $y^2(z + x^3)$

d $4x(3 - z) + y$

e $5(x^2 + y) + x(3x + 2)$

f $5y(x + y^3 + z) + 3y^2(x + 3z)$

g $y\sqrt{x}$

h $\sqrt[3]{xy} + z^2$

i $\sqrt{xyz + 76}$

Challenge   Use the values $x = 4$, $y = 9$, $u = -6$, $v = -2$ to write three expressions that will give each of these answers.

a   18   b   24   c   12   d   40

For example, $\dfrac{xy}{2}$ is one expression that gives an answer of 18.

$$\frac{xy}{2} = \frac{4 \times 9}{2} = \frac{36}{2} = 18$$

At least one of your expressions should involve a square or square root.

Reflect   Helga writes,

<u>When substituting into expressions, watch out for</u>
<u>brackets (HINT: work out whatever is in the brackets first)</u>

Hint You could begin with the same point as Helga.

Look back at the questions you answered in this lesson.
Write your own 'watch out for' list.
Write a short hint for each point in your list.

2.3 Writing and using formulae

- Write and use formulae

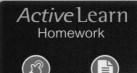

Active Learn
Homework

1 **Fluency**   Match each statement to the correct expression.

A 2 more than x	**1** $\frac{x}{2}$
B twice x	**2** $2x + 2$
C 2 less than x	**3** $2 - x$
D half x	**4** $x + 2$
E x less than 2	**5** $2x$
F 2 more than double x	**6** $x - 2$

2   Jake earns £9 per hour.
   a How much does he earn in 6 hours?
   b Write an expression for the amount he earns in h hours.
   c Write a formula for E, the amount he earns in h hours.

Key point   A **formula** is a rule that shows a relationship between two or more variables (letters).

Worked example

The cost of hiring a bike is £10 plus £5 an hour.
a   Write a formula for working out the cost, C, of hiring a bike for h hours.
b   What is the cost of hiring a bike for 8 hours?

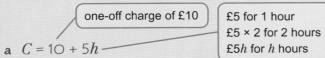

one-off charge of £10

£5 for 1 hour
£5 × 2 for 2 hours
£5h for h hours

a $C = 10 + 5h$

You are working out a formula for the cost, so write $C = \ldots$

b $C = 10 + 5 \times 8$
   $= £50$

Substitute $h = 8$ into the formula.

3   A plumber charges a call-out fee of £35, plus £20 per hour.
   a How much does he charge for a 2-hour job?
   b Write a formula to work out the total charge, C, for a job that takes h hours.

4 The cost of hiring a hall for a party is £80 plus £10 per person.
  a Write a formula for working out the cost, C, of hiring the hall for p people.
  b How much will it cost for a party with 50 people?

5 To cook a joint of beef takes 20 minutes per $\frac{1}{2}$kg, plus an extra 30 minutes.
  a Write a formula to work out the number of minutes, M, it takes to cook a joint of beef that weighs x kg.
  b Use your formula to work out M when $x = 3.8$ kg.
  c How long does it take to cook a 2.5 kg joint of beef?

6 **Reasoning** The graph shows the amount an electrician charges his customers.
  a How much does the electrician charge for
    i 1 hour's work
    ii 4 hours' work?
  b The electrician charges a call-out fee. How much is it?
  c Write a formula for the total amount, C, that the electrician charges his customers for h hours' work.
  d Use your formula to work out C when $h = 2\frac{3}{4}$ hours.

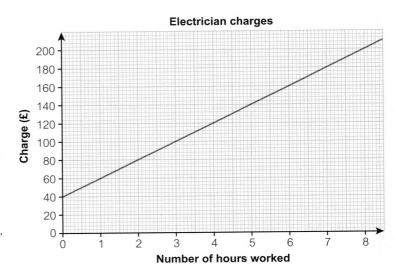

7 **Problem-solving** The graph shows the amount it costs to hire a bicycle.

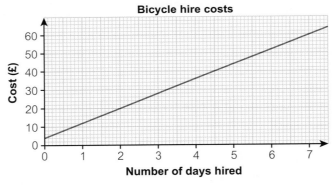

Write a formula for the total cost, C, to hire a bicycle for d days.

8 A riding stables charges £32 for an adult and £25 for a child to go riding.
  a How much does it cost a family of 2 adults and 2 children to go riding?
  b Write a formula for the total cost, T, for A adults and C children to go riding.

9 It costs £8 per adult and £5 per child to visit a museum.
  a Write a formula to work out the total cost, T, for a adults and c children.
  b Work out the cost for 4 adults and 6 children to visit the museum.

10 Problem-solving The table shows the results of an experiment in which a metal bar was heated. At 0 °C, the bar was exactly 10 m long. The increase in length of the bar was measured as the temperature increased.

Temperature of metal bar (°C)	0	1	2	3	4	5	6	7
Increase in length (mm)	0	0.12	0.24	0.36	0.48	0.60	0.72	0.84

a How much does the length of the bar increase with every 1 °C rise in temperature?

b Copy and complete the table showing how to work out the increase in length after a temperature increase of t °C.

Temperature of metal bar (°C)	0	1	2	3	t
Increase in length (mm)	0	0.12×1	0.12×2	$0.12 \times \square$	$0.12 \times \square$

c Write a formula for the total length of the bar in millimetres, L, after a temperature increase of t °C.

d Use your formula to work out the total length of the bar at a temperature of 15 °C.

> **Q10c hint** Add the increase in length to the original length of the bar.

11 You can use this formula to calculate the force acting on a body.

$$F = ma$$

where F is the force (in newtons), m is the mass of the body (in kilograms) and a is the acceleration (in metres per second per second).
Work out the value of F when

a $m = 6$ and $a = 5$ **b** $m = 2$ and $a = -4$ **c** $m = 0.6$ and $a = -9.8$

12 You can use this formula to work out the height of a ball when it is thrown upwards.

$$s = ut + \tfrac{1}{2}at^2$$

where s is the height (in m), u is the starting speed (in m/s), a is the acceleration (in m/s²) and t is the time (in s).
Work out the value of s when

a $u = 30$, $t = 6$ and $a = -10$ **b** $u = 40$, $t = 8$ and $a = -9.8$

13 The formula $E = mc^2$ gives the energy E (in joules) contained in a mass m kg.
The speed of light, c, is approximately 300 000 000 m/s.
Calculate the energy contained in a mass of 20 kg.
Write your answer using standard form.

14 Use the formula $M = \frac{rg}{h}$ to work out the value of M when

a $r = 8$, $g = -10$ and $h = 5$ **b** $r = 2$, $g = -12$ and $h = 4$
c $r = -6$, $g = 9$ and $h = 3$ **d** $r = -4$, $g = 15$ and $h = -12$

> **Q14a hint**
> $M = \dfrac{8 \times -10}{5} = \dfrac{\square}{5}$

Challenge These are two formulae that you might use in science.

$$T^2 = \frac{kx}{l} \qquad E = \frac{kx^2}{2l}$$

Use the values $T = 16$, $x = 0.6$ and $l = 3$ to work out the value of E.

Reflect What is different and what is the same about formulae and expressions?

2.4 Using and rearranging formulae

Active Learn
Homework

- Substitute into formulae and then solve equations to find unknown values
- Change the subject of a formula

Warm up

1 Fluency What is the formula for
  a area of a rectangle
  b area of a triangle
  c area of a trapezium?

2 Use the formula $S = nt$ to work out the value of S when
  a $n = 5$ and $t = 3$ **b** $n = 0$ and $t = 4$ **c** $n = -4$ and $t = \frac{1}{2}$

3 Solve
  a $x + 12 = 25$ **b** $3x - 4 = 11$ **c** $\frac{x}{2} = 12$

4 Calculate the area of each shape.

a
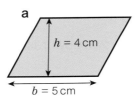
$h = 4\,\text{cm}$
$b = 5\,\text{cm}$

b
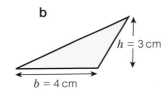
$h = 3\,\text{cm}$
$b = 4\,\text{cm}$

c
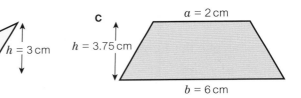
$a = 2\,\text{cm}$
$h = 3.75\,\text{cm}$
$b = 6\,\text{cm}$

Key point

You can use substitution to work out the unknown value in a formula.

Worked example

The area of this trapezium is $35\,\text{cm}^2$.
Work out the value of a.

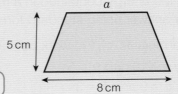
a
$5\,\text{cm}$
$8\,\text{cm}$

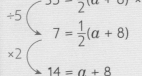

$\text{Area} = \frac{1}{2}(a + b)h$ — Write down the formula.

$35 = \frac{1}{2}(a + 8) \times 5$ — Substitute the values.
$\div 5$ $\div 5$

$7 = \frac{1}{2}(a + 8)$
$\times 2$ $\times 2$

$14 = a + 8$
-8 -8

$a = 6\,\text{cm}$

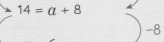

Solve the equation to find the value of a.

5 Use the formula $F = ma$ to work out the value of
   a m when $F = 24$ and $a = 10$
   b a when $F = 54$ and $m = 12$

6 The area of this triangle is $12\,\text{cm}^2$.

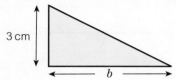

3 cm

b

   a Substitute the values into the area formula.
   b Work out the value of b.

7 A skate hire company uses the formula $C = 3h + 10$ to
   work out the cost, C, of hiring skates for h hours.
   a Soraya paid £16 to hire skates.
      How many hours did she hire them for?
   b Luke paid £21.50 to hire skates.
      How many hours did he hire them for?

8 A theme park charges $10 for entry plus $5 for each ride.
   a Write a formula to work out the total cost, C, for entering the theme park and going on
      r rides.
   b Suzie goes to the theme park and goes on 8 rides.
      How much does this cost?
   c Ahmed spends all day at the theme park and spends $85.
      How many rides does he go on?

9 Use the formula $v = u + at$ to work out the value of
   a u when $v = 34$, $a = 5$ and $t = 3$
   b t when $v = 50$, $u = 20$ and $a = 5$
   c a when $v = 22$, $u = 8$ and $t = 7$

10 Use the formula $s = ut + \frac{1}{2}at^2$ to work out the value of a when $s = 37$, $t = 5$, and $u = 5.6$

11 Use the formula $T = \frac{nP}{V}$ to work out the value of n when $T = 0.24$, $P = 4.2$ and $V = 7$.

12 The number of office chairs, N, that an online business should regularly

   order, is given by the formula

   $$N = \sqrt{\frac{2AP}{H}}$$

   where A is the number sold each year, H is the storage cost and P is the cost of processing
   an order.

   Work out the value of N, when $A = 100$, $P = £10$ and $H = £5$.

Worked example

Make m the subject of the formula $F = ma$

$F = m \times a$

$\div a \quad \dfrac{F}{a} = m \quad \div a$ — Use the inverse of '$\times a$' to get m on its own.

or $m = \dfrac{F}{a}$

---

13 Make x the subject of these formulae.

Q13 hint Rearrange each formula so it starts '$x = ...$'.

a $P = xh$ **b** $V = rx$ **c** $A = x + y$

d $F = x - r$ **e** $r = \dfrac{x}{2}$ **f** $M = \dfrac{x}{n}$

g $t = x - 2v$ **h** $Y = x + np$ **i** $R = 2x + 4$

14 Make the letter in brackets the subject of each of these formulae.

a $D = ST$ (T) **b** $D = ST$ (S)

c $F = T + R$ (T) **d** $h = m - n$ (m)

e $k = 2l + n$ (n) **f** $v = u + at$ (u)

g $v = u + at$ (a) **h** $F = T - mg$ (T)

i $K = \dfrac{m}{t}$ (m) **j** $K = \dfrac{m}{t}$ (t)

k $D = \dfrac{M}{V}$ (M) **l** $D = \dfrac{M}{V}$ (V)

Challenge

a Use the formula cards to work out the value of each letter.

| $I = 12$ | $K + I = G$ | $4H = I$ | $G + 4 = 2I$ |

| $N = H^3 - I$ | $A = (W - H)^2$ | $K + I = 4W$ |

b Write the letters in order of value from the smallest to the biggest. What famous scientist's surname do they spell?

Reflect   In this lesson, you have met or used some formulae used in different contexts.

Who uses formulae?

Why do you think formulae are useful?

2.5 Index laws and brackets

- Use the rules for indices for multiplying and dividing
- Simplify expressions involving brackets
- Factorise an expression by taking out an algebraic common factor

Active Learn
Homework

Warm up

1 **Fluency** Write as a single power
   a $2^3 \times 2^2$
   b $3^3 \times 3$
   c $3^4 \div 3^2$

2 a Write $x \times x \times x \times x$ in index form.
   b Write y^5 as a product.

3 Simplify
   a $x \times x \times z \times z \times z$ b $2n \times 3n$

4 Simplify by collecting like terms
   a $4a + 2b - 3 - a + 5b$
   b $2(x + 4) + 5(x - 1)$

Key point   When multiplying powers of the same letter, you add the indices.

5 Simplify.
   a $p^2 \times p^5$
   b $k^3 \times k^2$
   c $a^5 \times a$
   d $3 \times m^2 \times m^3$
   e $4 \times a \times a^2$
   f $b^3 \times b \times 4$
   g $4c^3 \times c$
   h $d^2 \times 4d^3$
   i $5e^3 \times 2e^2$
   j $6s^2 \times 3s$
   k $5g \times 2g$
   l $3p^3 \times 4p^2$

Key point   When dividing powers of the same letter, you subtract the indices.

6 Simplify.
   a $e^7 \div e^2$
   b $a^8 \div a^3$
   c $\dfrac{b^5}{b^2}$
   d $\dfrac{c^4}{c}$
   e $\dfrac{3c^4}{c}$
   f $\dfrac{5b^3}{b^2}$
   g $\dfrac{4a^8}{a^3}$
   h $3d^6 \div d^3$
   i $8m^3 \div m^2$
   j $4t^8 \div t^5$
   k $6r^2 \div r^2$
   l $\dfrac{7x^3}{x^3}$

7 Simplify these terms. Two are started for you.
   a $(2a)^2 = 2a \times 2a =$
   b $(5x)^2$
   c $(4y)^3$
   d $\left(\dfrac{a}{3}\right)^3 = \dfrac{a}{3} \times \dfrac{a}{3} \times \dfrac{a}{3} =$
   e $\left(\dfrac{x}{6}\right)^2$
   f $\left(\dfrac{y}{2}\right)^3$

8 **Reasoning** Write true (T) or false (F) for each of these statements.
   a $7^0 = 7$
   b $y^0 = 1$
   c $4p^0 = 1$
   d $3q^0 = 3$

9 **Reasoning** Simplify these expressions. The first one is started for you.

a $\dfrac{9x^2}{3x^2} = 3x^{\square} =$

b $\dfrac{24y^7}{4y^7}$

Q9d hint First simplify $4q^2 \times 5q^6$, then divide the answer by $10q^8$.

c $\dfrac{3p^5}{2p^5}$

d $\dfrac{4q^2 \times 5q^6}{10q^8}$

Q9e hint Write your answer as a fraction in its simplest form.

e $\dfrac{8r^5 \times 2r^9}{20r^{14}}$

f $\dfrac{3t^4 \times 4t^6}{15t^{10}}$

10 **Reasoning** Copy and complete

a $6^{-2} = \dfrac{1}{6^{\square}}$

b $3^{-3} = \dfrac{1}{3^{\square}}$

c $5^{-1} = \dfrac{1}{5^{\square}}$

d $x^{-2} = \dfrac{1}{x^{\square}}$

e $y^{-4} = \dfrac{1}{y^{\square}}$

f $z^{-1} = \dfrac{1}{z^{\square}}$

11 Simplify these expressions. Write each one as a negative power and as a fraction. The first one is started for you.

a $\dfrac{x^7}{x^{12}} = x^{7-12} = x^{\square} = \dfrac{1}{x^{\square}}$

b $\dfrac{y^3}{y^7}$

c $\dfrac{z^4}{z^{10}}$

d $\dfrac{w^2}{w^9}$

e $\dfrac{v}{v^3}$

f $t^5 \div t^{11}$

Q11e hint $v = v^1$

g $m^6 \div m^8$

h $n^4 \div n^5$

Key point 'Like terms' contain the same power of the same letter.

a^2 and $3a^2$ are like terms.

a^2 and a^3 are *not* like terms.

---

12 Simplify by collecting like terms.

a $a^2 + a^2 + a^2$

b $m^3 + m^3 + m^3 + m^3 + m^3$

c $a^2 + a^2 + b^2 + b^2 + b^2$

d $e^2 + e^2 + e^4$

e $y^5 + y^5 + y^3 + y^3$

f $5a^3 - 2a^3$

g $2p + 3p^2 + 5p^2 + 7p$

h $3h^2 + 4b^3 + 2b^3 + 5h^2$

13 Expand these brackets.

a $y(y^2 + 5)$

b $y(y^2 + 5y)$

c $x^2(x - 2)$

d $x^2(x - 2x)$

e $x^2(x^3 + 2x)$

f $3n(n^2 - 2)$

g $3n(n^2 - 2n)$

h $3n(5n^2 - 2n)$

14 **Reasoning** The diagram shows a cuboid.

Q14 hint 'Show that' means 'Show your working'.

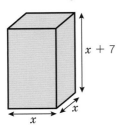

Show that an expression for the volume of the cuboid is $x^3 + 7x^2$.

15 Expand and simplify

a $m(3m - 4) + 5m$

b $8d^2 + 3d(d - 4)$

c $2s(s + 4) + 3(2s - 2)$

d $x(x^2 + 3x) + 2x(x^2 + 4x)$

e $4b(b^2 + 7b) - b(b^2 + 9b)$

f $5d(d^3 - 3) - d(2d^3 - 9)$

Key point To **factorise** an expression completely, take out the **highest common factor** (HCF) of its terms.

Worked example

Factorise $6x^2 + 12x$. Check your answer.

$6x^2 + 12x = 6x(x + 2)$ ———————— The HCF of $6x^2$ and $12x$ is $6x$.
$6x \times x = 6x^2$ and $6x \times 2 = 12x$

Check: $6x(x + 2) = 6x^2 + 12x$

---

16 Factorise each expression completely. Check your answers.

a $4x + 8$

b $4x^2 + 8$

c $4x^2 + 8x$

d $4x^3 + 8x^2$

e $y^2 - 5y^3$

f $9y^5 - 3y^3$

g $10y^4 - 5y^2$

h $12y^7 + 9y^5$

17 Factorise each expression completely.

a $xy + y$

b $xy - y$

c $x^2y - xy$

d $xy^2 + xy$

e $2xy^2 + 2xy$

f $2xy^2 + 4xy$

g $4xy^2 - 2xy$

h $4xy^2 - 6xy$

Challenge

Show that $3x^3 + x(4x^2 + 9x) = 7x^2(x + 3) - 12x^2$.

Hint Expand and simplify each side of the equation to show that both expressions are the same.

Reflect Kevin asks, 'Are the results of $x^2 \times x^2$ and $x^2 + x^2$ the same or different?' Answer Kevin's question, then explain your answer.

2.6 Expanding double brackets

* Multiply out double brackets and collect like terms

Active Learn
Homework

Warm up

1 Fluency Work out
a 3×-4 **b** -3×-2 **c** -5×7 **d** -4×-8

2 Simplify
a $a \times a$ **b** $x \times x$ **c** $4 \times a$
d $-2 \times x$ **e** $3a - a$ **f** $7x - 2x$
g $x^2 + 4x + 7x + 1$ **h** $x^2 - 3x + 5x + 12$ **i** $a^2 + 2a - 5a - 7$

3 Expand
a $4(x + 2)$ **b** $8(y - 1)$ **c** $z(z + 4)$ **d** $m(m - 4)$

4 a Copy and complete the expression for the area of this rectangle.

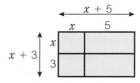

length × width = $(\Box + \Box)(\Box + \Box)$

b The rectangle can be divided into four smaller rectangles.

Work out the areas of the other two small rectangles.

c Add together the four areas from part **b**. Simplify by collecting like terms.

d Use your answers to parts **a** and **c** to write the area in two ways.
$(\Box + \Box)(\Box + \Box) = x^2 + \Box x + \Box$

5 Repeat Q4 for each of these rectangles.

a 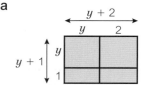 **b** 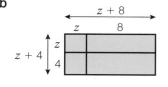 **c**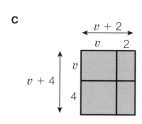

6 Problem-solving Work out an expression for the area of this rectangle.

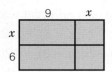

Worked example

Expand and simplify $(w + 6)(w + 12)$.

$(w + 6)(w + 12) = w^2 + 12w + 6w + 72$

$\qquad\qquad\quad = w^2 + \quad 18w \quad + 72$ ——— Simplify by collecting like terms.

7 Expand and simplify these double brackets.

a $(x + 3)(x + 7) =$ **b** $(y + 1)(y + 9)$ **c** $(m + 4)(m + 6)$

d $(p + 8)(p + 11)$ **e** $(q + 15)(q + 3)$ **f** $(n + 5)(n + 12)$

8 Expand and simplify
a $(x + 3)(x - 5)$ **b** $(y + 5)(y - 3)$ **c** $(p - 7)(p + 12)$
d $(q - 9)(q + 8)$ **e** $(s + 2)(s - 5)$ **f** $(t + 5)(t - 2)$

Q8a hint Watch out for the minus sign.

9 Expand and simplify
a $(m - 4)(m - 2)$ **b** $(n - 1)(n - 5)$

10 Problem-solving / Reasoning Kaira and Pawel both expand and simplify the quadratic expression $(x - 4)(3 + x)$.
Kaira says that the answer is $x^2 + x - 12$.
Pawel says that the answer is $x^2 - x - 12$.
Only one of them is correct. Who is it? What mistake was made?

11 When you square a number you multiply it by itself.
For example, $\qquad 5^2 = 5 \times 5 = 25$
or $\qquad\qquad 16^2 = 16 \times 16 = 256$
or $\qquad\qquad (x + 2)^2 = (x + 2)(x + 2) = x^2 + 2x + 2x + 4 = x^2 + 4x + 4$
Expand and simplify
a $(x + 3)^2$ **b** $(x + 5)^2$ **c** $(x - 4)^2$ **d** $(x - 8)^2$

12 Problem-solving Each diagram shows a blue rectangle with a shape cut out of it. Write an expression for the blue area. Simplify your expression.

a

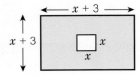

b

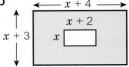

c

13 Copy and complete these expansions. Simplify each answer.

    a $(x + 6)(x - 3) + x(2x - 5)$

    b $(n - 5)(n - 8) - 12(n - 2)$

Challenge

Here is part of a number grid.

A block of four numbers is shaded green.

10	11
18	19

You can work out the answer to

    top right × bottom left − top left × bottom right

like this: $11 × 18 - 10 × 19 = 198 - 190 = 8$

1	2	3	4	5	6	7	8
9	10	11	12	13	14	15	16
17	18	19	20	21	22	23	24
25	26	27	28	29	30	31	32
33	34	35	36	37	38	39	40

1 Do the same for the block of four numbers shaded

    a red

7	8
15	16

    b blue

29	30
37	38

2 What do you notice about your answers?

3 A block of four squares is shaded yellow on the same number grid.

n	...
...	...

> **Q3 hint** Bottom left number is 8 more than top left number, so it will be $n + \square$.

The number in the top left-hand corner is n.

Copy the block of four squares and write an expression for each number in the block in terms of n.

4 For the block of four yellow squares, work out

    top right × bottom left − top left × bottom right

Expand and simplify your answer.

5 What do you notice about your answer?

6 Investigate blocks of four squares on different number grids: for example, rows of 6, 9, 12 etc.

7 What do you notice about your answers?

Reflect

Larry says, 'When expanding brackets, I like to draw Horace.'

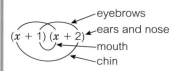

eyebrows

ears and nose

mouth

chin

$(x + 1)(x + 2)$

Does this work for expanding brackets?

Could 'Horace' help you to remember how to expand brackets?

If not, how might you remember?

What pictures (on paper or in your head) do you use to remember mathematics?

Compare with others in your class.

2 Check up

Solving equations

1 Solve

   a $\dfrac{x}{3} - 4 = 3$

   b $\dfrac{5n}{8} = 10$

   c $3r - 2 = r + 8$

   d $5(c - 2) = 2(c + 1)$

   e $\dfrac{x + 7}{8} = 3$

Substituting into expressions

2 Work out the value of these expressions.

   a $5ab^2$ when $a = 2$ and $b = 3$

   b $4 + (a^3 - b)$ when $a = 3$ and $b = 7$

   c $(a - b)^2 + 2c$ when $a = 13$, $b = 6$ and $c = 5$

   d $\dfrac{2a + 3b}{c - d}$ when $a = 7$, $b = 2$, $c = 7$ and $d = 3$

3 Find the value of each expression when $x = 2$, $y = -3$ and $z = 4$.

   a $5(x^2 + y)$

   b $y^2(4 + 2x^3)$

   c $5z(6 - x) - y$

Writing and using formulae

4 Use the formula $P = mgh$ to work out the value of P when

   a $m = 8$, $g = 10$ and $h = 2.5$

   b $m = 3$, $g = 9.8$ and $h = -4$

5 A car hire company charges £x per day to hire a car for d days.
They also charge a one-off fuel cost of £f.

   a Work out the total cost to hire a car for 7 days that costs £15 per day with a one-off fuel cost of £55.

   b Write a formula for the total amount a customer pays, T, in terms of x, d and f.

   c Use your formula to work out T when $x = 18$, $d = 10$ and $f = 65$.

6 Use the formula $P = mv + t$ to work out the value of t when $P = 50$, $m = 6$ and $v = 5$.

7 Use the formula $A = \frac{1}{2}(a + b)h$ to work out the value of a when $A = 30$, $b = 7$ and $h = 6$.

8 Make x the subject of each formula.

   a $y = kx$ **b** $n = \dfrac{x}{a}$ **c** $t = x - v$ **d** $u = 2x + d$

Indices, expanding and factorising

9 Expand
    a $y(y^3 + 7y)$
    b $3x(2x^3 + x)$

10 Expand and simplify $x(x + 5) + 3(x^2 + 9x)$.

11 Simplify
    a $(7y)^2$ **b** $\left(\dfrac{x}{5}\right)^3$

12 Simplify
    a $w^2 \times w^3$ **b** $4g^3 \times 3g^2$

    c $v^3 \div v$ **d** $y^2 \div y^3$

    e $\dfrac{15z^7}{3z^7}$ **f** $\dfrac{2a^2 \times 6a^5}{3a^6}$

13 Factorise each expression completely. Check your answers.
    a $9x - 3x^3$ **b** $20y^6 + 15y^4$

14 Expand and simplify
    a $(x + 4)(x + 8)$ **b** $(x + 9)(x - 3)$
    c $(m - 5)(m - 4)$ **d** $(x + 2)^2$

Challenge

1 Write down three expressions that simplify to give an answer of x^{-3}.

2 In this spider diagram, the four expressions with brackets expand to give the expression in the middle.

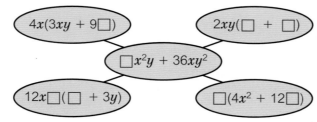 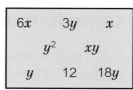

Use the terms in the box to fill in the spider diagram.

Reflect
How sure are you of your answers? Were you mostly

🙁 Just guessing   😐 Feeling doubtful   🙂 Confident

What next? Use your results to decide whether to strengthen or extend your learning.

2 Strengthen

Solving equations

1 Draw function machines to help you solve these equations.
Some are started for you.

a $\dfrac{3x}{2} = 6$ $x \rightarrow \boxed{\times 3} \rightarrow \boxed{\div 2} \rightarrow 6$
$\qquad\qquad\qquad\quad \square \leftarrow \boxed{\div \square} \leftarrow \boxed{\times \square} \leftarrow 6$

b $\dfrac{3x}{5} = 6$ $x \rightarrow \boxed{} \rightarrow \boxed{} \rightarrow \square$
$\qquad\qquad\qquad \square \leftarrow \boxed{} \leftarrow \boxed{} \leftarrow \square$

c $\dfrac{5x}{3} = 10$

d $\dfrac{x}{3} + 7 = 8$ $x \rightarrow \boxed{\div 3} \rightarrow \boxed{+7} \rightarrow 8$
$\qquad\qquad\qquad\qquad \square \leftarrow \boxed{} \leftarrow \boxed{} \leftarrow 8$

e $\dfrac{x}{2} + 3 = 7$

f $\dfrac{x}{2} - 3 = 7$

g $\dfrac{x + 7}{3} = 10$ $x \rightarrow \boxed{+7} \rightarrow \boxed{\div 3} \rightarrow 10$
$\qquad\qquad\qquad\quad \square \leftarrow \boxed{} \leftarrow \boxed{} \leftarrow 10$

h $\dfrac{x - 7}{3} = 10$

2 These scales are balanced. Each box weighs x grams.

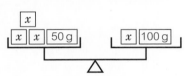

Use the balancing method to work out the weight of one box.

3 Use the balancing method to solve these equations with the unknown on both sides.
a $10r = 9r + 3$ $\underbrace{\quad 10r \quad}\qquad\qquad \underbrace{\quad 9r + 3 \quad}$

b $5s = 2s + 12$ **c** $7p - 2 = 4p + 4$ **d** $8f + 2 = 3f + 12$

4 Solve these equations. Expand the brackets first.
a $6g = 2(g + 4)$
b $5v = 3(v + 2)$
c $6(n - 1) = 5n + 4$
d $2(5h + 1) = 6h + 2$

Substituting into expressions

1 Use priority of operations to work out
a $4^2 + 1$ **b** $5^2 - 3$ **c** $2^2 + 5^2$ **d** $2^2 - 3$

2 Copy and complete, to work out the value of each expression when $x = 2$ and $y = 3$.
a $x^2 + 1 = \square^2 + 1 = \square + 1$ **b** $y^2 - 4 = \square^2 - 4 = \square - 4$
c $x^2 + y = \square^2 + \square$ **d** $y^2 - x = \square^2 - \square$

3 Use priority of operations to work out
   a 2×3^2
   b $3^2 \times 5$
   c $2 \times 3^2 \times 4$
   d $2^2 \times 3^2$

4 Copy and complete to work out the value of each expression when $a = 5$ and $b = 2$.
   a a^2
   b b^2
   c $2a^2 = 2 \times \square^2$
   d $4b^2 = 4 \times \square^2$
   e $a^2 \times b^2 = \square^2 \times \square^2$
   f $2a^2b = 2 \times \square^2 \times \square$
   g $3ab^2 = 3 \times \square \times \square^2$

5 Use priority of operations to work out
   a $2(5 + 7)$
   b $3(2 \times 4 - 1)$
   c $4(2^2 + 1)$
   d $5(3^2 - 2^2)$

6 Work out the value of each expression when $x = 3$ and $y = 4$.
   a $2(x + y)$
   b $3(4x - 1)$
   c $3(4x - y)$
   d $2(x^2 + 1)$
   e $5(x^2 + y)$
   f $3(x^2 + y^2)$
   g $2(y^2 - x^2)$
   h $\dfrac{4x}{6}$
   i $\dfrac{x^2 + 1}{5}$
   j $\dfrac{y^2 - 1}{x}$
   k $\dfrac{4x^2 + 3y}{8}$
   l $\dfrac{5y - 2x}{x + y}$

7 Work out
   a $4 + -1$
   b $-5 - -2$
   c 3×-2
   d -6×5
   e -3×-5
   f $(-1)^2 = -1 \times -1 =$

   Check your answers with a calculator.

8 Copy and complete to find the value of each expression when $a = 2$ and $b = -1$.
   a $2a + b = 2 \times 2 + -1 = 4 - 1 = \square$
   b $6a - 4b = 6 \times \square - 4 \times \square = \square + \square = \square$
   c $a^2 - b = \square^2 - \square = \square + \square = \square$
   d $3b^2 = 3 \times (\square)^2 = 3 \times \square = \square$
   e $4(b - a) = 4(\square - \square) = 4 \times \square = \square$
   f $6(b^3 + 2a) = 6((\square)^3 + 2 \times \square) = 6(\square + \square) = 6 \times \square = \square$

9 Find the value of each expression when $x = 5$, $y = 4$ and $z = -3$.
   a $xy + 2z$
   b $z^2 + 3xy$
   c $5y^2 - xz$
   d $6(4x - 9z)$
   e $3(y^3 + 4xz)$
   f $\dfrac{x - z}{2y}$

Writing and using formulae

1 **a** Copy and complete to write an expression for the cost of hiring a bicycle at £8 per day.
  b Write a formula for C, the cost of hiring a bicycle for n days.
     $C = \boxed{}$
  c Use your formula to work out the cost of hiring a bicycle for 10 days.

Number of days	Cost at £8 per day
1	$1 \times 8 = \square$
2	$\square \times 8 = \square$
3	$\square \times 8 = \square$
n	$\square \times 8 = \square$

2 Another bicycle hire company charges a one-off fee of £30, plus £5 per day.

a Copy and complete the table to write an expression for the cost of hiring a bicycle.

Number of days	Cost at £5 per day + one-off fee
1	$1 \times 5 + 30 = \square + 30$
2	$\square \times 5 + 30 = \square + 30$
n	$\square \times 5 + 30 = \square + \square$

b Write a formula for T, the total cost of hiring a bicycle for n days.

$T = \boxed{} + \square$

c Use your formula to work out the cost of hiring a bicycle for 5 days.

3 A surf shop charges an amount per hour to hire a surfboard. They also charge a one-off cost to hire a wetsuit.

a Work out the total cost to hire a surfboard for 3 hours at £6 per hour when the one-off wetsuit cost is £12.

b Write an expression for the total cost to hire a surfboard for h hours at £6 per hour when the one-off wetsuit cost is £w.

c Write an expression for the total cost to hire a surfboard for h hours at £x per hour when the one-off wetsuit cost is £w.

d Write a formula for the total cost, T, in terms of h, x and w.

e Use your formula to work out T when $h = 6$, $x = 5$ and $w = 8$.

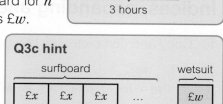

> **Q3a hint**
> surfboard   wetsuit
> £6 | £6 | £6 | £12
> 3 hours

> **Q3c hint**
> surfboard   wetsuit
> £x | £x | £x | ... | £w
> h lots of £x

4 Use the formula $M = Fd$ to work out the value of M. The first part is started for you.

a $F = 12$ and $d = 6$

$M = F \times d = \square \times \square = \square$

b $F = 25$ and $d = 3$

c $F = 8.5$ and $d = 0.2$

> **Q4 hint** Replace the letters with numbers.

5 Use the formula $T = 2P + 3R$ to work out the value of T. The first part is started for you.

a $P = 12$ and $R = -7$

$T = 2 \times \square + 3 \times \square$

b $P = -2$ and $R = 14$

c $P = -6$ and $R = -1$

6 Substitute the values given into the formula $A = bh$. Solve the equation to work out the value of b when

a $A = 12$ and $h = 3$ **b** $A = 10$ and $h = 25$

$12 = b \times \square$

7 Substitute the values given into the formula $R = mu + p$. Solve the equation to work out the value of

a p when $R = 20$, $m = 4$ and $u = 2$

$20 = \square \times \square + p$

b p when $R = 25$, $m = 2$ and $u = 7$

c m when $R = 23$, $u = 3$ and $p = 14$

d m when $R = 40$, $u = 5$ and $p = 20$

e u when $R = 28$, $m = 6$ and $p = 16$

f u when $R = 79$, $m = 8$ and $p = 7$

8 Use the formula $A = \frac{1}{2}(a + b)h$ to work out the value of b when $A = 24$, $a = 4$ and $h = 3$.

Q8 hint

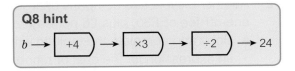

9 Copy and complete to make b the subject of the formula $A = bh$.

$$\div h \left(\begin{array}{c} A = b \times h \\ \frac{\Box}{\Box} = b \end{array} \right) \div h \qquad b \to \boxed{\times h} \to A \qquad b \leftarrow \boxed{\div h} \leftarrow A$$

10 a Make a the subject of the formula $v = at$.

b Make n the subject of the formula

$$\Box \left(\begin{array}{c} K = \frac{n}{t} \\ \boxed{} = n \end{array} \right) \Box \qquad n \to \boxed{\div t} \to K \qquad n \leftarrow \boxed{\times t} \leftarrow K$$

Indices, expanding and factorising

1 Copy and complete

a i $\overbrace{m^2}^{} \times \overbrace{m^3}^{}$
$\underline{m \times m} \times \Box \times \Box \times \Box = m^\Box$

ii $m^2 \times m^3 = m^{\Box + \Box} = m^\Box$

b i $\overbrace{b^3}^{} \times b$
$\underline{\Box \times \Box \times \Box} \times b = b^\Box$

ii $b^3 \times b = b^{\Box + \Box} = b^\Box$

2 Simplify.

a $a \times a^3$ **b** $c^2 \times c^2$ **c** $b \times b^2$ **d** $g^3 \times g^2$ **e** $d \times d^4$

3 Simplify these expressions. The first one is started for you.

a $4d^3 \times d^5 = 4 \times d^3 \times d^5 = 4 \times d^\Box$

b $p^2 \times 3p$ **c** $-5n \times 2n^3$ **d** $-2g^2 \times -3n^2$

4 Copy and complete

a $m^4 \times m^\Box = m^7$ **b** $m^7 \div m^4 = m^{\Box - \Box} = m^\Box$

c $h^2 \times h^\Box = h^6$ **d** $h^6 \div h^2 = h^\Box$

e $s \times s^\Box = s^5$ **f** $s^5 \div s = s^\Box$

g $7m^\Box \times m^2 = 7m^5$ **h** $7m^5 \div m^2 = 7m^\Box$

5 Simplify by collecting like terms.

a $a^2 + 2a + 3a$ **b** $a^2 + 5a - 2a$

c $a^2 + 2a - 5a$ **d** $2a^2 - 3a + 2a$

6 Expand, then simplify by collecting like terms. The first one is started for you.

a $d(d + 3) + d = d^2 + \Box d + d$ **b** $d(d + 3) + 2d$

c $d(d + 3) - 2d$ **d** $2d(d + 3) + d$ **e** $2d(d + 3) + 5d$ **f** $2d(d + 3) + 5d^2$

7 Copy and complete

a $2^{-2} = \frac{1}{2^\Box}$ **b** $x^{-2} = \frac{1}{x^\Box}$ **c** $2^{-3} = \frac{1}{2^\Box}$ **d** $y^{-3} = \frac{1}{y^\Box}$

8 Simplify these expressions. The first one is started for you.

a $\dfrac{x^2}{x^3} = x^{2-3} = x^{\square} = \dfrac{1}{x^{\square}}$　　b $\dfrac{y^4}{y^6}$　　c $\dfrac{z^3}{z^8}$　　d $\dfrac{w}{w^7}$

9 a What is the highest common factor of
　　i 3x and 6　　　ii 4x^2 and 12x　　　iii 10x^2 and 15x^3?
　b Factorise each expression completely.
　　Take out the highest common factor and put it in front of the brackets.
　　Check your answers by expanding the brackets.
　　i $10x + 5 = 5(\square + \square)$
　　ii $10x^2 + 5x = 5x(\square + \square)$
　　iii $12x - 9x^2 = 3x(\square - \square)$
　　iv $25y^5 + 10y^2 = 5y^2(\square + \square)$
　　v $14a^3 - 10a = \square(\square - \square)$
　　vi $b^2 + 3b^4 = \square(\square + \square)$
　　vii $12c^2 + 18c^3 = \square(\square + \square)$

> **Q9a ii hint** The HCF of 4 and 12 is 4.
> x is also a common factor.
> So $4x$ is the HCF of $4x^2$ and $12x$.

10 To expand $(a + 2)(a + 5)$, use a grid method like this:

×	a	+2
a	$+a^2$	$+2a$
+5	$+5a$	+10

Copy and complete to simplify the answer.
$a^2 + 2a + 5a + 10 = \square + \square + \square$

11 Use the grid method to expand and simplify
　a $(a + 3)(a + 5)$　　　b $(b + 9)(b + 4)$　　　c $(c + 1)(c + 2)$

12 Expand and simplify
　a $(a + 8)(a - 2)$　　　b $(b - 5)(b + 4)$　　　c $(c - 7)(c - 3)$

> **Q12a hint**
>
> | × | a | +8 |
> |---|---|---|
> | a | | $+8a$ |
> | −2 | $-2a$ | |

Challenge　　Find numbers to complete the power pyramids.
a For pyramid A, multiplying two adjacent powers on the same row gives the power above.
b For pyramid B, dividing two adjacent powers on the same row gives the power below.

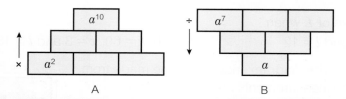

A　　　　　B

Reflect　　Ask someone in your class to show you a question they got wrong.
Try to work out what mistake they made.

2 Extend

1 Solve these equations. Check your solutions.

    a $\dfrac{2n}{5} = 8$ **b** $\dfrac{5x}{4} = 10$ **c** $\dfrac{4u}{3} = 12$ **d** $\dfrac{3n}{100} = 30$

2 Solve these equations. Check your solutions.

    a $\dfrac{m-5}{4} = 2$ **b** $\dfrac{2b+5}{3} = 7$ **c** $\dfrac{3k-4}{2} = 4$

3 Use the formula $T = \dfrac{kx}{l}$ to work out the value of T when

    a $k = 20$, $x = 0.6$ and $l = 3$ **b** $k = 50$, $x = -0.5$ and $l = 4$

4 Use the formula $L = \dfrac{5x^2}{v}$ to work out the value of L when $x = 4$ and $v = 10$.

5 Wooden flooring costs £35 per square metre.

The floor is then edged with a narrow wooden strip which costs £4 per metre.

    a How much does it cost for a 6 m by 4 m room, including the edging?

    b Write a formula for the cost, C, of a wooden floor in a rectangular room of width w and length l (remember to include the edging).

    c Use your formula to work out C when $w = 3.5$ m and $l = 5$ m.

6 The pressure, P, volume, V, and temperature, T, of a gas are related by the formula $\dfrac{PV}{T} = 6$.

Use the formula to find the value of V when $P = 3$ and $T = 40$.

7 An elastic string has natural length l metres.

When the string is stretched by x metres, the tension T newtons is given by the formula $T = \dfrac{60x}{l}$.

Use the formula to work out x when $T = 24$ newtons and $l = 15$ m.

8 Use the formula $X = hr^3$ to work out the value of X when

    a $h = 12$ and $r = 3$ **b** $h = 7$ and $r = 2$

    c $h = 100$ and $r = 5$ **d** $h = 36$ and $r = 4$

9 You can use this formula to calculate the energy stored in a stretched string.

    $E = \dfrac{kx^2}{2l}$

Work out the value of E when

    a $k = 30$, $x = 2$ and $l = 12$ **b** $k = 60$, $x = 3$ and $l = 18$

10 **Problem-solving** The diagram shows a shape made from two rectangles. All measurements are in centimetres.

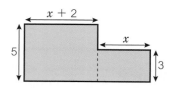

    a Write an expression for the total area of the shape.

    b The total area of the shape is 30 cm². Write an equation in terms of x, then solve it to find the value of x.

    c Work out the perimeter of the shape.

11 Make m the subject of each formula.

a $x = 2hm$ **b** $P = mgh$ **c** $r = \dfrac{m}{2l}$

d $y = \dfrac{3m}{4x}$ **e** $y = m^2$ **f** $x = m^2 + 2n$

Q11a hint

$m \longrightarrow \boxed{\times 2h} \longrightarrow x$

12 Simplify

a $-10t \times 3t^3$ **b** $-2a \times -3a^2$

c $m^2 \times m^3 \div m^4$ **d** $c^5 \times c \div c^2$

e $u^4 \div u^2 \times u^3$ **f** $\dfrac{p^6}{p^2}$

g $r^4 \times \dfrac{r^5}{r^3}$ **h** $\dfrac{s^4}{s} \times s^3$

i $4w^3 \times 2w^2 \div w$ **j** $d^6 \div -d^3 \times d^7$

k $2b^4 \times 3b \times b^3 \times 4b^2$ **l** $4x^4 \times -5x^2 \times -3x$

Q12d hint

$m \longrightarrow \boxed{\times 3} \longrightarrow \boxed{\div 4x} \longrightarrow y$

Q12f hint

$m \longrightarrow \boxed{\square^2} \longrightarrow \boxed{+2n} \longrightarrow x$

13 Expand

a $(5m)^3$ **b** $(10a)^2$ **c** $(2c)^4$ **d** $(3pq)^2$

14 Expand

a $x(x^3 + 3x + 7)$ **b** $a(a^2 - 8a + 1)$ **c** $b(b^3 + 5b^2 - 6)$ **d** $2p(4 + 5p + p^2)$

e $6z(z^3 - 4z^2 + 9)$ **f** $a^2(2a^2 + 3a - 4)$ **g** $3k(k^3 - 6k - 7)$

15 **Problem-solving / Reasoning**   Hannah and Barney both simplify the expression $\dfrac{6x^7}{3x^9}$.

Hannah says that the answer is $2x^{-2}$. Barney says that the answer is $\dfrac{1}{2x^2}$.

Only one of them is correct. Who is it? Explain your answer.

16 **Reasoning**   This is how Alisha factorises the expression $8x^2y^2 - 4xy^2z$ completely.

$8x^2y^2 - 4xy^2z = 2xy\,(4xy - 2yz)$

a Explain the mistake that she has made.

b Factorise the expression correctly and completely.

17 **Problem-solving**   The diagram shows a red square with a square hole cut out of it.

a Explain how you can work out the red area on the diagram.

b Write an expression for the red area on the diagram. Simplify your expression.

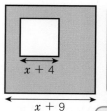

$x + 4$

$x + 9$

Q17 hint How would you work out the red area if the side length of the red square was 20 cm and the side length of the hole was 15 cm?

Q17a hint area of red square $= (x + 9)^2$

Reflect   Look back at the questions you answered in this Extend lesson.

Find a question that you could not answer straightaway, or that you really had to think about.

Why couldn't you immediately see what to do? How did this make you feel?

Did you keep trying or did you give up? Did you think you would get the answer correct or incorrect?

Write down any strategies you could use when answering tricky algebra questions.

Compare your strategies with others in your class.

2 Unit test

1   Use the formula $F = pm + r$ to work out the value of F when
    a $p = 7$, $m = 6$ and $r = 12$
    b $p = 6$, $m = 2.5$ and $r = -8$

2   Use the formula $M = \dfrac{3r}{t}$ to work out the value of M when $r = 18$ and $t = -6$.

3   Work out the value of these expressions.
    a $2a + b^2$ when $a = 5$ and $b = 2$
    b $40 - (a + b^3)$ when $a = 8$ and $b = 3$
    c $(a + b)^2 - 4c$ when $a = 3$, $b = 5$ and $c = 5$
    d $\dfrac{2a^2}{bc}$ when $a = 6$, $b = 4$ and $c = 3$

4   A wedding venue company charges an amount per person for food plus an amount per hour for the room hire.
    a Work out the total cost of food for 80 people at £30 per person plus room hire at £50 per hour for 6 hours.
    b Write an expression for the cost of food for p people at £x per person plus room hire for h hours at £y per hour.
    c Write a formula for the total cost, T, in terms of x, p, y and h.
    d Use your formula to work out T when $x = 35$, $p = 100$, $h = 8$ and $y = 30$.

5   Expand and simplify $x(x^2 + 15x) + 4x(2x^2 - 3x)$.

6   Simplify
    a $(3x)^3$
    b $\left(\dfrac{y}{4}\right)^2$

7   Work out the value of each expression when $x = 4$ and $y = -2$.
    a $2(3x + 2y)$
    b $x^2(3 - y)$
    c $\dfrac{2x - 3y}{y + 9}$

8   Use the formula $R = \dfrac{ax}{3}$ to work out the value of R when $a = 2$ and $x = 9$.

9   Simplify
    a $\dfrac{x^3}{x^5}$ **b** $\dfrac{y^2}{y^8}$ **c** $\dfrac{z}{z^3}$

10 Expand
    a $x^3(3x - 4x^2)$
    b $2y^2(5y^3 + y)$

11 Factorise each expression completely. Check your answers.
    a $24x + 8x^2$ **b** $12x^3 - 9x^5$

12 Solve

   a $\dfrac{x-2}{3} = 4$

   b $\dfrac{g}{3} + 2 = 7$

   c $\dfrac{2b}{5} = 6$

   d $3(x + 2) = 4x - 1$

13 Use the formula $A = bh$ to work out the value of

   a h when $A = 35$ and $b = 5$

   b b when $A = 20$ and $h = 8$

14 Use the formula $R = mg - T$ to work out the value of m when $R = 40$, $g = 12$ and $T = 8$.

15 Expand and simplify

   a $(x + 6)(x + 7)$

   b $(x + 12)(x - 9)$

   c $(m - 7)(m - 11)$

16 Make x the subject of each formula.

   a $F = x + p$

   b $M = xR$

   c $d = 5x + h$

17 Expand and simplify $(x + 6)^2$.

Challenge

a Show that $(y + 4)(y + 7) - y(y + 8) = (y + 4)(y - 8) - (y - 12)(y + 5)$.

b Explain the method that you used.

Reflect   This may be the first time you have done any algebra for a while.

Choose **A**, **B** or **C** to complete each statement.

In this unit, I did...	**A** well	**B** OK	**C** not very well
I think algebra is...	**A** easy	**B** OK	**C** difficult
When I think about doing algebra, I feel...	**A** confident	**B** OK	**C** unsure

If you answered mostly As and Bs, are you surprised that you feel OK about algebra? Why?
If you answered mostly Cs, look back at the questions in the lessons that you found most difficult. Ask a friend or your teacher to explain them to you. Then complete the statements above again.

3 Dealing with data

Master   Check up p71   Strengthen p73   Extend p78   Unit test p80

3.1 Planning a survey

- Identify sources of primary and secondary data
- Choose a suitable sample size and what data to collect
- Identify factors that might affect data collection and plan to reduce bias

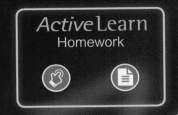

Active Learn
Homework

Warm up

1 **Fluency** Work out
   a 10% of 700   **b** 10% of 2000   **c** $\frac{37}{200}$ as a percentage.

2 The table shows the ages of visitors to a shopping centre on a Monday morning in November.
   a How many visitors were there in total?
   b How many visitors were 18 or under?
   c What percentage of visitors were 61 or over?
   d Which age group had the lowest frequency? Suggest a reason for this.

Age (years)	Frequency
0–5	23
6–18	5
19–30	9
31–45	34
46–60	87
61+	42

3 Henry wants to test whether a coin is biased.
   Should Henry flip the coin 10, 50 or 100 times?

Q3 hint A **biased** coin is not 'fair' – heads and tails are not equally likely.

4 Alpita wants to find out if young people use the swimming pool at her local sports centre more than adults.
   Which of these pieces of information should she collect?
   A Gender
   B Age
   C Distance of travel to sports centre
   D Activity chosen at the sports centre
   E Length of time spent in the sports centre

Key point
Primary data is data you collect yourself.
Secondary data is collected by someone else.

5 A town councillor wants to find out information about the ages of the people living in her town. Which of these sources use **secondary data**?
   A Carrying out a survey of the ages of people in the town centre.
   B Looking at the electoral roll (a list of the people registered to vote).
   C Looking at online records.

Q5 hint In a survey you collect information.

6 A journalist wants to find out information about the number of people in each household in the UK.
Decide whether each method will produce **primary** or **secondary** data.

   a She carries out a survey of the number of people in her town.

   b She looks at the most recent **census** results.

> **Q6 hint** In a **census**, data is collected from the whole population. The UK Government carries out a census every 10 years.

> **Key point** The total number of items a survey relates to is called the **population**.
> Sometimes you can't test every single item in a population, so you collect a **sample**.
> A good-sized sample is usually about 10% of the population.
> For a sample to be suitable it needs to be unbiased.

7 **Reasoning** For each survey, select the most appropriate **sample** size. Explain your choices.

   a There are 1000 students in a school. Peter wants to find out students' favourite drinks. How many students should he ask?

     A 4   **B** 100   **C** 500

   b A café gets 700 customers each week. The owner thinks that most customers order food to take away. How many customers should she sample?

     A 7   **B** 70   **C** 350

> **Key point** A **hypothesis** is a statement that you can test by collecting data in a questionnaire, survey or experiment.

8 **Reasoning** What data would you collect to test each **hypothesis**?

   a **i** 25% of children at a school walk to school.

     ii Most households have more than one TV.

     iii 40% of people eat at least five portions of fruit or vegetables a day.

   b How would you collect the data for each?
Would you use primary or secondary data?

9 **Reasoning** Match each investigation to the best way to obtain relevant data.

   a the age of students in your class   **A** experiment

   b who uses the local supermarket   **B** survey

   c the number of times an even number is rolled on a dice   **C** questionnaire

> **Q9a hint** A questionnaire is a set of questions for people to answer.

10 **Reasoning** Select an appropriate level of accuracy for the measurements in these investigations.

   a The lengths of worms in a flower bed.

     A nearest cm   **B** nearest mm   **C** nearest 0.1 mm

   b The times taken to run 100 m at your school sports day.

     A nearest minute   **B** nearest second   **C** nearest millisecond

   c The times taken for athletes to run 100 m in a world record attempt.

     A nearest minute   **B** nearest second   **C** nearest hundredth of a second

   d The masses of newborn babies.

     A nearest kg   **B** nearest 0.1 kg   **C** nearest gram

11 Reasoning A school wants to investigate the length of time students spend travelling to school. There are 1000 students at the school.

   a i Suggest the number of students that should be sampled.

     ii What level of accuracy should be used to record their times?

   b Which of these factors will affect the data?

     A Standing by a bus stop to collect the data.

     B Standing at the gates of the school to collect the data.

     C The gender of the students asked.

     D Asking only students who arrive at school early.

     E Asking only students who travel by train.

> **Key point** In order to reduce **bias**, a sample must represent the whole population.

12 Reasoning Callum wants to find out the favourite TV programme of people in his school. He asks his friends what their favourite TV show is. Explain why Callum's results will be biased.

13 Reasoning Here are four methods to find out a town's most popular shop.
Method 1: Amy interviews 100 randomly chosen students at her school.
Method 2: Rudi stands in the centre of town on a Saturday and asks 500 people that he chooses randomly.
Method 3: Helen asks everyone coming out of a particular shop.
Method 4: Paul asks his friends, family and neighbours.

   a Which is the best method and why?

   b What bias was there in the other methods?

   c How could you improve the method you chose in part **a**?

> **Key point** In a **random sample**, every item is equally likely to be chosen.

14 Reasoning A school wants to choose a **random sample** of students to take part in a competition. Which of these will give a random sample?

   A Students whose names begin with 'A'.

   B The oldest students.

   C Students' names placed into a hat and picked out.

   D Every 10th student on the whole school register.

> **Challenge** Choose a topic that you are interested in. It could be sport, music, school activities, where you live – anything you like. Write a hypothesis related to your topic. Plan how you will test your hypothesis.
> - Where and when will you collect your data?
> - What sample size will you use?
> - How will you avoid bias in your sample?

> **Reflect** How do you use mathematics when you plan a survey?
>
> **Hint** Look carefully at some of the questions you answered. What mathematical skills do you need? What mathematical words must you understand? What measures might you use?

3.2 Collecting data

- Design and use data collection sheets and tables
- Design a good questionnaire

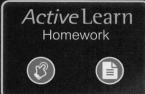

Active Learn
Homework

Warm up

1 Fluency In which class does 0.5 cm go for each of these grouped frequency tables?

a

Length, l (cm)	Frequency
$0 \leq l < 0.5$	
$0.5 \leq l < 1$	

b

Length, l (cm)	Frequency
$0 < l \leq 0.5$	
$0.5 < l \leq 1$	

2 Here are the ages of 24 users of a leisure centre.
18, 23, 36, 20, 8, 1, 23, 27, 29, 35, 33, 26, 25, 10,
19, 15, 23, 30, 36, 19, 26, 30, 34, 36

Copy and compete the tally chart for the data.

Age (years)	Tally	Frequency
0–10		
11–20		
21–30		
31–40		

Key point A **data collection sheet** is a table or chart for collecting **data**.

3 Mark recorded the colour of cars passing the school one morning.

red   blue   red   black   red   white   silver   red   blue   green   red   green
blue   blue   green   black   red   black   silver   black   green   blue   black   red

He plans to do a longer survey the next day.

a Copy and complete this **data collection sheet** for his survey.

Car colour	Tally	Frequency
red		
blue		

> **Q3 hint** Include all the colours.

b Would it be useful to have a row for 'other colours'?

Key point A **grouped frequency table** has several equal width classes. You can add a tally column for recording the data.

4 Problem-solving Fernando asked some of his classmates how many emails they sent last week. These are his results.

12   8   23   15   18   24   23   24
10   17   22   6   7   14   18   23

a Copy and complete this data collection sheet for his data.

b How many of his classmates did he ask?

c What is the modal class?

Number of emails	Tally	Frequency
0–4		
5–9		

5 The numbers of people using a supermarket each day in one month were

123	179	235	189	207	199	145	154	198	132
201	99	134	245	207	198	64	157	149	183
172	175	188	192	184	167	203	201	188	181

a Is the data discrete or continuous?

b Design a grouped frequency table to record this data.

c Which group has the highest frequency?

6 A post office employee recorded the masses in kilograms of 15 parcels.

2.00 4.54 9.75 8.21 4.53 3.45 6.00 1.24
5.22 3.30 0.99 6.12 5.44 6.23 7.12

a Is this data discrete or continuous?

b Design a grouped frequency table to record this data.

c Which group has the highest frequency?

7 Here are some records from a hospital database.

a Is the mass data discrete or continuous?

b Design a grouped frequency table to record the masses.

  i Copy and complete this two-way table with 4 or 5 classes to show the masses and ages of the patients.

Name	Age	Mass, m (kg)
Hall	35	63
Field	25	56
Aintree	17	67
Kingley	34	80
Firbrand	56	77
Ruvierra	72	66
Huckelberry	61	70
Tudoristo	43	56
Franklin	45	73
Murphy	81	80
Orringe	34	88
Fruitry	47	93
Smith	65	67
Frankless	32	82
Harrison	45	91
Amberly	63	110
Kingston	45	84
Ocra	35	92
Savile	72	72
Dengel	56	88

		Age (years)		
		10–29	30–49	50+
Mass, m (kg)	$50 \leqslant m < 70$			
	$70 \leqslant m < 90$			
	90+			

  ii How many patients who are 50+ have a mass less than 70 kg?

  iii What proportion of the patients are aged between 10 and 29 years?

  iv What proportion of patients are in the middle mass group?

8 Year 8 and Year 9 students choose to learn French, Spanish or Mandarin.
Copy this two-way table to record their choices and fill in the headings.

	Year	

9 A fair dice is rolled. The score is even or odd.
A coin is flipped.
Design a two-way table to show all the possible results, for example Odd, Head.

Here are three questions used in an online questionnaire.
Explain what is wrong with each question and rewrite it.

a How old are you?

☐ 0–10   ☐ 10–20   ☐ 20–30   ☐ 30–50   ☐ 50+

The groups overlap. For example, if you are 20 years old, which box do you tick?
Change to: ☐ 0–10   ☐ 11–20   ☐ 21–30   ☐ 31–50   ☐ 51+

b Do you agree that exercise is enjoyable?   ☐ Yes   ☐ No

Saying, 'Do you agree?' encourages the answer 'Yes'.
Change to: Do you enjoy exercise?

c Do you exercise enough?

'Enough' is not precise and means different things to different people.
Change to: How much exercise do you do each day?

☐ Less than 1 hour   ☐ 1–2 hours   ☐ More than 2 hours

10 Reasoning   Anti animal-cruelty campaigners want to find out how people feel about killing animals for fur. They ask, 'It is cruel to kill animals for fur, isn't it?'
  a What do you think most people will answer? Why is this a leading question?
  b Rewrite the question to find out what people really think about killing animals for fur.

11 Reasoning
  a Explain what is wrong with each of these questions and rewrite them.
    i How many portions of fruit or vegetables do you eat a day?   ☐ 0–2   ☐ 4–6   ☐ 6–8
    ii Do you eat enough fruit?   ☐ Yes   ☐ No
    iii Do you agree that fruit and vegetables are good for you?   ☐ Yes   ☐ No
  b Imagine you are carrying out a survey using your new questions.
    Design a data collection sheet to collect together all the answers.

12 Problem-solving   Write your own questionnaire to collect data to test this hypothesis.
  'Most people watch at least two hours of television a day.'

Challenge   Look at the hypothesis that you wrote in the investigation in lesson 3.1.
a Design a questionnaire to collect the information you need to test your hypothesis.
b Test your questionnaire on a friend.
c Design a data collection sheet to record the answers to your questionnaire.
d Collect data from a suitable sample.
e Record your findings.

Reflect   You have learned lots of new key words so far in this unit.
  • primary data   • bias
  • secondary data   • random samples
  • hypothesis   • discrete and continuous data

Work with a classmate. Discuss what you think 'primary data' and 'secondary data' are.
Now write definitions for 'primary' and 'secondary data'. Try to be as accurate as possible.
Do the same for the other words in the list.

3.3 Calculating averages

- Find the median from a frequency table
- Estimate the mean from a large set of grouped data

Active Learn
Homework

Warm up

1 **Fluency** In a set of 15 data values in order, which value is the median?

2 The table shows the number of goals scored by a football team in matches over one season.
   a What is the modal number of goals scored?
   b How many matches did the team play?
   c Work out the mean number of goals scored.
   d Work out the range of goals scored.

Number of goals	Frequency
0	5
1	6
2	3
3	2
4	3
5	1

Key point

You can find the median from a frequency table.

Worked example

The table shows the numbers of pets people own. Find the median number of pets.

Number of pets	Frequency
0	7
1	5
2	2
3	4
4	2
Total	**20**

1st–7th data values

8th–12th data values

Median is the $\frac{20+1}{2}$th $= \frac{21}{2} = 10.5$th value

Median is the $\frac{n+1}{2}$th value.

The median is 1 pet.

3 The table shows the numbers of cars per household in one street.
   Find the median number of cars.

Number of cars	Frequency
0	3
1	16
2	19
3	1

4 Use the table in Q2 to find the median number of goals scored by the football team.

Worked example

In a survey, people were asked their age. The table shows the results.

Age, a (years)	Frequency
$0 \leq a < 10$	12
$10 \leq a < 20$	15
$20 \leq a < 30$	2
$30 \leq a < 40$	11

1st–12th data values

13th–27th data values

a Find the class that contains the median.

Total frequency = 40

Median is the $\dfrac{40 + 1}{2}$th = 20.5th value

The median is in the class $10 \leq a < 20$

Add a column to calculate the midpoint of each class. This is an estimate for the ages, because you don't know the exact values in each class.

b Calculate an estimate for the mean age.

Age, a (years)	Frequency	Midpoint of class	Midpoint × frequency
$0 \leq a < 10$	12	$\dfrac{0 + 10}{2} = 5$	$5 \times 12 = 60$
$10 \leq a < 20$	15	$\dfrac{10 + 20}{2} = 15$	$15 \times 15 = 225$
$20 \leq a < 30$	2	25	$25 \times 2 = 50$
$30 \leq a < 40$	11	35	$35 \times 11 = 385$
Total	40		720

Add a column to calculate an estimate of the total age for each class.

$\text{mean} = \dfrac{\text{sum estimated of ages}}{\text{total number of people}}$

$= \dfrac{720}{40}$

$= 18$

Calculate the total number of people in the survey and the sum of their estimated ages.

5 **a** The table shows the lengths of a sample of grass snakes. Copy and complete the table.
  b Find the class that contains the median.
  c Calculate an estimate for the mean length.

Length, l (cm)	Frequency	Midpoint of class	Midpoint × frequency
$0 \leq l < 6$	8		
$6 \leq l < 12$	7		
$12 \leq l < 18$	2		
$18 \leq l < 24$	3		
Total			

6 The table shows the earnings of workers in a factory.
  a What is the modal class for this data?
  b Work out an estimate for the range.
  c Find the class that contains the median.
  d Calculate an estimate for the mean earnings. Round your answer to the nearest pound.

Earnings (per annum), e	Number of employees
£0 < e ⩽ £10 000	3
£10 000 < e ⩽ £20 000	52
£20 000 < e ⩽ £30 000	29
£30 000 < e ⩽ £40 000	27
£40 000 < e ⩽ £50 000	5

7 a What is the modal class for each of these data sets?

i

Class	Frequency
$0 \leqslant a < 2$	3
$2 \leqslant a < 4$	5
$4 \leqslant a < 6$	11
$6 \leqslant a < 8$	1

ii

Class	Frequency
$0 < b \leqslant 0.5$	2
$0.5 < b \leqslant 1$	1
$1 < b \leqslant 1.5$	7
$1.5 < b \leqslant 2$	0

iii

Class	Frequency
$0 \leqslant l < 0.4$	52
$0.4 \leqslant l < 0.8$	13
$0.8 \leqslant l < 1.2$	22
$1.2 \leqslant l < 1.6$	13

b Work out an estimate of the range for each data set.

c Find the class that contains the median for each data set.

d Calculate an estimate of the mean for each data set.

8 The grouped frequency table shows students' marks in a test.

a What is the modal class?

b Find the class that contains the median.

c Calculate an estimate for the mean mark.

Mark	Frequency
1–10	4
11–20	23
21–30	26
31–40	16
41–50	16

9 The distances d, in metres, achieved in a welly-throwing competition were

15.8   21.9   39.5   28.3   19.7   30.0   42.1   35.0   19.9   27.5

39.9   29.7   17.3   24.1   46.2   27.3   37.3   27.4   38.8   32.0

Distance, d (m)	Frequency
$10 \leqslant d < 20$	
$20 \leqslant d < 30$	
$30 \leqslant d < 40$	
$40 \leqslant d < 50$	

a Copy and complete the grouped frequency table.

b What is the modal group?

c Calculate an estimate of the mean from your grouped frequency table.

d Find the median from the ungrouped data.

10 A scientist is testing the hypothesis that each year tadpoles are bigger. She recorded the lengths of 100 of this year's tadpoles.

a What is the modal class?

b Estimate the range of lengths.

c Calculate an estimate for the mean length.

d **Reasoning**   Last year the estimate for the mean length was 5.92 mm. Is the scientist's hypothesis correct?

Length, l (mm)	Frequency
$3 < l \leqslant 4$	7
$4 < l \leqslant 5$	18
$5 < l \leqslant 6$	27
$6 < l \leqslant 7$	31
$7 < l \leqslant 8$	11
$8 < l \leqslant 9$	6

Challenge   Look at the data that you recorded in the investigation in lesson 3.2. Work out the modal class, the mean, the range and the class that contains the median for your data.

Reflect   Explain what is the same and what is different when calculating

- the mean of a set of data
- the mean from a frequency table
- an estimate of the mean from a grouped frequency table.

3.4 Displaying and analysing data

- Construct and use a line of best fit to estimate missing values
- Identify and suggest reasons for outliers in data
- Identify further lines of enquiry
- Draw line graphs to represent grouped data

*Active*Learn
Homework

Warm up

1 **Fluency** Find the midpoint of each class.

a $0 < e \leqslant 10$ **b** $2 < e \leqslant 8$ **c** $20\,000 < e \leqslant 30\,000$

2 The table shows the age and number of visits to a doctor's surgery from April to September for a sample of 19 people.

Age (years)	25	67	35	92	35	48	72	18	25	63	28	19	26	50	38	78	93	38	1
Number of visits	2	7	4	12	3	6	8	0	2	7	3	1	4	8	5	13	12	4	8

a Plot a scatter graph showing this data. Plot the values from the top row of the table on the horizontal axis.

b What type of correlation does the graph show?

c Draw a line of best fit.

d What is the population for this survey?

Key point

An **outlier** is a value that doesn't follow the trend or pattern.

Worked example

The scatter graphs show height above sea level and temperature in the west of Scotland on one day.

a Describe the correlation shown on the graph.
  negative correlation

b Use the line of best fit to predict the temperature at 1100 m.
  13 °C

c Identify an outlier and suggest what might have caused it.
  The point for 280 m, 15 °C is an outlier.
  The temperature or the height may have been recorded wrongly.

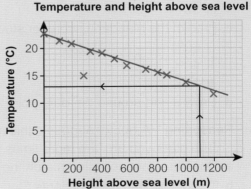
Temperature and height above sea level

An outlier may be from a recording error.

For part **b**, draw a line up from 1100 m to the line of best fit. Draw a line across to the temperature axis.

3 **Reasoning**

a Use your line of best fit in Q2 to estimate the number of visits a 40-year-old would make between April and September.

b Use your line of best fit to estimate the age of a patient who visited the doctor 11 times between April and September.

c Identify an outlier in the data and suggest what might have caused it.

Q3a hint Find 40 on the correct axis. Draw a line up to the line of best fit and then across to the other axis.

4 **Reasoning** Some Year 9 students took two English assessments – writing and comprehension. Here are their results.

Student	A	B	C	D	E	F	G	H	I	J	K	L	M
Writing	64	59	78	82	42	76	43	absent	15	38	45	68	72
Comprehension	60	absent	72	88	36	80	49	85	27	37	51	65	76

a Draw a scatter graph for this data. Put writing marks on the horizontal axis and comprehension marks on the vertical axis.
Ignore the data for students B and H.

b Draw a line of best fit on your graph.

c Describe the relationship between the marks for writing and marks for comprehension.

d Use your line of best fit to predict
  i the comprehension marks for student B
  ii the writing marks for student H.

5 **Reasoning** Here are 9 students' exam results in Mandarin and maths.

Mandarin	75%	81%	45%	24%	57%	91%	89%	93%	63%
Maths	83%	92%	35%	30%	62%	25%	80%	84%	59%

a Draw a scatter diagram for this data.

b Predict the maths score for students whose Mandarin score was
  i 30%
  ii 50%
  iii 90%

c Predict the Mandarin score for students whose maths score was
  i 60%
  ii 40%
  iii 70%

d Draw a ring around the data point that is an outlier.

6 **Reasoning** A doctor suggests this hypothesis for the data in Q2.
'The older you are, the more times you visit the doctor per year.'

a Does the data collected match the hypothesis?

b The doctor has 5000 patients.
Is the sample size large enough to represent this population?

c Explain what you would need to do to investigate this hypothesis further.

7   **Reasoning** The manager of
a shop wants to work out when
she needs the most staff in her
shop. She records the numbers of
customers in a shop at half-hour
intervals one Monday.
The graph shows her results.

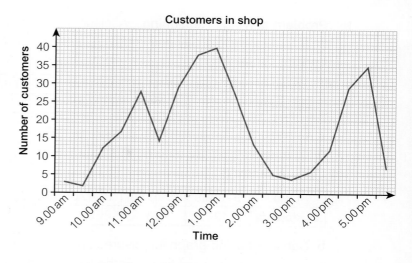

Customers in shop

a Which times is she most likely
to need extra staff?

b Suggest a reason why these
times might be the busiest.

c Do you think the pattern of
customer numbers is likely to
be the same

    i every weekday   ii on Saturdays and Sundays?
   Explain.

d How could she investigate further?

Key point To draw a line graph for grouped data, you need to plot the frequencies at the
midpoints of the classes.

Worked example

Draw a line graph to represent this data.

Age, a	Frequency	Midpoint
$0 \leqslant a < 10$	12	5
$10 \leqslant a < 20$	15	15
$20 \leqslant a < 30$	2	25
$30 \leqslant a < 40$	11	35

First work out the midpoint of each class.

Plot each frequency against the midpoint age.

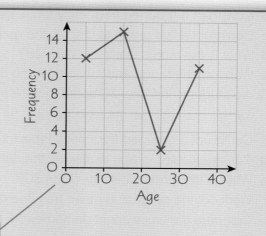

8   **Reasoning** Samarah draws a line graph for this data.

Earnings (per year), e	Number of employees
$£0 < e \leqslant £10\,000$	3
$£10\,000 < e \leqslant £20\,000$	52
$£20\,000 < e \leqslant £30\,000$	29
$£30\,000 < e \leqslant £40\,000$	27
$£40\,000 < e \leqslant £50\,000$	5
$£50\,000 < e \leqslant £60\,000$	3

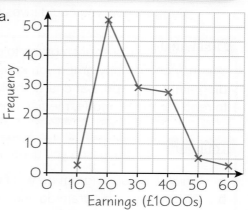

a Explain what she has done wrong.

b Construct an accurate line graph for the data.

9 **Problem-solving / Reasoning** A leisure centre records the number of customers each hour throughout the day one Friday.

Leisure centre A

Time	9–10 am	10–11 am	11–12 pm	12–1 pm	1–2 pm	2–3 pm	3–4 pm	4–5 pm
Customers	35	79	182	23	31	245	90	118

a Construct a line graph for the data.

Another leisure centre records this data.

Leisure centre B

Time	9–10 am	10–11 am	11–12 pm	12–1 pm	1–2 pm	2–3 pm	3–4 pm	4–5 pm
Customers	127	23	65	213	189	34	21	17

b Construct a line graph for leisure centre B on the same axes as in part **a**.

c Compare the busiest times for the two leisure centres.

d The leisure centres are open 7 days a week, from 7 am to 11 pm.
Suggest how the leisure centres could investigate further.

10 **Problem-solving / Reasoning** A teacher recorded the times (in minutes) that some students in Class 2B spent on their maths homework.

34 29 3 55 16 23 30 39 59 45 35 48 33 56 29 51 23 41 31 45

a Identify any outliers in the data. Suggest a reason for them

b Construct a grouped frequency table, ignoring any outliers.

c Construct a line graph to display the data from your frequency table.

d What is the modal class for Class 2B?

e Work out the range and mean from the data, ignoring any outliers.

Some students in Class 3C spent these lengths of time on their homework.

44 51 34 62 34 56 49 44 48 23 54 34 35 36 55 56 47 44 41 20

f Construct a grouped frequency table for this data.

g Construct a line graph to display the data from your frequency table.

h What is the modal class for Class 3C?

i Work out the range and mean from the data.

j Compare the times spent on homework by the two classes.

k The teacher's hypothesis is 'The students in Class 3C spend more time on homework than the students in Class 2B.'
Suggest how you could investigate the teacher's hypothesis further.

Challenge Construct a graph to present your findings from your investigation in lesson 3.2. You may choose any graph you know how to draw: scatter graph, pie chart, frequency diagram, line graph, bar chart. Think about what you wish to display and how easy it will be to read the mean, mode, median and range from it.

Reflect In this lesson you used scatter diagrams (for Q2–5) and line graphs (for Q7–10)

a Which type of diagram do you find easiest? Why?

b Which type of diagram do you find hardest? Why?

c What could you do to make it easier to work with the diagram you chose in part **b**?

3.5 Presenting and comparing data

Active Learn
Homework

- Draw back-to-back stem and leaf diagrams
- Write a report to show survey results

Warm up

1 Fluency Work out the midpoint of each class.
  a 0–5   **b** 1–5   **c** 0–4   **d** 1–6

2 The table shows the languages studied by students in two Year 9 classes.
  a Draw a dual bar chart to show this data.
  b Which average can you find from the chart?

Language	Number of students in Class 9A	Number of students in Class 9B
German	18	12
Spanish	5	9
French	13	14

Key point

A report could include
- the hypothesis or what you are investigating
- the data shown in a graph or chart
- averages and range
- a conclusion
- what else you could investigate.

3 Reasoning This dual bar chart shows the child population (in millions) by age in the USA for 1950 and 2017.
  a What is the modal age group for
    i 1950   **ii** 2017?
  b Copy and complete the frequency table for 1950.

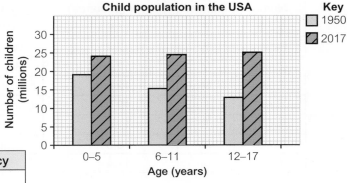

Child population in the USA

Key
☐ 1950
▨ 2017

Source: www.childstats.gov

Age	Midpoint	Frequency
0–5		
6–11		
12–17		

  c Use the frequency table to calculate an estimate of the mean age of a child in 1950. Give your answer to 1 decimal place.
  d Calculate an estimate of the mean age in 2017. Use the method from part **b**.
  e Write a sentence comparing the ages of children in the USA in 1950 and 2017.

4 Reasoning 'GDP per capita' means 'Gross Domestic Product per person'. This is an average, worked out by calculating how much the country earns as a whole and dividing by the population. The table shows the GDP per capita of nine countries in 2018.

Country	GDP per capita ($)
Congo, Democratic Republic of	449
Burundi	307
Central African Republic	430
Sierra Leone	516
Afghanistan	544
Mozambique	476
Nepal	972
Guinea	883
Mali	927

  a Draw a bar chart for this data.
  b Write two sentences about what the bar chart shows.
  c Explain whether you think your results are a good representation of GDP per capita across the world.
  d Describe how you could investigate this further.

5 Reasoning A group of Year 9 students were tested on their knowledge of countries of the world before and after watching a video. This back-to-back stem and leaf diagram shows their test marks.

Before video		After video
8 5 3 2	1	2
9 6 6 4 1 0	2	1 7 9
2 0	3	0 6 7 7 8
8 4 3	4	2 2 5 9
	5	0 0

Key: 2 | 3 means 32   3 | 6 means 36

  a Work out the median and range before and after the students watched the video.
  b Write two sentences comparing the median and range for before and after.
  c Does the data suggest that watching the video increased the students' knowledge?
  d How many students took part in this experiment?
  e How could you investigate further whether watching this video increases students' knowledge?

6 Reasoning Here are some records from a running club's 100 m sprint.

Name	Gender	Time, t (seconds)
Jones	F	11.9
Peters	F	12.2
Clarke	M	12.0
Scott	M	12.5
Lee	F	12.0
Smith	F	12.8
Akbar	M	13.6
Ford	M	11.4

Name	Gender	Time, t (seconds)
Pitt	F	12.9
Wang	M	12.5
Henry	M	11.8
Moss	F	13.0
Campbell	F	12.8
Khalid	F	13.1
Lott	M	13.2

  a Draw a back-to-back stem and leaf diagram for the data.
  b Copy and complete this two-way table to record the times.

	$11 < t \leqslant 12$	$12 < t \leqslant 13$	$13 < t \leqslant 14$	Total
Male				
Female				
Total				

  c The club's hypothesis is 'Male runners are faster than female runners.' Does the data support this hypothesis?

7 Reasoning A scientist suggests this hypothesis.

'Coffee cools faster than tea.'

She measures the temperature of cooling cups of tea and coffee over 30 minutes.

Time (minutes)	0	5	10	15	20	25	30
Temperature of tea (°C)	91	81	72	64	57	51	45
Temperature of coffee (°C)	91	80	74	67	60	59	55

a Plot two line graphs for this data on the same axes. Plot time on the horizontal axis.

b Write a report based on this data.

> **Q7b hint** What do the results show? Do the results support her hypothesis? How could she investigate further?

8 Reasoning A geography student wants to find out how far people are willing to travel to visit the cinema. He asks 100 customers at cinema A,

'How far is this cinema from your home?'

The table shows his results.

Cinema A

Distance, d (miles)	Frequency
$0 < d \leqslant 5$	21
$5 < d \leqslant 10$	32
$10 < d \leqslant 15$	23
$15 < d \leqslant 20$	15
$20 < d \leqslant 25$	7
$25 < d \leqslant 30$	2
$30 < d \leqslant 35$	0
$35 < d \leqslant 40$	0
$40 < d \leqslant 45$	1

a Write a report on the data he has collected. Make sure you

- include at least one graph – think carefully about which type to use

- identify any outliers and suggest how they might have occurred

- include an estimate of the mean, range and modal class (ignore any outliers)

- suggest what else the student could investigate.

The student completed a second survey at another cinema.

The table shows his results.

Cinema B

Distance, d (miles)	Frequency
$0 < d \leqslant 5$	0
$5 < d \leqslant 10$	8
$10 < d \leqslant 15$	34
$15 < d \leqslant 20$	15
$20 < d \leqslant 25$	7
$25 < d \leqslant 30$	19
$30 < d \leqslant 35$	17
$35 < d \leqslant 40$	0
$40 < d \leqslant 45$	0

b Draw two line graphs on the same axes to show the data for both cinemas.

c For Cinema B

  i calculate an estimate of the mean distance people travel

  ii calculate an estimate of the range of distances

  iii find the modal class.

d Compare the averages and range for the two cinemas.

Cinema A is a town centre cinema with three screens. Cinema B is in a leisure complex and has ten screens.

e Write a conclusion to explain what the student has found out about the distances people will travel to large and small cinemas.

Challenge Write a report on your findings from the hypothesis you have been investigating throughout this unit.

Reflect Why do you think people use mathematical diagrams or graphs when they write reports? Write down at least two ideas. Compare them with your classmates.

3 Check up

Surveys

1 A student wants to find out about the type of food students prefer. She collects two sets of data.

    A A survey of students about the food they like.

    B A record of food sold in the canteen.

    a Are **A** and **B** primary data or secondary data?

    b There are 1500 students at the school.
      What size sample should she use: 15, 150 or 500?

2 Explain what is wrong with each question.

    a What is your shoe size?

       ☐ 1–3   ☐ 3–5   ☐ 5–7   ☐ 7+

    b Do you agree that it is harder to buy shoes for larger feet?

3 Which units, m, cm or mm, should you use to measure these?

    a the lengths of the long jump at a school sports day

    b the length of a screw

    c the length of a swimming pool

4 A farmer records the masses (in grams) of 20 eggs laid by her chickens.
    70.5 61.2 75.3 77.7 79.7 80.0 84.3 69.9 70.5 91.3
    90.0 68.9 73.8 80.4 78.4 81.9 70.1 73.3 82.3 79.9

    a Is this data discrete or continuous?

    b Design a grouped frequency table to record the data.

    c Complete your frequency table.

5 At a stage school the head teacher records the gender (male or female) and the course (singing, dancing, acting) of all the students.

    M – singing   F – dancing   M – dancing   M – acting   F – acting
    F – singing   F – acting   M – singing   M – acting   M – singing
    M – singing   M – acting   F – acting   F – acting   F – dancing
    M – dancing   M – dancing   M – dancing   M – singing   F – acting

    a Put the data into a two-way table.

    b Which course has most boys?

    c Which course has fewest girls?

6 You want to find out the most popular clothing brand. You are going to survey 200 people in a town.
    Which is the best sample to reduce bias?

    A customers in one shop

    B females

    C people over 60

    D 200 people randomly selected

Calculating averages

7 The table shows the lifespan of a sample of insects.
  a Calculate an estimate for the mean lifespan.
  b Which is the modal class?
  c Which class contains the median?
  d Estimate the range.

Lifespan, w (days)	Frequency
$0 < w \leq 5$	3
$5 < w \leq 10$	91
$10 < w \leq 15$	96
$15 < w \leq 20$	80

Displaying and analysing data

8 a Draw two line graphs on the same axes to show the lifespans of butterflies and moths.

Lifespan, w (days)	Butterflies	Moths
$0 < w \leq 5$	3	1
$5 < w \leq 10$	88	123
$10 < w \leq 15$	76	91
$15 < w \leq 20$	83	35

  b Describe the main differences.

9 The scatter graph shows the number of driving tests taken plotted against the number of driving lessons before a successful pass.
  a Identify an outlier.
  b Suggest a reason for this outlier.
  c Adil has 36 lessons. Estimate how many tests he would take before passing.

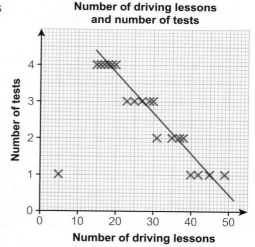

Number of driving lessons and number of tests

Challenge The mean of a set of five positive whole numbers is 20.
The mode, median and range are all 25.
Suggest as many possible different whole number values for the numbers as you can.

Reflect How sure are you of your answers? Were you mostly

😟 Just guessing   😐 Feeling doubtful   🙂 Confident

What next? Use your results to decide whether to strengthen or extend your learning.

3 Strengthen

Surveys

1 Rahni is doing a geography investigation on soil types in her area.
  a She tests 10 different samples of soil.
  Is this primary or secondary data?
  b She uses data from the Environment Agency website.
  Is this primary or secondary data?

> **Q1 hint I** collect primary data for my investigation. **S**omeone else collects secondary data.

2 The head teacher of a school wants to find out how long students spend on their homework. There are 1000 students in the school.
  a What is the population for this survey?
  b He asks a sample of 100 students.
  What percentage of the population is this?
  c What should he ask pupils to round their answers to?
    A the nearest hour
    B the nearest 10 minutes
    C the nearest minute
  d He decides to ask only students from Year 11.
  Is this a good idea? Explain your answer.

> **Q2c hint** Think about how long you spend on your homework. What would you answer?

3 A village has 800 residents.
The council wants to find out what people think of the local bus service.
How many people should they sample?

4 A researcher measures the lengths of a sample of 100 caterpillars using a ruler.

What level of accuracy should the lengths be measured to?
  A the nearest millimetre   **B** the nearest centimetre   **C** the nearest metre

5 A student wants to record the lengths of pebbles in a stream to the nearest centimetre.
He suggests the following groups.
    0–10 cm   10–20 cm   20–30 cm
  a In which groups could he record a 10 cm long pebble?
  b What is the problem with his choice of groups?
  c He redesigns his groups.
  Copy and complete the new groups.
    0–9 cm   ☐–19 cm   ☐–29 cm

6 The times (in minutes) that 10 people spent in the gym are
65, 34, 49, 58, 23, 45, 40, 36, 55, 69
Copy and complete the frequency table.
All groups must be the same width.

Time, t (minutes)	Tally	Frequency
$20 < t \leqslant 30$		
$30 < t \leqslant \square$		
$\square < t \leqslant \square$		
$\square < t \leqslant \square$		
$60 < t \leqslant 70$		

7 Design a frequency table to record the answers to this question.
'How many minutes did you spend cooking dinner tonight?'

Q7 hint Think about the answers you would expect to get to the question.

8 In a canteen you can choose
- beef or chicken
- chips, jacket potato or mashed potato.

a Copy the two-way table and fill in the headings.

b Put this data in your table.

beef and chips	20
beef and jacket potato	15
beef and mashed potato	13
chicken and chips	35
chicken and jacket potato	13
chicken and mashed potato	17

	Beef	

9 At GCSE, students can choose one language (Spanish, German or Mandarin) and one humanities subject (History or Geography).

a Design a two-way table to record students' choices.

Q9a hint Write all the language choices down the side of the table. Write the humanities along the top.

b Here are the choices of ten students.

Spanish and History
Mandarin and History
Spanish and History
German and Geography
German and History
German and History
German and History
Spanish and Geography
Mandarin and History
German and Geography

Record these choices in your two-way table.

c Which combination is the most popular choice for these 10 students?

d Is there any combination that none of these students chose?

10 A company is carrying out a survey about pet insurance.

a The company surveys everyone who brings their pet to the vet on one day.
Why will this give a biased result?

b The survey includes the question,
'Do you want the best possible treatment for your pet if it becomes ill?'
What are people likely to answer?
Explain why this question will result in a biased survey.

c **Reasoning** Which question would you choose for the survey? Explain why.

A Your pet is an important part of your household.
Do you have pet insurance?

B Do you love your pet and want the best for him/her?

C Do you currently have pet insurance?

D Do you agree that insurance is a waste of money?

Calculating averages

1 Rebecca records the ages of people in a squash club in a frequency table.

Age (years)	Frequency
10–19	3
20–29	12
30–39	8
40–49	2

  a Work out the total frequency, n.

  b Use $\frac{n+1}{2}$ to work out the position of the median.

  c Write down the class containing the median value.

Q1c hint

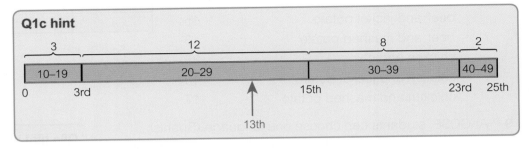

2 In a survey, 12 people said they spent 0–20 minutes on the phone each day.
Which of these is the best estimate for the average time?

  A 2 minutes   **B** 5 minutes   **C** 10 minutes   **D** 20 minutes

  Explain your decision.

3 A phone company recorded the lengths of time some people spent on the phone in a day.

Time, t (minutes)	Midpoint	Frequency	Midpoint × frequency
$0 < t \leqslant 20$	10	5	10 × 5 = 50
$20 < t \leqslant 40$	30	12	
$40 < t \leqslant 60$	☐	19	
$60 < t \leqslant 80$	☐	8	
$80 < t \leqslant 100$	☐	6	
	Total	☐	☐

  a Copy and complete the table.

  b What is the total number of people?

  c Estimate the total time.

  d Work out an estimate for the mean $= \dfrac{\text{total time}}{\text{total number of people}}$

> **Q3d hint** It is an estimate because you are using the midpoints to calculate the time.

4 A theatre manager recorded the number of audience members at a theatre over 10 nights.

Number in audience, a	Frequency
$100 < a \leqslant 150$	5
$150 < a \leqslant 200$	2
$200 < a \leqslant 250$	2
$250 < a \leqslant 300$	1

  a What columns do you need to add to the table to calculate an estimate of the mean?

  b Copy the table and add the extra columns from part **a**.
Complete the table.

  c Find an estimate for the mean number of people in the audience.

  d Find the class that contains the median.

5 The table shows the projected population for the UK in 2025. What is the modal class of this data?

Q5 hint The **modal** class has the **most** in it.

Age (years)	Population (thousands)
0–9	7905
10–19	8346
20–29	8061
30–39	9088
40–49	8484
50–59	8834
60–69	8125
70–79	6175
80–89	3210
90+	698

Source: ONS

Displaying and analysing data

1 A vet recorded the masses of some puppies in a litter.

Mass, m (kg)	Midpoint	Frequency	Coordinates
$0.4 \leqslant m < 0.6$	0.5	1	(0.5, 1)
$0.6 \leqslant m < 0.8$	☐	6	(☐, 6)
$0.8 \leqslant m < 1$	☐	2	(☐, ☐)

a Work out the midpoints and coordinates.
b Copy the axes.
c Draw a line graph for this data.

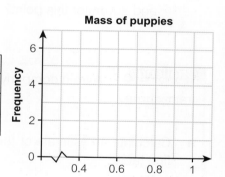

Mass of puppies

2 The table shows the heights of 14 children in Year 3.
a Copy the axes.
b Draw a line graph for this grouped data.

Height, h (cm)	Frequency
$120 < h \leqslant 130$	3
$130 < h \leqslant 140$	4
$140 < h \leqslant 150$	7

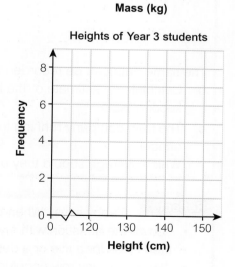

Heights of Year 3 students

3 Draw a line graph for the grouped data in
a Q1   **b** Q3   **c** Q4
in *Calculating averages* on page 75.

4 The scatter graph shows the times taken for 20 students to run 200 m plotted against their times taken to run 100 m.

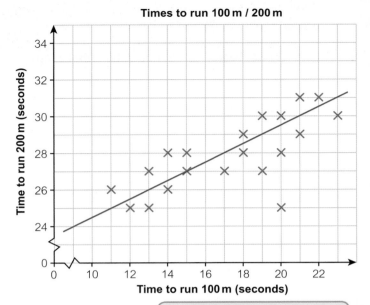

Times to run 100 m / 200 m

a Find 100 m in 16 seconds on the correct axis.

b Draw a line up to the line of best fit and then across to the other axis.
Read off the time to run 200 m.

c Use the line of best fit to predict the 200 m time for a student who ran the 100 metres in
  i 19 seconds
  ii 17 seconds.

d One point shows an outlier. What were the times for 100 m and 200 m for this point?

> **Q4d hint** Outliers are points that don't follow the trend, so are not close to the line of best fit.

Challenge A train company records the numbers of passengers on a regular train journey.

a Calculate an estimate of the mean using the first table.

Number of passengers, n	Frequency
$0 < n \leqslant 30$	1
$30 < n \leqslant 60$	3
$60 < n \leqslant 90$	2
$90 < n \leqslant 120$	4

The same data can be recorded in a different way.

b Calculate an estimate of the mean using the second table.

c The train company running the train wants to cancel it.
Which average should they use to support their argument?

Number of passengers, n	Frequency
$0 < n \leqslant 40$	4
$40 < n \leqslant 80$	3
$80 < n \leqslant 120$	3

Reflect Gabby says, 'When I see a question with a table:
- I cover the question with my hand, so I can only see the table
- then I look for a title or a description of the table
- then I read any row or column headings
- finally, I randomly pick a number in the table and ask myself what this number tells me.

It only takes a minute, and stops me panicking about all the information I am being given.'
Look back at any Strengthen question that has a table in it. Use Gabby's method.
Now find an Extend question with a table. Use Gabby's method again.
Is Gabby's method helpful?

3 Extend

1 **Problem-solving**   The owner of a beauty salon thinks that the average age of her customers is decreasing.
Suggest ways in which she could collect primary data to support her hypothesis.

2 **Reasoning**   A company is designing an online survey to find out whether their employees are happy in their work.
Which data should they collect about each employee? Explain why you did or didn't choose each one.
A name   **B** age
C level of satisfaction with the company   **D** number of years with the company
E how their working conditions should be improved

3 **Reasoning**   Which is the most dangerous job?
a What type of data would you need to investigate this?
b List some sources for this data.
   State whether they are primary or secondary sources.
c What kind of organisation might need to know this?

4 A driving school wanted to find out whether students who revised were more likely to pass their driving theory test.
120 students were surveyed. 98 of them had passed.
Of the 98 who passed, 75 said they had revised.
Of those who failed, 20 said they had revised.
a Construct a two-way table to show this information.
b What do you think the problem might be with a survey like this?

5 **Problem-solving**   What is the missing number if
a the mode is 11
b the mean is 10
c the range is 10?

| 12 | 13 | 8 | 11 | ? |

6 **Problem-solving / Reasoning**   Five whole numbers have mode 10, median 12 and mean 12.
Work out what they are.

7 This spreadsheet shows the results (in %) that students in a Year 10 class received in their end-of-term exams in English and maths.
a Construct a back-to-back stem and leaf diagram for the data.
b Write two sentences to compare the distributions.
c Construct a scatter graph for this data. Describe what it shows.

	A	B	C
1	**Student**	**English (%)**	**Maths (%)**
2	Ali	90	47
3	Allan	73	84
4	Anderly	47	57
5	Avery	92	90
6	Blick	47	85
7	Brainchild	83	66
8	Brierly	79	46
9	Brown	78	90
10	Emmery	82	84
11	Mercal	83	55
12	Murphy	72	73
13	Oxbury	68	57
14	Rothchild	41	94
15	Shilpa	46	49
16	Shunnington	73	75
17	Wilson-Smith	50	86

8 **Reasoning** A political party uses a phone-in poll to find out what is important to voters.
Why does a phone-in poll usually produce biased results?

Q8 hint A 'phone-in poll' is when people are asked to phone in to say what they think.

9 **Reasoning** A council wants to find out what facilities the people living in the town would like to improve.
a Explain what is wrong with this question.
'Do you agree this town needs more play parks for children?'
b Write some questions you might ask instead.

10 **Reasoning** The table gives the prices of cars with different-sized engines for one manufacturer.

Engine size (litres)	1	1.5	1.25	1.6	1.2	1.6	2	1.5	1.6	2	1.6	2.2
Price (£ thousands)	13.5	15.5	13.5	17.3	11.5	18.5	22.3	18	20	23.5	8.8	27.9

a Plot a scatter graph using this data.
b Describe the correlation shown on the graph.
c Identify an outlier. Suggest a reason for this data item.
d Predict the price of a car with engine size 1.4 litres.
e Jeremy says, 'Cars with larger engines cost more.'
Does the data support his hypothesis?
f Suggest how he could investigate further.

11 **Problem-solving / Reasoning**
The scatter graph shows the times it took children of different ages to complete a puzzle.
Explain what the data shows.

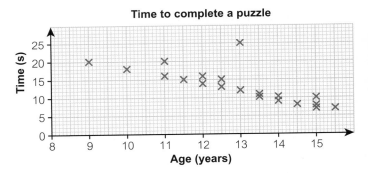

Time to complete a puzzle

12 **Problem-solving** The table shows the frequency of heights of students in a class.
a Copy and complete the frequency diagram.
b What is the modal class?
c How many students were taller than 149 cm?

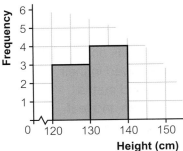

Height, h (cm)	Frequency
$120 \leqslant h < 130$	3
$130 \leqslant h < 140$	4
$140 \leqslant h < 150$	6
$150 \leqslant h < 160$	8
$160 \leqslant h < 170$	5

Q12 hint For continuous data there are no spaces between the bars.

Reflect A census is a survey of all the people and households in a country on a particular date.
Who do you think uses census data? What do you think they use it for?
What skills have you learned in this unit to help you plan a census?

3 Unit test

1   You are going to investigate this hypothesis.
    'Buttered toast always lands butter-side down.'
    How many times should you drop a piece of buttered toast?
    A 10 times   **B** 100 times   **C** 1000 times

2   An insurance company suggests, 'Men are better drivers than women.'
    It uses these questions in a survey.
      A How many accidents have you had in the last 10 years?
        ☐ 0–2   ☐ 2–4   ☐ 4–6   ☐ 6+
      B Would you agree that women have more accidents than men?
    a Explain what is wrong with the questions.
    b Rewrite the questions.

3   You are investigating the average daily temperature in July.
    You collect data by:
    A Recording the temperature using a thermometer every morning, midday and evening.
    B Getting the average temperature from the Met Office website.
    Which is secondary data?

4   'Girls at St Margaret's School score better in Maths exams than in English exams.'
    a Describe how you would collect data to test this hypothesis.
    There are 400 girls at St Margaret's.
    b How large a sample should you use?

5   For a 'Stop Speeding' campaign, Brendan measures the speed that cars travel along his
    road. The road has a 30 mph limit.
    a How accurately should he record the data to state his case to the council?
      A nearest 10 mph   **B** nearest 1 mph   **C** nearest 0.1 mph
    b Design a data collection sheet to record his data.

6   Students at a school can choose one sport from each group.
    Group A Tennis, Badminton, Squash
    Group B Swimming, Athletics, Gymnastics
    Design a two-way table to record the results.

7   A supermarket wants to find out how much its customers spend on ready meals.
    Which is the most appropriate sample?
    A customers who bought a ready meal in the last week
    B customers who spend over £100 in the shop
    C the next 100 customers through the tills

8   Janice plays football. She recorded the number of goals
    she scored per match in her last 20 matches.
    Work out
    a the range
    b the median number of goals.

Goals	Frequency
1	1
2	4
3	3
4	3
5	4
6	5

9 The scatter graph shows the relationship between the maximum daily temperature and the number of ice creams sold in a shop.

a What type of correlation does the graph show?

b What is the temperature for the outlier?

c Use the line of best fit to estimate

   i the maximum daily temperature when the shop sells 20 ice creams

   ii the number of ice creams the shop will sell when the temperature is 30 °C.

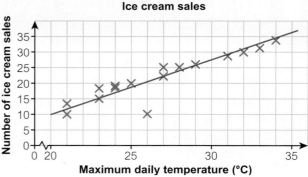

Ice cream sales

10 Two airline companies record the numbers of people travelling on their Airbus 320s for 200 flights.

Airline A

Number of passengers, p	Frequency
$0 \leqslant p < 40$	20
$40 \leqslant p < 80$	43
$80 \leqslant p < 120$	112
$120 \leqslant p < 160$	25

Airline B

Number of passengers, p	Frequency
$0 \leqslant p < 40$	0
$40 \leqslant p < 80$	44
$80 \leqslant p < 120$	54
$120 \leqslant p < 160$	102

a Which is the modal class of passengers for

   i Airline A   **ii** Airline B?

b Calculate an estimate of the mean number of passengers for each airline.

c Estimate the range for each airline.

d Find the class that contains the median for each airline.

e On the same set of axes construct two line graphs to show both airlines.

f Write two sentences comparing the data for each airline.

4 Multiplicative reasoning

Master   Check up p98   Strengthen p100   Extend p105   Unit test p107

4.1 Enlargement

- Enlarge 2D shapes using a positive whole number scale factor and centre of enlargement
- Find the centre of enlargement by drawing lines on a grid
- Understand that the scale factor is the ratio of corresponding lengths

*Active*Learn
Homework

Warm up

1   **Fluency**   In each diagram, shape B is an enlargement of shape A.
What is the scale factor of the enlargement?

   a

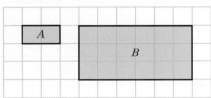

   b

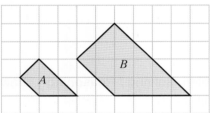

2   Copy this shape onto squared paper.
Now enlarge the shape by scale factor 4

3   **a**   Write the ratio of length A to
length B.
Give the ratio in its simplest form.
    b   Write the ratio as a unit ratio in the form $1 : n$.

A _____ B _____

4 cm   10 cm

> **Key point**   When you enlarge a shape by a scale factor from a **centre of enlargement**, the distance from the centre to each point on the shape is multiplied by the scale factor.

Worked example

Enlarge this triangle using a scale factor 2 and the marked centre of enlargement.

> Count the squares from the centre of enlargement to each vertex on the original shape.
> Then multiply the distances by the scale factor.

   original shape

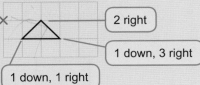

2 right
1 down, 3 right
1 down, 1 right

   enlarged shape

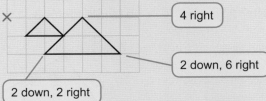

4 right
2 down, 6 right
2 down, 2 right

4 Copy these shapes and the centres of enlargement onto squared paper.
Enlarge them by the scale factors given, using the marked centres of enlargement.

a scale factor 2   **b** scale factor 4   **c** scale factor 3   **d** scale factor 3

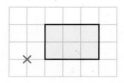 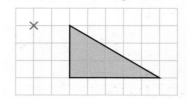 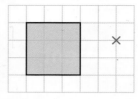 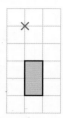

5 **a** Copy this diagram onto squared paper.
   b Mark a centre of enlargement at (9, 5).
   c Enlarge the rectangle by scale factor 2, with
     centre of enlargement (9, 5).

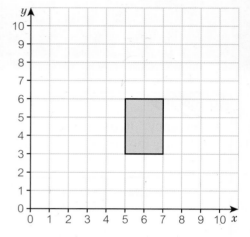

6 **Problem-solving / Reasoning** Draw a pair of axes
from 0 to 10.
Draw a triangle A with vertices at (3, 2), (5, 2) and (3, 4).
Draw a triangle B with vertices at (8, 6), (9, 6) and (8, 7).
   a Draw an enlargement of triangle A with scale factor 2 and centre of enlargement (1, 1).
   b Draw an enlargement of triangle B with scale factor 4 and centre of enlargement (9, 7).
   c What do you notice about your answers to parts **a** and **b**?
   d Triangle C has vertices at (3, 6), (4, 6) and (3, 7).
     Draw triangle C on the grid.
   e Salim says, 'If I enlarge triangle C by a scale factor of 3 and
     centre of enlargement (2, 7), it will give exactly the same triangle
     as my answers to parts **a** and **b**.'
     Is Salim correct? Explain your answer.

7 Copy these shapes and the centres of
enlargement onto squared paper.
Enlarge them by the scale factors given, using
the marked centres of enlargement.

> **Q7 hint** When the centre of enlargement lies
> on a vertex of the shape, the distance from
> the centre of enlargement to this point on the
> shape is 0. This point is in the same place on
> the grid in the enlarged shape.

a scale factor 2   **b** scale factor 3   **c** scale factor 2

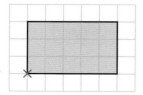 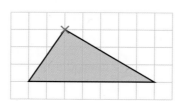 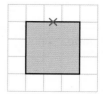

8 **a** Draw a pair of axes from −10 to 10.

   b Plot the points (−4, 2), (−6, 2) and (−5, 4) and join them to form a triangle.

   c Enlarge the triangle by scale factor 3, with centre of enlargement (−5, 4).

9 **a** Copy this trapezium onto a coordinate grid.
         Enlarge it by scale factor 2, with centre of enlargement (4, 1).

   b Measure the angles in the trapezium and in its enlargement.
         What do you notice?

   c Measure the sides in the trapezium and in its enlargement.
         What do you notice?

   d **Reasoning**   Is this true for all enlargements of shapes?

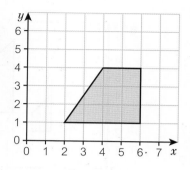

10 Copy these shapes onto squared paper.
   Enlarge them by the scale factors given, using the marked centres of enlargement.

> **Q10 hint** Follow the same method: multiply the distance from the centre of enlargement to each vertex by the scale factor.

   a scale factor 2

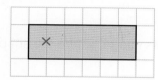

   b scale factor 3

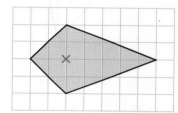

   c scale factor 4

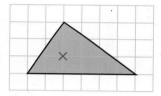

11 Draw a pair of axes from 0 to 10.
   Draw a square with vertices (3, 3), (3, 5), (5, 5) and (5, 3).
   Enlarge the square by scale factor 4, with centre of enlargement (4, 4).

12 **Problem-solving / Reasoning**   Shape *A* has been enlarged to give shape *B*.

   a What is the scale factor of the enlargement?

   b Copy the diagram and use straight lines to join together corresponding corners of the two shapes. Extend these lines across the whole grid. The first one is shown in red on the diagram. These lines are called **rays**.

   c What are the coordinates of the centre of enlargement? Use the rays you drew in part **c**.

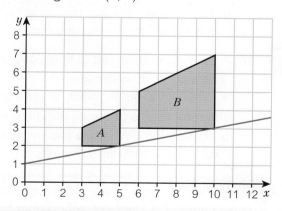

> **Key point**   To describe an enlargement, give the scale factor and the coordinates of the centre of enlargement.

13 Describe the enlargement that takes shape A to shape B in each of these diagrams.

Q13 hint Use the method in Q12 to work out the coordinates of the centre of enlargement.

a
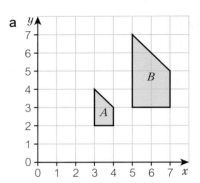

b
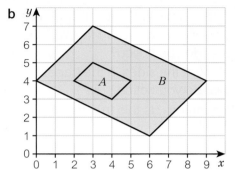

14 Reasoning The diagram shows two rectangles.

a What is the scale factor for enlarging rectangle A to give rectangle B?

b Write the ratio, in its simplest form, of

  i the height of rectangle A to rectangle B

  ii the length of rectangle A to rectangle B.

c What do you notice about your answers to parts **a** and **b**?

d What is the ratio of corresponding sides in a shape and its image, where the shape has been enlarged by

  i scale factor 3   **ii** scale factor 4   **iii** scale factor 7?

15 A model of a sports car is 12 cm long. The real car is 4.8 m long.

a Write the ratio of the length of the model to the length of the real car.

b Write your answer as a ratio in the form $1 : n$.

c Reasoning What is the scale factor for enlarging the model to give the real car?

Q15a hint You must work in the same unit of measure. For example 4.8 m = ☐ cm

16 A painting is enlarged to fit exactly on the side of an office building. A ratio of 1 : 35 is used.

a What is the scale factor for enlarging the painting to fit on the building?

The dimensions of the painting are length 508 mm and height 610 mm.

b Reasoning What are the length and height of the office building? Give your answers in metres.

Challenge   Draw a shape on a coordinate grid and enlarge it using your own scale factor and centre of enlargement. Don't mark the centre of enlargement. Swap with a partner and ask them to work out the scale factor and centre of enlargement.

Reflect   This unit is called 'Multiplicative reasoning'.

Multiplicative means using multiplication and/or division.

How is enlargement multiplicative?

Why is it good to use reasoning in mathematics?

4.2 Negative and fractional scale factors

Active Learn
Homework

- Enlarge 2D shapes using a negative whole number scale factor
- Enlarge 2D shapes using a fractional scale factor

Warm up

1 Fluency What is

a $\frac{1}{2}$ of 4   **b** $\frac{1}{4}$ of 4   **c** $\frac{1}{3}$ of 9?

2 Draw a pair of axes from 0 to 8.

a Draw triangle A with vertices (4, 5), (6, 5) and (6, 7).

b Rotate triangle A 180° about the point (3, 5). Label your rotated triangle B.

3 Copy these diagrams. Enlarge each shape by the scale factor given, using the marked centre of enlargement.

a scale factor 3   **b** scale factor 2   **c** scale factor 4

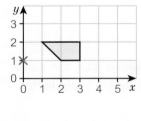 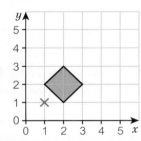 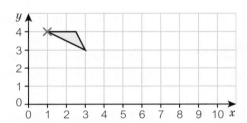

Key point

A **negative scale factor** takes the image to the opposite side of the centre of enlargement.

Worked example

Enlarge this triangle using scale factor −2, using the marked centre of enlargement.

Count the squares from the centre of enlargement to each vertex on the original shape.
Then multiply the distances by the scale factor, but in the **opposite direction**.

original shape

2 left   1 left

1 down, 2 left

enlarged shape

2 up, 4 right

2 right   4 right

Unit 4 Multiplicative reasoning   86

4   Copy these diagrams.
    Enlarge the shapes by the **negative scale factors** given, using the marked
    centres of enlargement.
    a scale factor −3   b scale factor −2   c scale factor −3

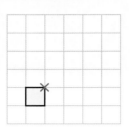
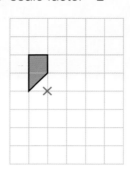
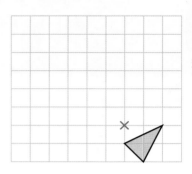

5   **Problem-solving / Reasoning**   What is the effect on the side lengths and angles of
    enlarging a shape by scale factor −1?

6   **Reasoning**   Draw a pair of axes from 0 to 12.
    Draw shape A with vertices at (3, 3), (4, 3), (5, 4), (5, 5) and (3, 5).
    a Enlarge shape A using scale factor −2 and centre of enlargement (6, 6).
    b Enlarge shape A using scale factor 2 and centre of enlargement (6, 6), then rotate the
       enlarged shape 180° about the point (6, 6).
    c What do you notice about your answers to parts **a** and **b**?

> **Key point**   You can enlarge a shape using a **fractional scale factor**. Use the same
> method of multiplying the distances from the centre of enlargement by the scale factor.

7   Copy these diagrams.
    Enlarge the shapes by the **fractional scale factors** given, using the marked centres of
    enlargement.
    a scale factor $\frac{1}{2}$ b scale factor $\frac{1}{4}$ c scale factor $\frac{1}{3}$

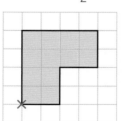
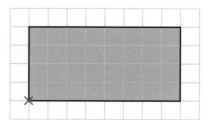
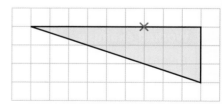

8   **Reasoning**   What happens to the side lengths and angles of a shape when you enlarge it
    by a positive number less than 1?

> **Key point**   The word 'enlarge' is used for fractional scale factors, even though the image
> is smaller.

9 For each of these diagrams work out the scale factor for

    i enlarging shape A to give shape B **ii** enlarging shape B to give shape A.

a
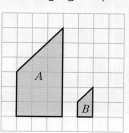

b
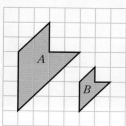

c
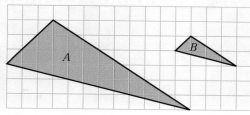

10 Copy these diagrams.

    i Enlarge each shape by the scale factor given, using the centre of enlargement (7, 1). Label the enlargement B.

    ii Write the ratio of the lengths of shape A to the lengths of shape B. Write the ratio in its simplest form.

    iii Write the enlargement that takes shape B back to shape A.

> **Q10iii hint** Remember to include the scale factor and the centre of enlargement.

a scale factor $\frac{1}{2}$

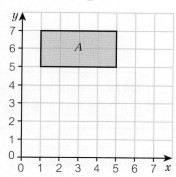

b scale factor $\frac{1}{3}$

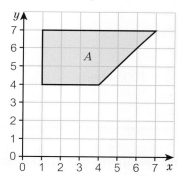

c scale factor $\frac{1}{3}$

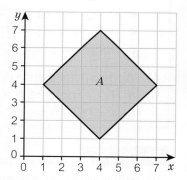

Challenge Make three copies of this diagram.

a Carry out each of the following combined transformations.

    i Translate the shape 4 squares left and 1 square down, then enlarge it by scale factor 2, centre of enlargement (0, 12).

    ii Rotate the shape 180° about the point (6, 8), then enlarge it by scale factor $\frac{1}{2}$, centre of enlargement (0, 0).

    iii Reflect the shape in the line $x = 9$, then enlarge it by scale factor $\frac{1}{2}$, centre of enlargement (10, 8).

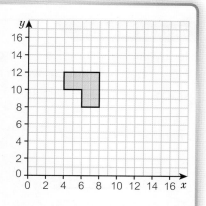

b Describe a combined transformation that will take the image in part **a ii** to the position of the image in part **a iii**.

Reflect What is the same and what is different when enlarging shapes using

a a positive whole number scale factor and a positive fractional scale factor

b a positive whole number scale factor and a negative whole number scale factor?

4.3 Percentage change

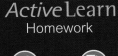
Active Learn
Homework

- Find an original value using inverse operations
- Calculate percentage change

Warm up

1 Fluency Here is an answer on a calculator.   `16.85011942`
What is the answer
   a to the nearest whole number   **b** to 3 significant figures
   c to 2 significant figures   **d** to 2 decimal places
   e to 1 decimal place   **f** to 3 decimal places

2 What multiplier would you use to work out
   a a decrease of 20%   **b** an increase of 15%   **c** an increase of 3%?

3 a Increase 23 g by 25%.
   b Decrease 576 km by 35%.
   c Decrease £24 by 2%.

4 Work out the percentage $\frac{A}{B} \times 100$, when
   a $A = 27$ cm and $B = 50$ cm
   b $A = £54.99$ and $B = £85.9$

> **Q4 hint** Round your answer to the nearest whole number.

Key point

You can use **inverse operations** to find the original amount after a percentage increase or decrease.

Worked example

In a year the value of a car dropped by 15% to £4760.
How much was the car worth at the start of the year?

100% − 15% = 85% = 0.85

Original number → [× 0.85] → 4760 ——— Draw a function machine.

5600 ← [÷ 0.85] ← 4760

The car was worth £5600 at the start of the year.

5 A hedge has been reduced in height by 10%.
Now it is 1.8 m tall. What was its original height?

6 There is a 20% discount in a sale.
A coat has a sale price of £38.
What was its original price?

7 A shop has three items on sale.
The table shows the discount for each item and the sale price.

	Original price	Discount	Sale price
Item 1		12%	£66.00
Item 2		35%	£53.30
Item 3		65%	£99.75

Work out the original price for each item.

8 **Problem-solving** Jessica bought a computer for £420. It had been reduced by 25%.
   a What was the original price of the computer before the reduction?
   Sam bought a computer for £483. It had been reduced by 30%.
   b Who saved more money?

9 In its second year of trading, a company's profits fell by 8% and the company made
£1.38 million.
How much did it make in its first year of trading?

10 A seal pup gains 28% of its birth weight each
day for the first 10 days of its life.
A one-day-old pup weighs 17.92 kg.
How much did it weigh at birth?

> **Q10 hint**
> Birth weight ⟶ ×1.28 ⟶ 17.92 kg

11 In 20 years, the population of a town has increased by 30% to 156 000.
What was the population of the town 20 years ago?

12 Between 2012 and 2018, average weekly earnings in a British city increased by 5% to £522.90.
What was the average weekly earnings in this city in 2012?

> **Key point**   You can calculate a **percentage change** using the formula
> $$\text{percentage change} = \frac{\text{actual change}}{\text{original amount}} \times 100$$

13 Maggie's hourly rate of pay increases from £12 to £12.90.
Copy and complete the working to calculate her percentage increase in pay.

   actual change = £12.90 − £12 = £☐

   $$\text{percentage change} = \frac{\text{actual change}}{\text{original amount}} \times 100 = \frac{☐}{12} \times 100 = ☐\%$$

14 An investment 'matures' when the investment period ends.
Maya invests £2400.
When her investment matures she receives £2592.
Work out
   a the actual increase in her investment
   b the percentage increase in her investment.

15 Sim invests £3500.
When his investment matures he
receives £3430.
Calculate the percentage decrease in
his investment.

> **Q15 hint** Use the same formula,
> $$\text{percentage change} = \frac{\text{actual change}}{\text{original amount}} \times 100$$

Key point Percentage profit is the percentage change between cost price and selling price.

16 The table shows the price a shopkeeper pays for some items (cost price) and the price he sells them for (selling price).

Item	Cost price	Selling price	Actual profit	Percentage profit
hoody	£12	£21		
T-shirt	£5	£8		
fleece	£30	£45		
polo shirt	£8	£18		

   a Work out the percentage profit (percentage change) on each item he sells.

   b **Reasoning** Is the item with the greatest actual profit the item with the greatest percentage profit?

17 Hannah bought a flat for £125 000. She sells it for £110 000.
What percentage loss has she made on the flat?

18 The estimated UK cost of the HS2 high speed rail link increased from £32.7 billion to £42.6 billion in June 2013.
What is the percentage increase in the estimated cost?
Give your answer to the nearest whole number.

> **Q18 hint** You don't need to write the zeros.
> 42.6 − 32.7 = ☐ billion

Challenge The table shows the number of people at a music festival between 2013 and 2018.

Year	2013	2014	2015	2016	2017	2018
Number of people	33 450	38 568	33 851	37 589	44 328	41 678

a **i** Between which two years was the greatest percentage increase in the number of people?

   ii What was this percentage increase to 3 significant figures?

b In 2013 each person paid a £185 entrance fee.
In 2018 each person paid a £210 entrance fee.
What was the percentage increase in total entrance fee takings between 2013 and 2018? Give your answer to 2 significant figures.

Reflect Marcia says, 'I find it difficult to remember the percentage change formula. Is it actual change divided by original amount or the other way round?'
Andrew says, 'I know that if I invest £2 and get £3 in return, I've made £1, which is 50% of £2 or a 50% change. That helps me to remember the formula.'

£2	+ £1

50%

Try both of Marcia's formulae suggestions using Andrew's numbers.
Which is the correct formula?
What do you think of Andrew's strategy? Do you have another way of remembering the formula? If so, what is it?

4.4 Compound measures

- Solve problems using compound measures
- Solve problems using constant rates and related formulae

Active Learn
Homework

Warm up

1　Fluency　What is

　a　$2\frac{1}{2}$ as a decimal　　**b**　1 km in metres　　**c**　1 kg in grams

　d　$1\frac{1}{4}$ hours in minutes　**e**　$\frac{3}{5}$ hour in minutes　**f**　1 hour in seconds?

2　Solve each equation to find the value of a.

　a　$b = \dfrac{a}{c}$ when $b = 25$ and $c = 5$　　　　**b**　$c = \dfrac{b}{a}$ when $b = 30$ and $c = 6$

3　Work out

> **Q3a hint** Convert the mm measures to cm. Then find the area.

　a　the area of this rectangle　　　　　　**b**　the volume of this cuboid.

6 mm
10 mm

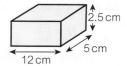
2.5 cm
5 cm
12 cm

　　Give your answer in cm².

4　Change
　a　20 000 cm² to m²　　**b**　5 cm² to m²　　**c**　25.3 cm² to m²

Key point

Compound measures combine measures of two different quantities. For example, speed is a measure of distance travelled and time taken. It can be measured in metres per second (m/s), kilometres per hour (km/h) or miles per hour (mph). You can calculate **speed** if you know the **distance** and the **time**.

$$\text{speed} = \frac{\text{distance}}{\text{time}} \quad \text{or} \quad S = \frac{D}{T}$$

5　Work out the **speed** for these journeys.
　a　A car travels 180 km in 3 hours.
　b　A train travels 300 km in 4 hours.
　c　A jogger runs 10 miles in 2 hours.
　d　A cyclist rides 24 miles in $1\frac{1}{2}$ hours.

> **Q5 hint** Substitute distance and time into the formula. Give answers using the correct speed measure, for example km/h or mph.

6　**a**　Work out the **distance** travelled for these journeys.
　　i　A car travels for 4 hours at a speed of 88 km/h.
　　ii　A motorcycle travels for $\frac{3}{4}$ of an hour at a speed of 72 km/h.
　b　Work out the **time** taken for these journeys.
　　i　A car travels 210 km at a speed of 70 km/h.
　　ii　A cyclist travels 18 miles at a speed of 12 mph.

> **Q6 hint** Substitute the numbers you know into the formula. Solve the equation to find the value of D (for part **a**) or T (for part **b**).

Worked example

Convert 8 m/s into km/h.

$$\begin{array}{l}
8\text{ m/s} \\
\times 60 \Big\downarrow \\
480\text{ m/min} \\
\times 60 \Big\downarrow \\
28\,800\text{ m/h} \\
\div 1000 \Big\downarrow \\
28.8\text{ km/h}
\end{array}$$

Convert seconds to minutes.

Convert minutes to hours.

Convert metres to kilometres.

---

7 Convert these speeds.
  a 6 m/s into km/h   **b** 25 m/s into km/h
  c 72 km/h into m/s   **d** 162 km/h into m/s

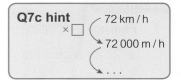

Q7c hint
$$\begin{array}{l}
72\text{ km/h} \\
\times\square \Big\downarrow \\
72\,000\text{ m/h} \\
\Big\downarrow \\
\dots
\end{array}$$

8 **Problem-solving**   The distance by train from Haverfordwest to Swansea is 64 miles. Lynn leaves Haverfordwest train station at 1723 and arrives at Swansea train station at 1853.
  a How long is the train journey?
  b Calculate the speed of the train in km/h.

Q8 hint 1 mile = 1.6 km. The distance is in miles, but you are asked for the speed in km/h.

Key point   **Density** is a compound measure.

Density is the **mass** of substance contained in a certain **volume**.

$$\text{density} = \frac{\text{mass}}{\text{volume}} \text{ or } D = \frac{M}{V}$$

Density is usually measured in grams per cubic centimetre (g/cm³).
To calculate it, you need mass in g and volume in cm³.

Worked example

A silver pendant has a mass of 31.5 g and a volume of 3 cm³.
Work out the density of the silver.

$$D = \frac{M}{V}$$

Write the formula first.

$$D = \frac{31.5}{3} = 10.5\text{ g/cm}^3$$

Substitute the numbers into the formula.
Don't forget the units: g/cm³.

---

9 A piece of gold has mass 48.5 g and volume 2.5 cm³.
  Work out the density of the gold.

10 **Problem-solving**   The diagram shows a wooden cuboid.
  The block has a mass of 20.8 kg.
  Work out the density of the wood.
  Give your answer in g/cm³ to 2 significant figures.

11 **Reasoning**   1 cm³ of graphite has mass 2.25 g.
  1 cm³ of diamond has mass 3.51 g.
  Which is more dense? Explain your answer.

Q11 hint Write down the density of each substance.

12 A block of lead has volume $880\,cm^3$ and density $11.35\,g/cm^3$.
Work out the mass of the lead. Give your answer in grams.

> **Q12 hint** Substitute the numbers you know into the formula.

 13 A sheet of copper has mass $3.76\,kg$. Copper has a density of $8.96\,g/cm^3$.
Work out the volume of the copper sheet. Give your answer to the nearest cm^3.

> **Key point** **Pressure** is a compound measure. It is the **force** applied over an **area**.
>
> $$\text{pressure} = \frac{\text{force}}{\text{area}} \text{ or } P = \frac{F}{A}$$
>
> Pressure is usually measured in newtons (N) per square metre.
> To calculate it, you need pressure in N and area in m^2.

 14 A **force** of $56\,N$ is applied to an **area** of $3.5\,m^2$.
Work out the **pressure** in N/m^2.

 15 **Problem-solving** The diagram shows the dimensions of a rectangular piece of metal.
A force of $45\,N$ is applied to the piece of metal.
Work out the pressure in N/cm^2 to 1 significant figure.

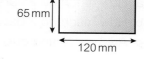

 16 Copy and complete this table.

Force	Area	Pressure
120 N	1.25 m²	☐ N/m²
☐ N	0.75 m²	15 N/m²
☐ N	3.6 cm²	20 N/m²
40 N	☐ m²	16 N/m²

> **Q16 hint** Substitute the numbers you know into the formula. Solve an equation if necessary.
> Look carefully at the units of measurement.
>
>

Challenge Lisa sits on a chair with four identical legs. The foot of each chair leg is a square measuring $3\,cm$ by $3\,cm$. The force produced by the mass of Lisa and the chair is $522\,N$. Work out

a the total area of the floor covered by the feet of the chair

b the pressure on the floor when Lisa sits on the chair with all four chair feet flat on the floor.

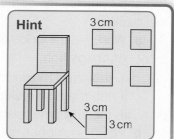

Reflect Jesse says, 'A compound measure combines measures of two different quantities. A rate of change describes exactly how one of the quantities changes in relation to another.'
Jesse starts this table to show what he means.

> **Hint** Look back at the compound measures and rates of change you worked with in this lesson. Can you think of other examples? Think about subjects like science and geography, or activities outside school.

Compound measure	Rate of change (example)
Speed – measure of distance and time	40 miles per hour

Copy the table and add more examples.

4.5 Direct and inverse proportion

- Solve best-buy problems
- Solve problems involving inverse proportion

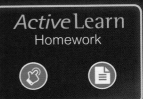
*Active*Learn
Homework

Warm up

1 **Fluency**   Work out
   a £2.40 ÷ 4   **b** £4.50 ÷ 3
   c £3.12 ÷ 3   **d** 2 hours ÷ 3

> **Q1d hint** 2 hours = ☐ minutes

2 1 bar of chocolate weighs 210 g and costs 98p.
   a How much do 2 bars of chocolate weigh?
   b How much do 2 bars of chocolate cost?
   c Are weight and cost in direct proportion? Explain.

3 4 tickets to the cinema costs £46.
   a How much do 6 tickets cost?
   b Are number of tickets and cost in direct proportion? Explain.

Key point

You can use direct proportion to work out the best value for money.

4 **Reasoning**   Here are some multipacks of crisps.
   Each multipack is the same brand
   and contains the same size smaller
   packets.
   a Work out the price of one packet
      of crisps from
      i the small multipack
      ii the medium multipack
      iii the large multipack.
   b Which multipack is the best value for money?
      Explain your answer.
   c What other calculations could you do to compare
      the prices of these multipacks and work out which
      is the best value for money?

SMALL MULTIPACK — 6 packets of crisps — £1.68
MEDIUM MULTIPACK — 12 packets of crisps — £3.24

LARGE MULTIPACK — 18 packets of crisps — £4.50

> **Q4c hint** How do the numbers
> of packets of crisps in each
> size pack relate to each other?

5 **Reasoning**   Here are some jars of honey at different
   prices from different producers.
   a Work out the cost of 10 g of honey from
      each jar.
   b Which jar of honey is the best value for
      money?
      Explain your answer.

HONEY A — 40 g — £0.74
HONEY B — 250 g — £1.75

HONEY C — 340 g — £2.89

6 Problem-solving A supermarket has three different offers on washing tablets.

Offer A
24 tablets for £4.32

Offer B
16 tablets for £3.20

Offer C
40 tablets for £7.50

Show two different ways to work out the best value offer.

7 Reasoning Here are three different makes of compost, sold at different prices.

| Green's compost 99 litres £11 | Tip top compost 120 litres £10 | Sunshine compost 125 litres £12.50 |

a Greg says he is going to work out the cost of 9 litres of compost for each make.
Audrey says she is going to work out the number of litres she gets for £1 for each make.
Whose method is better? Explain why.

b Which bag of compost is the best value for money? Show working.

c Which bag of compost is the worst value for money? Show working.

8 Reasoning Bob, Ellen and Ali are gardeners.
Bob charges £140 for a full day's work (7 hours).
Ellen charges £45 for 2 hours' work.
Ali charges £65 for 3 hours' work.

a Which gardener is the best value for money?

b Did you work out exact or approximate charges per hour for each of the gardeners? Explain.

9 Reasoning Bob and Ellen from Q8 sometimes work together.
They each estimate it will take 3 days to lay a grass tennis court, working alone.
How long should it take if they work together?

> **Q9 hint** 1 gardener takes 3 days.
> Will 2 gardeners take twice as long or half as long?

Key point When two quantities are in **inverse proportion**, as one increases, the other decreases at the same rate. This means that
- when one doubles, the other halves
- when one triples, the other is divided by 3
- and so on.

Worked example

It takes 2 people 6 days to lay out a new garden.
How long does it take

a 4 people

b 1 person?

a Number of people   Time (days)

$$×2 \binom{2 \quad 6}{4 \quad 3} ÷2$$

> The more people there are, the less time it takes. Doubling the number of people halves the time.

It takes 3 days.

b Number of people   Time (days)

$$÷2 \binom{2 \quad 6}{1 \quad 12} ×2$$

> Halving the number of people doubles the time.

It takes 12 days.

10 Problem-solving 4 mechanics can repair a coach in 2 hours.
How long would it take
  a 2 mechanics
  b 1 mechanic
  c 8 mechanics?

Q10 hint Use a table to set out your working.

Number of people	Time (hours)
4	2
2	☐

11 Problem-solving It takes 60 minutes to empty a pool with 2 pumps.
  a How long would it take with 3 pumps?
  b How many pumps are needed to empty the pool in 30 minutes?

Q11a hint Work out how long it would take with 1 pump first.

12 Problem-solving 5 workers can dig a 48 m trench in 4 days.
  a How long would it take 10 workers to dig a 48 m trench?
  b How long would it take 10 workers to dig a 12 m trench?

13 Problem-solving A printer prints 1000 leaflets in 5 minutes.
  a How long will it take the printer to print 5000 leaflets?
  b Is the number of printed leaflets directly or inversely proportional to time? Explain.

Q13a hint Will it take more time or less time?

14 Problem-solving It takes a team of 6 builders 90 days to build a house.
  a The client wants the house built in 60 days.
  How many more builders are required in the team to achieve this?
  b Is the number of builders directly or inversely proportional to time? Explain.

Q14a hint Work out how many builders for 30 days first. Will it take more builders or fewer builders?

Challenge Which of these pairs of variables are
  a directly proportional   **b** inversely proportional   **c** not proportional?
  A The number of litres of fuel put in a car and the cost
  B The number of students in a class and the length of time given to complete a test
  C The number of identical textbooks in a pile and the weight of the pile
  D The number of people delivering leaflets and the time it takes
  E The speed of a train and the time it takes to cover a distance
  F The length of a rectangle and its length when enlarged by a scale factor

Reflect Describe to a classmate what is the same and what is different about direct and inverse proportion.

4 Check up

Enlargement

1 Copy these shapes on to coordinate grids and then enlarge them, using the scale factors and centres of enlargement given.

   a scale factor 3

   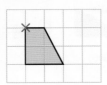

   b scale factor −2

   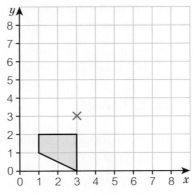

2 Describe the enlargement that takes shape A to shape B.

   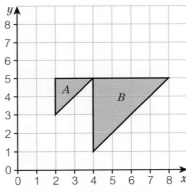

3 Copy the diagram and enlarge the triangle using scale factor $\frac{1}{2}$ and the given centre of enlargement.

   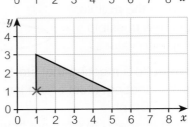

4 A model helicopter is made using a ratio of 1 : 48.
   The width of the model helicopter is 9.9 cm.
   What is the width of the real helicopter? Give your answer in metres.

Compound measures and proportionality

5 Convert 36 km/h into m/s.

6 **a** Sol takes 2 hours to drive 114 miles. Work out the speed of his journey.
   b Mair cycles at a speed of 12 mph for $1\frac{3}{4}$ hours. How far does she cycle?

7 Copy and complete this table to show the mass, volume and density of beech.

Tree	Mass (g)	Volume (cm³)	Density (g/cm³)
beech	402	600	

8 A force of 370 N is applied to an area of 8 m².
Work out the pressure in N/m².
Give your answer to 2 significant figures.

9 Toilet rolls come in three different size packs.
Which pack is the best value for money?
Show working to explain your answer.

10 3 students can put away all the chairs in the school hall in 18 minutes.
How long would it take 6 students?

Percentage change

11 There was a 30% discount in a sale. A bag had a sale price of £28.
What was the original price?

12 Ellie invests £3200. When her investment matures she receives £3584.
Work out
a the actual increase in her investment
b the percentage increase in her investment.

13 Jane buys a car for £9075. She sells it for £6171.
What percentage loss has she made on the car?

Challenge

1 In this spider diagram, the four calculations give the amount in the middle. Work out three possible sets of missing values.

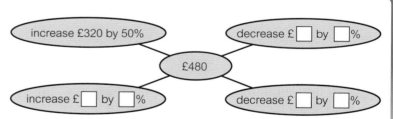

2 Jon has to go to a meeting that starts at 10.30 am. He plans to drive the 150 miles from home to the meeting. Most of the journey is on the motorway. The speed limit on the motorway is 70 mph.
Use a suitable speed to work out how long the journey will take and what time he should leave home when
a there is not much traffic on the roads
b there is a lot of traffic on the roads.

Reflect How sure are you of your answers? Were you mostly

☹ **Just guessing**   😐 **Feeling doubtful**   ☺ **Confident**

What next? Use your results to decide whether to strengthen or extend your learning.

4 Strengthen

Enlargement

1   Copy these shapes onto coordinate grids.
    Complete the enlargements using the marked
    centres and scale factors.

> **Q1 hint** Count the squares (up/down and
> left/right) from the centre of enlargement to
> each vertex. Then multiply each distance by
> the scale factor.

a scale factor 2

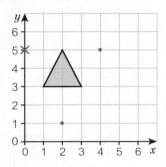

b scale factor 3

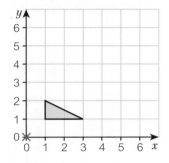

c scale factor 3

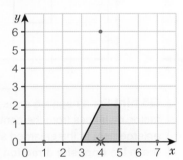

d scale factor 2

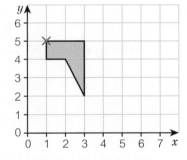

2   Shape A has been enlarged to shape B.
    The corresponding vertices of the original shape A and the
    enlarged shape B are shown with the same colour dots.
    a Copy the shapes onto a coordinate grid and join the
       corresponding vertices with straight lines.
       Write down the coordinates of the point where the lines cross.
       This is the centre of enlargement.
    b What is the scale factor of the enlargement?
    c Count the squares (up/down and left/right) from the centre
       of enlargement to each corresponding vertex on A
       and B. Write a sentence describing how you can use
       this to find the scale factor.

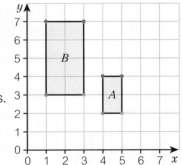

> **Q2a hint** Make sure the lines are
> long enough to cross each other.

3 Copy and complete to describe the enlargement that takes shape C to shape D.
Shape C is enlarged by scale factor $\square$, with centre of enlargement ($\square$, $\square$).

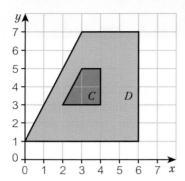

Q3 hint Follow the instructions in Q2 parts **a** and **b**.

4 Copy these shapes onto coordinate grids.
Complete the enlargements using the marked centres and scale factors.

Q4 hint Follow the method you used in Q1. As the scale factors are fractions you will need to work out, for example,
$\frac{1}{2} \times 2 = \square$ $\frac{1}{3} \times 3 = \square$

a scale factor $\frac{1}{2}$

b scale factor $\frac{1}{3}$

c scale factor $\frac{1}{2}$

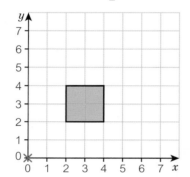
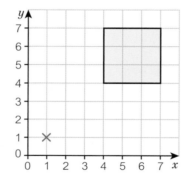
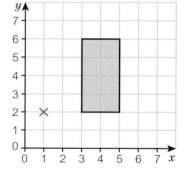

5 What are the missing words in these sentences?
When enlarging a shape by a negative scale factor

Q5 hint For a negative scale factor, distances from the centre of enlargement to the enlarged shape are in the **opposite direction** from distances to the original shape.

a a distance left from the centre of enlargement becomes a distance _____

b a distance right from the centre of enlargement becomes a distance _____

c a distance up from the centre of enlargement becomes a distance _____

d a distance down from the centre of enlargement becomes a distance _____ .

6 Copy these shapes onto coordinate grids. Complete the enlargements using the marked centres and scale factors.
a scale factor −2   **b** scale factor −3

Q6 hint Count the squares (up/down and left/right) from the centre of enlargement to each vertex. Then multiply each distance by the scale factor, but in the **opposite direction**.

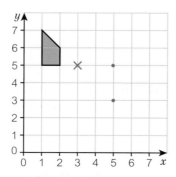
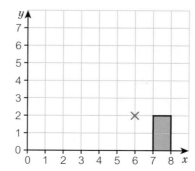

7 A photograph is enlarged using the ratio 1 : 2.

    a The height of the original photograph is 4 inches. What is the height of the enlarged photograph?

    b The width of the original photograph is 6 inches. What is the width of the enlarged photograph?

Q7 hint
original : enlargement
      1 : 2
This is an enlargement with scale factor 2.

8 **Problem-solving** A model farmhouse is made using a ratio of 1 : 76. The height of the model is 85 mm.

    a What is the scale factor?

    b What is the height of the real farmhouse? Give your answer in

      i millimetres   **ii** metres.

Compound measures and proportionality

1   **a** Convert 9 km/h into m/h.

    b Convert your answer to part **a** from m/h into m/min.

    c Convert your answer to part **b** from m/min into m/s.

    d Convert 108 km/h into m/s.

kilometres (km) × ☐ gives metres (m).

hours (h) ÷ ☐ gives minutes (min).

minutes (min) ÷ ☐ gives seconds (s).

Q1d hint Follow the steps in parts **a** to **c**.

2 Copy and complete this table of distance, time and speed.

Distance (miles)	Time (hours)	Speed (mph)
	3	55
	$1\frac{1}{2}$	68
120	4	
144	$2\frac{1}{4}$	
70		35
180		48

Q2 hint

speed = $\dfrac{\text{distance}}{\text{time}}$

distance = speed × time

time = $\dfrac{\text{distance}}{\text{speed}}$

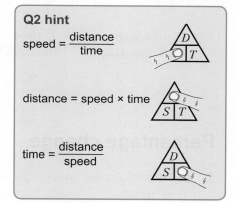

3 Copy and complete this table of mass, volume and density.

Metal	Mass (g)	Volume (cm³)	Density (g/cm³)
tin		100	7.31
iron	472.2		7.87
nickel	311.5	35	

Q3 hint

Use your finger to cover the quantity you want to find.

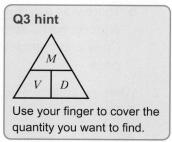

4 Copy and complete this table showing force, area and pressure.

Force (N)	Area (cm²)	Pressure (N/cm²)
	12	7
45	15	
56		14

Q4 hint

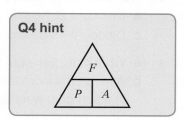

5 Pasta is sold in three different size bags.

500 g £0.76
1 kg £1.45
3 kg £4.26

Q5a hint

×2 (500 g = £0.76) ×2
1 kg = £☐

÷☐ (3 kg = £4.26) ÷☐
1 kg = £☐

a Work out the price of 1 kg of pasta based on the 500 g bag and the 3 kg bag.

b Reasoning Which bag is the best value for money? Explain your answer.

6 The price of a pack of 16 bars of soap is £4.
The price of a pack of 20 bars of soap is £5.

a Work out the price of one bar of soap from the pack of 16.
Then work out the price of 20 of these bars of soap.

b Reasoning Which pack is the better value for money?

7 2 gardeners can plant a flower bed in 40 minutes.

a Would it take 1 gardener a longer or a shorter time?

b Would it take 4 gardeners a longer or a shorter time?

c Copy and complete to work out how long it takes

  i 1 gardener   **ii** 4 gardeners.

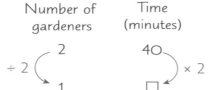 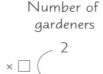

Percentage change

1 a What multiplier would you use to work out a decrease of 10%?

b There was a 10% discount in a sale.
A jacket had a sale price of £36.
Copy and complete the working to find the original price.

Q1 hint
100% − 10% = ☐% = 0.☐

original price ☐
× multiplier ( ) ÷ multiplier
sale price £36

2 What multiplier would you use for a decrease of

  a 20%   **b** 40%   **c** 15%   **d** 30%?

3 Work out the original price for each of these items

  a Discount 20%, sale price £48   **b** Discount 40%, sale price £72

  c Discount 15%, sale price £68   **d** Discount 30%, sale price £63

4 a What multiplier would you use to work out an increase of 25%?

b After a 25% increase in membership, the number of members in a surf club went up to 20.
Copy and complete the working to find the original number of members in the club.

Q4a hint
100% + 25% = ☐% = 1.☐

original membership ☐
× multiplier ( ) ÷ multiplier
membership now 20

5 What multiplier would you use for an increase of
  a 10%   **b** 30%   **c** 45%   **d** 6%?

6 Work out the original number of members in each of these clubs.
  a Increase of 10%, up to 66 members
  b Increase of 30%, up to 195 members
  c Increase of 45%, up to 174 members
  d Increase of 6%, up to 477 members

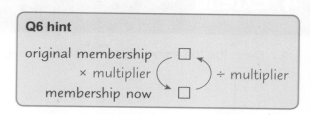

Q6 hint

original membership ☐
  × multiplier   ÷ multiplier
membership now ☐

7 Anil invests £6000. When his investment matures he receives £6240.
  a Copy and complete the working to calculate his percentage increase.
    original amount = 6000
    actual change = 6240 − 6000 = 240
    percentage change = $\frac{\text{actual change}}{\text{original amount}} \times 100$
    $= \frac{240}{6000} \times 100 = \square\%$

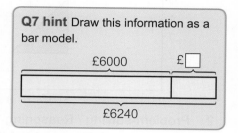

Q7 hint Draw this information as a bar model.

£6000   £☐

£6240

  b Check your answer by increasing £6000 by the percentage you calculated.

8 Work out the percentage profit made on each of the items. For each part, copy and complete the following working. Check your answers.
    original amount = ☐   actual change = ☐
    percentage profit = $\frac{\text{actual change}}{\text{original amount}} \times 100 = \frac{\square}{\square} \times 100 = \square\%$
  a Bought for £6, sold for £7.50
  b Bought for £15, sold for £19.50
  c Bought for £120, sold for £222

9 Work out the percentage loss made on each of these items. Check your answers.
  a Bought for £12, sold for £9
  b Bought for £360, sold for £306
  c Bought for £42, sold for £26.46

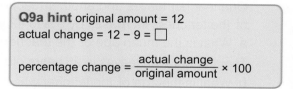

Q9a hint original amount = 12
actual change = 12 − 9 = ☐

percentage change = $\frac{\text{actual change}}{\text{original amount}} \times 100$

Challenge

1 Lowri and Tyler take a typing test. Lowri types 312 words in 8 minutes. Tyler types 220 words in 5 minutes. Who types faster?

2 The area of the yellow rectangle is 60% of the area of the blue rectangle.

area = 42 cm²

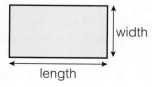

width

length

  a Work out the area of the blue rectangle.
  b Work out a possible length and width of the blue rectangle.

Reflect   Write a sentence describing how you use multiplication or division in questions about
a enlargement   **b** compound measures   **c** percentage change.

4 Extend

1 Describe the enlargement that takes shape A to shape B in each of these these diagrams.

a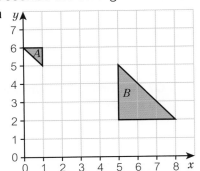

b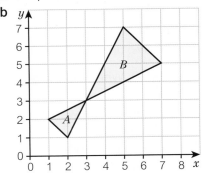

2 **Problem-solving / Reasoning** Hassan makes a model of Buckingham Palace using a scale of 1 : 12. The height of the real palace is 24 m.

a What is the height of the model?

Hassan then makes a doll's house of the palace to go inside his model.
The scale of the doll's house compared to the model is 1 : 10.

b What is the height of the doll's house?

Hassan says, 'The scale of the doll's house to Buckingham Palace is 1 : 22 because 12 + 10 = 22.'

Raj says, 'The scale of the doll's house to Buckingham Palace is 1 : 120 because 12 × 10 = 120.'

c Who is correct? Explain your answer. Check your answer by comparing the real height of Buckingham Palace with your answer to part **b**.

3 **Problem-solving** There are 10 teachers in a primary school. One teacher leaves and another teacher arrives. The mean age of the teachers increases by 5% to 42 years old.

a What is the mean age of the teachers before the teacher leaves?
The teacher who leaves is 25 years old.

b What is the age of the teacher who arrives?

> **Q3b hint** Work out the total age of the teachers before the teacher leaves and after the other teacher arrives.

4 **Problem-solving** A car travels at a speed of 24 m/s. Work out the time it takes to travel 325 km. Give your answer in hours and minutes, to the nearest minute.

5 **Problem-solving / Reasoning** It is 235 miles from London to Manchester by train.
The table shows the top speed and average speed of a high-speed train and an Intercity train.

	Top speed	Average speed
High-speed train	200 mph	185 mph
Intercity train	125 mph	110 mph

a How much quicker is the journey from London to Manchester on a high-speed train than an Intercity train when you use

  i the top speeds   ii the average speeds?
  Give your answers to the nearest minute.

b Which answer is more realistic? Explain why.

6 Reasoning The line graph shows the mean household mortgage and rent payments from 2008 to 2010.

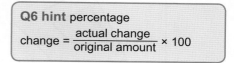

Average household mortgage and rent payments

a Work out the percentage increase, to the nearest 1%, in rent payments for the average household between
   i 2008 and 2009
   ii 2009 and 2010
   iii 2008 and 2010.

b Explain why the sum of your answers to parts **i** and **ii** is not the same as your answer to part **iii**.

c Work out the percentage decrease, to the nearest 1%, in mortgage payments for the average household between
   i 2008 and 2009   ii 2009 and 2010.

> **Q6 hint** percentage
> change = $\dfrac{\text{actual change}}{\text{original amount}} \times 100$

7 Problem-solving The block of wood (A) has a mass of 1.44 kg. The wooden cube (B) is made from wood with a density 50% greater than the block of wood.
Work out the mass of the wooden cube.
Give your answer in grams to three significant figures.

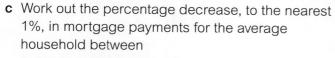

8 Problem-solving The diagram shows a piece of plastic cut into the shape of a trapezium.
Work out the force required to create a pressure of 12 N/cm² on the trapezium.

> **Q8 hint** Work out the area of the trapezium in cm² first.

62 mm
50 mm
84 mm

9 Problem-solving The diagram shows a piece of metal.
When a force of 328 N is applied to the metal, it creates a pressure of 16 N/cm².
Work out the length, x, of the rectangle.

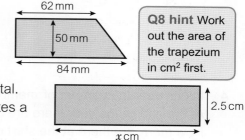

2.5 cm
x cm

10 Problem-solving 4 gardeners can plant 120 daffodil bulbs in 1 hour 15 minutes and 200 snowdrop bulbs in 1 hour 30 minutes.
How long would it take 6 gardeners to plant 96 daffodil bulbs and 300 snowdrop bulbs?

11 Problem-solving A pentagon has vertices at (8, 3), (8, 5), (9, 5), (10, 4) and (10, 3).
a Draw the pentagon on a coordinate grid with x axis from 0 to 20 and y axis from 0 to 10.
b Transform the pentagon using a rotation of 180° about (10, 5) then enlarge by scale factor −2 using centre of enlargement at (13, 5).
c Describe the single enlargement that will take the finishing pentagon back to the starting pentagon.

> **Q11c hint** Work out the scale factor.
> Use rays to work out where the centre of enlargement is.

Reflect   Look back at the questions in this Extend lesson.
Write down the question that you found most difficult to answer.
What made it most difficult?
What could you do to make this type of question easier to answer?

4 Unit test

1   Copy this shape onto squared paper and then enlarge it, using the marked centre of enlargement and scale factor 3.

2   In each of these diagrams describe the enlargement from A to B.

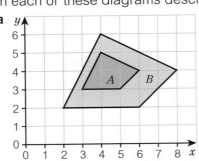   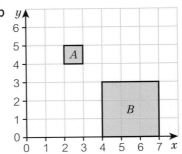

3   Copy this shape onto squared paper and then enlarge it, using the marked centre of enlargement and scale factor -3.

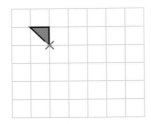

4   In one year the number of members in a chess club increases by 20%.
    At the end of the year there are 30 members.
    How many are there at the start of the year?

5   Chan invests £2800. When his investment matures he receives £2968.
    Work out
    a how much his investment increased by
    b the percentage change in his investment.

6   A secondhand car dealer buys a car for £3500.
    He sells the car for £4270.
    What percentage profit does he make?

7   a Joel takes 4 hours to drive 188 miles. Work out his speed.
    b Ava walks at a speed of 8 km/h for $3\frac{1}{4}$ hours.
       How far does she walk?
    c Rowan flies a helicopter at a speed of 115 mph for 92 miles. How long does it take him?
       Give your answer in minutes.

8 This table shows the mass, volume and density of two pieces of plastic.
Work out the missing values in the table.

Mass (g)	Volume (cm³)	Density (g/cm³)
	280	1.15
846	450	

9 A force of 84 N is applied to an area of 15 cm². Work out the pressure in N/cm².

10 Cartons of fruit juice come in different size multipacks.

Pack of 4
FRUIT JUICE
£1.18

Pack of 6
FRUIT JUICE
£1.68

Pack of 10
FRUIT JUICE
£2.85

Which pack is the best value for money? Explain your answer.

11 Copy this diagram and enlarge the triangle, using scale factor $\frac{1}{3}$ and centre of enlargement (7, 1).

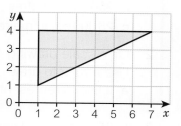

12 A model of a building is 40 cm high. The real building is 6.4 m high.
Work out the scale factor of the model to the building.
Write your answer as
   a a number   **b** a ratio, in the form 1 : n.

13 Jan bought a camper van for £28 000. She sold it for £16 800.
Work out her percentage loss.

Challenge The diagram shows a triangle, some scale factor cards and some area cards.

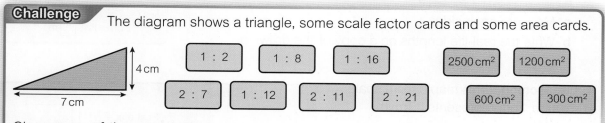

Choose one of the area cards.
Then work out which scale factor card, if used to enlarge the triangle, would give the closest possible area to the one on your card.
Try again with a different card.

Reflect   Make a list of all the topics you have worked on in this unit where you have used multiplicative reasoning.
Look back at other units you have studied in this book.
List some other mathematics topics that use multiplicative reasoning. Compare your list with those of your classmates.

Hint Remember that 'multiplicative' means 'involving multiplication or division'. Reasoning is being able to explain why.

5 Constructions

5.1 Using scales

- Use scales on maps and diagrams
- Draw diagrams to scale

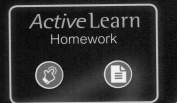

Active Learn
Homework

Warm up

1   **Fluency**   What is
    a 250 cm in metres
    b 2500 cm in metres
    c 25 000 cm in metres
    d 2500 m in kilometres?

2   On a scale drawing 1 cm represents 1 m.
    Use a ruler to draw
    a a line to represent 5 m
    b a line to represent 3.5 m.

3   In this diagram, 1 cm represents 2 m in real life.

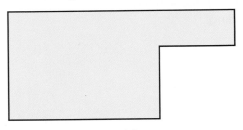

    a Measure each side.
    b Write the real-life lengths on a copy of the drawing.

Q3b hint

Diagram		Real life
1 cm	is	2 m
2 cm	is	☐ m

×2   ×2

4   **Reasoning**   This map uses a scale where 1 cm represents 20 m in real life.
    a Measure the distance on the roads between
       i the newsagent and the zebra crossing
       ii the school and the post office.
    b Work out the real-life distances for parts **a i** and **a ii**.
    c Alix walks along the roads from the newsagent's to the post office. How far does she walk?

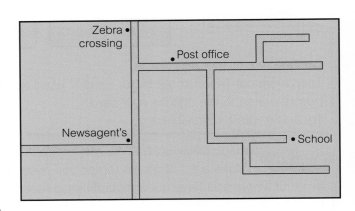

5 **Reasoning** This map of a city centre uses a scale of 1 cm for every 200 m. Use the map to estimate as accurately as possible the real distance in metres between the

a Town Hall and Art Gallery

b Museum and Theatre

c Cathedral and School.

d Why can you only estimate the distances from the map?

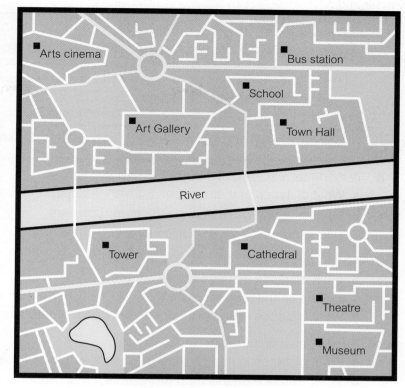

6 **Problem-solving** Neeta has drawn this scale diagram showing a design for her garden. The length of the fence is 4 m in real life.

a Work out the scale of the diagram. Write the scale as 1 cm to _____.

b Use this scale to find

  i the length of the pond

  ii the length of the border

  iii the area of the border

  iv the area of the decking.

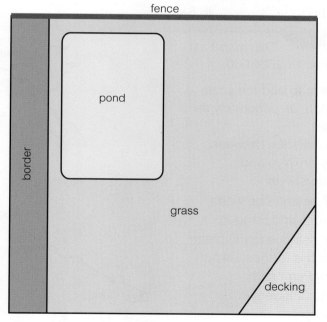

7 Draw a floor plan on cm squared paper for the kitchen and utility room of this house. Use a scale of 1 cm to 0.5 m.

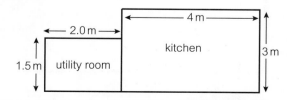

A map has scale 1 : 25 000. What distance in metres does 3 cm on the map represent?

Map		Real life
1 cm	is	25 000 cm
1 cm	is	250 m
3 cm	is	750 m

×3 ⟨ ⟩ ×3

> Work out what 1 cm represents in centimetres.

> Convert to metres.

8 A map has a scale of 1 : 25 000.
  a What distance in metres does 5 cm on the map represent?
  b What distance does 8 cm on the map represent
    i in metres   ii in kilometres?

9 A map has a scale of 1 : 50 000.
  a What distance in metres does
    i 1 cm on the map represent   ii 4 cm on the map represent?
  b What distance in kilometres does 6 cm on the map represent?

10 A map has a scale of 1 : 30 000.
  a What distance in metres does 1 cm on the map represent?
  b What distance on this map represents a real distance of
    i 600 m   ii 6 km

This map has a scale of 1 : 2 500 000.

Use the map and the scale to estimate as accurately as possible
a the distance between Hay-on-Wye and Aberystwyth
b the distance between Cardiff and Bangor
c the distance to the place which is furthest away from Pembroke.
Give your answers in kilometres.

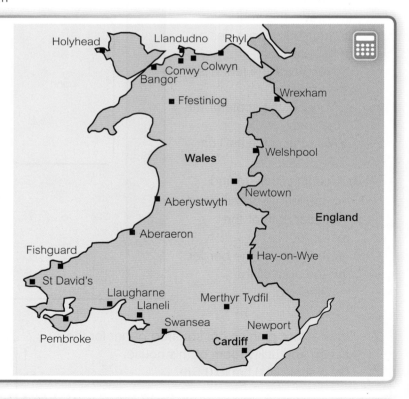

Santiago says, 'When working with scales on maps and diagrams, one of the most important things is multiplying by the correct scale factor.'
a Do you agree with him? Explain.
b What else is important when working with scales on maps and diagrams?

5.2 Basic constructions

• Make accurate constructions using drawing equipment

Active Learn
Homework

1 Fluency

a What does 'perpendicular' mean?   **b** In a circle, what is the radius?

2 Use a ruler and a sharp pencil to draw lines with these lengths.

a 6.5 cm   **b** 10.6 cm   **c** 27 mm

3 Draw an angle of 40°.

4 Use compasses to draw accurately
  a a circle of radius 5 cm
  b a circle of radius 8 cm.

Q4a hint

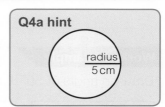

radius
5 cm

Key point   **Construct** means draw accurately using a ruler and compasses.
Perpendicular means 'at right angles'.
Bisect means 'to cut in half'.
A **perpendicular bisector** is a line that cuts another line in half at right angles.

Worked example

Draw a line 5 cm long.
Construct its perpendicular bisector.

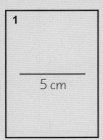 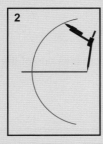 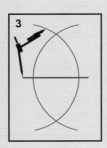 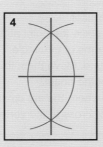

5 cm

1 Use a ruler to draw the line.
2 Open your compasses greater than half the length of the line.
  Place the point on one end of the line and draw an arc above and below.
3 Keeping the compasses the same, move them to the other end of the line and draw another arc.
4 Join the points where the arcs intersect. The vertical line divides the horizontal line exactly in half.
Do not rub out the arcs.

5 **a** Draw a line 7.5 cm long. Construct its perpendicular bisector.

    b Check by measuring that your line cuts the original line in half.

    c Check the angle where the lines cross.

6 **Problem-solving**

    a Draw a straight line using the straight edge of a protractor.

    b Without using a ruler, draw a construction to find the midpoint of your line.

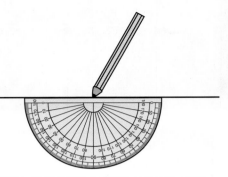

Key point   An **angle bisector** cuts an angle in half.

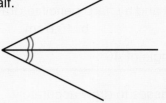

Worked example

Draw an angle of 50°. Construct the angle bisector.

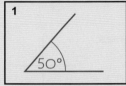 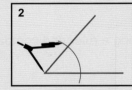 

 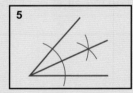

  1 Draw the angle using a protractor.

  2 Open your compasses and place the point at the vertex of the angle.
     Draw an arc that cuts both arms of the angle.

  3 Keep the compasses the same. Move them to a point where the arc crosses one of the arms.
     Make an arc in the middle of the angle.

  4 Do the same from the point where the arc crosses the other arm.

  5 Join the point where the arcs cross to the vertex of the angle.

---

7 **a** Draw an angle of 60°. Construct the angle bisector.

    b Use a protractor to check that it cuts the angle in half.

8 Draw an angle of 75°. Construct the angle bisector.

9 Use a protractor to draw an obtuse angle of any size.
Construct the angle bisector.

10 Follow these instructions to draw a perpendicular from a point to a line.

a Draw a line 12 cm long.

b Mark a point above the line.

c Put your compasses on the point. Draw an arc that crosses the line.

d Construct the perpendicular bisector of the straight line segment between the arcs.

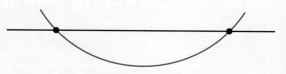

11 Problem-solving

a Trace this diagram.

P

b Construct a perpendicular line from the point to the horizontal line.

---

12 Problem-solving

a Trace this diagram.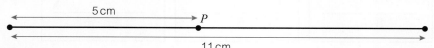

b Put your compasses on P and draw arcs so that P is the midpoint of a line segment between the arcs.

c Construct the perpendicular bisector for this line segment.

13 Problem-solving   Copy this diagram and then draw a line perpendicular through P.

5 cm

P

11 cm

Challenge

a Draw a line segment and construct the perpendicular bisector.

b Choose any point on the bisector. Measure the shortest distance to each end of the line segment.

c Repeat this for other points on the bisector.

d What do you notice? Is this always true? Why?

Reflect   Miguel says, 'Constructions in maths are all about drawing accurate diagrams with only a pair of compasses and a straight edge or ruler. No measurement of lengths or angles is allowed.'

Look back at the constructions you did in this lesson. Do you agree?

Which do you find easier:
- using compasses and a straight edge to construct, or
- using a ruler and a protractor to measure lengths and angles accurately?

Explain why.

5.3 Constructing triangles

- Construct accurate triangles
- Construct accurate nets of solids involving triangles

Active Learn
Homework

Warm up

1 Fluency What shapes are the faces of a triangular prism?

2 Sketch a possible net for this square-based pyramid.

3 Draw a 9 cm line. Construct the perpendicular bisector.

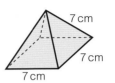

7 cm
7 cm
7 cm

Key point

Construct means draw accurately using ruler and compasses.

Worked example

Construct a triangle with sides of 8 cm, 6 cm and 9 cm.

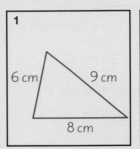

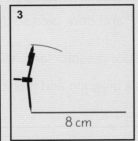
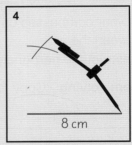

1 Sketch the triangle first.
2 Draw an 8 cm line.
3 Open your compasses to 6 cm. Place the point at one end of the 8 cm line. Draw an arc.
4 Open the compasses to 9 cm. Draw an arc from the other end of the 8 cm line.
5 Join the intersection of the arcs to both ends of the 8 cm line.

4 A triangle has sides of 5 cm, 6 cm and 7 cm.
    a Sketch this triangle.
    b Use a ruler and compasses to construct this triangle accurately.

5 A triangle has sides of 7 cm, 4 cm and 10 cm.
    Construct an accurate drawing of the triangle.

6 This picture shows some soundproofing material.
    Each triangle in the soundproofing has these measurements.
    a Construct an accurate diagram of one triangle in the soundproofing.
    b Measure the angle at the top of the triangle.

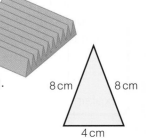

8 cm   8 cm
4 cm

7 Follow these instructions to construct this right-angled triangle.

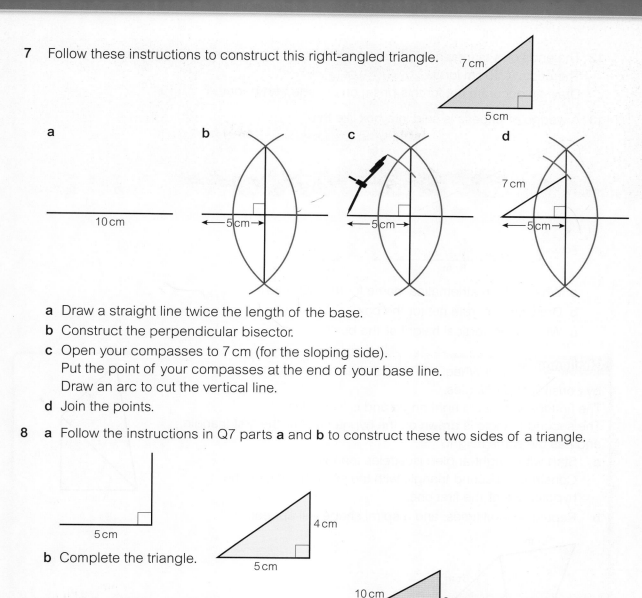

a Draw a straight line twice the length of the base.
b Construct the perpendicular bisector.
c Open your compasses to 7 cm (for the sloping side).
   Put the point of your compasses at the end of your base line.
   Draw an arc to cut the vertical line.
d Join the points.

8 **a** Follow the instructions in Q7 parts **a** and **b** to construct these two sides of a triangle.

b Complete the triangle.

9 **a** Construct this triangle accurately.
   b How long is the other side in the triangle?

> **Q9b hint** Rotate the triangle so the 6 cm side is the base.

10 Here is a sketch of the net for a triangular prism.
   a Draw the rectangles accurately on cm squared paper.
   b Construct the triangles accurately.

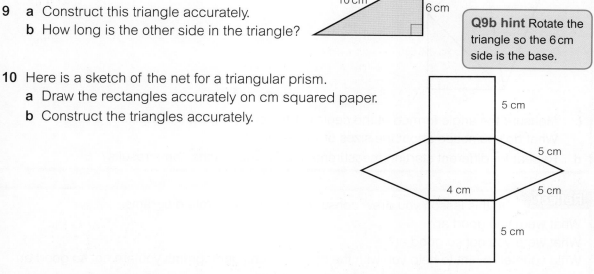

11 Draw an accurate net, on cm squared paper, for the square-based pyramid in Q2.

12 The ends of a triangular prism are equilateral triangles of side length 6 cm.
The prism is 10 cm long.
Draw an accurate net for this prism on cm squared paper.

13 A wedge of cheese is sold in a box like this.

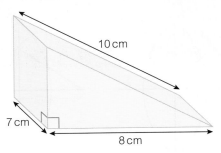

    a What is the mathematical name for this 3D solid?

    b Draw an accurate net for the box.

    c What is the vertical height of the box?

Challenge   The Wheel of Theodorus is a spiral formed
by constructing triangles.
The first triangle has a right angle and is isosceles.
The second triangle is drawn on the hypotenuse of the first triangle,
and has the same height.

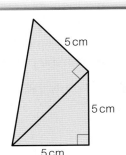

a   Start with a right-angled isosceles triangle.
Construct a second triangle with the same height, on the
hypotenuse of the first one.

b   Repeat several times, and a spiral shape will appear.

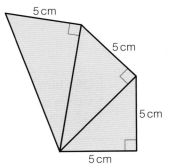

c   Measure the angle formed at the centre of the spiral by each triangle.
What do you notice about the sizes of the angles?

d   Repeat for different starting measurements. Do you get the same results?

Reflect   In this lesson you drew constructions and accurate diagrams.
What were you good at?
What were you not so good at?
Write yourself a hint to help you with the constructions or diagrams you are not so good at.
You could ask your classmates for ideas for your hint.

5.4 Using accurate scale diagrams

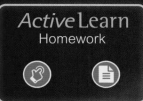

*Active*Learn
Homework

- Construct and draw accurate scale diagrams
- Use scale diagrams to solve problems

1   **Fluency**   The scale of a drawing is 1 cm to 2 m.
   a What length is represented by 5 cm on the drawing?
   b How long on the drawing is a real-life distance of 6 m?

2   Draw a straight line. Mark a point *P* on your line.

   Construct the perpendicular at *P*.

3   Use a protractor and ruler to draw this triangle accurately.

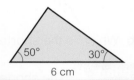

4   Follow the steps to draw this triangle accurately.
   a Draw a base 4 cm with a 110° angle at   b Measure 6 cm up the line. Join the ends
      the right-hand end.   of the two lines.

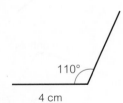

   c Measure the third side of the triangle.

Key point   **Accurate drawings** are drawn to scale, with accurate angles.
Use a ruler and protractor to make accurate drawings.

5   The diagram shows a sketch of a skateboard ramp.
   Use a scale of 1 cm to 1 m to make an accurate drawing
   of the ramp.

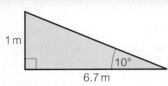

6   A shop has an access ramp for wheelchairs.
   The ramp makes an angle of 5° with the ground and has a height of 50 cm.
   The wall of the shop is at right angles to the ground.
   a Sketch the side view of the ramp. Label all three angles, and the side length you know.
   b Draw a scale diagram of the side view of the ramp.
      Use a ruler and protractor. Use the scale 1 : 10.

   Q6b hint Start by drawing the
   side whose length you know.

   c Use your diagram to work out
      i how far the ramp will stick out from the shop
      ii how long the ramp surface will be.

7 A new road is to be built at right angles to a dual carriageway. Construct an accurate scale drawing of this sketched plan.
Use a scale of 1 cm to 1 km.

8 **a** On this diagram, measure the distances from Y to different points on the line.

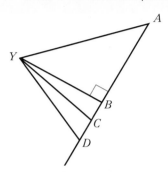

b Which is the shortest distance: YA, YB, YC or YD?

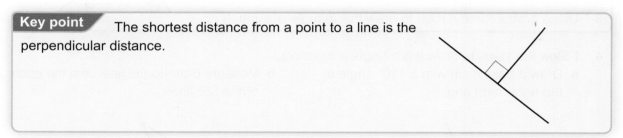

Key point   The shortest distance from a point to a line is the perpendicular distance.

9 The sketched plan shows the path of a new drain from a manhole that meets the main drain at right angles.

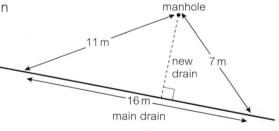

   a Construct an accurate plan showing the path of the new drain. Use a scale of 1 : 100.
   b How long will the new drain be?
   c **Reasoning** Explain why this is the shortest possible length for the drain.

10 **Problem-solving**   The sketch shows the positions of a wind turbine, two paths and a road.
   a Construct a scale diagram to show the shortest possible distance between the wind turbine and the road. Use a scale of 1 cm to 100 m.
   b Work out the shortest distance from the wind turbine to the road.

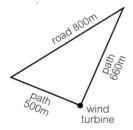

11 Problem-solving Malachi walks 3 km south.
Then he walks 6 km west.

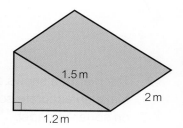

  a Draw an accurate scale diagram using a suitable scale.

  b Draw in the line for the shortest distance Malachi can walk back to the start.

  c Work out the shortest distance in kilometres.

12 Reasoning A carpenter is drawing plans for a roof truss.
The roof truss is an isosceles triangle made from two 10 m lengths and a 15 m length.

  a Construct a scale drawing of the roof truss. Use a scale of 1 : 200.

  b Bisect the angle enclosed between the equal sides.

   i What angle does the bisector make with the opposite side?

   ii Explain why.

13 Problem-solving A garden storage box is made in the shape of a right-angled triangular prism.
The longest side of the triangle is 1.5 m.
The base of the triangle is 1.2 m.
The length of the box is 2 m.

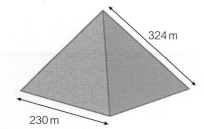

  a Draw an accurate net of the storage box. Use a scale of 10 cm to 1 m.

  b Work out the vertical height of the storage box.

Challenge   The Great Pyramid of Giza in Egypt is a square-based pyramid with base length 230 m.

Hint Add tabs like this to join the edges.

Each triangular face is an isosceles triangle with two sides of 324 m.

a   Draw an accurate net of the pyramid. Use a scale of 1 cm to 20 m.

b   Add tabs to the edges and glue the net together to make a scale model of the pyramid.

Reflect   Abbie looks back at this lesson. She says, 'This lesson is about scale drawing, but I have also used lots of other mathematics knowledge and skills.' She begins to make two lists.

Knowledge (what is)	Skills (how to)
measure (e.g. cm, m)	construct a perpendicular bisector
perpendicular	construct an angle bisector

Look back at all the questions in this lesson and make lists of all the knowledge and skills you have used. You might begin in the same way as Abbie.
Read your lists.
Put a star beside any of the knowledge or skills that you do not feel confident about.

5 Check up

Using scales

1 Here is a plan of a bedroom, drawn accurately to a scale of 1 cm to 50 cm.
   a How wide is the bedroom, from the door to the opposite wall?
   b How wide is the door?

2 The diagram shows a plan of Mary's garden. Make an accurate scale drawing of the garden on squared paper.
   Use a scale of 2 cm to 1 m.

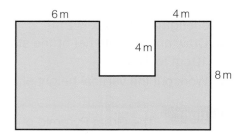

3 The map below has a scale of 1 : 25 000. Use the map to find the distance, in metres
   a from the Ice Rink to the Swimming Pool
   b from the Cinema to the Museum
   c from the Library to the Town Square.

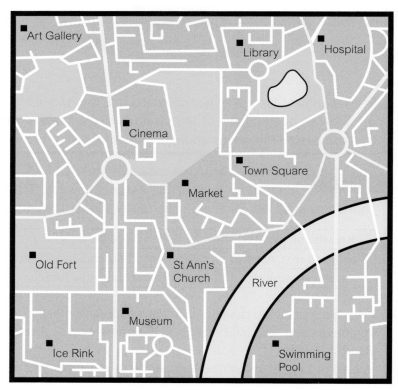

Basic constructions

4 Draw a line 11 cm long. Use a ruler and compasses to construct the perpendicular bisector.

5 Draw an angle of 80° using a protractor.
Construct the bisector of this angle.

6 The diagram shows a line
with a point marked above it.
Trace this diagram.
Construct a perpendicular
line from the point to the line.

7 Draw a line 9 cm long.
Mark point P exactly 3.5 cm from one end of the line.
Construct a line perpendicular to the line from point P.

Constructing triangles

8 A triangle has sides of length 6.5 cm, 8 cm and 9 cm.
Construct this triangle.

9 **a** Construct this right-angled triangle.
b What is the length of the other side of the triangle?

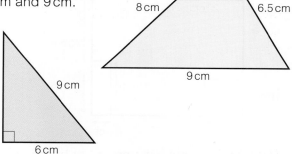

Using scale diagrams

10 a Make an accurate scale drawing of this ramp. Use a scale of 1 : 20.

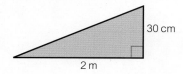

b Work out the length of the ramp.
c Find the angle the ramp makes with the ground.

Challenge   A manufacturer sells a chocolate bar in a box that is an equilateral triangular prism.
Each edge of the triangle is 5 cm long, and the box is 12 cm long overall.
Draw an accurate net for the box.

Reflect   How sure are you of your answers? Were you mostly

☹ Just guessing   😐 Feeling doubtful   ☺ Confident

What next? Use your results to decide whether to strengthen or extend your learning.

5 Strengthen

Using scales

1 David has designed this logo for a magazine.
Make an accurate drawing of the logo.
Use a scale of 1 cm to 2 cm.

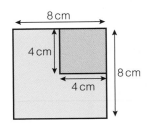

> **Q1 hint** Use a double number line.
>
> drawing $\div 2$ — 1 cm
>
> real life — 2 cm 4 cm 6 cm 8 cm

2 Marina is designing a new board game.
She makes a sketch.

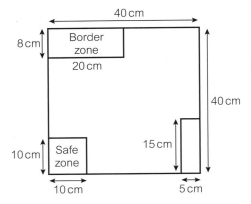

> **Q2 hint**
>
> drawing $\div \square$ — 1 cm   ?
>
> real life — 4 cm   40 cm

Make an accurate drawing of her board on squared paper.
Use a scale of 1 cm to 4 cm.

3 Chan has drawn a scale plan of his new garden.
The scale is 1 cm to 2 m. (1 square = 1 cm)

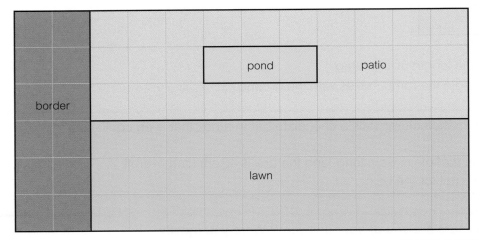

Work out these real-life measurements.
a the length and width of the border
b the length and width of the pond
c the length and width of the lawn

> **Q3 hint**
>
> drawing 0   1 cm 2 cm 3 cm
>
> real life 0   2 m

4 Mikel's garden is shown in this plan.
The scale is 1 cm to 3 m.

a How long is the fence

    i on the plan   **ii** in real life?

b The decking is a square shape.
How long is each side of the square

    i on the plan   **ii** in real life?

c How wide and how long is the
vegetable patch in real life?

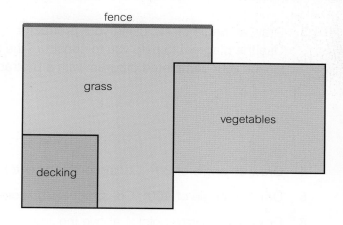

5 A map has a scale of 1 : 100 000.

a Copy and complete this double number line.

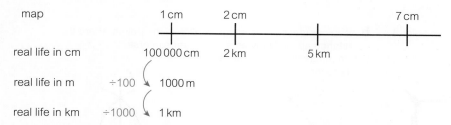

b A distance is 5 cm on the map. How far is it in kilometres in real life?

6 A map of the UK has a scale of
1 : 50 000.
Copy and complete this double
number line.

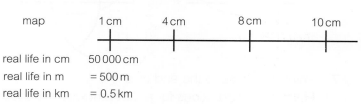

7 A map has a scale of 1 : 50 000.
Copy and complete this double
number line.

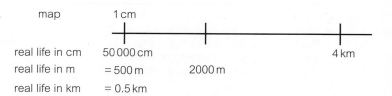

Basic constructions

1 Draw a line 6 cm long and label it AB.
Use this diagram to help you to
construct the perpendicular
bisector of AB

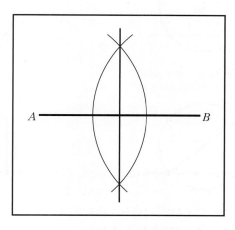

2 Draw a line that is 14 cm long. Construct the perpendicular bisector.

3 Draw an angle of 72° using your protractor.
Use the diagram to help you to construct the angle bisector.
Check your completed diagram with a protractor.

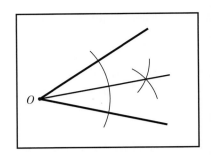

4 Draw an angle of 30°. Construct the bisector of this angle.

5 Draw an angle of 100°. Construct the bisector of this angle.

> **Q5 hint** Sketch what you think it will look like first.

6 Draw a line. Draw point A above the line.
Follow these instructions to construct a perpendicular line from point A to the line.

a Draw an arc from point A.

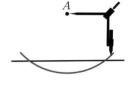

b Keep compasses the same distance apart. Draw an arc from each of the two points where the arc crosses the line.

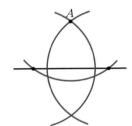

c Join the points where the arcs intersect.

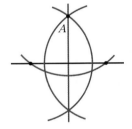

7 Point P is close to the end of a line.
Follow the instructions for a different way to construct a perpendicular to the line at point P.

a Mark point A to the right of point P. Point A should be near to, but not on the line. Put your compasses on point A and draw a circle through point P.

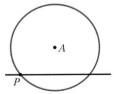

b Mark point B where your circle crosses the line again.

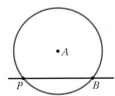

c Draw a line across the circle through point A and point B.

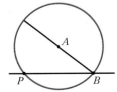

d Join point P to the circle.

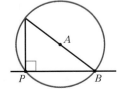

Constructing triangles

1 Follow these instructions to construct accurately a triangle with sides 6 cm, 7 cm and 8 cm.

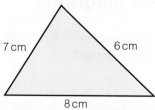

a Use a ruler to draw accurately the first side. The 7 cm side starts at the left-hand end of this line.

b Open your compasses to exactly 7 cm and draw an arc from the left-hand end of the line.

c Open your compasses to exactly 6 cm and draw an arc from the other end.

d Use the point where the arcs cross to create the finished triangle.

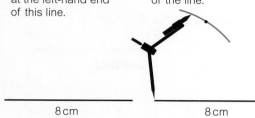

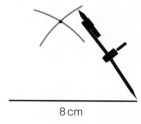

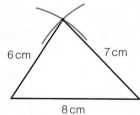

2 **a** Sketch a triangle with sides 5 cm, 8 cm and 9 cm.
   b Construct accurately a triangle with sides 5 cm, 8 cm and 9 cm.

3 **a** Copy this sketch of the net of this triangular prism.

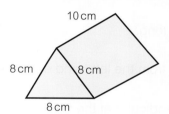

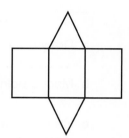

   b Write all the measurements on your net.
   c Draw the rectangles accurately on cm squared paper.
   d Construct the triangles using compasses.

4 Follow these instructions for a different way to construct this right-angled triangle.

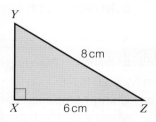

a Use a ruler to draw the horizontal side length (*XZ*).

b Construct a perpendicular line at *X*. (Follow the instructions in Basic constructions Q7.)

c Open your compasses to 8 cm. Draw an arc from point *Z*. Join the intersection of the arc and the perpendicular (*Y*) to point *Z* to form the triangle.

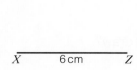

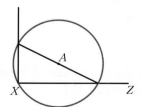

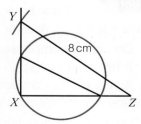

5 **a** Construct this right-angled triangle.
   b Measure the third side of your triangle.

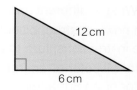

Using scale diagrams

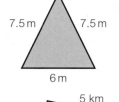

1 Draw a scale diagram of this triangle.
Use the scale 1 cm to 1 m.

> **Q1 hint** Use the method in Constructing triangles Q1.

2 Draw a scale diagram of this triangle.
Use the scale 1 cm to 1 km.

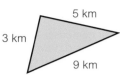

3 Follow the instructions to make an accurate scale drawing of this diagram.
Use a scale of 1 cm to 1 m.

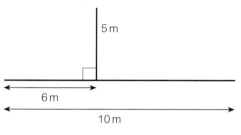

> **Q3a hint**
>
> $\times 10 \left(\begin{array}{c} \text{1 cm to 1 m} \\ \text{10 cm to 10 m} \end{array} \right) \times 10$

a Draw a line 10 cm long.

10 cm

b Mark a point 6 cm from the left-hand end.

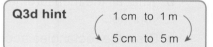

6 cm

c Construct a perpendicular at the point.
(Follow the instructions in Basic constructions Q7.)

d Measure 5 cm along the perpendicular.

> **Q3d hint**
>
> $\left(\begin{array}{c} \text{1 cm to 1 m} \\ \text{5 cm to 5 m} \end{array} \right)$

Challenge The diagram shows a crop circle that was found in Wiltshire in May 2011.

a Using compasses and a ruler, create a plan of the crop circle.
Make sure the triangle is equilateral, and the small circles are evenly spaced and all the same size.

b Design your own crop circle design using accurate constructions.

Reflect **a** Look back at the steps in Q1 of the Basic constructions section.
For each step, answer these questions.

- Do I need compasses?
- If no, what tool(s) do I need?
- If yes, where do I put the point of the compasses? Where do I draw?

b Repeat for the steps in Basic constructions Q3.

c Both of these questions show steps for constructing bisectors.
Compare the steps. What is different and what is the same?

d Do you think you can now construct bisectors without the instructions?
Have a go! Cover the instructions, turn to a new page of your book, and construct

   i the perpendicular bisector of an 8 cm line

   ii the angle bisector of an 80° angle.

5 Extend

1 Trace the diagram.
Find the shortest distance from B to the line.

• B

___

2 Construct an accurate net for a four-sided dice.
Each edge of the dice should be 3 cm long.

3 Bill is planning to build a child's swing.
He has started by making this sketch.
Choose a suitable scale and create
an accurate scale drawing of Bill's design.

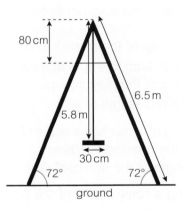

4 **Problem-solving**   A map has a scale of 1 : 25 000.
Seeta says that 4 km is represented by 10 cm.
Is she right? Show your working.

5 **Reasoning**   The map shows the route of a 10 km run.

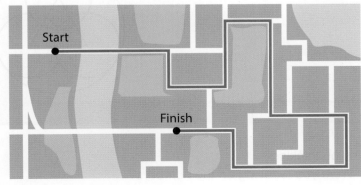

What is the scale of the map?

6 Problem-solving The plan shows Seera's design for a garden.

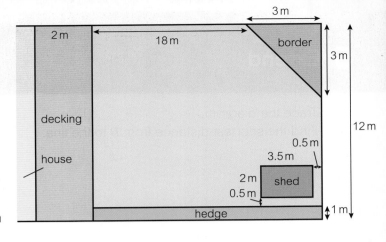

a Make an accurate scale drawing of her design on cm squared paper.

b How long is the sloping edge of the border in real life?

c What is the area of the decking in real life?

The shed needs a concrete base underneath. It must stick out 20 cm all around the shed.

d What area of concrete is needed?

7 Problem-solving A ship leaves a port and sails north for 10 km before turning and sailing east for 15 km. How far away is the ship from the port?

8 a Construct this triangle.

b How long is the other side?

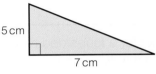

9 Problem-solving The diagram shows a sketch of a playground.

a Work out the size of the angle marked a.

b Use a scale of 1 cm to 4 m to make an accurate scale drawing of the playground.

c Work out the real length of y.

10 A scale drawing of a car has a scale of 1 : 32.
The length of the drawing is 109 mm.
What is the length of the real car? Give your answer in metres, correct to 1 decimal place.

11 Harry is making a scale model of the Angel of the North sculpture using the ratio 1 : 200.
The sculpture is 54 m wide.
How wide is the model? Give your answer in centimetres.

Challenge Explain how you might construct this pattern just using compasses and a ruler.

Reflect Re-read Q7.
While you were reading, what were you thinking?
Were you visualising any images? Were you focusing on the numbers?
How did your initial thoughts help you to answer this question?

5 Unit test

1 Descheeta has drawn a plan of her desk.
The scale is 1 cm to 15 cm.
In real life,
  a how wide is the desk?
  b how long is the desk?
  c how long and wide is the in-tray?

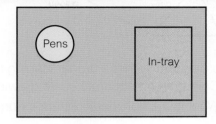

2 In this map 1 cm represents 200 m.

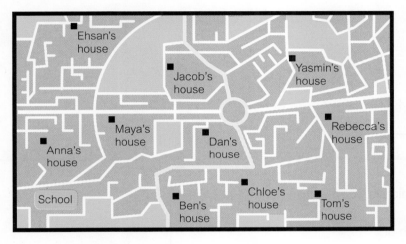

Use the map to estimate the distance between
  a Ben's house and Ehsan's house
  b Yasmin's house and Rebecca's house.

3 Draw a line 13 cm long.
Use a ruler and compasses to construct the perpendicular bisector of the line.

4 Draw an angle of 42° using a protractor. Construct the angle bisector.

5 Draw a straight line. Draw a point P 4 cm away from the straight line.
Construct a perpendicular from point P to the line.

6 A map has a scale of 1 : 25 000.
  a What real distance is represented by a distance of 5 cm on the map?
  b The distance between two towns is 15 km. How far is this distance on the map?

7 Use a ruler and compasses to construct a triangle with sides
10 cm, 12 cm and 8 cm.

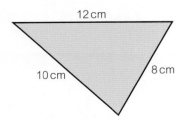

8 Draw an accurate net of this triangular prism.

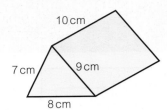

10 cm
7 cm
9 cm
8 cm

9 The diagram shows a ladder leaning against a wall.
 a Construct an accurate scale drawing of the diagram.
 b What is the horizontal distance from the foot of the ladder to the wall?

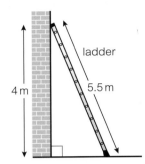

ladder
4 m
5.5 m

Challenge

a Draw a straight line which is 16 cm long.

b Draw a perpendicular bisector half the length of the first line.

c Draw a perpendicular bisector half the length of the second line and to its left.

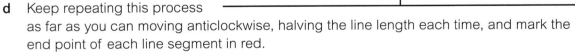

d Keep repeating this process as far as you can moving anticlockwise, halving the line length each time, and mark the end point of each line segment in red.

e What shape would be formed if the process was continued and all the red points were joined together?

Reflect For this unit, copy and complete these sentences.

I showed I am good at _____.

I found _____ hard.

I got better at _____ by _____.

I was surprised by _____.

I was happy that _____.

I still need help with _____.

6 Sequences, inequalities, equations and proportion

Master   Check up p148   Strengthen p150   Extend p155   Unit test p158

6.1 nth term of arithmetic sequences

*Active*Learn
Homework

- Use the nth term to generate an arithmetic sequence
- Find and use the nth term of an arithmetic sequence

Warm up

1 **Fluency** Which of these are arithmetic sequences?
Find the common differences of the ones that are.
   a 1, 5, 9, 13, ...   **b** 2, 4, 8, 18, ...   **c** 10, 8, 6, 4, ...   **d** 0.7, 1.2, 1.7, 2.2, ...

2 Copy and complete the tables to work out the first five terms of each sequence.
   a General term $3n$

Position (n)	1	2	3	4	5
Term ($3n$)					

   b General term $n + 4$

Position (n)	1	2	3	4	5
Term ($n + 4$)					

3   **a** For each sequence, work out what you do to the position number to get the term.

   i

Position	1	2	3	4	5
Term	3	4	5	6	7

   ii

Position	1	2	3	4	5
Term	8	16	24	32	40

   b Write your answers to part **a** using algebra to give the nth term of each sequence.

4 Copy and complete the tables to work out the first five terms of each sequence.
   a nth term $= 2n + 1$

Position (n)	1	2	3	4	5
Term ($2n + 1$)	$2 \times 1 + 1 = 3$	$2 \times \square + 1 = \square$			

   b nth term $= 10n - 10$

Position (n)	1	2	3	4	5
Term ($10n - 10$)	$10 \times 1 - 10 = \square$	$10 \times \square - \square = \square$			

   c nth term $= 3n - 9$

Position (n)	1	2	3	4	5
Term ($3n - 9$)					

   d nth term $= 2n - 0.5$

Position (n)	1	2	3	4	5
Term ($2n - 0.5$)					

5 Work out the 10th term and the 100th term of the sequence with nth term

   a $4n + 3$ **b** $7n - 2$ **c** $5n + 9$

   d $6n - 18$ **e** $3n - 1.5$ **f** $2n + 0.5$

Q5 hint To find the 10th term, substitute $n = 10$.

6 Write the first five terms of the sequence with nth term

   a $4n$ **b** $2n + 1$ **c** $3n - 2$

   d $\frac{1}{2}n + 1$ **e** $20 - 5n$ **f** $-2n + 3$

   g Reasoning Look at the common difference for each sequence and its nth term. What do you notice?

7 Problem-solving a Match each sequence to its nth term.

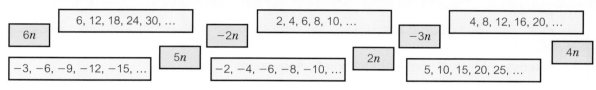

   b What is the name for the sequence generated by $2n$? ... by $5n$?

Key point   To find the nth term of an arithmetic sequence:

1   Find the common difference.

2   If the common difference is 3, compare with the sequence for $3n$.

3   If the common difference is 4, compare with the sequence for $4n$.

And so on.

Worked example

Work out the nth term of this sequence.

7, 9, 11, 13 ...

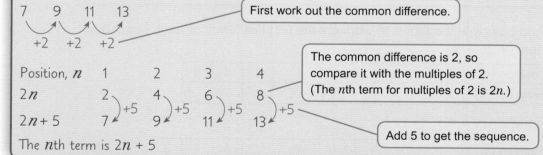

First work out the common difference.

The common difference is 2, so compare it with the multiples of 2. (The nth term for multiples of 2 is $2n$.)

Add 5 to get the sequence.

The nth term is $2n + 5$

---

8 Find the nth term of each sequence. The first one has been started for you.

   a 11, 16, 21, 26, ...

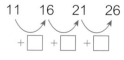 

   b 2, 5, 8, 11, 14, ...   **c** 5, 7, 9, 11, 13, ...

   d 1, 5, 9, 13, 17, ...   **e** 21, 16, 11, 6, 1, ...

   f 3, 1, -1, -3, -5, ...   **g** -4, -7, -10, -13, -16, ...

Q8e hint When the common difference is negative, compare with the multiples of a negative number.

The nth term of a sequence is $4n + 5$.

Mike says, '44 is a term of this sequence.' Is he correct? Explain.

$4n + 5 = 44$

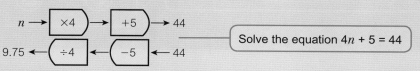

Solve the equation $4n + 5 = 44$

Position numbers are always integers.

9.75 is not an integer, so 44 cannot be a term of the sequence.

9   **Reasoning**   For each sequence, decide whether 42 is one of its terms.
State its position in the sequence if it is.
  a $2n + 12$ **b** $5n - 3$ **c** $4n + 4$
  d $10n + 2$ **e** $6n - 1$ **f** $9n + 8$

10 **Problem-solving**   The nth term of a sequence is $-3n + 16$.
  a Is the sequence ascending or descending?
  b Work out the 12th term.
  c How many terms of this sequence are positive?

11 Here is a sequence of patterns made from dots.
  a Draw the next pattern in the sequence.
  b Copy and complete this table for the sequence
    of numbers of dots.
  c Work out the nth term of this sequence.
  d How many dots will there be in the 40th pattern?
  e **Problem-solving**   Which pattern has 46 dots?

Pattern number	1	2	3	4	5
Number of dots	4	7			

12 Here is a sequence of patterns made from lines.
Work out
  a the nth term for the number of lines
  b the number of lines in the 20th pattern
  c **Problem-solving**   the number of the largest pattern you can make using 50 lines.

  a Copy and complete the table for the first five terms of the sequence $2n + 5$.
b Draw a pair of axes with the x-axis from
0 to 6 and the y-axis from 0 to 20.

n	1	2	3	4	5
$2n + 5$	7				

Plot the values from your table on your axes. Join the points.
c In the same way, plot the first five points of the sequences with nth term
    i $3n + 3$ **ii** $5n - 6$ **iii** $10 - 2n$
d Why do you think arithmetic sequences are also called linear sequences? Test your idea
  with some of the other sequences from this lesson.

Look back at Q3 and Q8. What was the same and what was different about
finding the nth terms for the sequences in Q3 and the sequences in Q8?

6.2 Non-linear sequences

Active Learn
Homework

- Recognise and continue geometric sequences
- Recognise and continue quadratic sequences

Warm up

1 Fluency What is the missing number in each statement?

a Multiplying by $\frac{1}{2}$ is the same as dividing by $\square$.

b Multiplying by $\frac{1}{10}$ is the same as dividing by $\square$.

2 Work out the value of
a $2x^2$, when $x = 5$ **b** $3x^2$, when $x = -2$ **c** $-4x^2$, when $x = 3$ **d** $\frac{1}{2}x^2$, when $x = 6$

Key point

In a **geometric sequence**, the term-to-term rule is 'multiply by a number'.

3 All these sequences are **geometric sequences**.
For each one, write the term-to-term rule 'multiply by …' and find the next two terms.
a 1, 2, 4, 8, …   **b** 50, 25, 12.5, …   **c** 1, 4, 16, 64, …
d −2, −6, −18, −54, …   **e** 120, 60, 30, 15, …   **f** 2, 3, 4.5, 6.75, …
g 600, 200, $66\frac{2}{3}$, $22\frac{2}{9}$, …   **h** 1000, 100, 10, 1, …   **i** −5, −25, −125, −625, …
j 3, −6, 12, −24, …   **k** 1, −1, 1, −1, …   **l** −24, 12, −6, 3, …

4 Reasoning Sort these sequences into two sets: arithmetic sequences and geometric sequences.

| **A** 500, 50, 5, 0.5, … | **B** 1.8, 3.6, 5.4, 7.2, … | **C** 1, 5, 9, 13, … |

| **D** 2, 4, 8, 16, … | **E** 0.3, 1.2, 4.8, 19.2, … | **F** 10, 25, 62.5, 156.25, … |

5 Problem-solving For each geometric sequence, find the first term that is less than 1.
a 3296, 329.6, 32.96, …   **b** 1000, 500, 250, …
c 30, 10, $3\frac{1}{3}$, …   **d** 10^5, 10^4, 10^3, …
e Will there be negative terms in these sequences? Explain.

6 Problem-solving
a Write the first five terms of a geometric sequence and the
term-to-term rule to match each description.

Description A	all the terms are positive
Description B	all the terms are negative
Description C	the first term is negative, second is positive, third is negative and so on
Description D	all the terms are less than 1

Q6 hint Choose an easy starting number. Try out different term-to-term rules.

b Which of your sequences are increasing? Write decreasing sequences that match the same descriptions.

c Which of your sequences are decreasing? Write increasing sequences that match the same descriptions.

7   A ball is dropped on to a hard surface from a height of 300 cm.
    It bounces back up to half the previous height each time.
    a Copy and complete the table.

Bounce number	1	2	3	4	5
Height of bounce (cm)	150	75			

   b **Problem-solving**   Which is the first bounce that is less than 1 cm?

8   **Problem-solving**   Each day, a doctor recorded the number of patients with a throat infection.

Day	Mon	Tue	Wed
Number of patients	5	15	45

The doctor said, 'If the number of cases continues to grow in the same way, there will be over 1000 cases by the end of the week.'
Is the doctor correct? Explain.

> **Key point**   An nth term that includes n^2 (and no higher power of n) generates a **quadratic sequence**.

9   Write down the first five terms of the sequence with nth term
    a n^2 **b** $2n^2$ **c** $n^2 + 3$ **d** $\frac{1}{2}n^2$

10 Here is the sequence $n^2 + 1$.

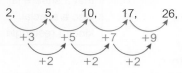

   2,   5,   10,   17,   26, ...
   +3 +5 +7 +9   1st difference: the difference between terms
   +2 +2 +2   2nd difference: the difference between differences

   a What is the pattern in the 1st differences?
   b Use the pattern to work out the next term.

11 Some baked bean tins in a supermarket are stacked like this.
    a Copy and complete this table.

Number of rows	2	3	4	5
Number of tins	3	6		

   + ☐

   b **Problem-solving**   Pete wants to make a display of baked bean tins 8 rows high. How many tins does he need?

12 All these nth terms generate quadratic sequences.

> **A** $n^2 + 2$ **B** $n^2 + 5$ **C** $n^2 - 4$

  a For each one

    i write down the first five terms

    ii write down the 1st differences

    iii write down the 2nd differences.

  b Reasoning   What do you notice about the 2nd differences of sequences with n^2 in the nth term?

  c Work out the 1st and 2nd differences of these sequences.

    i $2n^2 + 1$

    ii $3n^2$

    iii $4n^2 - 1$

  d Reasoning   What do you notice about the 2nd differences of sequences with a multiple of n^2 in the nth term?

  e Reasoning   Explain how you can tell if a sequence is quadratic by looking at its 2nd differences.

13 Reasoning

  a Write down the first five terms of the sequence with nth term $(n + 4)(n - 1)$.

  b What type of sequence is it?

  c Jenny says, 'This sequence is not quadratic because the nth term does not include n^2.' Explain why she is incorrect.

> **Q13c hint** Can you write $(n + 4)(n - 1)$ in another way?

Challenge   The patterns in this sequence are made from squares.

Pattern 1   Pattern 2   Pattern 3

> **Hint** Don't forget that a square is also a special kind of rectangle.

  a Draw the fourth pattern in the sequence.

  b Count the number of rectangles you can see in each pattern.

  c Copy and complete the table.

Pattern number (n)	1	2	3	4
Rectangles				

  d Continue the sequence to find the number of rectangles in pattern 6. Check your answer by drawing the pattern.

  e What type of sequence is it?

  f How will your answers change if you only count rectangles that are not squares?

Reflect   Copy and complete this sentence.

I know when a sequence is linear because _____.

Write sentences like this for a geometric sequence and a quadratic sequence.

6.3 Inequalities

- Represent inequalities on a number line
- Find integer values that satisfy an inequality

Active Learn
Homework

Warm up

1 Fluency
 a What is an integer?
 b An integer is < 5. Write three possible values.
 c An integer is $\geqslant 2$. Write three possible values.

2 Solve these equations.
 a $3x + 5 = 29$ **b** $5x - 6 = 42$ **c** $6x + 11 = 32$

3 In a survey, people were asked their age.
 Here is a table to collect the results.
 a In which class does age 10 go?
 b Write down all the possible ages in the class $20 \leqslant x < 30$.

Age, x (years)	Frequency
$0 \leqslant x < 10$	
$10 \leqslant x < 20$	
$20 \leqslant x < 30$	

> **Key point**   'Satisfy' means 'make the statement true'.

4 Write down the integer values of x that satisfy each inequality.
 a $5 < x < 10$ **b** $6 < x \leqslant 14$ **c** $-5 \leqslant x < 5$ **d** $-8 < x < -2$

> **Key point**   You can also show inequalities on a number line.
> An empty circle shows that the value is not included.
> A filled circle shows that the value is included.
> An arrow shows that the values continue to infinity or negative infinity.
> These include the integers, and all the numbers in between.

Worked example

Use a number line to show the values that satisfy the inequalities

a $x < 4$

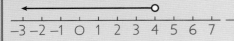

This includes all the numbers less than 4 (*excluding* 4).

b $2 < x \leqslant 6$

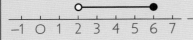

This includes all the numbers greater than 2 (*excluding* 2) and less than or equal to 6 (*including* 6).

5 Show these inequalities on a number line.

  a $x < 3$ **b** $x \leqslant 8$ **c** $x > 5$

  d $x \geqslant 4$ **e** $x > -3$ **f** $x < -2$

  g $0 < x \leqslant 5$ **h** $-3 \leqslant x < 2$ **i** $-3 < x \leqslant 2$

6 Write the inequalities shown by each of these number lines.

  a

  b

  c

  d

  e

  f

  g

  h

7 Show these inequalities on number lines.
Write down the integer values that satisfy each one.

  a $2 < x < 7$ **b** $-3 < x \leqslant 2$ **c** $-1 < x < 1$

  d $-5 \leqslant x < 2$ **e** $-9 \leqslant x \leqslant -1$ **f** $-5 < x < -1$

8 Write inequalities for each of these sentences and show them on number lines.

  a 4 is less than n

  b n is less than -5

  c n is greater than or equal to -6

  d 6 is more than n

  e A number is less than 5 and greater than or equal to -2

  f A number is greater than or equal to 0 and less than or equal to 5

  g A number is less than or equal to -2 and greater than -7

  h A number is greater than or equal to -5 and less than 2

  i A number is between 3 and 7 (excluding 3 and 7)

  j A number is between -5 and 0 (including -5 and 0)

  k A number is between -5 and 0 (excluding 0)

> **Q8 hint** Choose a letter to represent the number.

9 Reasoning $n > 5$

Write an inequality for

a $2n$ b $3n$

c $4n$ d $2n + 1$

10 I think of a number. My number plus 7 is less than 12.

a Write an inequality to show this.

b What is the largest integer value for my number?

11 I think of a number, multiply it by 2, and add 7.

My answer is less than 15. Write an inequality.

Find three possible values for my number.

12 Reasoning $-1 < x \leqslant 4$

Write an inequality for

a $2x$ b $5x$

c $2x - 1$ d $5x + 2$

13 Reasoning Show these two inequalities on the same number line.

$x \geqslant 4$ and $-3 \leqslant x < 7$

Write down the integer values that satisfy *both* inequalities.

Challenge   On a number line you can see that $-6 < -2$.

a Add 4 to both sides of the inequality $-6 < -2$.

b Subtract 1 from both sides of the inequality $-6 < -2$.

c Multiply both sides of the inequality by 3.

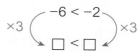

d Divide both sides of the inequality by 2.

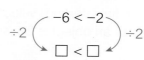

e Do the operations in parts **a** to **d** give correct inequalities?

f Multiply both sides of the inequality by -1.
What do you notice?

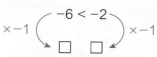

Reflect   Why are pictures like these good for representing inequalities?

Hint Write down how the circles, lines and arrows help you to understand the inequality.

6.4 Solving equations

- Construct and solve equations including fractions or powers

Warm up

1 **Fluency**

   a $x^2 = 16$

   Give two possible values of x.

   b $x^2 = 121$

   Give two possible values of x.

2 Solve these equations.

   a $5x + 8 = 53$　　**b** $6 - 2x = -2$　　**c** $\dfrac{x}{5} - 6 = -3$　　**d** $\dfrac{x + 2}{7} = 3$

3 Solve these equations.

   a $5x = 3x + 12$

   b $8n + 9 = 6n + 3$

   c $3(4n - 2) = 10n + 4$

   d $5(3x + 2) = 7(2x + 1)$

4 Solve these equations. The first one is started for you

   a $\times 3 \left(\dfrac{4x + 3}{3} = 9 \right) \times 3$

   $4x + 3 = \square$

   b $\dfrac{5x - 4}{9} = 4$

   c $\dfrac{14 - 2x}{8} = 2$

   d $\dfrac{6x + 7}{5} = 2$

5 The formula $a = \dfrac{v - u}{t}$ is used to calculate the acceleration of an object, where v is the final velocity, u is the initial (starting) velocity and t is the time taken.

The acceleration of an object is $2\,\text{m/s}^2$, the final velocity is $20\,\text{m/s}$ and the time taken is 6 seconds.

What was the initial velocity of the object?

Worked example

Solve the equation $\dfrac{3x - 2}{2} = 2x - 3$

$\times 2 \left(\dfrac{3x - 2}{2} = 2x - 3 \right) \times 2$

$3x - 2 = 2(2x - 3)$

$-3x \left(\begin{array}{l} 3x - 2 = 4x - 6 \\ -2 = 4x - 3x - 6 \end{array} \right) -3x$

$+6 \left(6 - 2 = x \right) +6$

$4 = x$

LHS: If $x = 4$, $\dfrac{3x - 2}{2} = \dfrac{12 - 2}{2} = \dfrac{10}{2} = 5$

RHS: If $x = 4$, $2x - 3 = 8 - 3 = 5$

> Multiply both sides by the denominator.

> Expand the brackets.

> Solve.

> Substitute your solution back into the original equation. If it is correct, both sides of the equation will have the same value.

6 Solve these equations.

a $\dfrac{2x + 7}{3} = x$

b $\dfrac{3a + 2}{4} = 2a - 7$

c $\dfrac{4b - 1}{3} = b + 2$

d $3y - 16 = \dfrac{5y - 1}{4}$

7 Solve these equations.

a $\dfrac{3n + 4}{2} = 2n + 3$

b $\dfrac{4d + 2}{3} = 2d + 2$

c $\dfrac{2n - 4}{3} = 3n + 8$

d $2p + 10 = \dfrac{3p + 1}{5}$

8 **Problem-solving** Shakira and Tal start with the same number. Shakira doubles this number, adds 6 and then divides the result by 2.
Tal multiplies the number by 4, then subtracts 6.
They both get the same answer.
What number did they start with?

> **Q8 hint** Use a letter for the number. Write expressions for Shakira and Tal's calculations.

9 Solve these equations.

a $\dfrac{3y + 2}{5} = 4y - 1$ **b** $\dfrac{2y + 3}{4} = 5y - 2$ **c** $4x + 1 = \dfrac{2x - 1}{3}$ **d** $6x + 4 = \dfrac{4x - 1}{3}$

Worked example

Solve the equation $x^2 + 9 = 90$, giving the positive and negative solutions.

$$x^2 + 9 = 90$$
$$-9 \qquad \qquad -9$$
$$x^2 = 81$$

$x = \pm\sqrt{81}$ ——————— Square root.

$x = +9$ or $x = -9$

---

10 Solve these equations. Give the positive *and* negative solutions.

a $x^2 + 5 = 21$ **b** $x^2 + 9 = 58$ **c** $x^2 - 5 = 95$

d $\dfrac{x^2}{2} = 32$ **e** $x^2 = 3^2 + 4^2$ **f** $x^2 - 5^2 = 12^2$

11 **Problem-solving**   **a** Find the missing length in each diagram.

> **Q11a hint** Write an equation using the area.

i
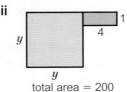
x
area = 225

ii
y — 1 — 4
y
total area = 200

iii

z, 1, 4
z
green area = 252

iv
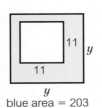
11, y
11
y
blue area = 203

b Explain why $x \neq -15$ in Q11 part **a i**.

> **Q11b hint:** $\neq$ means 'is not equal to'

12 For each equation, find the positive solution.
Give your answers correct to 1 decimal place.

a $x^2 = 28$

b $y^2 - 7 = 16$

c $24 = z^2 - 15$

d $200^2 = a^2 + 13^2$

13 Problem-solving Electrical power can be calculated using the
formula $P = \dfrac{V^2}{R}$, where V is the voltage and R the resistance in a circuit.

Use this formula to complete the table below.

Circuit	Power (watts)	Voltage (volts)	Resistance (ohms)
Circuit 1		5	10
Circuit 2	51.2		20
Circuit 3		24	16
Circuit 4	72		8
Circuit 5	31.25		20

Challenge

- I think of a number.
- I add 3 to it.
- I double the result.
- I take 2 away from this.
- I halve the result.
- I take away the number I originally thought of.

a Write this using algebra.

b Work out the answer for different starting numbers.

c Use algebra to show why this happens.

Part c hint Collect like terms.

d Make up similar puzzles where the answer will always be the same.

e Can you make one where the answer is the number you first thought of?

Reflect   Roshan says, 'When solving equations, I always check that my solution is
correct. If it isn't, then first of all I check my check! Then, I cover my original working, and try
to solve the equation again.'
Did you check your solutions to the equations in this lesson? If so, how?
What do you think of Roshan's strategy when he gets an incorrect solution?
What is your strategy when you get an incorrect solution?
Compare your strategy with those of others in your class.

6.5 Proportion

- Write formulae connecting variables in direct or inverse proportion
- Use algebra to solve problems involving direct or inverse proportion

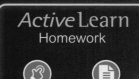

Active Learn
Homework

Warm up

1 **Fluency** Apples cost £1.50 per kg.
What is the cost of   **a**   3 kg   **b** $\frac{1}{2}$ kg of apples?

2 4 machines make 6000 chocolates in 1 hour.
   a How long does it take 2 machines to make 6000 chocolates?
   b How many chocolates can 3 machines make in 1 hour?

3   **a** Work out the gradient of this line.

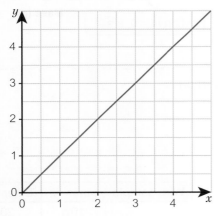

   b Write down the equation of this line.

4   **i** Work out the gradient of each line.
     ii Write down the equation of each line

   a   **b**   **c**   **d**

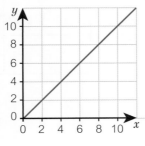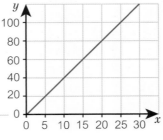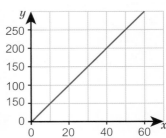

5   In a science experiment Akmal measures how far a wire extends when he adds different masses to it. The table shows his results.

Mass, m	10 g	20 g	30 g	40 g	50 g
Extension, e	12 cm	24 cm	36 cm	48 cm	60 cm

a Show that m and e are in direct proportion.

b Work out $\frac{e}{m}$ for each pair of values in the table.

The first two are started for you.

$\frac{e}{m} = \frac{12}{10} = \square$ $\frac{e}{m} = \frac{24}{20} = \square$

What do you notice about the value of $\frac{e}{m}$?

c Draw a graph for these results.
Plot m on the x-axis and e on the y-axis.

d Work out the gradient of your graph.

e Compare your answers to parts **b** and **d**.
What do you notice?

f Write down the equation of your line.

g Use your equation to work out
   i the extension e when $m = 35$ g
   ii the mass m that gives an extension of 18 cm.

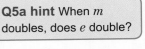

Q5a hint When m doubles, does e double?

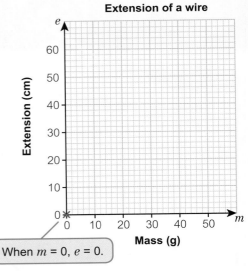

Extension of a wire

When $m = 0$, $e = 0$.

Key point   For two quantities x and y in direct proportion

• $\frac{x}{y}$ has constant value k

• the graph of y against x has gradient k

• the relationship between x and y is $y = kx$.

---

6   Other students conduct the same experiment but with different wires.
For each wire sample

   i work out $\frac{e}{m}$ to find k

   ii write a formula $e = \square m$ for the relationship between the extension and the mass.

Wire sample	Mass, m	Extension, e
A	10 g	20 cm
	15 g	30 cm
B	25 g	20 cm
	45 g	36 cm
C	20 g	25 cm
	32 g	40 cm
D	40 g	30 cm
	60 g	45 cm
E	40 g	70 cm
	75 g	131.25 cm

7 **Reasoning** The graph shows an object moving at a constant speed.

a Is the distance travelled in direct proportion to the time taken? Explain.

b Work out the gradient of the graph.

c Write a formula connecting distance (d) and time (t).

d If the object continues at the same speed, how long will it take to travel 750 metres?

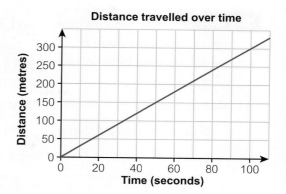

Distance travelled over time

8 For each pair of quantities, check whether they are in direct proportion.

If they are, write a formula for the relationship.

a 10 oranges cost £3
15 oranges cost £4

b 6 plants cost £48
21 plants cost £168

c 5 sacks weigh 15 kg
12 sacks weigh 35 kg

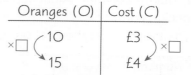

Worked example

One day 8 dollars ($) will buy 48 Argentinian pesos.
The number of pesos (P) is in direct proportion to the number of dollars (D).
How many pesos will $200 buy?

$P = kD$ ——————— Write the equation for the relationship.

When $D = 8$, $P = 48$

$48 = k \times 8$ ——————— Substitute the values given to find k.

$k = 6$

$P = 6D$ ——————— Write the equation using the value of k.

When $D = 200$

$P = 6 \times 200$

$= 1200$ ——————— Use your equation to answer the question.

$200 will buy 1200 pesos.

9 UK pounds (£) are in direct proportion to Bulgarian lev.
£15 buys 36 lev.
How many lev will £500 buy?

10 **Reasoning** The number of painters, and the time taken to paint a building, are in inverse proportion.

Number of painters, n	1	2	4	8
Hours to paint building, h	56			

a Copy and complete this table of values.

b Work out nh for each pair of values in the table.
What do you notice about the value of nh?

c Write the relationship $nh = \square$

d Rearrange to make h the subject.

11 Reasoning In each table, x and y are in inverse proportion. For each table

    i write the relationship $y = \dfrac{k}{x}$ and use values from the table to work out the value of k

    ii write the formula connecting x and y.

a

x	1	2	3
y	12	6	4

b

x	2	4	5
y	10	5	4

c

x	2.5	3.6	4.5
y	7.2	5	4

12 Problem-solving A cricket club asks its players to share the cost of improving the cricket pitch.

The table shows the cost per player when different numbers of players share the cost.

Number of players, n	8	10	16
Cost per player, £C	£56	£44.80	£28

    a Write a formula connecting C and n.

    b Work out the cost per player when

        i 14 players share the cost   **ii** 25 players share the cost.

> **Q12a hint** $C = ...$

13 Problem-solving It takes 30 seconds to fill a 6 litre bucket from a garden tap.
The time taken to fill a bucket with water is proportional to the capacity of the bucket.
How long will it take to fill a 10 litre bucket?

14 Problem-solving x and y are in inverse proportion.
When $x = 9.2$, $y = 14$.
Work out the value of y when $x = 20$.

15 Problem-solving In a set of Russian dolls the height is proportional to the width.
The tallest doll is 12 cm tall and 5 cm wide.
The smallest doll is 2.5 cm tall. How wide is it?

Challenge

- Take a piece of A4 paper. Measure the dimensions carefully.
- Cut the A4 paper precisely in half by halving the longer side. You now have A5 paper.
- Measure the dimensions carefully.
- Continue this process for different sizes.

a What do you notice about the relationships between the dimensions?

b Start again with a different sized rectangular piece of paper and repeat this experiment. Do you get the same result?

Reflect Tom says, 'Direct proportionality is all about multiplying and dividing.'
What do you think he means?

> **Hint** Look back at some of the questions you answered in this lesson. How did you use multiplying and dividing?

6 Check up

Sequences

1 Generate the first three terms of the sequences with these nth terms.

a $4n$ **b** $3n + 1$ **c** $10 - 3n$

d $n^2 + 2$ **e** $3n^2$ **f** $2n^2 - 2$

2 Find the 100th term of the sequence with nth term

a $5n + 6$ **b** $3 - 2n$

3 Find the nth term of each sequence.

a 6, 12, 18, 24, …   **b** −5, −10, −15, −20, …

c 8, 9, 10, 11, …   **d** 2, 6, 10, 14, …

e 11, 9, 7, 5, …   **f** 2, 1, 0, −1, …

4 Work out the next two terms of each sequence.

a 4, 9, 14, 19, …   **b** 7, 14, 28, 56, …

c 4, 5, 7, 10, …   **d** 800, 400, 200, 100, …

e 1, 2, 5, 10, …   **f** 0.1, 0.3, 0.9, 2.7, …

5 Look at the sequences in Q4.

a Which ones are arithmetic sequences?

b Which ones are geometric sequences?

6 The nth term of a sequence is $6n + 2$.
Is 52 a term of the sequence? Explain.

Solving equations and inequalities

7 Solve these equations.

a $\dfrac{3x + 5}{2} = 4$ **b** $\dfrac{4x + 1}{3} = x + 4$

8 Solve these equations. Give both possible values of x.

a $x^2 + 14 = 78$ **b** $\dfrac{x^2}{2} = 50$

     $x = \square$ or $x = \square$ $x = \square$ or $x = \square$

9 Show each inequality on a number line.
Write down the integers that satisfy each inequality.

a $n > 7$ **b** $-5 < n \leqslant 2$

10 Write the inequalities shown by these number lines.

a

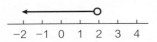

b

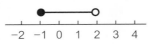

Proportion

11 Meena weighed different length wooden planks.
    Here are her results.

Length	Mass
3 cm	51 g
5 cm	85 g
8 cm	136 g

Is the mass in direct proportion to the length?
Explain your answer.

12 Distance travelled at a constant speed is in direct proportion to time taken.
    It takes 45 minutes to travel 25 miles.
    a How long would it take to travel 40 miles at the same speed?
    b How far would you travel in 2 hours?

13 The price of oranges varies in proportion to the number sold.
    The price of 15 oranges is £3.90.
    a Write a formula for the relationship between the price (P) and the number sold (n).
    b What is the price of 98 oranges?

14 The time taken to load a lorry is in inverse proportion to the number of people loading it.
    3 people take 40 minutes to load the lorry.
    a Write a formula connecting the time (t) and the number of people (n).
    b Work out how long it takes 4 people to load the lorry.

Challenge

a Make up four different sequences, each with 4th term 10. Try to include a decreasing
   sequence.
b Write the nth term next to each sequence.
c How many different sequences with a 4th term of 10 can you make?
d What type of sequences have you used?

Reflect

How sure are you of your answers? Were you mostly

😕 Just guessing   😐 Feeling doubtful   🙂 Confident

What next? Use your results to decide whether to strengthen or extend your learning.

6 Strengthen

Sequences

1 **a** Copy and complete the tables to show the first five terms of each sequence.
The first one is partly done for you.

i $6n - 2$

Position number (n)	1	2	3	4	5
$6n$	6				
-2	-2	-2			
Term	4				

← Work out $6 \times n$ for each value of n.

← Subtract 2.

← Add the numbers in the middle two rows to find each term.

ii $4n - 10$

Position number (n)	1	2	3	4	5
$4n$					
-10					
Term					

b Work out the 10th term of each sequence.

2 **a** Copy and complete the table to show the first five terms of the sequence $-3n + 12$.

Position number (n)	1	2	3	4	5
$-3n$	-3				
$+12$	$+12$	$+12$			
Term	9				

← Work out $-3 \times n$ for each value of n.

← Add 12.

← Add the numbers in the middle two rows to find each term.

b Work out the 10th term of the sequence.

3 Copy and complete this method to work out the nth term of the sequence 6, 11, 16, 21, …

a Sequence   6   11   16   21

Differences $+\square$ $+\square$ $+\square$

The sequence goes up in $\square$s.

b The $\square$ times table is: $\square, \square, \square, \square, …, \square n$.

c Each term in the sequence is $\square$ more than $\square n$.

d The nth term is $\square n + \square$

e Check: Substitute $n = 1$ into your nth term. Do you get 6 (the first term)?

4 Work out the nth term of each sequence.
    a 11, 14, 17, 20, …   **b** 8, 13, 18, 23, …   **c** 4, 6, 8, 10, …
    d 1, 7, 13, 19, …   **e** $-3, -1, 1, 3, …$ **f** 8, 6, 4, 2, …
    g 5, 2, $-1, -4, …$ **h** $-7, -4, -1, 2, …$

5 a Draw the next two patterns in this sequence.

b Copy and complete the table to show the number of squares in each pattern.

Position number (n)	1	2	3	4	5
Number of squares	5	9			

c Work out the differences between terms.

d Work out the nth term.

e Use your nth term to work out the number of squares in the 10th pattern.

6 Reasoning The nth term of a sequence is $5n - 1$.

a Copy and complete the table for the first five terms.

Position (n)	1	2	3	4	5
Term ($5n - 1$)					

b Look at the numbers in the sequence. Explain why 16 cannot be a term of the sequence.

c i Solve the equation $5n - 1 = 16$.

  ii How does your answer show that 16 is not a term of the sequence?

7 The nth term of a sequence is $2n + 9$.

Work out the position number n for each of these terms.

a 25   **b** 31   **c** 55

> **Q7a hint** Solve the equation $2n + 9 = 25$

8 Work out the term-to-term rule for each sequence.

a 1, 3, 9, 27, ...
   $\times \square$ $\times \square$ $\times \square$

b 2, 6, 18, 54, ...
   $\times \square$ $\times \square$ $\times \square$

c 27, 9, 3, 1, ...
   $\times \dfrac{1}{\square}$ $\times \dfrac{1}{\square}$ $\times \dfrac{1}{\square}$

d 54, 18, 6, 2, ...
   $\times \dfrac{1}{\square}$ $\times \dfrac{1}{\square}$ $\times \dfrac{1}{\square}$

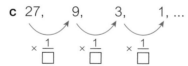 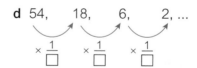

9 Copy these sequences and fill in the boxes to show how to get from one term to the next.

a 25, 31, 37, 43, ...
   $\square$ $\square$ $\square$

b 7, 8, 10, 13, 17, ...
   $\square$ $\square$ $\square$ $\square$

c 5, 10, 20, 40, ...
   $\square$ $\square$ $\square$

d 19, 16, 13, 10, ...
   $\square$ $\square$ $\square$

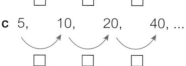

e 5000, 500, 50, 10, ...
   $\square$ $\square$ $\square$

f 1, 4, 9, 16, ...
   $\square$ $\square$ $\square$

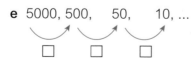

10 Look back at Q9.

a i Which sequences are arithmetic (add or subtract the same number each time)?

  ii Write the term-to-term rule for the arithmetic sequences.

b i Which sequences are geometric (multiply by the same number each time)?

  ii Write the term-to-term rule for the geometric sequences.

c Which sequences are neither arithmetic nor geometric?

Inequalities

1 To show $x \leqslant 2$ on a number line:
   a draw a number line including 2
   b draw a circle above 2
   c fill in the circle to show that 2 is included
   d draw an arrow above numbers less than 2.

                         −1 0 1 2 3

2 Show these inequalities on number lines.
   a $x < 2$ **b** $x > 2$ **c** $x \geqslant 2$

3 Write down the inequality shown on each number line.

a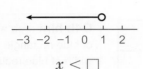

$x < \square$

b

$x \geqslant \square$

c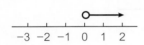

d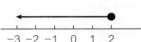

4 To show $-1 \leqslant x < 3$ on a number line:
   a draw a number line including −1 and 3
   b draw circles above −1 and 3
   c fill in the circle to show that −1 is included
   d draw a line between the two circles.

                        −2 −1 0 1 2 3 4

5 Show these inequalities on number lines.
   a $-1 \leqslant x \leqslant 3$ **b** $-1 < x \leqslant 3$ **c** $-1 < x < 3$

6 Write down the inequality shown on each number line.

a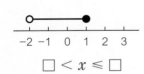

$\square < x \leqslant \square$

b

$\square \leqslant x < \square$

Solving equations

1 Copy and complete the working to solve these equations.

a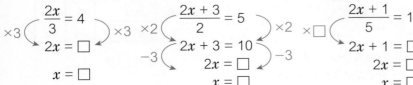

b

$$\frac{2x + 3}{2} = 5$$

c

$$\frac{2x + 1}{5} = 1$$

d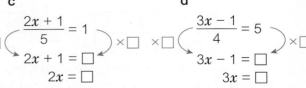

2 Solve these equations.

a $\dfrac{5x + 1}{4} = x + 2$ **b** $\dfrac{3x + 1}{4} = 3x$ **c** $\dfrac{3y + 2}{3} = 2y + 1$

d $4x + 3 = \dfrac{5x + 6}{4}$ **e** $5a + 6 = \dfrac{2a + 1}{3}$ **f** $\dfrac{3x + 3}{4} = 4x + 7$

3 a Work out

  i $(-5)^2$ and 5^2 **ii** $(-7)^2$ and 7^2

  b Solve these equations. Give both possible values of x.

  i $x^2 = 81$ **ii** $x^2 = 16$ **iii** $x^2 + 3 = 67$

  iv $x^2 - 17 = 83$ **v** $x^2 - 13 = 12$ **vi** $x^2 + 4 = 40$

> **Q3b iii hint** Rearrange to get x^2 on its own.

4 Write an equation for each diagram.
Solve it to find the length x.

a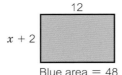
12
$x + 2$
Blue area = 48

b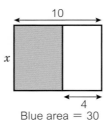
10
x
4
Blue area = 30

c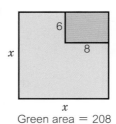
6
8
x
x
Green area = 208

> **Q4b hint** area = length of blue rectangle × width of blue rectangle

Proportion

1 The table shows a gardener's charges.

Hours, h	4	7
Charge, C	£60	£105

a Work out $\dfrac{\text{charge } (C)}{\text{hours } (h)}$ for each pair of values.

Is the value of $\dfrac{C}{h}$ the same for both pairs?

b Are h and C in direct proportion?

> **Q1b hint** h and C are in direct proportion if $\dfrac{C}{h}$ always has the same value.

2 The table shows plumber's charges.

Hours, h	2	3
Charge, C	£45	£55

a Is $\dfrac{C}{h}$ the same for both pairs?

b Are h and C in direct proportion?

3 In each table, the variables are in direct proportion.
Copy and complete the formula connecting the two variables.

a

x	1	2	4
y	2	6	8

$\times \square$

$y = \square x$

b

h	2	5	8
t	3	7.5	12

$\times \square$

$t = \square h$

c

p	3	4	7
q	18	24	42

$\times \square$

$q = \square p$

4 A and B are in direct proportion.

When $A = 3$, $B = 5$.

Copy and complete this formula connecting A and B.

$B = \square A$

5 I can buy 1040 Hong Kong dollars (HKD) with £80.

   a How many HKD can I buy with £1?

   b Copy and complete this equation relating HKD to £.

     $h = \square p$, where h is HKD and p is pounds

   c How many HKD can I buy with £150?

6 I can buy 5760 Icelandic kroner with £30.

How many kroner can I buy with £75?

7 The table shows the number of days to build a house.

Number of builders, n	2	3	4
Number of days, d	18	12	9

   a Work out $n \times d$ for each pair.

     Is the value of $n \times d$ the same for each pair?

   b Are n and d in inverse proportion?

> **Q7b hint** n and d are in inverse proportion if $n \times d$ always has the same value.

8 In each table, the variables are in inverse proportion.

Copy and complete the formula connecting the two variables.

a

x	3	4	6
y	2	1.5	1

$xy = \square$

$y = \dfrac{\square}{x}$

b

s	5	12	16
v	9.6	4	3

$sv = \square$

$v = \dfrac{\square}{s}$

Challenge Two music download websites have different pricing structures.

Website A charges 49p per download with a monthly fee of £1.

If you buy 10 tracks in a month you get the 11th free.

Website B charges 59p per download only.

Three friends discuss which website is better value for money.

Match their statements to the number of tracks they buy per month.

Rachel: 'Website A is better value.'	8 tracks
Anita: 'Website B is better value'	20 tracks
Peter: 'Both websites cost the same.'	10 tracks

Reflect For these Strengthen lessons, copy and complete these sentences:

I found questions _____ easiest. They were on _____ (list the topics).

I found questions _____ most difficult. I still need help with _____ (list the topics).

6 Extend

1 **Problem-solving** Here are some arithmetic sequences.
   a 1, ☐, ☐, 10, 13, ...　**b** 2, ☐, ☐, 14, ...　　**c** 12, ☐, 8, 6, ...　　**d** ☐, 5, ☐, 9, ...
   For each sequence, work out
   　　i the missing terms　**ii** the nth term　　　**iii** the 20th term.

2 Show these inequalities on number lines.
   Write down the integer values that satisfy each of them.

   a $-2 \leqslant x < 1.5$　　　**b** $\frac{1}{2} \leqslant x < 6$　　　**c** $-0.5 < x \leqslant 3$　　　**d** $-2.5 \leqslant x \leqslant 4$

3 **Reasoning** Explain why there are no integer values that satisfy $5 < x < 6$.

4 **Problem-solving / Reasoning**
   a There are 2 chairs in a room. Terry and Alan sit on a chair. In how many different ways
   can this happen?
   b There are 3 chairs in a room. In how many different ways can Terry and Alan sit on a chair?
   c Copy and complete this table.
   d In how many ways can they sit on
   10 chairs?

Number of chairs	2	3	4	5
Number of ways to sit				

5 The graphs show the terms of two sequences.
   a Work out the nth term of each
   sequence.
   b Work out the 20th term of each
   sequence.

6 Write each statement as an equation
   showing direct proportion.
   The first one has been done for you.
   a The cost (C) of sending a text
   message (t) at 7p a text.
   $C = 7t$ (Or $C = 0.07t$, if C is in £.)
   b The perimeter (P) of a regular hexagon with sides of length k.
   c Weekly earnings (E) for 37 hours at y pounds an hour.
   d The cost (c) in pounds of x calculators at £5 each.
   e The number of miles (m) travelled in 3.5 hours at a speed of y miles per hour.

7 **Problem-solving** Describe in a statement what each
   formula shows. The first one has been done for you.
   a $C = 35b$　　　C is cost in pence, b is number of bananas.
   　　The cost of bananas at 35p per banana.
   b $P = 8s$　　　P is perimeter, s is length of side.
   c $W = 9h$　　　W is wage, h is hours.
   d $E = 30w$　　　E is weekly earnings in pounds, w is
   　　　　　　hourly rate.
   e $d = 60h$　　　d is distance in miles, h is hours.

> **Q7 hint** $P = 5s$ could be
> 'What is the total cost in pence
> of s sweets at 5p each?'
> or 'What is the total amount of
> paint in s 5-litre cans?'
> or 'What is the perimeter of a
> regular pentagon with sides of
> length s?'

8 **Problem-solving** Josh thinks of a number. He adds 3 to it and multiplies the result by 4. Then he divides this new number by 5.

He finds that he gets the same result by doubling the same original number, adding 2 to it, trebling this number, then dividing the result by 6.

a Write an equation to express this.

b Solve the equation to find the number that Josh first thought of.

9 Shapes B and C are enlargements of Shape A.

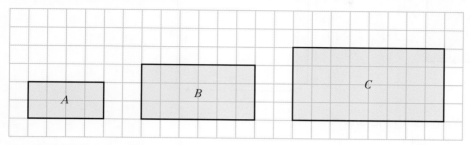

a Copy and complete this table.

Shape	Length (l)	Width (w)	Area (A)
A			
B			
C			

b Write a formula $l = \ldots$ for the relationship between the length (l) and the width (w).

c Use your formula from part **b** to write a formula connecting the area (A) and the width (w).

10 Solve these equations.

a $-5(x - 3) = 29 + 2x$

b $2(10 - x) = -3x + 50$

c $-3(x - 5) + 2 = 18 - x$

d $4(-2x - 4) - 2x = 62 + 3x$

e $4(-3x + 3) = x - 1$

f $-3(-4x - 2) = -2x - 36$

11 Solve these equations.

a $4(3a - 6) = 100 - 2(a - 1)$

b $86 - 2(2p + 1) = 9(3p - 1)$

c $-2(6x + 5) = 54 - 2(2x + 12)$

d $40 - 2(t + 6) = -2(4 - 2t)$

12 **Problem-solving** One hundred and twenty-eight women play in the Wimbledon Women's Singles Tennis Tournament each year. They each play one first-round match.

a How many matches are there in the first round?

b The winning players from the first round go through to the second round.

  i How many players go through to the second round?

  ii How many matches are there in the second round?

c After every round, the winning players go through to the next round. How many rounds will there be?

d How many matches does the overall winner play?

e How many matches are there in the tournament?

> **Q12a hint** How many women play in each singles match?

> **Q12c hint** Continue the sequence for the number of matches in each round.

13 Problem-solving Write the next three terms in this sequence.

10, 11, 9, 12, 8, 13, 7, ...

14 Problem-solving Shape A has 3 times the area of shape B.

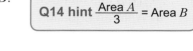

Q14 hint $\dfrac{\text{Area } A}{3} = \text{Area } B$

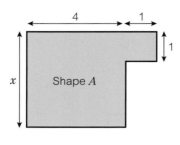

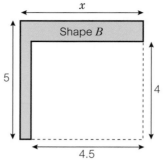

Write an equation using the areas.
Solve it to find length x.

15 Reasoning $-x < 8$
    a Write down three possible values for $-x$.
    b Use your answers to part **a** to write down three possible values for x.
    c Write an inequality for x.

16 Reasoning $x \leqslant 2$
Write an inequality for $-x$.

Challenge

1 The nth term of a sequence is $2n + a$, where a is an integer.
One of its terms is 20.
    a Choose a value for a.
    b What position is the term 20 with your choice of a?
    c How can you make the term 20 appear earlier in the sequence?

2 The nth term of a sequence is $an + 4$, where a is an integer.
One of its terms is 20.
    a Choose a value for a.
    b What position is the term 20 with your choice of a?
    c How can you make the term 20 appear earlier in the sequence?

3 The nth term of a sequence is $an + b$, where a and b are integers.
One of its terms is 20.
    a Choose a value for a.
    b What position is the term 20 with your choice of a?
    c How can you make the term 20 appear earlier in the sequence?

Reflect   In this unit you have used algebra in sequences, inequalities, equations and
proportion problems.
Which topic did you find easiest? Which did you find hardest?
For the one you found hardest, make up some hints or practice questions to help you.

6 Unit test

1 Work out the nth term of the sequence 5, 11, 17, 23, … .

2 Write down the first three terms of the sequences with nth term
   a $8n - 3$ **b** $6 - 2n$ **c** $n^2 + 5$ **d** $3n^2$

3   **a** Draw the next two patterns in this sequence.

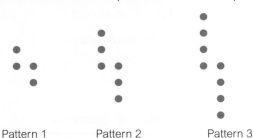

Pattern 1   Pattern 2   Pattern 3

   b Copy and complete the table to show the number of dots in each pattern.

Pattern number (n)	1	2	3	4	5
Number of dots					

   c Work out the nth term.
   d Work out the number of dots in the 10th pattern.
   e Which pattern has 100 dots?

4 These patterns are made from black and white counters.

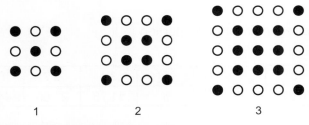

1   2   3

   a Copy and complete the table.

Pattern number	1	2	3	4	5
White counters					
Black counters					

   b Work out the nth term for the sequence of white counters.
   c Is the sequence of white counters an arithmetic sequence or a geometric sequence? Explain how you know.
   d How many white counters will there be in the 10th pattern?
   e Is there a pattern with 68 white counters? Show working to explain.
   f What type of sequence is the sequence of black counters?
   g Find the nth term of the sequence of black counters.

5 Write down the integer values that satisfy the inequality $-5 \leqslant x < 3$.

6 $x > 4$

Write an inequality for $3x$.

7 Solve these equations.

a $\dfrac{8x - 3}{2} = 2x + 1$

b $\dfrac{6x + 3}{4} = 2x - 3$

8 Solve these equations.

a $x^2 + 5 = 21$

b $\dfrac{x^2}{3} = 12$

9 The formula $a = \dfrac{v - u}{t}$ is used to calculate the acceleration of an object,

where v is the final velocity, u is the initial velocity and t is the time taken.
The acceleration of an object is $3 \, \text{m/s}^2$, the initial velocity is $5 \, \text{m/s}$
and the time taken is $5 \, \text{s}$.
What is the final velocity of the object?

10 In an experiment, Emma records the time taken to travel different distances.

a The time and distance are in direct proportion.
Write a formula to show the relationship.

b Use your formula to calculate the time taken to travel $54 \, \text{m}$.

Time (t)	Distance (d)
3 seconds	13.5 m
7 seconds	31.5 m
5 seconds	22.5 m

11 p and q are in inverse proportion.
Work out the value of A in this table.

p	q
7.6	3.9
A	8

12 For each table

i work out whether x and y are in direct or inverse proportion

ii write a formula connecting x and y.

a

x	2.5	3.68	5
y	1.84	1.25	0.92

b

x	3.1	5.7	11.6
y	11.78	21.66	44.08

Challenge In each of these squares, different combinations of
the three values $a = 3$, $b = 5$ and $c = 4$ have been used to generate
numbers.
Suggest expressions for each number, using a, b and c, that would
give the correct value in each of these squares. Use each letter at
least once.
For example, this expression would work for square A.
$$bc - (a + b) = 5 \times 4 - (3 + 5) = 12$$

A	B	C
12	15	9

D	E	F
2	125	6

G	H	I
4	20	11

Reflect All the lessons in this unit used algebra.
Which lessons involved solving equations?

7 Circles, Pythagoras and prisms

Master   Check up p176   Strengthen p178   Extend p184   Unit test p186

7.1 Circumference of a circle

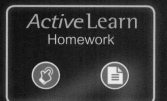

Active Learn
Homework

- Calculate the circumference of a circle
- Estimate calculations involving pi (π)
- Solve problems involving the circumference of a circle

Warm up

1 Fluency

a Round 2.6637 to

  i 1 decimal place   ii 2 decimal places.

b Round 9.458 to

  i 1 significant figure   ii 2 significant figures.

2 A measure is 3.505 m.

a Round the measure to the nearest cm.   b Change the measure into mm.

3 Here are two formulae.

$a = 2b$ $c = 3d$

a What is the value of a when b is 9 cm?   b What is the value of b when a is 10 cm?

c What is the value of c when $d = 11$ cm?   d What is the value of d when $c = 12$ cm?

Key point

The **circumference** (C) is the perimeter of a circle.
The **centre** of a circle is marked using a dot.
The **radius** (r) is the distance from the centre to the circumference.
The plural of radius is **radii**.
The **diameter** (d) is a line from one side to the other through
the centre.

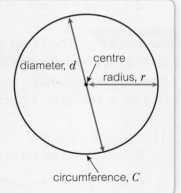

4 a Use compasses to draw accurately a circle of radius 6 cm.

b Use this information to mark the points O, A, B and T on your circle.

  O is the centre.

  OT is a radius.

  AB is a diameter.

c Mark any other point S on the circumference.

5 a The radius of a circular button is 7 mm. Work out its diameter.
   b The radius of a dinner plate is 12.7 cm. Work out its diameter.

Q5 hint
diameter = □ × radius

6 a The diameter of a circular Mexican hat is 42 cm. What is its radius?
   b The diameter of a circular pond is 1.9 m. What is its radius?

7 Reasoning A standard international dartboard has a diameter of 18 inches.
   Jamie says, 'The radius is 36 inches.' Is Jamie correct? Explain.

8 a r is the radius of a circle. Write a formula to give its diameter, d.
   b d is the diameter of a circle. Write a formula to give its radius, r.

9 Problem-solving The 22 balls of a snooker game are placed along the edge of the table, touching each other. Their total length is 1.115 m.
   Work out the radius of a snooker ball to the nearest mm.

10 Reasoning The table shows the diameters and approximate circumferences of some fishing reels.

Diameter, d (mm)	Circumference, C (mm)	$\dfrac{C}{d}$
51	160	
57	179	
65	204	
71	223	

   a Copy and complete the table.
      Round the values of $\dfrac{C}{d}$ to 2 decimal places.

   b What do you notice about the value of $\dfrac{C}{d}$?

   c Copy and complete the formula $C = □ × d$.

   d Use your formula to estimate the circumference of a fishing reel with diameter 77 mm.

Key point The Greek letter π (pronounced pi) is a special number 3.141 592 6535....
To find the circumference C of a circle with diameter d, use the formula $C = \pi d$.
If you know the radius r you can use the equivalent formula $C = 2\pi r$.
Use the π key on your calculator.

---

11 Use your calculator to work out the circumference of each circle.
   Round your answers to an appropriate degree of accuracy.

Q11a hint 8.2 cm is measured to the nearest mm (or 1 decimal place) so your answer should have the same degree of accuracy.

a

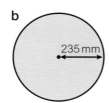

8.2 cm

b

235 mm

c

0.45 m

12 Calculate the circumference of each circular object.
Round your answers to an appropriate degree of accuracy.

   a The lens of a mobile phone camera with a diameter of 3.85 mm.

   b A bass drum with a diameter of 56 cm.

   c A GPS satellite's circular orbit with a diameter of 40 360 km.

13 Reasoning A circular saw blade has a radius of 80 mm.
Maria works out that its circumference is approximately 250 mm.
Is Maria correct? Explain.

14 Problem-solving The radius of the Earth is approximately 3950 miles.
Use this radius to work out the circumference of the Earth.
Give your answer to the nearest mile.

> **Q14 hint**
> Round π to the nearest integer.

Key point   Half a circle is called a **semicircle**.

---

15 Work out the perimeter of this semicircle, correct to the nearest cm.

> **Q15 hint** Find the circumference of half a circle. Add the diameter.

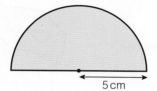

5 cm

16 Problem-solving The diagram shows a semicircular Victorian window frame.
Work out the total length of the frame, including all of the radii.

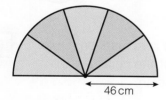

46 cm

17 Reasoning Monty has to estimate the length of edging needed for a circular lawn with a diameter of 9.4 m.
He forgot to bring his calculator to the store.

   a Calculate an estimate by rounding the numbers to 1 significant figure.

   b Is your answer an underestimate or an overestimate? Explain why.

   c Estimate how much edging Monty should buy.

18 Europe's largest stone circle is at Avebury in Wiltshire.
It has a radius of 175 m.

   a Estimate the circumference of the circle.

   b Write the circumference in terms of π.

   c Calculate the circumference to the nearest metre.

> **Q18a hint** Round the numbers to 1 significant figure.

> **Q18b hint** Your answer should be written as ☐π m.

19 Problem-solving The diameter of the sun is approximately 1 400 000 km.
Estimate the circumference of the sun.

20 a Work out, to 2 significant figures, the diameter of a circle
   with circumference
   i 20 cm   **ii** 2.5 m

b Work out, to 2 significant figures, the radius of a circle
   with circumference
   i 150 mm   **ii** 4000 km

> **Q20a hint** Start by writing the value you know in the formula $C = \pi d$.

21 Problem-solving A cake is removed from a circular cake tin.
   A ribbon 56.5 cm long fits exactly around the outside of the cake.
   What diameter cake tin was used to bake the cake?
   Give your answer to the nearest cm.

22 Problem-solving
   a i How far does a wheel of radius 48 cm travel in one revolution?
     ii How many times will it rotate when travelling a distance of 15 m?
   b A tractor wheel travels 4 m in 1 revolution. What is its radius?
   Round your answer to an appropriate degree of accuracy.

Challenge

1 The string of a yo-yo is wound around a spool of diameter d.
   When fully wound, the yo-yo rotates 25 times before it reaches the
   end of the string.
   a Write a formula for the length L mm of the string in terms of π.
   b Work out the length of the string for a spool of diameter 13 mm.
   Give your answer in terms of π.
   c Is your formula a good model for the length of string?
   Explain your answer.

2 a i Mark a dot on the edge of a 2p coin and align it with the zero mark on a ruler.
     ii Roll the coin along the ruler to find the circumference of the coin.
    iii Use the circumference to estimate the diameter of the coin.
   b Make a better estimate by rolling the coin further.
   c Check your estimate using a ruler.
   d Explain how you can estimate the diameter of a football or other spherical shape.

Reflect   Close your book and write down as many facts about circles as you can.
Make sure you include all the facts you remember from this lesson.
Then open your book again and look back at the lesson.
Did you miss any facts? If so, add them to your list.
Did you make any spelling mistakes? If so, correct them.

7.2 Area of a circle

- Calculate the area of a circle
- Solve problems involving the area of a circle

Active Learn
Homework

Warm up

1 Fluency
 a How can you find the diameter if you know the radius?
 b What is an easy estimate for π when working without a calculator?

2 Work out
 a 8^2 **b** 30^2 **c** 0.5^2 **d** $\sqrt{36}$
 e $250\,\text{cm} = \square\,\text{m}$ **f** $1\,\text{m}^2 = \square\,\text{cm}^2$ **g** 0.075 written in standard form: $\square \times 10^{\square}$

3 Substitute into each formula to work out the unknown quantity.
 Give your answers to 2 decimal places, where necessary.
 a $A = 3r^2$, where $r = 4$
 b $s = 9.81t^2$, where $t = 12$
 c $r = \sqrt{A}$, where $A = 14$

Key point

The formula for the area A of a circle with radius r is $A = \pi r^2$.

4 The radius of a circular rug is 0.5 m.
 Use the formula $A = \pi r^2$ to estimate its area.

> **Q4 hint** $A = \pi r^2$
> $\approx 3 \times \square \times \square$

5 Work out the area of each circle.
 Round your answers to an appropriate degree of accuracy.

a    7.2 m

b 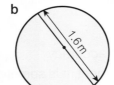   1.6 m

c 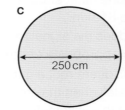   250 cm

> **Q5 hint** Use the π key on your calculator.

> **Q5a hint** Round your answer to the nearest $0.1\,\text{m}^2$.

6 a Estimate the area of each circular object.
 i The head of a screw with a radius of 2.8 mm.
 ii A serving plate with a diameter of 42 cm.
 iii The Mach crater on the Moon with a diameter of 180 km.
 b Calculate the areas in part **a** using the π key of your calculator.
 Round your answers to 2 significant figures.
 c Work out the area of the Mach crater in m^2.
 Give your answer in standard form, correct to 2 significant figures

> **Q6a hint** Round each measure to 1 significant figure.

> **Q6c hint** $1\,\text{km} \times 1\,\text{km} = 1\,\text{km}^2$
> $1000\,\text{m} \times 1000\,\text{m} = \square\,\text{m}^2$

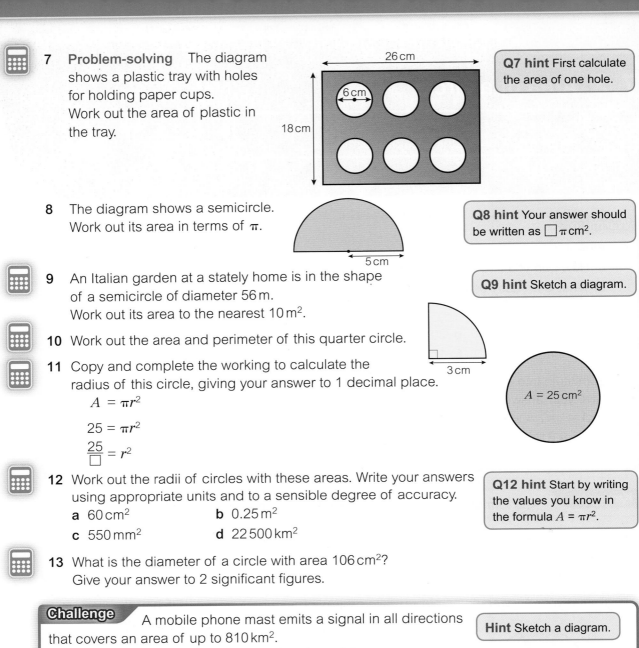

7 **Problem-solving** The diagram shows a plastic tray with holes for holding paper cups.
Work out the area of plastic in the tray.

26 cm

6 cm

18 cm

Q7 hint First calculate the area of one hole.

8 The diagram shows a semicircle. Work out its area in terms of π.

5 cm

Q8 hint Your answer should be written as $\square\,\pi\,cm^2$.

9 An Italian garden at a stately home is in the shape of a semicircle of diameter 56 m.
Work out its area to the nearest 10 m^2.

Q9 hint Sketch a diagram.

10 Work out the area and perimeter of this quarter circle.

3 cm

11 Copy and complete the working to calculate the radius of this circle, giving your answer to 1 decimal place.

$A = 25\ cm^2$

$$A = \pi r^2$$

$$25 = \pi r^2$$

$$\frac{25}{\square} = r^2$$

12 Work out the radii of circles with these areas. Write your answers using appropriate units and to a sensible degree of accuracy.
   a 60 cm^2 **b** 0.25 m^2
   c 550 mm^2 **d** 22 500 km^2

Q12 hint Start by writing the values you know in the formula $A = \pi r^2$.

13 What is the diameter of a circle with area 106 cm^2?
Give your answer to 2 significant figures.

Challenge   A mobile phone mast emits a signal in all directions that covers an area of up to 810 km^2.

Hint Sketch a diagram.

a How far from the mast does the signal reach?
Write your answer to an appropriate degree of accuracy.
b Rohan says, 'When you square root a measurement, it is sometimes a good idea to write the answer more accurately than the measurement itself.'
Explain why Rohan says this is sometimes a good idea.

Reflect   Which of these calculations involves the most steps? Explain.
   • Working out the area of a circle, given its diameter
   • Working out the area of a circle, given its radius
   • Working out the diameter of a circle, given its area
   • Working out the radius of a circle, given its area

7.3 Pythagoras' theorem

Active Learn
Homework

- Find the length of an unknown side of a right-angled triangle
- Solve problems involving right-angled triangles

Warm up

1 Fluency Work out

   a $\sqrt{81}$ **b** $\sqrt{121}$ **c** $3^2 + 4^2$ **d** $5^2 - 2^2$

2 Work out the area of each shape.

   a

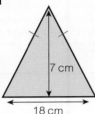

     7 cm

     18 cm

   b

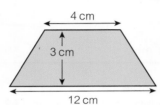

     4 cm

     3 cm

     12 cm

3 Work out these calculations.
Give your answers correct to 3 significant figures where necessary.

   a $7^2 + 14^2$ **b** $2.5^2 + 4.2^2$ **c** $\sqrt{5^2 + 8^2}$ **d** $\sqrt{3.2^2 - 1.8^2}$

4 Find the positive solution of each equation.
Give your answers correct to 3 significant figures where necessary.

   a $a^2 = 45$ **b** $a^2 = 324 + 841$ **c** $a^2 = 6^2 + 5^2$ **d** $6.25 = b^2 + 2.25$

   e $13^2 = b^2 + 12^2$

Key point   The longest side of a right-angled triangle is called the **hypotenuse**.

5 a Draw this right-angled triangle on centimetre squared paper.
   b i Measure the lengths of the three sides to the nearest mm.
     ii What is the length of the hypotenuse?
   c i Measure the three angles of the triangle.
     ii Look at each angle and the length of its opposite side.
     What do you notice?

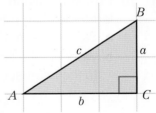

6 Write down the length of the hypotenuse for each of these triangles.

   a

     13 cm   5 cm

     12 cm

   b

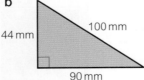

     44 mm   100 mm

     90 mm

   c

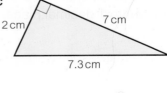

     2 cm   7 cm

     7.3 cm

   d

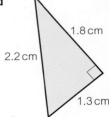

     1.8 cm

     2.2 cm

     1.3 cm

Worked example

Work out the length of the hypotenuse of this right-angled
triangle, correct to the nearest mm.

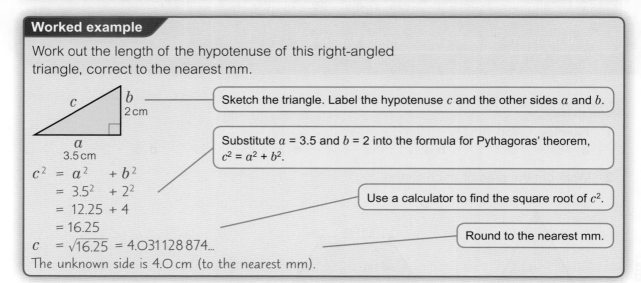

Sketch the triangle. Label the hypotenuse c and the other sides a and b.

Substitute $a = 3.5$ and $b = 2$ into the formula for Pythagoras' theorem, $c^2 = a^2 + b^2$.

$$c^2 = a^2 + b^2$$
$$= 3.5^2 + 2^2$$
$$= 12.25 + 4$$
$$= 16.25$$
$$c = \sqrt{16.25} = 4.031128874...$$

Use a calculator to find the square root of c^2.

Round to the nearest mm.

The unknown side is 4.0 cm (to the nearest mm).

7 **Reasoning** Look at the worked example.
Does it matter which way round you label the sides a and b?

8 Work out the length of the hypotenuse in each of these right-angled triangles,
correct to the nearest mm.

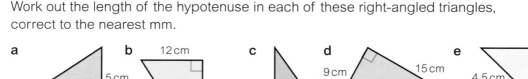

9 **Reasoning** Do you need to give the negative square root of c? Explain.

10 **Problem-solving** The diagram shows a
ladder leaning against the wall of a house.
a Sketch the triangle.
b Work out the length of the ladder,
to the nearest cm.

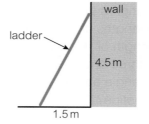

Q10a hint Label
the lengths a, b
and c, and label
the right angle.

11 Work out the diagonal, x, of this tablet screen.
Give your answer to 1 decimal place.

12 Work out the length of the unknown side of each right-angled triangle. Give your answers to an appropriate degree of accuracy. Part **a** has been started for you.

Q12 hint Label the sides a, b, c. Substitute into Pythagoras' theorem $c^2 = a^2 + b^2$. Solve the equation.

a

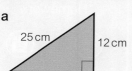

$$25^2 = 12^2 + b^2$$
$$25^2 - \square = b^2$$
$$b = \sqrt{\square}$$

b

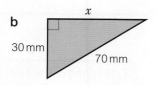

c

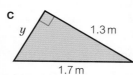

d

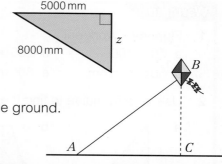

13 Problem-solving A person at point A is flying a kite B. The length of string is 75 m and the kite is 48 m above the ground. The kite falls vertically to point C on the ground. How far is it from point A?

14 Problem-solving Work out the area of this triangle.

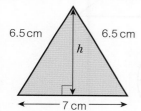

Q14 hint Sketch one right-angled triangle. Use Pythagoras' theorem to work out the height.

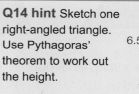
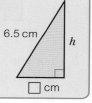

15 Problem-solving The diagram shows a trapezium. Work out

a the length labelled w

b the height of the trapezium, h

c the area of the trapezium in m².

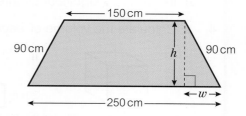

Challenge A football club plans to build a rectangular pitch of length 105 m and width 68 m. The lengths of the diagonals can be used to check if the rectangle has been marked out accurately.

1 Work out the length of the diagonal joining two corners, writing your answer

a as a surd   b to the nearest m

c to the nearest 10 cm   d correct to 5 decimal places.

Key point A **surd** is a square root $\sqrt{\square}$ that cannot be simplified any further.

2 a Which of your answers is the most accurate? Explain why.

b Which of your answers is the most useful? Explain why.

Reflect Look at the worked example. In your own words, list the steps to solve the problem. Look back at Q8. Do your steps work to solve these problems? If not, change them. Look back at Q12 and do the same, and then look back at Q13.

7.4 Prisms and cylinders

- Calculate the volume and surface area of a right prism
- Calculate the volume and surface area of a cylinder
- Convert between m³, cm³ and mm³

*Active*Learn
Homework

Warm up

1 Fluency Work out
a 50 × 1000
b 250 000 ÷ 1000
c 1 ÷ 1000
d 60 mm in cm
e 600 mm² in cm²
f 2500 cm³ in litres

> **Q1f hint** 1 cm³ = 1 ml
> so   1000 cm³ = 1 litre

2 Use area formulae to find the area of each shape.

a

5 cm
2 cm

b
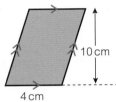
10 cm
4 cm

c
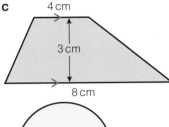
4 cm
3 cm
8 cm

3 For this circle, work out
a its radius
b its circumference to 2 decimal places
c its area to 3 significant figures.

10 cm

4 a Calculate the volume of each 3D solid.

i
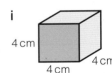
4 cm
4 cm
4 cm

ii
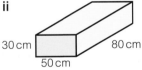
30 cm
50 cm
80 cm

iii
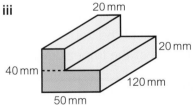
20 mm
20 mm
40 mm
120 mm
50 mm

b Calculate the total surface area of solids **i** and **ii**.

5 a A cube measures 1 cm by 1 cm by 1 cm. What is its volume in cm³?
b The same cube measures 10 mm by 10 mm by 10 mm. What is its volume in mm³?
c Another cube measures 1 m by 1 m by 1 m. What is its volume in m³?
d The same cube measures 100 cm by 100 cm by 100 cm. What is its volume in cm³?
e Use your answers to parts **a** to **d** to copy and complete
   i 1 cm³ = ☐ mm³   **ii** 1 m³ = ☐ cm³   **iii** 1 m³ = ☐ litres

> **Key point**   1 cm³ = 1000 mm³   1 m³ = 1 000 000 cm³   1 litre = 1000 cm³ = 0.001 m³

6 Look back at the 3D solids in Q4a. Write the volume of
   a solid **i** in mm³   **b** solid **ii** in m³   **c** solid **iii** in cm³.

A **right prism** is a 3D solid that has the same **cross-section** throughout its length.

The cross-section can be any polygon. It is at right angles to the length of the solid.

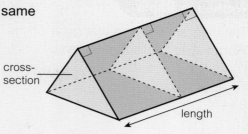

cross-section

length

7   Which of these solids are right prisms?
What shapes are their cross-sections?

a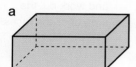

b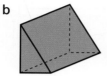

c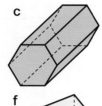

d

e

f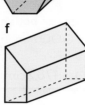

8   **Reasoning**   If you cut a right prism in half, do you get two prisms? Explain.

9   Look back at the 3D solids in Q4**a**. For each solid
a   work out the area of the darker shaded cross-section
b   multiply the area of the cross-section by the length of the solid
c   compare the result with the volume found in Q4.
What do you notice?

> **Q9c hint** $V = l \times w \times h$
> Which part of the formula gives the area of the cross-section?

Key point   Volume of a right prism = area of cross-section × length

Worked example

The diagram shows a triangular prism.

> Cross-section is a right-angled triangle.

Work out its volume.

153 mm
30 mm
40 mm
150 mm

> Length of prism

area of cross-section = $\frac{1}{2}$ × base × height

= 0.5 × 150 mm × 30 mm

= 2250 mm²

30
150

volume of prism = area of cross-section × length

= 2250 mm² × 40 mm = 90 000 mm³

90 000 mm³ ÷ 1000 = 90 cm³

> 90 000 has too many figures, so mm is not a sensible unit to use. Convert to cm³ instead.

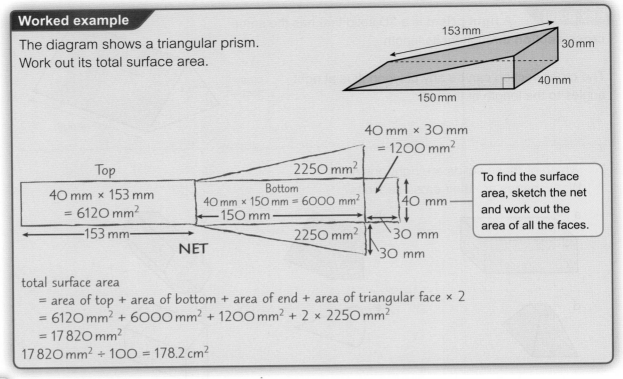

Worked example

The diagram shows a triangular prism.
Work out its total surface area.

153 mm
30 mm
40 mm
150 mm

40 mm × 30 mm = 1200 mm²

Top
40 mm × 153 mm = 6120 mm²

2250 mm²

Bottom
40 mm × 150 mm = 6000 mm²
←150 mm→

40 mm

←153 mm→
NET

2250 mm²
30 mm
30 mm

To find the surface area, sketch the net and work out the area of all the faces.

total surface area
= area of top + area of bottom + area of end + area of triangular face × 2
= 6120 mm² + 6000 mm² + 1200 mm² + 2 × 2250 mm²
= 17 820 mm²
17 820 mm² ÷ 100 = 178.2 cm²

10 For each solid, work out
  i its volume in cm³ **ii** its total surface area in cm².
  Give your answers to an appropriate degree of accuracy.

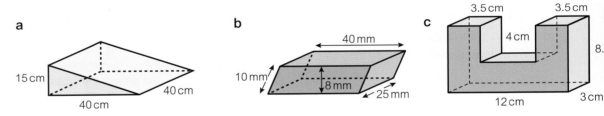

a

15 cm
40 cm
40 cm

b

40 mm
10 mm
8 mm
25 mm

c

3.5 cm   3.5 cm
4 cm
8.2
12 cm
3 cm

11 The diagram shows the cross-section of water in a pool.
The pool is 8 m wide.
  a Work out the volume of water in the pool in
    i m³   **ii** litres
  b How many hours would it take to fill the pool
    at a rate of 5 litres per second?

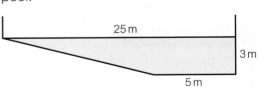

25 m
3 m
5 m

12 a Write an expression for the area of the circular
    cross-section of the cylinder.
  b Write an expression for the volume of the cylinder.
  c Write a formula for the volume of a cylinder, $V =$.

Q12 hint Think of a **cylinder**
as a right prism with a circular
cross-section. The height, h,
could also be the length.

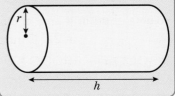

r

h

13 Work out the volume of this cylinder.
Give your answer to an appropriate degree of accuracy.

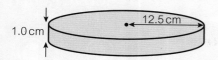

14 Work out the volume of this cylinder.
Give your answer in cm³ to 2 decimal places.

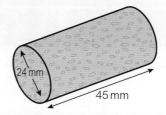

Worked example

Work out the area of the label on this tin of tuna to the nearest cm².

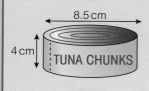

length of label = circumference of tin
$$= \pi \times 8.5 \text{ cm}$$

area of rectangular label = base × height
$$= \pi \times 8.5 \text{ cm} \times 4 \text{ cm}$$
$$= 107 \text{ cm}^2 \text{ (to the nearest cm)}$$

---

15 The cardboard inner from a toilet roll has a diameter of
3.5 cm and height 10.5 cm. Work out the area of cardboard.

> **Q15 hint** Sketch a diagram.

16 The diagram shows a closed cardboard poster tube.
  a Sketch the net of this cylinder. Mark the dimensions on
    your diagram.
  b Work out the circumference of the tube to the nearest mm.
  c Work out the area of cardboard needed to make the tube,
    to the nearest 100 cm².

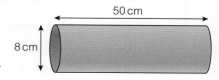

Challenge The curved surface of a circular jam jar has a label stuck on it.
The label fits the surface exactly, with no overlap.
The area of the label is 240 cm².
Sketch three possible jam jars. Mark the radius and height of each jar.

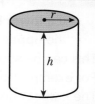

Reflect Toby says, 'A right prism always has two end faces that are exactly the same.'
Ed says, 'The faces that are not at the ends are always rectangles.'
Issy says, 'It is called a *right* prism because the end faces and other faces are always at
right angles to each other.'
Mel says, 'The shapes of the end faces give the prism its name.'
Look carefully at the pictures of the right prisms you identified in Q7.
Are all the students correct?

7.5 Errors and bounds

- Find the lower and upper bounds for a measurement
- Calculate percentage error intervals

*Active*Learn
Homework

Warm up

1 Fluency

a What is 18.2 cm to the nearest
   i cm   **ii** 10 cm?

b What is 428 g to the nearest
   i 10 g   **ii** 5 g   **iii** 100 g?

c What is 10% of 70 g?

2 a Increase 40 cm² by
   i 10%   **ii** 5%   **iii** 1%

   b Decrease 1800 g by
   i 10%   **ii** 2%   **iii** 0.5%

3 This tin has a diameter of 8.0 cm and a height of 15 cm.
Work out
   a its circumference   **b** the area of the top   **c** its volume.

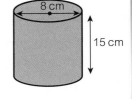

4 a What is the smallest possible value that rounds up to 5 cm, to the nearest cm?

   b What is the smallest possible value that rounds up to 6 cm?

Q4 hint

Key point   For a number that is rounded

- the **lower bound** is the smallest possible value that rounds up to that number
- the **upper bound** is the smallest possible value that rounds up to the next number.

This can be shown as an inequality.
For example, for Q4 the inequality is $4.5 \leqslant x < 5.5$.
The lower bound is 4.5 cm. The upper bound is 5.5 cm.

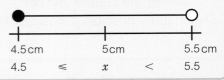

5 Draw a number line and write an inequality to show the lower and upper bounds for each measurement.

   a A length l is 15 cm, to the nearest cm.

   b A mass m is 4 kg, to the nearest kg.

   c A length x is 60 cm, to the nearest 10 cm.

   d A number n is 120, to the nearest 20.

   e A mass m is 400 g, to the nearest 50 g.

   f A length l is 3 cm, to the nearest 1 mm.

Q5c hint

Q5f hint 3 cm = ☐ mm

6 **Problem-solving** A novel is wrapped in a rectangular sheet of brown paper.

a The width of the sheet is 30 cm, to the nearest cm.
What are the lower and upper bounds?

b The length of the sheet is 90 cm, to the nearest 2 cm.
What are the lower and upper bounds?

Q6b hint

c Work out the lower and upper bounds for the
area A of the paper. Write your answer as an
inequality, using 3 significant figures.

Q6c hint Sketch and label the smallest
and largest possible rectangles.

7 A circular flower bed has a radius of 180 cm to the nearest 10 cm.
Write an inequality for

a the lower and upper bounds of the radius, r, of the flower bed

b the lower and upper bounds of the circumference, C, of the flower bed.
Write your answer as an inequality, using 3 significant figures.

8 **Problem-solving** A label is wrapped around this cardboard
tube with no overlap.
The diameter of the tube is 10 cm, to the nearest cm.
The height of the tube is 25 cm, to the nearest cm.
Work out the lower and upper bounds of the area, A,
of the label.
Write your answer as an inequality, using
3 significant figures.

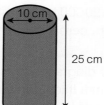

Q8 hint Work
out the lower and
upper bounds for
the diameter and
the height.

Key point An **error interval** tells you the minimum and maximum possible
measurements.

Worked example

A mass m is 500 g to within a 2% error interval.
Use an inequality to describe the range of possible values for m.

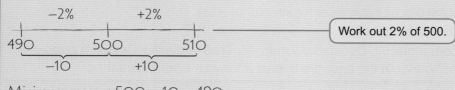

Work out 2% of 500.

Minimum mass = 500 − 10 = 490 g

Maximum mass = 500 + 10 = 510 g

$490 \leqslant m \leqslant 510$ ← Write an inequality.

---

9 Use an inequality to describe the range of possible values for

a a length, l, when l is 50 cm to within a 10% error interval

b a height, h, when h is 3 m to within a 10% error interval

c a capacity, c, when c is 40 litres to within a 5% error interval

d a mass, m, when m is 100 kg to within a 0.5% error interval

e a number, n, when n is 240 to within a 2% error interval.

10 a The mass m of a 200 g block of cheese has a 5% error interval.
   Work out the minimum and maximum possible masses of the cheese.
   Write your answer as an inequality.

b The number n of matches in a box of 300 matches has an 8% error interval.
   Work out the minimum and maximum possible values for n.
   Write your answer as an inequality.

> **Key point**   An error interval can be written using a 'plus or minus' sign, $\pm$.
> For example, $\pm1\%$ means the maximum possible error is +1% and the minimum possible error is −1%.

11 The number, n, of pins in a box of 1000 pins is $\pm3\%$.
   Work out the minimum and maximum possible values for n.
   Write your answer as an inequality.

12 Problem-solving   A machine fills 500 g cereal boxes with a $\pm2\%$ error.
   One day it fills 20 000 boxes with the maximum error possible.
   How much extra cereal (in grams) does it use than if it had been filling at the minimum?

> **Challenge**   The diagram shows a cereal biscuit with semicircular ends.
> Each biscuit is 22 mm thick. Ten biscuits are stacked together in plastic and
> placed inside a cuboid cardboard box.
>
>
>
>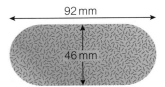
> 92 mm
> 46 mm
>
> **a**   Work out
>   **i** the area of plastic, assuming no overlaps
>   **ii** the area of cardboard, assuming no overlaps.
> **b**   The dimensions of the biscuit have an error interval of $\pm5\%$.
>   What size of box should be used?
> **c**   Design your own cereal biscuit. Decide how many to wrap in plastic. Design a cuboid
>   box to contain them. Work out the answers to part **a** for your box of cereal.

> **Reflect**   List all the previously learnt maths topics you have used in this lesson.
> Compare your list with others in your class.

7 Check up

Circles

1   The diagram shows a circle with a diameter of 7.5 cm.
    Calculate the circumference of the circle, correct to 1 decimal place.

2   A circular steering wheel has a radius of 20 cm.
    Work out the circumference of the wheel.
    Give your answer in terms of π.

3   The diagram shows a circular disc with a diameter of 15 mm.
    Work out the area of the disc.
    Give your answer to the nearest mm^2.

4   The diagram shows a semicircle.
    a   Work out the area to the nearest cm^2.
    b   Work out the perimeter, correct to
        1 decimal place.

12 cm

5   A circle has a diameter d and circumference 30 cm.
    Work out the value of d, correct to the nearest mm.

6   A circle has a radius r and an area of 200 m^2.
    Work out the value of r, correct to the nearest cm.

Pythagoras' theorem

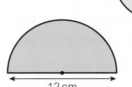

12 cm l 18 cm

7   Work out the length l, correct to the nearest mm.

8   a   Work out the length of the unknown side in this triangle.
    b   Write down the length of the hypotenuse.

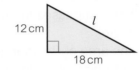

30 mm   24 mm x

9   Work out the area of this triangle.
    Give your answer to a sensible
    degree of accuracy.

0.9 m   1.8 m

Prisms and cylinders

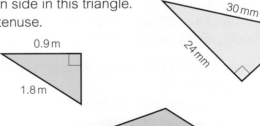

10 The diagram shows a triangular prism.
    a   Work out the volume.
    b   Work out the surface area.

6 cm   4 cm   12 cm

11 Work out the volume of this cylinder.
    Give your answer in cm^3 to
    2 decimal places.

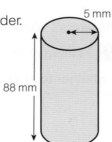

5 mm   88 mm

12 The diagram shows a packet of biscuits wrapped in plastic.
Work out the total surface area of plastic.

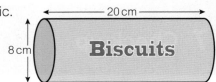

13 The diagram shows a metal drinking trough on a farm.
How many litres of water can the trough hold?

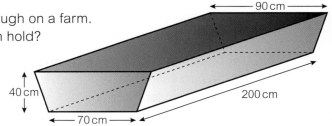

Errors and bounds

14 A square has sides of length 20 cm, to the nearest cm.
  a Work out the lower and upper bounds for the length d of the side of the square.
  b Work out the lower and upper bounds for the area A of the square.

15 The number n of paper clips in a box of 200 paper clips has a 5% error interval.
Work out the possible values for n. Write your answer as an inequality.

Challenge

1 **a** **i** Draw a triangle by joining grid line intersections (where the lines cross ⊢⊣)
      on centimetre squared paper. Here is one possibility.
   ii Calculate the perimeter of the triangle.
  iii Use a pair of compasses to draw a circle with the
      same perimeter.
  b **i** Calculate the area of the triangle.
   ii Use a pair of compasses to draw a circle with the
      same area.
  c Repeat parts **a** and **b** with a different shape.
    Try starting with a rectangle, parallelogram or trapezium.

2 The diagram shows a wheelchair ramp and wheelchair.
The ramp length is 3 m.
The wheelchair moves from the top of the ramp to the bottom.
  a Work out the number of complete wheel revolutions.
  b The small wheel at the front rotates 8 times.
    Work out its diameter.

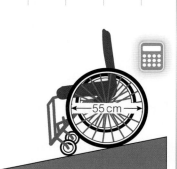

Reflect   How sure are you of your answers? Were you mostly

    ☹ Just guessing   😐 Feeling doubtful   🙂 Confident

What next? Use your results to decide whether to strengthen or extend your learning.

7 Strengthen

Circles

1   Use your calculator to work out
  a π   b $2 \times \pi$ c $\pi \times 5^2$
  d 4π e $\pi \times 2^2$

> **Q1a hint** Find the π key on your calculator.

2   Circumference C, $= \pi \times$ diameter
  a What is the diameter of this circle?
  b Copy and complete.
     $C = \pi \times \square$
  c Use a calculator to work out the circumference.
     Give your answer to 1 decimal place.

3   Work out the circumference of each circle using the formula $C = \pi \times d$.
   Give your answers to 1 decimal place.

  a   b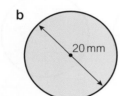

4   Work out the circumference of these objects.
   Give your answers to 1 decimal place.
  a A circular button with diameter 8 mm.
  b A circular tin lid with diameter 12.5 cm.

> **Q4 hint** Draw a sketch. Label the measurements you know.

5   A circle has a diameter of 5 cm.
   Copy and complete to write its circumference in terms of π.
     $C = \square \pi$

6   Diameter $= 2 \times$ radius
  a What is the diameter of this circle?
  b Copy and complete.
     $C = \pi \times \square$
  c Use a calculator to work out the circumference.
     Give your answer to 1 decimal place.

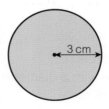

7   Work out the circumference of each circle using the formula $C = \pi \times d$.
   Give your answers to 1 decimal place.

> **Q7 hint** Work out the diameter first.

  a 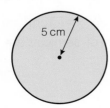   b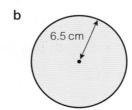

8 A circle has a radius of 8 cm.
   a Work out its diameter.
   b Copy and complete to write its circumference in terms of π.
      $C = \square\,\pi$

9 Work out the diameter d of the circles with these circumferences.
Give your answers to 1 decimal place.
   a 12 mm   **b** 8 cm   **c** 25 m
   d 1.8 m   **e** 300 km   **f** 0.5 mm

Q9a hint Use an inverse function machine.

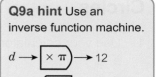

10 Area $= \pi \times \text{radius}^2$
   a What is the radius of this circle?
   b Copy and complete.
      $A = \pi \times \square^2$
   c Work out the area. Give your answer to 1 decimal place.

4 cm

11 Work out the area of each circle.

a   **b**   **c**   **d**

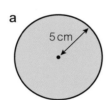 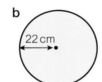 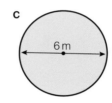 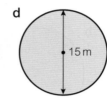

5 cm   22 cm   6 m   15 m

Q11c hint Work out the radius first.

12 A circle has a radius of 11 cm.
Write down its area in terms of π.

Q12 hint Substitute $r = 11$ into $A = \pi \times r^2$. Write your answer as $A = \square\,\pi$.

13 Work out the radius of each circle from its area.
Give your answers to 1 decimal place.
   a 31 cm^2 **b** 12 cm^2 **c** 100 cm^2
   d 2.5 m^2 **e** 500 mm^2 **f** 0.6 m^2

Q13a hint Use an inverse function machine.

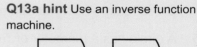
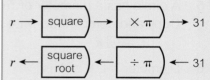

14 Here is a semicircle.
It is half a circle with a diameter of 30 cm.
Copy and complete.

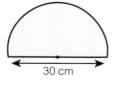

30 cm

   a Radius $= \square$ cm

   b Area of semicircle $= \frac{1}{2} \times \pi r^2$
                         $= \frac{1}{2} \times \pi \times \square^2$
                         $= \square$ cm^2

   c Curved perimeter of semicircle $= \frac{1}{2} \times \pi \times d$
                                   $= \frac{1}{2} \times \pi \times \square$
                                   $= \square$ cm

   d Total perimeter of semicircle $= \square + 30$
                                  $= \square$ cm

Pythagoras' theorem

1 **a** Copy these right-angled triangles.

   i 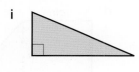   ii

   iii 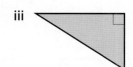   iv

Q1b hint The hypotenuse is the longest side and is opposite the right angle.

Q1c hint

 or

It doesn't matter which side length is a and which is b.

   b Label the hypotenuse of each triangle c.

   c Label the two shorter sides a and b.

2 Use the formula $c^2 = a^2 + b^2$ to find the hypotenuse c of each triangle.
   Give your answers to the nearest mm.
   The first one has been started for you.

Q2 hint Follow the same steps for the other two triangles.

   a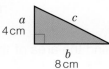

   $a = 4, b = 8$
   $c^2 = a^2 + b^2$
   $c^2 = \square^2 + \square^2 = \square$
   $c = \sqrt{\square} = \square$ (to nearest mm)

   b   **c**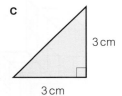

3 Use the formula $c^2 = a^2 + b^2$ to find the unknown side of each triangle.
   Give your answers to the nearest mm, where necessary.
   The first one has been started for you.

   a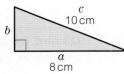

   $c^2 = a^2 + b^2$
   $10^2 = 8^2 + b^2$
   $\square = \square + b^2$
   $\square - \square = b^2$
   $b^2 = \square$
   $b = \sqrt{\square} = \square$ cm

   b 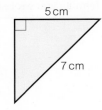   **c**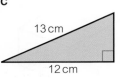

4 Problem-solving For each shape
  i use Pythagoras' theorem to work out the height, h
  ii work out the area, correct to 1 decimal place.

a
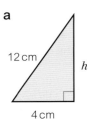
12 cm
h
4 cm

b
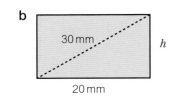
30 mm
h
20 mm

c
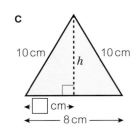
10 cm   10 cm
h
☐ cm
8 cm

d
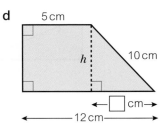
5 cm
h 10 cm
☐ cm
12 cm

Prisms and cylinders

1 Here is a cube with width, length and height of 10 mm.
  a Work out the volume of the cube.
  b Sketch the cube with its width, length and height in cm.
  c Work out the volume of the cube in cm^3.
  d Use your answers to parts **a** and **c** to copy and complete

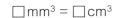
10 mm
10 mm
10 mm

   ☐ mm^3 = ☐ cm^3

  e Copy and complete
    i 2000 mm^3 = ☐ cm^3 **ii** 500 mm^3 = ☐ cm^3
    iii 2500 mm^3 = ☐ cm^3 **iv** ☐ mm^3 = 3.5 cm^3

2 **a** These prisms are made using centimetre cubes. For each prism find the area of the darker shaded surface (the cross-section) and the volume.

i
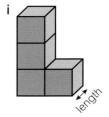
length

ii

length

iii
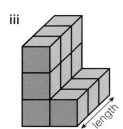
length

iv
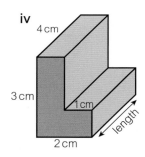
4 cm
3 cm
1 cm
2 cm
length

  b Copy and complete.
    Volume of prism = area of cross-section × ......

3 For each prism
  i sketch the cross-section
  ii work out the area of the cross-section
  iii work out the volume.

> **Q3 hint** The cross-sections are trapezia.

> **Q3iii hint** Use the formula you wrote in Q2b.

a
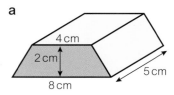
4 cm
2 cm
5 cm
8 cm

b
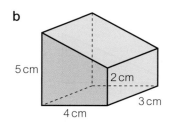
5 cm
2 cm
4 cm
3 cm

4 Work out the volume of this prism.

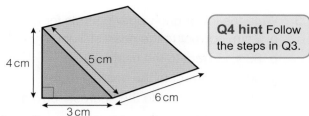

Q4 hint Follow the steps in Q3.

5 **a** How many faces does the prism in Q4 have?
   b Sketch all the faces. Label the measurements.
   c Work out the area of each face.
   d Work out the surface area of the prism.

Q5d hint The surface area is the total area of all the faces.

6 Work out the surface area of each prism.

Q6 hint Follow the same steps as in Q5.

a

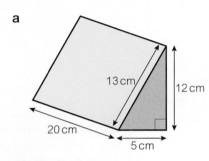

b

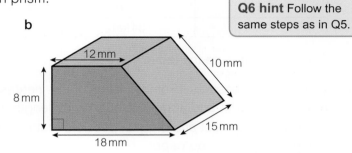

7 For each cylinder

a

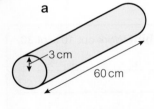

b

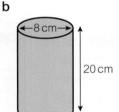

c

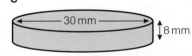

   i sketch the cross-section and label the radius
   ii work out the area of the cross-section
   iii work out the volume of the cylinder, correct to 1 decimal place.

Q7 hint
radius = half of diameter = ☐
area of circular cross-section
  = π × ☐² = ☐
volume
  = area of cross-section × height
  = ☐ × ☐ = ☐

Errors and bounds

1 Which of these measurements round to 9 cm, to the nearest cm?
   A 8.1 cm   **B** 5.2 cm   **C** 8.4 cm   **D** 9.6 cm
   E 8.6 cm   **F** 8.8 cm   **G** 9.1 cm   **H** 9.4 cm

Q1 hint Look at a ruler to help you.

2 **a** Copy this number line.

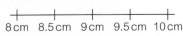

   Shade the part where all the values round to 9 cm, to the nearest cm.

Q2b hint

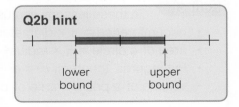

   b Write down the lower and upper bounds for the measurement.

3 Write the lower and upper bounds for each measurement.

    a 8 cm, correct to the nearest 1 cm

    b 80 g, correct to the nearest 10 g

    c 60 cm, correct to the nearest 5 cm

    d 300 cm² , correct to the nearest 100 cm²

    e 1000, correct to the nearest 50

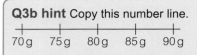

Q3b hint Copy this number line.

70 g   75 g   80 g   85 g   90 g

Shade the part where all the values round to 80 g, to the nearest 10 g.

4 The table shows the lower and upper bounds for the value x.

Q4 hint The upper bound is not included, so the 'less than' symbol is used.

Lower bound	Upper bound	Inequality
10 cm	20 cm	10 cm $\leqslant x <$ ☐
6.5 g	7.5 g	☐ $\leqslant x <$ ☐
30 km	34 km	

    Copy and complete the table.

5 A rectangle measures 15 cm by 10 cm, to the nearest 2 cm.

    a Write the lower and upper bounds for the length and the width.

    b Draw the smallest and biggest possible rectangles on centimetre squared paper.

    c Work out the area of each of your two rectangles.

    d Copy and complete the inequality for the area A.

        ☐ cm² $\leqslant A <$ ☐ cm²

Q5b hint The smallest height and width will give the smallest rectangle.

6 Use an inequality to describe the range of possible values.

    a The length x is 30 cm, to within a ±10% error interval.

    b The length x is 100 cm, to within a ±5% error interval.

    c The weight w is 200 g, to within a ±2% error interval.

    d The number n is 500, to within a ±1% error interval.

Q6a hint Work out 10% of 30.

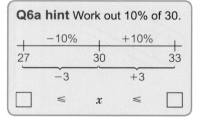

−10%   +10%

27   30   33

−3   +3

☐ $\leqslant x \leqslant$ ☐

Challenge

a How many different ways can you make this statement true?

    square number = square number + square number

b Write your answers to part **a** in the form of Pythagoras' theorem: $c^2 = a^2 + b^2$.

c Sketch and label right-angled triangles with these sides.

Part a hint Make a list of square numbers to help you.

Reflect   In these lessons you used these formulae:

- circumference = π × diameter (in Circles Q2–9)
- area of a circle = π × radius² (in Circles Q10–13)
- Pythagoras' theorem: $c^2 = a^2 + b^2$ (in Pythagoras' theorem Q2–Q4)
- volume of a prism = area of cross-section × length (in Prisms and cylinders Q2–4)

Which formula was easiest to use? Explain why.

Discuss the formula you found most difficult with a classmate.

Ask them to explain questions they answered using this formula.

7 Extend

1 Work out the area and perimeter of this shape.

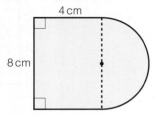

4 cm

8 cm

2 **Problem-solving** The diagram shows how three rows of four equally-spaced biscuits have been cut from a rectangular sheet of dough.
The rows and columns are 1 cm apart.
The top and bottom rows are 1 cm from the edge and so are the first and last columns.
Work out the area of dough left over.

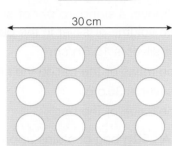

30 cm

Q2 hint Work out the diameter of a biscuit first.

3 **Problem-solving** A hedge trimmer runs on a mixture of petrol and oil in the ratio 40 : 1.
The fuel tank has the shape of a right-angled triangular prism.

a Work out the capacity of the tank.

b **i** How much oil is used to fill the tank?
  ii How much petrol is used to fill the tank?
After 10 minutes of use, the tank had 100 ml of fuel left in it.

c Work out the depth d of fuel.

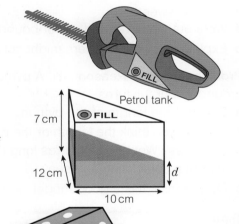

Petrol tank

7 cm

FILL

12 cm

d

10 cm

4 **Problem-solving** A 3D printer prints layers of plastic particles to build solid objects like this hexagonal prism dice.

a Work out the area of the cross-section.

b The prism has a volume of 2 cm³. Work out the length of the prism.
Each hexagonal layer is 50 μm thick.

c Work out the number of hexagonal layers needed to make the prism.

d Each layer takes 2 seconds to print.
How long does it take to print the prism?

8.7 mm

5 mm

Q4a hint Split the hexagon into two trapeziums or six equilateral triangles.

5 **Problem-solving** The diagram shows a wooden gate, where AC = 2.4 m and AD = 1 m.
Work out the total length of wood needed to make the gate.

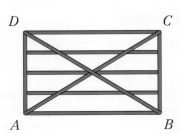

D   C

A   B

6 These lines were drawn on centimetre squared paper. Work out the length of each line, correct to 1 decimal place.

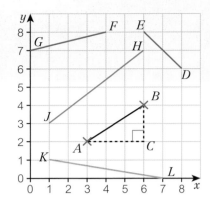

Q6 hint For the line AB, use the coordinates of A and B to find lengths AC and BC.

7 The diagram shows a standard bar of silver in the shape of a prism.
  a Work out the volume of silver in the bar.
  The density of silver is $10.5\,\text{g/cm}^3$.
  b Work out the mass of the bar, to the nearest 1 g.
  The price of silver is 35 p/g.
  c Work out the value of the bar.

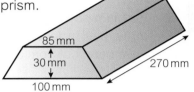

8 **Reasoning** A 250 g bag contains approximately 120 sweets.
There is a ±10% error interval in the weight of the bag and a ±5% error interval in the number of sweets.
  a Work out the lower and upper bounds for the mass m of a sweet.
  b Explain why your answers might not be accurate.

9 **Problem-solving / Reasoning** A python is tightly coiled on the ground in four full turns.
  a Estimate the length of the python.
  b How do you think the length of the python depends upon its thickness? Would it be half as long if it was half as thick? Try out a calculation and see.
  c Do you think this a good model for the length of a python?

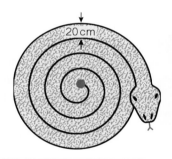

Challenge The diagram shows the inner and outer lanes of a circular race track. The tracks are 5 m apart. The finish line is shown in red.
  a The length of the inner track is 400 m. Work out its radius.
  b In a 400 m race, the runner on the inner track starts from the red line. How far in front of the red line should the runner on the outer track start?
  c How far in front of the red line should the runner on the outer track start for
    i an 800 m race   **ii** a 1500 m race?

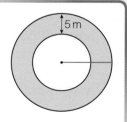

Reflect In problem-solving in mathematics and other sciences, you are not always told the steps to follow or the formula to use. You have to think of them for yourself.
Look back at Q6.
Why do you think the hint suggests that your first step is to work out the length of AC?
What formula did you use? Why?

Hint If you find AC, then you can ____. Then, this means you can ____.

7 Unit test

1 A circle has a radius of 4.2 cm.
  a Work out the diameter of the circle.
  b Work out the circumference of the circle.
     Use a sensible degree of accuracy for your answer.

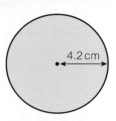

2 A circle has a circumference of 45 m.
  Work out
  a the diameter   **b** the radius   **c** the area.
  Give your answers to an appropriate degree of accuracy.

3 Calculate the length of the unknown side of each triangle.

  a 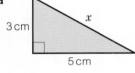   **b**

  Give your answers to the nearest mm.

4 A circle has an area of 2 m².
  a Work out the radius of the circle, correct to 2 decimal places.
  b Work out the circumference, correct to the nearest cm.

5 Work out the volume of this prism. Write your answer
  a in cm³   **b** in mm³.

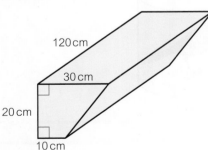

6 A wheel has a diameter of 40 cm, to the nearest 10 cm.
  Write an inequality to show
  a the lower and upper bounds for the diameter d of the wheel
  b the lower and upper bounds for the circumference C of the wheel.

7 A rectangle has length 5 m and height 3 m, measured to the nearest 1 m.
  Work out the lower and upper bounds for the area A of the rectangle.
  Write your answer using an inequality.

8   A pack of mixed flower bulbs contains 20 bulbs, to within a ±10% error interval.
    a Work out the minimum and maximum possible number of bulbs in a pack.
    b Write the number of bulbs n in a pack using an inequality.

9   **a** Work out the area of the cross-section of this prism.
    b Work out the length of the sloping side, l.
    c Work out the total surface area of the prism.

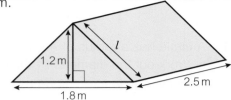

10 A cylinder has a radius of 5 cm and a height of 12 cm.
    a Work out the volume of the cylinder, correct to the nearest cm^3.
    b Work out the total surface area of the cylinder, correct to the nearest cm^2.

11 The world's biggest coin is an Australian $1 million pure gold coin.
    It has a diameter of 80 cm and a thickness of 12 cm.
    a Work out the volume of the coin, to the nearest cm^3.
    b The density of gold is 19.3 g/cm^3.
       Work out the mass of the coin, to the nearest kg.
    c The price of pure gold is $44.50 per gram.
       Is the coin worth $1 million?
       Explain your answer.

Challenge   A garden centre sells bird food in cylindrical tubs.
Which tub provides the best value for money?
Which is the worst value?

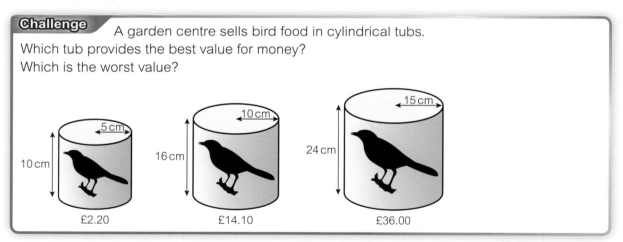

Reflect   This unit is called 'Circles, Pythagoras and prisms'.
Which of these topics did you like best? Why?
Which of these topics did you like least? Why?

8 Graphs

Master   Check up p203   Strengthen p205   Extend p210   Unit test p213

8.1 Using $y = mx + c$

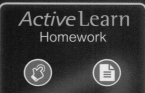

Active Learn
Homework

- Draw a graph from its equation, without working out points
- Write the equation of a line parallel to another line
- Compare graph lines using their equations

Warm up

1 Fluency

a Which graph has positive gradient?
Which has negative gradient?

b What are the x- and y-intercepts of each graph?

2 For each line

a work out the gradient

b write down the y-intercept

c write down the equation.

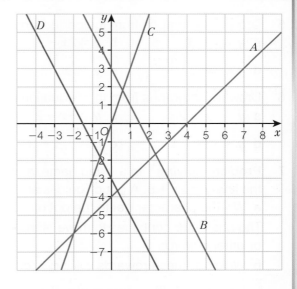

3 Reasoning

a Look at lines A and C in Q2.
Which line is steeper?

b How can you tell which line is steeper just by looking at the equations?

c Look at lines B and D in Q2.
What can you say about the gradients of parallel lines?

4 Fluency

a What is the gradient of the graph of $y = 2x + 5$?

b What is the y-intercept?

Key point You can identify the y-intercept and gradient from the equation of a straight line, and use these to draw its graph.

Worked example

Draw the graph of $y = 2x - 1$ from its equation.

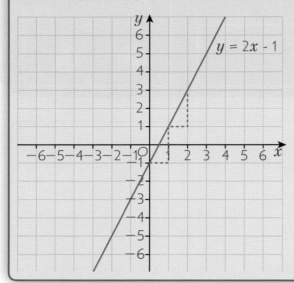

Identify the y-intercept from the equation. Plot the y-intercept.

Identify the gradient from the equation. Decide if the gradient is positive or negative. Draw a line with this gradient, starting from the y-intercept.

Extend your line to the edges of the grid. Label the graph with its equation.

5   Draw these graphs from their equations.
   a $y = x + 3$ **b** $y = 2x - 2$ **c** $y = 3x$

   d $y = 3x - 1$ **e** $y = \frac{1}{2}x$ **f** $y = \frac{1}{2}x + 3$

6   Draw these graphs from their equations.
   a $y = -x + 2$ **b** $y = -x - 2$ **c** $y = -2x + 2$

   d $y = -3x + 1$ **e** $y = -\frac{1}{2}x + 3$ **f** $y = -\frac{1}{2}x - 3$

> **Q6a hint** Gradient −1 means 1 down for every 1 across to the right.

7   **Problem-solving**   In a video game, a character moves along on the line $y = 2x + 5$. A pot of gold is at the point (3, 8).
   a Will the character get to the pot of gold?
   The character continues to move along the same line in search of other rewards.
   b Which of these rewards will it get to?

   axe at (−1, 3)   crown at (−2, −1)   shield at (−2.5, 0)

8   **Reasoning**
   a Without drawing the graphs, sort these equations into pairs of parallel lines.

   A $y = -2x + 3$ **B** $y = \frac{1}{2}x + 3$
   C $y = 2x - 3$ **D** $y = -2x - 23$
   E $y = 2x + 3$ **F** $y = 0.5x - 3$

   b Which of the equations in part **a** give lines that intercept the y-axis in the same place?

9 **Problem-solving**   Write the equation of a line parallel to
   a $y = 3x + 4$ **b** $y = -2x + 6$

Q9 hint What has to be the same in the equation? What has to be different?

10 **Problem-solving**   Write the equation of the line
   a parallel to $y = 3x + 5$ with y-intercept $(0, -2)$
   b parallel to $y = -4x + 6$ that passes through $(0, 3)$
   c parallel to $y = 2x - 3$ that passes through the origin.

11 **a** What is the x-coordinate of every point on the line $x = 4$?
   b Where does the line $y = 2x + 1$ cross the line $x = 4$?

Q11 hint Substitute your x-value from part a into the equation of the line to get the y-value. Write the x- and y-values as coordinates.

12 **Problem-solving**   In a video game, a hungry caterpillar
   moves along the line $y = 3x + 2$. An apple moves along the line $x = 3$.
   Where could the caterpillar eat the apple?

13 **Problem-solving**   Find the coordinates of the point
   a where the line $y = x + 4$ crosses the line $y = 5$
   b where the line $y = 2x + 5$ crosses the line $y = -3$.

14 A sales team boss uses a graph of this equation to work out
   the monthly pay for his staff.
   $y = 25x + 1500$
   where x is the number of items sold and y is the total monthly
   pay (£).
   a Draw the graph of this equation.
   The pay includes a basic payment (£), and then an amount (£) for each item they sell.
   b What is the basic payment?
   c How much do they get for each item they sell?

Q14a hint Choose scales for your axes so that your graph will fit on the page.

Challenge   A games designer has an alien moving on the line $y = 3x - 1$,
a spaceship on the line $y = 2x + 3$ and a stormtrooper on the line $y = 3x + 2$.
a   Can the alien get back to the spaceship?
b   Can the stormtrooper catch the alien? Explain.

Reflect   Write down, in your own words, as many facts about gradients of straight lines
as you can.
Compare your facts with your classmates'.

8.2 More straight-line graphs

- Draw graphs with equations in the form $ax + by = c$
- Rearrange equations of graphs into the form $y = mx + c$

*Active*Learn
Homework

Warm up

1 Solve

a $2x = -6$ **b** $-3y = 15$ **c** $-4z = -12$

2 Make y the subject of

a $2x + y = 3$ **b** $2x - y = 5$ **c** $3y - x = 4$

3 **a** What is the value of x at any point on the y-axis?

   b What is the value of y at any point on the x-axis?

   c Copy and complete.

     i The y-intercept of a graph has x-coordinate ☐.

     ii The x-intercept of a graph has y-coordinate ☐.

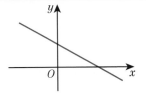

Key point

Graphs with equations of the form $ax + by = c$ are linear.

To find the y-intercept of a graph, find the y-coordinate where $x = 0$.

To find the x-intercept of a graph, find the x-coordinate where $y = 0$.

Worked example

Draw the graph of $3x + 4y = 6$.

When $x = 0$,

$3 \times 0 + 4y = 6$ To find the y-intercept, substitute $x = 0$ into the equation. Solve to find the value of y.

$4y = 6$

$y = \dfrac{6}{4} = \dfrac{3}{2} = 1\dfrac{1}{2}$

When $y = 0$,

$3x + 4 \times 0 = 6$ To find the x-intercept, substitute $y = 0$ into the equation. Solve to find the value of x.

$3x = 6$

$x = 2$

x	0	2
y	$1\dfrac{1}{2}$	0

Draw a table of values with $x = 0$ and $y = 0$.

Plot the points and join them with a straight line. Label the graph with its equation.

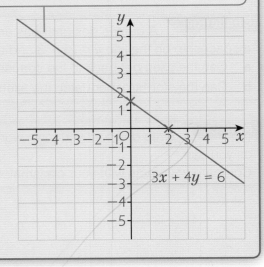

4 Draw these graphs.

   a $x + y = 3$ **b** $2x + y = 1$ **c** $3x + y = 3$

   d $3x + 2y = 3$ **e** $x + 3y = 6$ **f** $2x + 3y = -12$

5 Draw these graphs.

    a $x - y = 3$ **b** $2y - x = 2$ **c** $2x - y = -4$

6 **Problem-solving / Reasoning** The equation $36x - 5y = 160$ links the temperature in degrees Celsius (x) to the number of times a cricket chirps in 1 minute (y).

    a Draw a graph for this equation.

      Draw your x-axis from 0 to 20 and your y-axis from −40 to 140.

> **Q6a hint** Round your values for x and y to the nearest whole number if necessary.

    b Do crickets chirp more or less as it gets hotter?

    c Use your graph to estimate

      i the number of times a cricket chirps when the temperature is 20 °C

      ii the temperature when a cricket chirps 80 times per minute.

    d Why can't you use the graph to estimate the number of cricket chirps when the temperature is less than 5 °C?

7 **a** Rearrange $2y - x = 8$ to make y the subject.

    b Use your rearranged equation to find the gradient of the graph of $2y - x = 8$.

> **Key point**   To find the gradient or y-intercept of a straight-line graph with an equation $ax + by = c$, rearrange its equation into the form $y = mx + c$.

8 Which is the steepest line?

    A $y = 2x + 3$ **B** $3x + 2y = 5$ **C** $y = \frac{1}{4}x - 5$ **D** $10x + 5y = 7$ **E** $2y - 7x = 8$

9 **Problem-solving** Are any of these lines parallel? If so, which ones? Show your working.

    A $5x + 2y = 10$ **B** $2y - x = 5$ **C** $2x - y = 5$ **D** $2x + 12y = 4$

10 **a** Rearrange $x + 3y = 6$ to make y the subject.

    b Use your rearranged equation to find the gradient of the graph of $x + 3y = 6$.

11 **Problem-solving** Which of these lines pass through $(0, -2)$? Show how you worked it out.

    A $y = -2x + 2$ **B** $2y - 3x = -4$ **C** $3x + 2y = 4$ **D** $5x + y = -10$ **E** $y = 3x - 2$

12 **Reasoning** Here are two ways to draw graphs of linear equations.

    • The worked example in lesson 8.1 suggested that you plot the y-intercept, and then draw a line from the y-intercept with the correct gradient.

    • The worked example in lesson 8.2 suggested that you draw and complete a table, like the one shown here, and then plot the points and join them with a straight line.

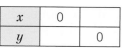

x	0	
y		0

    Which method is better for each of these equations?

    a $y = 4x + 1$ **b** $2x + 3y = 5$

    Explain why.

> **Challenge**   Explain why each of these equations could be the odd one out.
>
>   **A** $y = 2x - 3$ **B** $y = 2x$ **C** $y + 2x = 4$ **D** $2y = 5 + 4x$

> **Reflect**   Is it enough to plot only one point to draw a straight-line graph? What about two points? Explain. What is the advantage of plotting three points?

8.3 Simultaneous equations

Active Learn
Homework

- Solve simultaneous equations by drawing graphs
- Solve problems using simultaneous equations

Warm up

1 **Fluency** Which of these lines has a gradient of $-\frac{3}{2}$?

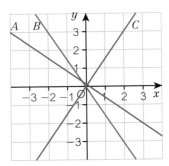

2 a On the same grid, plot the graphs of $y = 5$ and $2x + y = 8$.
   b Write down the coordinates of the point where they cross.

3 Write an equation for each of these situations.
   a It costs £41 for 2 adults and 3 children to go to the cinema.
     Use x for adults and y for children.
   b 3 ice lolly sticks and 2 cocktail sticks measure 40 cm in total.
     Use x for ice lolly sticks and y for cocktail sticks.
   c 5 LED lightbulbs and 3 halogen bulbs cost £12.
     Use x and y, and explain what they represent in your equation.

> **Key point** The point where two (or more) graphs cross is called the **point of intersection**.

4 a Plot each pair of graphs on the same grid.
     i $x + y = 6$ ii $2x + y = 4$ iii $2x + y = 6$
        $y = 2x$ $x - y = 2$ $x - 2y = 8$
   b Write down the coordinates of their point of intersection.

> **Key point** **Simultaneous equations** are two or more equations that, when solved, have the same values for all the unknowns. You can find the solution to a pair of simultaneous equations by
> - drawing the graphs on the same coordinate grid
> - then finding the point of intersection.

Worked example

Draw graphs to solve the simultaneous equations

$x + 2y = 10$
$2x - y = 5$

For $x + 2y = 10$ —————— Consider the first equation.

When $x = 0$, —————— Find the value of y when $x = 0$.
$0 + 2y = 10$
$2y = 10$
$y = 5$

When $y = 0$, —————— Find the value of x when $y = 0$.
$x + 2 × 0 = 10$
$x = 10$

x	0	10
y	5	0

Consider the second equation.

For $2x - y = 5$ —————— Rearrange to make y the subject.
$y = 2x - 5$

the y-intercept is at $(0, -5)$ —————— Identify the y-intercept and gradient.
the gradient is 2. (Instead, you could find the value of y when $x = 0$ and the value of x when $y = 0$.)

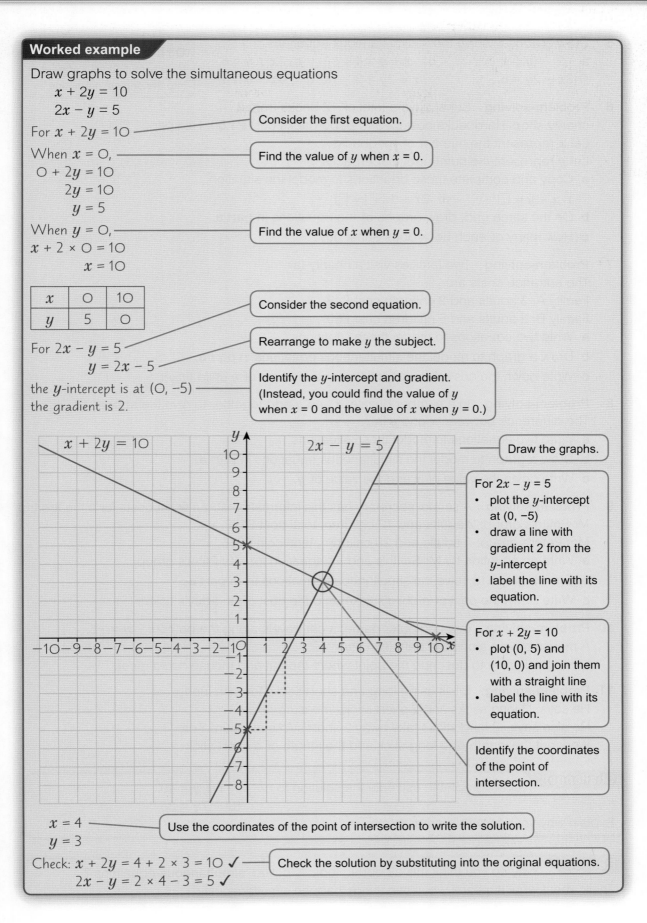

Draw the graphs.

For $2x - y = 5$
• plot the y-intercept at $(0, -5)$
• draw a line with gradient 2 from the y-intercept
• label the line with its equation.

For $x + 2y = 10$
• plot $(0, 5)$ and $(10, 0)$ and join them with a straight line
• label the line with its equation.

Identify the coordinates of the point of intersection.

$x = 4$ —————— Use the coordinates of the point of intersection to write the solution.
$y = 3$

Check: $x + 2y = 4 + 2 × 3 = 10$ ✓ —————— Check the solution by substituting into the original equations.
$2x - y = 2 × 4 - 3 = 5$ ✓

5   Draw graphs to solve these simultaneous equations.

   a $y = x$ **b** $x + y = 4$ **c** $3x + y = 6$
         $3x - 2y = 6$ $x + 2y = 3$ $4x - y = 1$

> **Q5 hint** Check your solution by substituting your answer into the original equations.

6   **Problem-solving**   Suhal buys a total of 12 books from a
    charity shop. Hardbacks cost £2 and paperbacks cost £1.50. He spends £21.
    Let x represent the number of hardbacks.
    Let y represent the number of paperbacks.
    a Copy and complete these equations to model the situation.
       i $x + y = \square$ **ii** $2x + 1.5\square = \square$
    b On the same grid, draw graphs of the equations in part **a**.
    c How many of each book does Suhal buy?

7   **Problem-solving**   Two families visit a charity fair.
    The entrance costs are:
    Family A: 3 adults and 2 children cost £42.
    Family B: 2 adults and 5 children cost £50.
    a Write two equations to model these situations.
    b Draw a graph to model the simultaneous equations in part **a**.
    c Write down the cost of an adult ticket and the cost of a child ticket.

8   **Problem-solving**   In a number puzzle, x and y add together to give the answer 18.
    The difference between x and y is 7.
    a Write two equations to model these situations.
    b Draw a graph to model the simultaneous equations in part **a**.
    c Write down the value of x and the value of y.

9   **Problem-solving**   A school secretary has this information about ticket costs for a theatre trip.
    Mr Smith's group: 2 adults and 12 children, total cost £150.
    Mrs Patel's group: 5 adults and 20 children, total cost £275.
    a Write an equation for Mr Smith's and an equation for Mrs Patel's group.
    b Draw a graph to solve the simultaneous equations from part **a**.
    c Write down the cost of a child's ticket and the cost of an adult's ticket.

10 **Problem-solving**   In a computer game, a cat travels along the path $2x - y = -6$.
    A mouse travels along the path $3x + 2y = 12$.
    Use coordinates to describe the point where the cat and mouse could meet.

11 **Problem-solving**   Bill is using long and short sticks for measuring.
    He says, '3 long sticks and 2 short sticks measure 48 cm.'
    He also says, '2 long sticks take away 2 short sticks measure 7 cm.'
    Work out the length of a long stick and the length of a short stick.

Challenge   Draw graphs to estimate the solution to $x + y = 40$
                                                            $5x - 7y = 35$
Explain why your answer is an estimate.

Reflect   Why do you think this algebraic topic is called '**simultaneous** equations'?
Think about what it means when two things happen simultaneously.

8.4 Graphs of quadratic functions

Active Learn
Homework

- Draw graphs with quadratic equations in the form $y = x^2$
- Interpret graphs of quadratic functions

Warm up

1 **Fluency** What is the formula for the area, $A \, cm^2$, of
  a a square with side length $l \, cm$
  b a circle with radius $r \, cm$?

2 Work out the value of $3x^2$ when
  a $x = 1$
  b $x = 4$
  c $x = -1$

3 Solve
  a $x^2 = 16$
  b $x^2 + 4 = 40$

Key point
A **quadratic equation** contains a term in x^2 but no higher power of x.
The graph of a quadratic equation is a curved shape called a **parabola**.

4 **a** Copy and complete this table of values for $y = x^2$.

x	−4	−3	−2	−1	0	1	2	3	4
y									

  b Draw a coordinate grid with x-axis from −5 to +5 and y-axis from 0 to 20.
  c Plot the points for $y = x^2$ using your table of values from part **a**.
  d Draw the graph of $y = x^2$ by joining the points with a smooth curve.
  e Label your graph $y = x^2$.

5 **a** Copy and complete this table of values for $y = 4x^2$.

x	−2	−1	0	1	2
y					

  b Draw the graph of $y = 4x^2$. Label your graph with its equation.

> **Q5b hint** Use axes like the ones in Q4.

6 **Reasoning** Look at your graphs from Q4 and Q5.
  a What is the same about them?
  b Describe the symmetry of each graph by giving the equation of its mirror line.

7 The graph shows the area, $A\,cm^2$, of squares with different side lengths, $l\,cm$.
   a What is the equation of the curve?
   b Use the graph to estimate
      i the area of a square of side length 5.5 cm
      ii the side length of a square of area 10 cm².
   c **Problem-solving** How accurate is your answer
      i to part **b i**   ii to part **b ii**?
   d **Reasoning** Why is the graph only plotted for positive values of l?

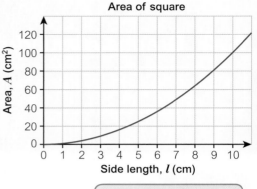
Area of square

Q7c hint How could you calculate these answers accurately without using the graph?

8 The approximate area, $A\,cm^2$, of a circle with radius $r\,cm$ is given by the formula $A = 3r^2$.
   a Copy and complete this table of values for $A = 3r^2$.

r	0	1	2	3	4	5
A						

   b Draw the graph of $A = 3r^2$.
   c Use your graph to estimate
      i the area of a circle with radius 2.5 cm
      ii the radius of a circle with area 45 cm².
   d **Problem-solving** How accurate is your answer
      i to part **c i**   ii to part **c ii**?

9 a Copy and complete this table of values for $y = x^2 - 1$.

x	−3	−2	−1	0	1	2	3
x^2							
−1	−1	−1	−1	−1	−1	−1	−1
y							

Q9a hint For quadratic functions with more than one step, you can include a row for each step in the table.

   b Draw the graph of $y = x^2 - 1$.

10 Draw the graph of $y = x^2 + 3$.

Q10 hint Draw and complete a table as in Q9.

11 **Problem-solving** Look at your graphs from Q4, Q9 and Q10.
    a What is the same about them?
    b What is different about them?
    c Describe what the graph of $y = x^2 + 7$ will look like.

Q11c hint Describe the shape, the symmetry and where it crosses the y-axis.

12 a Draw the line $y = 7$ on the same grid as your graph of $y = x^2 + 3$.
    b Write down the coordinates of the points of intersection with the parabola.
       The x-coordinates are the solutions to the equation $x^2 + 3 = 7$.
    c i Use your graph to estimate two solutions to the equation $x^2 + 3 = 9$.
       ii Use algebra to solve the equation $x^2 + 3 = 9$.
          Give your answer to 1 decimal place.
       iii How close was your estimate from your graph?
    d **Reasoning** Are there any solutions to the equation $x^2 + 3 = 1$? Explain.

Q12c i hint Draw the line $y = \square$.

13 Problem-solving

A sports coach videos players kicking a ball. He uses a computer to plot the paths of the ball for kicks at different angles.

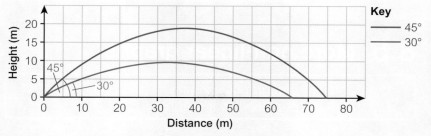

Key
— 45°
— 30°

a What is the maximum height reached by the ball kicked at a 45° angle?

b How far does the ball kicked at 30° travel?

c Rugby goal posts have a cross bar 3 m above the ground. Write some tips for rugby players on how to kick the ball to clear the cross bar.

> **Q13c hint** Think about the angle of kick and the distance from the posts.

14 Problem-solving / Reasoning

A scientist studying the effect of gravity measures the distance fallen each second by an object dropped from the top of a tall building.

Time (s)	1	2	3	4	5	6	7
Distance (m)	5	20	45	80	125	180	245

a Draw a graph for this data.

b What type of graph do you think this is?

c When is the object falling fastest?

> **Q14a hint** Choose your axes so that your graph will fit on the page.

d A bungee jumper uses a bungee that stretches to 200 m.
   Use the graph to estimate how many seconds the bungee jumper will fall before they bounce back up again.

Challenge

a Draw a table of values for $y = -x^2$.

b i Plot the graphs of $y = x^2$ and $y = -x^2$ on the same axes.
   ii What do you notice?

> **Part a hint** You could use a table like the one in Q4.

c Look at your graph of $y = 4x^2$ that you drew in Q5.
   i Predict what the graph of $y = -4x^2$ will look like.
   ii Draw a table of values for $y = -4x^2$ and plot the graph to check your prediction.

d If you are given the graph of $y = 2x^2$, how can you draw the graph of $y = -2x^2$?
   Write an explanation.

> **Part d hint** Use the correct language to describe a transformation.

Reflect

Use what you have learned so far in this unit to write an equation that could fit each of these graphs.
How did you decide on an equation for each of the graphs?

A

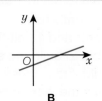

B

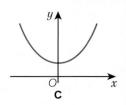

C

Compare your equations with a classmate. In what ways are your equations the same? In what ways are they different?

8.5 More non-linear graphs

- Draw and interpret graphs showing inverse proportion.
- Draw and interpret non-linear graphs

Active Learn
Homework

Warm up

1 **Fluency** Which integers are included in the inequality shown on this number line?

2 Work out the volume of this cylinder. Give your answer to the nearest cm^3.

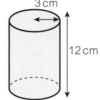

3 cm

12 cm

3 It takes 3 thatchers 30 days to thatch a cottage roof.
Is the number of days in direct or inverse proportion to the number of thatchers? Explain.

4 In each table, x and y are in inverse proportion. For each table

    i write the relationship $y = \dfrac{k}{x}$ and use values from the table to work out the value of k

    ii write the formula connecting x and y.

a
x	1	3	5
y	15	5	3

b
x	2	4	8
y	4	2	1

5 **Reasoning** The graph shows the number of days it takes different numbers of workers to build a theatre set.

    a How long would it take

      i 2 workers

      ii 3 workers?

    b How many workers are required to build the theatre set in 1 day?

    c The theatre currently has 1 full-time worker and 1 half-time worker available to build the set. How long would it take these workers to build the theatre set?

    d Write the relationship $y = \dfrac{k}{x}$ and use values you found in parts **a** and **b** to work out the value of k.

    e Write a formula connecting number of days and number of workers.

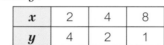

Days taken to build
a theatre set

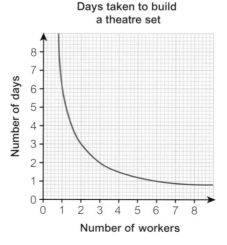

Number of days

Number of workers

Q4c hint This is the same as 1.5 workers.

Q4d hint y is number of days and x is number of workers.

6 The graph shows the relationship between the pressure P, in bar, and the volume V, in cm³, of gas in a petrol-engine cylinder.

Engine cylinder pressure

a Copy and complete this table of values.

Volume, V (cm³)	20	40	50	100
Pressure, P (bar)				

b Write the relationship $y = \dfrac{k}{x}$ and use values from your table to work out the value of k.

c Write an equation connecting P and V.

7 A scientist recorded the number of bacteria in a sample.

Time (hours)	0	1	2	3	4	5
Number of bacteria	1	2	4	8	16	32

a How many bacteria would you expect there to be after 6 hours?

b Draw a pair of axes with Time (x) from 0 to 10 and Number of bacteria (y) from 0 to 1100.

c Plot the points on the axes from your table and join them with a smooth curve.

d Continue the curve up to 10 hours.

e Use your graph to estimate how many bacteria there will be after
  i $6\frac{1}{2}$ hours   **ii** $8\frac{1}{2}$ hours.

> **Q6d hint**
> Extend the table of values up to 10 hours.

> **Key point**   When two quantities are in inverse proportion
> - plotting them on a graph gives a curve
> - when one variable doubles, the other halves
> - when one triples, the other is divided by 3, and so on.

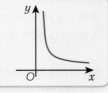

8 Look back at the graphs in Q5, Q6 and Q7.
Which graphs show values in inverse proportion? Explain.

9 **Problem-solving**   The graph shows the count rate against time for iodine-128, which is a radioactive material.
The count rate is the number of radioactive emissions per second.

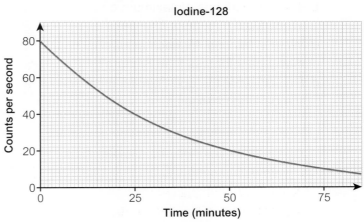

a What is the count rate after 50 minutes?

b After how many minutes is the count rate 50?

c The half-life of a radioactive material is the time it takes for the count rate to halve.
What is the half-life of iodine-128?

d **Reasoning**   Does the count rate ever reach zero?

10 Problem-solving A scientist counts the number of bacteria in a culture every hour.

Time (hours)	0	1	2	3	4	5
Number of bacteria	2	4	7	14	27	53

The table shows her results.

a Draw a graph to show these results.

b How many bacteria are there after $2\frac{1}{2}$ hours?

c The scientist says, 'A model for the growth of these bacteria is 'double every hour'.'
On the same grid, draw a graph starting with 2 bacteria at time 0 hours, and doubling every hour.

d How good is the scientist's model?

11 Problem-solving The table gives the volumes of cylinders with height 15 cm and radius r, for different values of r.

Radius, r (cm)	0	1	2	3	4	5
Volume of cylinder with radius r and height 15 cm (cm³)	0	47	188	424		

The volumes are rounded to the nearest cm³.

a Copy and complete the table.

b Plot a graph for these values.
Put radius on the horizontal axis and volume on the vertical axis.

c A cylinder 15 cm high has a radius 2.5 cm.
Estimate its volume from your graph.

d 250 cm³ of stainless steel is melted down and made into a cylinder with height 15 cm.
Estimate the radius of the cylinder using your graph.

> **Key point** A **step graph** has a constant value for given intervals. Empty circles show that a value is not included in an interval.
> A step graph is an example of a **piecewise graph**, as it is made up of pieces.

12 Problem-solving / Reasoning The graph shows the charges for a car park.

a How much do you pay to park for $3\frac{1}{2}$ hours?

b The car park has a maximum charge. What is the maximum charge?

c What is the cost for each additional hour if you park for less than 8 hours?

d Explain what the open circles mean for the parking charges.

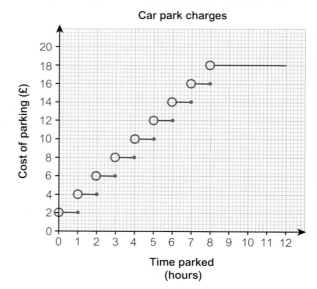

Car park charges

13 **Problem-solving / Reasoning**   A phone contract includes up to 1 GB of free data each month.
The graph shows how much you pay if you reach the
1 GB limit (1 GB = 1000 MB).

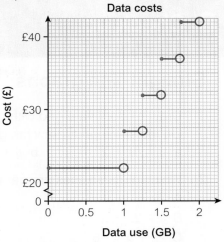

Data costs

  a How much is the phone contract each month if you
     use less than 1 GB of data?

  b How much do you pay if you use these amounts of
     data in a month?

     i 1 GB   ii 1.25 GB
     iii 1.5 GB   iv 1.4 GB

  c After the first gigabyte, how much does each extra
     250 MB of data cost?

  d Saleem paid £42.
     Can you tell exactly how much data Saleem used?
     Explain.

14 The table below shoes the cost of sending parcels of different weights, up to 15 kg.

Weight	Cost
2 kg or below	£12
5 kg or below	£14
10 kg or below	£18
15 kg or below	£24

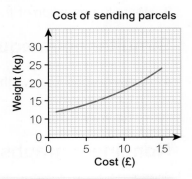

Cost of sending parcels

  a **Reasoning**   Jonathan uses the table to draw this graph.
     Explain why Jonathan's graph is not correct.

  b Draw the correct graph for the information in the table.

8 Check up

Straight-line graphs

1   Draw a coordinate grid with both axes from −10 to +10.
    On the same grid, draw the graphs of
    a $y = 4x - 2$ **b** $y + 2x = -4$

2   Which of these lines are parallel?
    A $2x + 3y = 10$
    B $y = 2x + 3$
    C $2x + y = -6$
    D $3y = 6x + 18$

3   Write the equation of the line parallel to $y = -2x + 5$ with y-intercept (0, 3).

Simultaneous equations

4   Draw graphs to solve these simultaneous equations.
    $$x + 2y = 8$$
    $$6x + 2y = 18$$

Non-linear graphs

5   Draw the graph of $y = 5x^2$.

6   The graph shows the number of days it takes different numbers of volunteers to set up tents in a festival field.
    a How long would it take
       i 2 volunteers
       ii 3 volunteers
       iii 2 full-time volunteers and 1 half-time volunteer
    b The organiser wants the tents set up in 2 days.
       How many volunteers does she need?
    c Write the relationship $y = \dfrac{k}{x}$ and work out the value of k.
    d Write a formula connecting the number of the days and the number of volunteers.
    e Describe the relationship between the number of volunteers and the number of days.

Days taken to set up tents

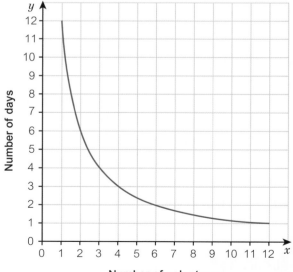

Number of volunteers

7 The graph shows an online company's
charges for parcel postage and packing.

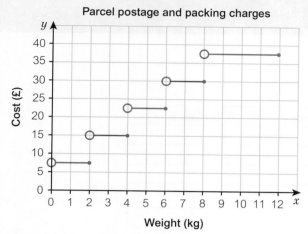

Parcel postage and packing charges

a How much is postage and packing for a parcel that is
   i 3 kg
   ii 8 kg
   iii 7.5 kg?
b What is the cost for each additional 2 kg, for parcels up to 8 kg?

8 Strengthen

Straight-line graphs

1　a Copy and complete the table.

$y = mx + c$	Gradient m	y-intercept $(0, c)$
$y = 3x - 4$		
$y = 5x + 4$		
$y = -2x + 1$		
$y = \frac{1}{2}x - 4$		
$y = 3x - 3$		

b Write down the equations of the lines that are parallel.

c Write down the equations of the lines that have the same y-intercept.

d Which line slopes in the opposite direction to the others? What is different about its equation?

> **Q1b hint** Parallel lines have the same _____.

2　a **Problem-solving** Sort these equations of straight-line graphs into two sets: one set with y-intercept $(0, 1)$ and the other set with y-intercept $(0, -1)$.

　　A $y = \frac{1}{2}x + 1$　　**B** $y = 2x - 1$　　**C** $y = 2x + 1$　　**D** $y = -x - 1$

b Next to each equation write the gradient and its direction: positive ⟋ or ⟍ negative

> **Q2b hint** $-x = -1 \times x$

c Match each graph to an equation from part **a**.

i 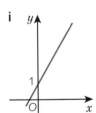　**ii** 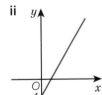　**iii** 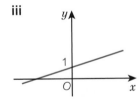　**iv**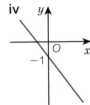

3 On squared paper, draw lines with these gradients. The first one is done for you.

a gradient $-\frac{1}{2}$

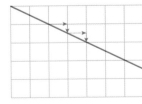

Gradient $-\frac{1}{2}$

b gradient $\frac{1}{2}$　　　**c** gradient 2　　　**d** gradient -2

4 Draw a coordinate grid with both axes from -10 to $+10$. On the same grid, draw the graphs of

a $y = -\frac{1}{2}x + 1$　　**b** $y = \frac{1}{2}x - 1$

c $y = 2x + 4$　　　　**d** $y = -2x - 3$

> **Q4 hint** Use your answers to Q2 and Q3 to help you identify and draw the y-intercept and gradient.

5 **a** **i** **Reasoning** What is the same about these lines?

   ii What is different about them?

Q5a hint Use these words: gradient, y-intercept.

   b Which of these equations give lines parallel to $y = 4x - 3$?

   A $y = 4x - 5$ **B** $y = 2x + 4$
   C $y = 4x + 5$ **D** $y = 10x - 4$

   c Which of lines A to D is parallel to $y = 4x - 3$ and has y-intercept (0, 5)?

   d Write the equation of the line parallel to $y = 4x - 3$ with y-intercept (0, 10).

   e Write the equations of three more lines parallel to $y = 4x - 3$.

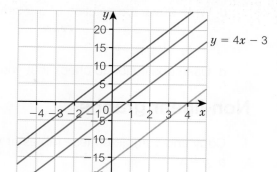

6 **a** For the equation $x + 2y = 6$

   i When $x = 0$, what is the value of y?
   Write the y-intercept as coordinates $(0, \square)$.

   ii When $y = 0$, what is the value of x?
   Write the x-intercept as coordinates $(\square, 0)$.

   b Plot the points you found in part **a**, and join them with a straight line.

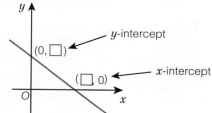

7 Draw a coordinate grid with both axes from -10 to $+10$.
On the same grid, draw the graphs of

   a $x + 3y = 6$ **b** $2x + y = 5$

Q7 hint Use the method in Q6. Label each graph with its equation.

8 **a** A, B and C are equations of straight lines.
   Rearrange each equation to make y the subject.

   A $y - 3x = 4$ **B** $y + 3x = 2$ **C** $6x + 2y = -2$

   b Write down the gradient of each line.

   c Which lines are parallel?

Simultaneous equations

1 **a** Draw the graph of $x + y = 6$.

   b On the same grid, draw the graph of $x + 2y = 8$.

   c Draw a small circle around the point of intersection.
   (This is where the two lines cross.)

Q1c hint

   d Write down the coordinates of the point of intersection.

   e The coordinates of the point of intersection give the solution to the simultaneous equations

   $x + y = 6$
   $x + 2y = 8$

   Copy and complete the solution: $x = 4$, $y = \square$

   f Check that your solution is correct by substituting your values of x and y from part **e** into

   i $x + y$ **ii** $x + 2y$

2 **a** Draw these graphs on the same grid.

    i $2x + 3y = 6$ **ii** $4x + 2y = -8$

  b Write down the coordinates of their point of intersection.

  c Write down the solution of the simultaneous equations

$$2x + 3y = 6$$
$$4x + 2y = -8$$

  d Use substitution to check that your solution is correct.

Non-linear graphs

1 Copy and complete these tables of values.

  a $y = x^2$

x	−3	−2	−1	0	1	2	3
x^2							

  b $y = 2x^2$

x	−3	−2	−1	0	1	2	3
x^2							
$2x^2$							

  c $y = 3x^2$

x	−3	−2	−1	0	1	2	3
x^2							
$3x^2$							

2 **a** Copy this coordinate grid.

  b Draw the graphs of $y = x^2$, $y = 2x^2$ and $y = 3x^2$ on the same grid.

  c Using a different coloured pencil, sketch $y = 5x^2$ on your grid.

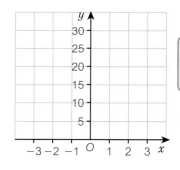

> **Q2b hint** Use the tables in Q1. Label your graphs.

3 Copy and complete these tables of values.

  a $y = x^2 + 1$

x	−3	−2	−1	0	1	2	3
x^2	9						
+1	+1	+1	+1	+1	+1	+1	+1
$x^2 + 1$	10						

  b $y = x^2 + 2$

x	−3	−2	−1	0	1	2	3
x^2	9						
+2	+2	+2	+2	+2	+2	+2	+2
$x^2 + 2$	11						

4 a Copy this coordinate grid.

b Draw the graphs of $y = x^2 + 1$ and $y = x^2 + 2$ on the same grid.

c Using a different coloured pencil, sketch $y = x^2 + 3$ on your grid.

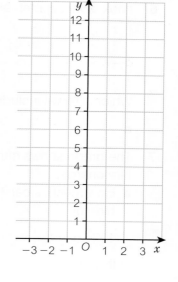

5 The graph shows the number of days it takes a team of decorators to paint a flat.

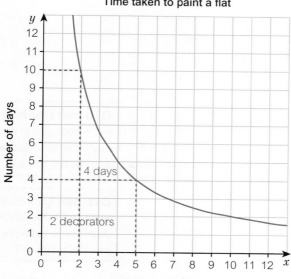

a How long would it take
  i 2 decorators   ii 4 decorators?

b How many decorators would be required to paint the flat in
  i 4 days   ii 2 days?

c Use your answers to parts **a** and **b** to copy and complete this table.

Number of decorators (x)	2	4		
Number of days (y)			4	2

d Write the relationship $y = \dfrac{k}{x}$ for each column in your table.

e Work out the value of k.

f Copy and complete to write a formula connecting number of days and number of decorators.

$$y = \frac{k}{x}$$

$$y = \frac{\square}{x}$$

$$\text{number of days} = \frac{\square}{\text{number of decorators}}$$

g Is the relationship between the number of decorators and the number of days directly proportional or inversely proportional? Give a reason.

Q5d hint $2 = \dfrac{k}{10}$

6 Look at these intervals.

A B C

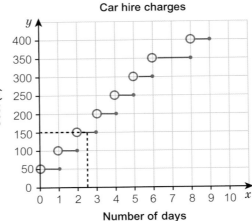

Which interval includes

a $2\frac{1}{2}$ **b** 3   **c** 2?

Q6 hint An empty circle means a number is *not* included in the interval.

7 The graph shows car hire charges.

  a How much is car hire for

    i $2\frac{1}{2}$ days

    ii 3 days

    iii 2 days?

  b What is the cost of each additional day's hire?

  c The car hire company offers one free day. When does this happen?

Q7b hint How much extra does it cost each day? Use your answers to parts **a ii** and **a iii**.

Q7c hint Look carefully at the lines. On which day do you not have to pay extra money?

Challenge

a Draw graphs of $y = 2x$ and $y = -2x$ on the same grid.

b What transformation takes $y = 2x$ on to $y = -2x$?

c Repeat for $y = x + 1$ and $y = -x + 1$.

d Repeat for $y = x^2$ and $y = -x^2$.

Part b hint There are four types of transformation: translation, reflection, rotation and enlargement.

Reflect

Sholly describes what she does when she sees a question with a graph.

> I cover the question with my hand, so I can only see the graph.
>
> I read the graph title.
>
> I read the titles of the axes.
>
> I make sure I know what one square on each axis represents.
>
> Finally, I randomly pick a point on the graph and ask myself, 'What does this point tell me?'
>
> It is really quick and always helps me to understand and answer the question.

Look at the graph in the Extend lesson, Q10.

Use Sholly's method to help you to understand the graph.

Does this help you to answer Q10a?

Is Sholly's method helpful? Explain why.

8 Extend

1 A straight-line graph has gradient 3. It goes through the point $(-2, 4)$.
   Write the equation of the line in the form $y = mx + c$ by following these steps.
   a Substitute the value for m.
   b Substitute the values of x and y for the point $(-2, 4)$.
   c Solve the equation you got in part **b** to find the value of c.
   d Write the equation of the line.

2 A straight-line graph has gradient -2. It goes through the point $(1, 3)$.
   What is the equation of the line?

3 **Problem-solving** A straight-line graph has gradient 2.
   It goes through the point $(1, 4)$ and the point $(2, a)$.
   What is the value of a?

4 **Reasoning** There is a linear relationship between the price P charged by a cleaning
   company and the number of hours h spent cleaning. The company charges £60 for 2 hours
   of cleaning and £99 for 5 hours of cleaning.
   a Copy and complete.
      Two points on the graph $P = mh + c$ are $(2, \square)$ and $(\square, 99)$.
   b Work out the equation of the line.
   c What does the gradient represent?
   d What does the y-intercept represent?

5 **Problem-solving** Here is a linear relationship between the value V of a car and its age a.
   A 5-year-old car is worth £14 000.
   The same car is worth £11 400 2 years later.
   a Work out an equation in the form $V = ma + c$.
   b What was the value of the car when it was new?

6 Copy and complete these equations so that their lines are parallel.
   $$\square x + 2y = 4 \qquad y - 2x = \square \qquad 3x - \square y = 8$$

7 **Reasoning** Adam is trying to solve this pair of simultaneous equations:
   $$2y - 6x = 2 \text{ and } y - 3x = 8$$
   Draw graphs to show why there are no solutions.

8 **Reasoning / Problem-solving** This is the graph of $y = x^2 + 2$.
   Write down the equation of a line that will never intersect
   $y = x^2 + 2$.

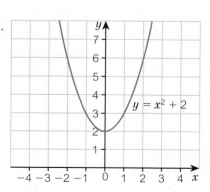

9 **Problem-solving** A teacher making a worksheet on symmetry draws two sides of a shape using a graph plotting package. Work out the equations of the two lines she needs to draw to make a shape that is symmetrical about the line $y = x$.

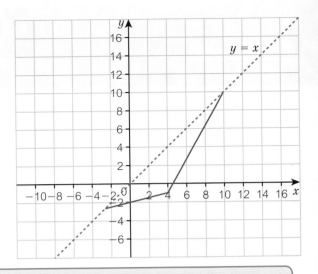

Q9 hint You could start by finding the equations of the two lines already drawn and using inverse operations, or by drawing your own diagram.

10 The tap on this water butt is opened and the water drains out. The graph shows the depth of water in the water butt over 10 minutes.

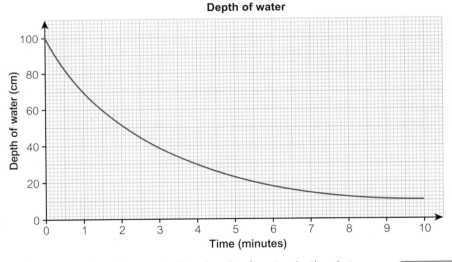

a Compare the change in the depth of water in the 1st minute with the 5th minute.

b When is the water flowing fastest? Explain how you can tell from the graph.

c How high is the tap above the bottom of the water butt?

Q10a hint The 1st minute is from 0 to 1 minute, the 5th minute is from 4 to 5 minutes.

Q10c hint What is the depth when the water stops flowing?

11 **Reasoning** Match each equation to one of the graphs below.

    i $y = x^2$ **ii** $y = -x^2$ **iii** $y = -x^2 - 2$

    iv $y = 2x^2$ **v** $y = x^2 + 2$

A 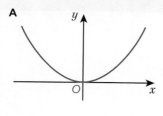   **B** 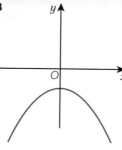   **C**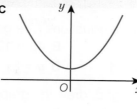

D 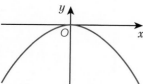   **E**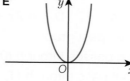

12 Sketch the graphs of
    a $y = x^2 + 5$ **b** $y = -x^2 - 5$

13 **Problem-solving** Jenni invests some money in a savings bond with a fixed rate of interest. This graph shows how her investment will grow.

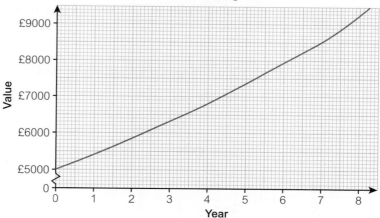

Jenni's savings bond

    a How much money will she have after 3 years?

    b When will she have £8000? How accurate do you think your answer is?

    c How much money did Jenni invest?

    d How much money did she have after 1 year?

    e Use your answers to parts **c** and **d** to work out the annual interest rate as a percentage.

> **Q13e hint** Work out the percentage change from 0 years to 1 year.

Challenge
Point A (5, □) lies on the straight line with equation $y = 4x - 11$.

a Show that Point A also lies on the straight line with equation $y = 2x - 1$.

b Write the equation of another straight line on which Point A lies.

Reflect Look back at the graphs in Q11.

a What steps did you take to match the graphs to the equations? You could begin with, 'Step 1: I looked for the U-shaped graphs, because …'

b How would you change your steps if Q11 also included the equations $y = 2x + 3$ and $2x + y = 3$ and their graphs?

> **Part b hint** What is the shape of these graphs?

8 Unit test

1 Which of these equations give parallel lines?
A $y = 3x + 2$ **B** $4y - 12x = 3$
C $5y + 15x = 1$ **D** $y = 3x + 5$

2 On the same grid, draw the graphs of
a $y = 4x - 1$ **b** $x + y = 2$

3 Which of these equations
A $y = 3x - 5$ **B** $2y - 4x = 5$
C $3y + 2x = -4$ **D** $y = 2x + 5$

  a gives the steepest graph
  b is a line that passes through (0, 5)
  c are lines that pass through (1, −2)?

4 **a** Draw the graph of $y = x^2 - 2$.
  b Use your graph to estimate two solutions to the equation $x^2 - 2 = 3$.

5 Draw graphs to solve these simultaneous equations.
$$2x - y = 9$$
$$x + 2y = 2$$

6 The graph shows a tour guide's charges for different length tours.

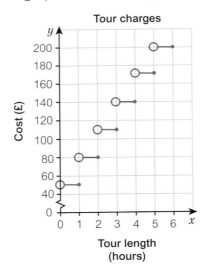

Tour charges

a How much is a tour of
  i $2\frac{1}{2}$ hours
  ii 3 hours
  iii 5 hours
  iv 30 minutes?
b What is the cost of each additional hour, after the first hour?

7 The graph shows the count rate against time for chromium-51, which is a radioactive material.

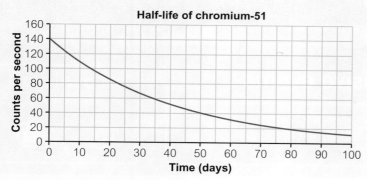

Half-life of chromium-51

a What is the count rate after 25 days?

b After how many days does the count rate reach 50?

The half-life of a radioactive material is the time it takes for the count rate to halve.

c What is the half-life of chromium-51?

The graph shows the power density P, emitted by a wi-fi router at a distance of d metres.

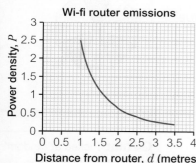

Wi-fi router emissions

a Estimate the power density at a distance of 1.5 m.

b Safety guidelines suggest that a person should not be exposed to a power density above 1 unit. Estimate the recommended minimum distance between a router and a person.

c The formula connecting the power density, P, and the distance d is

$$P = \frac{2.5}{d^2}$$

Use the formula to calculate P when $d = 0.5$ m.

d Use the formula to check your estimate to part **a**.

> **Part c hint** Substitute $d = 0.5$ into the formula $P = \dfrac{2.5}{d^2}$

Reflect Look back at the questions you answered in this unit test.

- Which took the shortest time to answer? Why?
- Which took the longest time to answer? Why?
- Which took the most thought to answer? Why?

9 Probability

Master　　Check up p230　　Strengthen p232　　Extend p237　　Unit test p239

9.1 Mutually exclusive events

Active Learn
Homework

- Identify mutually exclusive outcomes and events
- Work out the probabilities of mutually exclusive outcomes and events

Warm up

1　**Fluency**　What is the numerical probability of
　a　an event that is certain to happen
　b　an event that is impossible
　c　an event that is as likely to happen as not happen?

2　Here is a spinner. Work out
　a　P(red)　　　　b　P(blue)　　　c　P(red or blue)
　d　P(white)　　　e　P(not yellow)　f　P(not red)

3　Tina spins the spinner in Q2 40 times.
　How many times would you expect it to land on
　a　blue　　　　b　yellow　　　c　red or yellow?

4　Each of these cards has shapes and a number.

> **Q4 hint** 'Picked at random' means that each item is equally likely to be picked.

　Lucy picks one card at random.
　What is the probability that her card has
　a　circles　　　　　b　triangles　　　　c　an even number
　d　an even number *and* triangles　　　e　an even number *or* triangles *or* both
　f　an even number *or* circles *or* both?

> **Key point**　Events are **mutually exclusive** if they cannot happen at the same time. For example, when you roll a dice, you cannot get 3 and an even number on the same roll.

5　**Reasoning**　Look back at the cards in Q4.
　Which of these pairs of events are mutually exclusive?
　A　picking an even number and picking an odd number
　B　picking triangles and picking circles
　C　picking an even number and picking triangles
　D　picking an even number and picking circles

6 **Reasoning**   Which of these possible pairs of events from rolling a dice are mutually exclusive?
   A rolling a 1 and rolling a 2
   B rolling a 3 and rolling a prime number
   C rolling an odd number and rolling an even number
   D rolling a 1 or 6 and rolling a prime number
   E rolling an even number and rolling a square number

Q6 hint List the possible outcomes for each event. Can they both happen at the same time?

Q6 hint 1 is not a prime number.

7 **a** For this spinner, are the results red (R), white (W) and blue (B) mutually exclusive?
   b Work out
   i P(R)   **ii** P(B)   **iii** P(W)
   iv P(W or B)   **v** P(R or B)   **vi** P(not B)
   c Does P(R or B) = P(R) + P(B)? Explain.

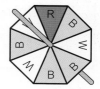

> **Key point**   For two mutually exclusive events, you can work out the probability that one or the other happens by adding together their probabilities.

8 The school canteen has to serve one vegetable with every main meal choice. The probabilities of a student choosing each vegetable are:
   P(sweetcorn) = 0.15   P(tomatoes) = 0.1
   P(green beans) = 0.2   P(peas) = 0.3
   P(cabbage) = 0.1   P(carrots) = 0.15
   a Explain why the choices of vegetables are mutally exclusive.
   b What is the probability that a student chooses:
   i tomatoes or cabbage
   ii any vegetable that is not tomatoes or cabbage
   iii a vegetable that is not green
   iv a vegetable that does not begin with the letter 'c'?

9 **Reasoning**   You need a handful of counters of different colours, for a game of 'pick a counter'.
   a Write all your colours (the possible outcomes) in a table like this.

Colour				
Probability				

   b Are all the possible outcomes mutually exclusive? Explain your answer.
   c Count the total number of counters in your handful.
      For your set of counters, work out the probability of picking each colour. Write the probabilities in your table.
   d Work out the total of the probabilities in your table.
   e Repeat for another handful of coloured counters.
   f Compare your total probabilities with someone else's. What do you notice?

> **Key point**   The probabilities of all the mutually exclusive outcomes of an event add to 1.

Worked example

A bag contains red, blue, yellow and green counters. A counter is picked at random.
The table shows the probability for each colour.

Colour	red	blue	yellow	green
Probability	0.4	0.2	0.1	

a Work out the probability that a green counter is picked.

$0.4 + 0.2 + 0.1 = 0.7$ —— The colours in the table are the only four colours possible. They are mutually exclusive, so their probabilities must add up to 1.

$1 - 0.7 = 0.3$

b There are 20 counters in the bag. How many are red?

$0.4 \times 20 = 8$ —— 0.4 (or $\frac{4}{10}$) of the 20 balls in the bag are red.

---

10 A packet contains red, pink, blue and green sweets. A sweet is picked at random. The table shows the probability for each colour.

Colour	red	pink	blue	green
Probability	0.3		0.2	0.4

  a Work out the probability that a pink sweet is picked.

  b There are 30 sweets in the packet. How many are blue?

11 The table shows the probabilities of buses arriving early, on time or late.
Work out the probability that the bus arrives late.

Bus arrives	early	on time	late
Probability	6%	80%	

12 Reasoning A spinner has sections labelled 'win', 'lose' and 'try again'.
The table shows the probability of it landing on each section.

Section	win	lose	try again
Probability	$\frac{1}{8}$	$\frac{5}{8}$	

  a Are the three outcomes 'win', 'lose' and 'try again' mutually exclusive?

  b What is the probability that it lands on 'try again'?

  c The spinner is spun 40 times. How many 'wins' would you expect?

13 Problem-solving A biscuit tin contains three different types of biscuit.
The table gives the probability of choosing different types.

  a Work out the probability of picking a jam biscuit.

  b Which type of biscuit is there most of?

  c There are 60 biscuits in the tin. How many are chocolate?

Biscuit	Probability
shortbread	$\frac{1}{4}$
chocolate	$\frac{2}{5}$
jam	

Challenge There are an equal number of red and white counters in a bag.
Milo adds some blue counters to the bag. A counter is picked at random.
  P(blue) = 0.4.   What is P(red)?

Reflect Sami works out that the probability of this spinner landing on an even number is $\frac{1}{2}$, and the probability of it landing on red is $\frac{2}{3}$.
Use what you have learned in this lesson to explain why the probabilities do not add up to 1.

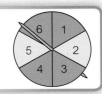

9.2 Experimental and theoretical probability

Active Learn
Homework

- Calculate estimates of probability from experiments
- Decide whether a dice or spinner is unbiased

Warm up

1 Fluency

a Which of $\frac{29}{90}$ and $\frac{4}{9}$ is closer to $\frac{1}{3}$?

b Which of $\frac{49}{200}$ and $\frac{16}{60}$ is closer to $\frac{1}{4}$?

2 The table shows the results of an experiment rolling a 4-sided dice.

a How many times in total was the dice rolled?

b From these results

   i work out the experimental probability of rolling a 3

   ii estimate the probability of rolling a 1.

c How many 4s would you expect in 200 throws?

Score	Frequency
1	13
2	12
3	11
4	14

3 Darryl rolled two 4-sided dice and calculated the difference between the numbers on the dice each time.

He did this many times and recorded his results in a frequency table.

Difference	0	1	2	3
Tally	卌 卌 卌 卌 卌	卌 卌 卌 卌 卌 卌 卌 I	卌 卌 卌 卌 卌 II	卌 卌 II
Frequency	25	36	27	12

a How many times did the difference equal 2?

b How many times did Darryl roll the dice?

c Which outcome is most likely?

d Estimate the probability of getting a difference of 2.
Give your answer as a fraction.

4 a Look again at Darryl's game in Q3.
How many times would he expect to get a difference of 0 if he rolled the dice 1000 times?

b Imagine a set of results showing that a difference of 3 occurs 30 times.
Roughly how many times might Darryl have rolled the dice?

5 Elodie rolled two 6-sided dice 80 times and added up the numbers each time.
She got a total of 7 on 13 occasions.

a Use a calculator to decide whether $\frac{1}{4}$, $\frac{1}{5}$ or $\frac{1}{6}$ is the best estimate for the probability of rolling a total of 7.

b Elodie rolls the dice 360 times. How many totals of 7 do you expect?

6 Reasoning A teacher has a set of red, blue and green pens. He says, 'There are three colours, so the probability of picking each colour is $\frac{1}{3}$.'

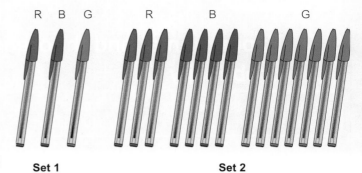

R B G   R   B   G

Set 1   **Set 2**

  a Use these sets of pens to explain why this might not be true.

  b Explain how to design a set of pens so the probability of picking each colour is $\frac{1}{3}$.

  c Design a set of pens where the probability of picking green is twice the probability of picking red.

7 Reasoning Every year, all the players in a darts competition are entered into a prize draw. There is one prize draw for the men and one for the women.
Explain why this might not give everyone a fair chance of winning.

Key point

The **theoretical probability** of an event is $\dfrac{\text{number of successful outcomes}}{\text{total number of possible outcomes}}$.

8 Reasoning Eluned records the results of rolling an ordinary 6-sided dice 100 times.

Score	Frequency
1	18
2	15
3	17
4	18
5	15
6	17

  a Calculate the experimental probability of rolling

    i a 2   **ii** a 6.

    Give your answers as decimals.

  b What is the theoretical probability of rolling

    i a 2   **ii** a 6?

    Give your answers as decimals.

  c Compare the experimental and theoretical probabilities for this dice. Are they close?

Key point   For an **unbiased** or 'fair' dice or spinner
* the theoretical probabilities are close to the experimental probabilities
* the theoretical number of times an outcome is expected to occur is close to the experimental number of times the outcome occurs.

9 Sara spins each of these spinners 120 times.

Spinner P

Spinner Q

Spinner R

Spinner S

Spinner	P	Q	R	S
Frequency	59	30	32	75

The table shows the number of times each spinner lands on green.

  a Calculate the experimental probability of 'green' for each spinner.

  b Calculate the theoretical probability of 'green' for each spinner.

  c Reasoning Compare the experimental and theoretical probabilities of each spinner, to decide if it is unbiased.

10 a Reasoning Each spinner in Q9 is spun 120 times. Use the theoretical probability to calculate the expected number of times the spinner will land on green.

   b Compare your results from part **a** with the number of 'green' results in Q9. Do you think each spinner is unbiased?

   c Is your decision for each spinner the same as in Q9?

11 Reasoning Angus rolls a 4-sided dice 50 times and records his results in this table.

Score	Frequency
1	9
2	14
3	15
4	12

Is the dice biased? Explain.

12 Reasoning / Problem-solving Jessica spins a fair 3-coloured spinner 80 times.
Her results are shown in the table.
Sketch a possible spinner.

Colour	Frequency
Blue	18
Red	41
Green	21

Challenge

1 Roll an ordinary dice 60 times and record the scores.
Do you think the dice is biased? Explain.

2 Work with a partner.

   a Roll two unbiased dice and add their scores.
   What scores are possible?
   Repeat this at least 50 times.
   Record your results in a table like this.
   Make sure you include columns for all the possible scores.

Score			
Tally			
Frequency			

   b Which score did you get most? What is the estimated probability?

   c Which score did you get least? How many times would you expect to get this score in 200 throws?

   d Combine your results with another pair's. Which is the least frequent score now? What is its estimated probability?

In a game, Player 1 wins if they score a total of 2 or 3. Player 2 wins if they score a total of 7.

   e Which player is most likely to win? Use the results of your experiment to explain.

   f Why do you think some scores are more likely than others?

Reflect   Sam and Misha are playing a game with a fair 6-sided dice.
Sam needs a 6 to win, but he rolls a 2.
Sam says, 'It's not fair. It's harder to roll a 6 than a 2.'
Use what you have learned about probability to decide whether Sam is correct. Explain.

9.3 Sample space diagrams

- List all the possible outcomes of one or two events in a sample space diagram
- Decide if a game is fair

*Active*Learn
Homework

Warm up

1 **Fluency** What are the possible outcomes for
   a rolling a dice   **b** flipping a coin?

2 Ann spins this spinner and records the score.
   a Write down all the possible outcomes.
   b Which outcome is most likely?
   c Which outcomes are least likely?
   d Is she more likely to spin an odd number or an even number?

3 For an ordinary fair dice, work out
   a P(even number)   **b** P(prime number)   **c** P(square number)
   d P(multiple of 3)   **e** P(factor of 10)   **f** P(odd number)

4 These two spinners are spun at the same time.
   a Copy and complete this list of possible outcomes.

   A green   B blue
   A green   B _____

   b Work out the probability of getting yellow on spinner A and red on spinner B.

Spinner A

Spinner B

5 **Reasoning** Helen flips a coin and rolls a 6-sided dice. List all the possible outcomes.

> **Q5 hint** Each outcome is a pair of events, e.g. (heads, 1).

Key point
A **sample space diagram** shows all the possible outcomes of two events.

6 Rory spins these two spinners.
   Copy and complete this sample space diagram for all the possible outcomes.

Spinner 1

Spinner 2

Spinner 1			
A	A, 1		
B			
C			
	1	2	3

Spinner 2

7 **Reasoning** These dominoes are placed face down.
   Danielle picks one from each set.
   She adds the numbers of spots on the two dominoes.

Set 1

Set 2

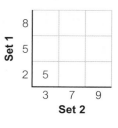

Set 1			
8			
5			
2	5		
	3	7	9

Set 2

   a Copy and complete this sample space diagram to show the total for each outcome.
   b From your diagram, which score is most likely to occur?

Sally spins these two spinners and adds the scores.
What is the probability of getting a total score of 8?

Spinner 1   Spinner 2

Spinner 1	4	8	9	10
	3	7	8	9
	2	6	7	8
		4	5	6

Spinner 2

Draw a sample space diagram and fill in the total score for each outcome.

3 outcomes give a total score of 8.

Probability of 8 = $\dfrac{\text{number of outcomes with a score of 8}}{\text{total number of possible outcomes}}$ = $\dfrac{3}{9} = \dfrac{1}{3}$

All of the outcomes are equally likely.

8 These dominoes are placed face down.
Alice picks one black and one white domino.
She multiplies the total number of spots on the white
domino by the total number of spots on the black domino.

a Draw a sample space diagram to show all the possible outcomes.

b Work out

   i P(5)   ii P(10)   iii P(more than 15)   iv P(even)

9 **Problem-solving** Two dice are rolled and their scores are added.

a Copy and complete this sample space diagram to show all
the possible outcomes.

b Work out

   i P(2)   ii P(3)

   iii P(5)   iv P(7)

c Work out the probability that at least one dice lands on 3.

d The two dice are rolled 180 times.
How many totals of 6 would you expect?

10 **Problem-solving** Two dice are rolled together 100 times.
The number of doubles (1, 1, or 2, 2, or 3, 3 and so on) is
recorded. Here are the results.

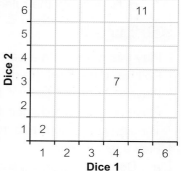

Doubles	Not doubles
33	67

a What is the experimental probability of rolling a double?

b Work out the theoretical probability of rolling a double.

c How many doubles would you expect from 100 rolls of two dice?

d Do you think these dice are fair? Explain your answer.

Q10b hint You could
use your sample space
diagram from Q9.

11 **Reasoning** Seema and Gavin play a game where they roll two dice and work out the difference between the scores.

Seema gets a point if the difference is even and Gavin gets a point if the difference is odd. Neither gets a point if the difference is zero.

a Copy and complete this sample space diagram.

b What is the probability of

  i Seema getting a point

  ii Gavin getting a point?

c Is the game fair? Explain.

d Gavin and Seema play a similar game where they work out the sum of the scores. Is this game fair?

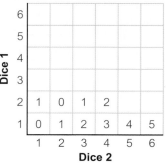

12 **Problem-solving** A 12-sided dice has the initial letter from the months of the year on each side. Greg challenges Amy to play a game he's invented called JAM FONDS.

If he rolls two of these dice and both land on a letter from J, A or M, then he gets a point.

If both dice land on a letter from F, O, N, D or S, then Amy gets a point.

Amy refuses, saying the game is not fair.

a Explain why Amy is correct.

b Is it possible for Amy to win?

c How could the rules be changed to make it fair?

Challenge

Play this game with a partner. Decide who will be Player 1 and Player 2.
Roll two dice. Find the difference between the two numbers.
Player 1 scores 1 point if the difference is a prime number.
Player 2 scores 1 point if the difference is a square.
The first player to reach 10 points wins.
Play a few times.

a Does the same person win more often?

b Do you think the game is fair?

c Draw a sample space diagram to show all the possible scores from rolling two dice and finding the difference.

d Calculate the probability of winning for each player.

e Is the game fair? Explain your answer.

Reflect Suzi has a fair 6-sided dice and a fair spinner with three sections numbered 1, 2 and 3.
She rolls the dice and spins the spinner.
Suzi wants to find the probability of the total score being 6. She could make a list of all the possible outcomes, or she could make a sample space diagram.
Which method would you choose and why?

9.4 Two-way tables

- Show all the possible outcomes of two events in a two-way table
- Calculate probabilities from two-way tables

Active Learn
Homework

Warm up

1 **Fluency**   A phone manufacturer tested 5000 phones at a factory.
They found that 200 were faulty.
Estimate the probability that a phone from that factory is faulty.

2 The table shows how Year 9 students at two different schools travel to school.

	Bus	Car	Walk	Cycle	Other
School A	17	13	28	19	5
School B	31	19	13	6	8

   a Which school has the most Year 9 students who walk to school?

   b How many Year 9 students are there in each school?

   c How many students in School B walk or cycle?

   d How many students in School A go by car or bus?

   e What fraction of the total number of students use the bus?

Key point   When the outcomes of an experiment or survey are pairs of results, you can show the frequencies in a **two-way table**.

3   **a** Copy and complete this two-way table for the outcomes of flipping two coins.

	Head (H)	Tail (T)
Head (H)	H, H	
Tail (T)		

   b What is the theoretical probability of flipping
   i two heads   **ii** two heads or two tails   **iii** a head and a tail (in any order)?

4 Zach flips a gold coin and a silver coin at the same time. He records his results in a two-way table.

		Silver coin		
		Heads	Tails	Total
Gold coin	Heads	23	30	
	Tails	26	21	
	Total			

   a Copy and complete the table.

   b How many times did Zach flip the coins in total?

   c How many times did he get two heads?

   d Work out the experimental probability of getting two heads with these coins.

   e Work out the experimental probability of getting

   i heads with the gold coin and tails with the silver coin

   ii tails with the gold coin.

5 The table shows some information about Year 9 students.

	Age 13	Age 14	Total
Male	48	56	104
Female	49	47	96
Total	97	103	200

A student is picked at random.
What is the probability that this student is

a female   b male

c aged 14   d aged 13

e a girl aged 14   f a 13-year-old boy?

> **Q5a hint** $\dfrac{\text{total number of females}}{\text{total number of students}}$

> **Q5e hint** $\dfrac{\text{total number of females aged 14}}{\text{total number of students}}$

6 **Problem-solving** Tom carries out a survey on the languages students are learning. Here are his results. Tom picks one of these students at random.

	French	German
Year 8	76	52
Year 9	59	68

a What is the probability that he picks a Year 8 student who learns French?

b Which is he more likely to pick: a Year 8 student who learns German or a Year 9 student who learns French? Show your working.

7 **Problem-solving** The table shows students' choices for an extended learning day.

	Drama	Science	Art	Totals
Y7	10	41	36	87
Y8	30	33	32	95
Y9	12	28	38	78
Totals	52	102	106	260

A student is picked at random to write an article for the school website about the extended learning day.

a What is the probability that the student is

   i a Year 7 student who chose Drama

   ii a Year 9 student who chose Science?

The headteacher picked a student from Year 9 at random.

b What is the probability that this student chose Art?

8 Alice spins these two spinners at the same time.
This two-way table shows her results.

		Spinner B		
		Blue	**Red**	**Green**
Spinner A	**Blue**	7	6	11
	Red	5	9	12
	Green	8	4	10

Spinner A

Spinner B

Work out the experimental probability of getting

a red with both spinners

b blue with spinner A and green with spinner B

c green with spinner A

d green with one spinner and blue with the other.

9 Reasoning Approximately 1000 babies are born each month at a hospital. Researchers recorded the day of the week and the time of birth over a month.

	0001–0600	0601–1200	1201–1800	1801–0000
Weekday	250	168	176	273
Weekend	42	28	30	33

a Copy the table and add an extra column and row for totals.
   Work out the totals.
b Are babies more likely to be born at the weekend or on a weekday? Explain.
c Estimate the probability that a baby is born between 0601 and 1200 on any day.
   Give your answer to 2 decimal places.
d Over a year, how many babies would you expect to be born
   i on a weekday   ii between 0601 and 1800?

10 Reasoning / Problem-solving In the game of 20s, each player throws three darts at a dartboard and counts the number of 20s that they hit.
George has eight attempts.
For George, $P(3) = \frac{3}{4}$ and $P(1) = \frac{1}{4}$.
Fiona has eight attempts: $P(0) = P(1) = P(2) = P(3) = \frac{1}{4}$
Anya has six attempts: $P(0) = \frac{1}{3}$, $P(1) = \frac{2}{3}$.
For everyone's attempts, $P(0) = \frac{2}{11}$.
Copy and complete the table. Add a column for the totals.

	Number of 20s			
	0	1	2	3
George				
Fiona				
Anya				

400 customers were randomly telephoned in a follow-up satisfaction survey.
Based on previous surveys, the probability of calling
• someone aged 20–39 is $\frac{2}{5}$
• a 'completely satisfied' customer aged over 60 is $\frac{1}{4}$
• a 'dissatisfied' customer aged 40–59 is the same as that of calling a 'mostly satisfied' customer aged 60 or over.

Copy and complete this table using the information given above.

	Completely satisfied	Mostly satisfied	Dissatisfied
20–39	80	40	
40–59	60		12
60 or over			28

Reflect Look back at Q8 in this lesson.
How do you know which total to choose for calculating probabilities from tables?
Write a hint for calculating probabilities from tables.

9.5 Venn diagrams

*Active*Learn
Homework

- Draw Venn diagrams
- Calculate probabilities from Venn diagrams

Warm up

1 **Fluency** For this spinner, what is
   a P(red)   b P(blue)   c P(red or blue)?

2 For the spinner in Q1, are the two events 'land on red' and 'land on blue' mutually exclusive? Explain.

3 The Venn diagram shows the factors of 20 and the factors of 6.
   a How many factors does 20 have?
   b What are the common factors of 6 and 20?
   c How many factors of 20 are *not* also factors of 6?

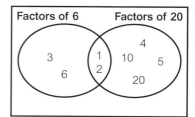

Key point
A **Venn diagram** shows sets of data in circles inside a rectangle. Data that is in both sets is written in the **intersection** – the part where the circles overlap.

4 The Venn diagram shows two events when a 6-sided dice is rolled: square numbers and numbers less than 4.

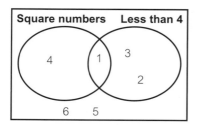

   a Explain why the two events are *not* mutually exclusive.
   b Why are 5 and 6 outside the circles?
   c How many square numbers are there in the diagram?
   d How many numbers are there in the diagram?
   e What is the probability of rolling a square number?
   f What is the probability of rolling a number less than 4?
   g What is the probability of rolling a square number or a number less than 4?
   h What is the probability of rolling a square number that is less than 4?

5 Reasoning An ordinary 6-sided dice is rolled once. The Venn diagram shows two events: square numbers and multiples of 3.

a Explain why the two events are mutually exclusive.

b What is the probability of rolling a square number?

c What is the probability of rolling a multiple of 3?

d What is the probability of rolling a square number or a multiple of 3?

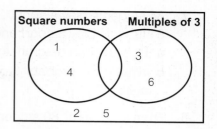

Worked example

20 students study French, 30 study German and 5 of them study both French and German.

a Show this information in a Venn diagram.

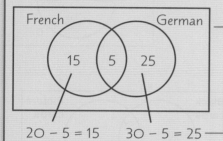

Draw two overlapping circles, one for each set of data.
5 students study French and German, so put 5 in the intersection.

$20 - 5 = 15$ $30 - 5 = 25$

Work out how many are left in the rest of each set and write the values in.
30 students study German, but 5 of these also study French. So 25 study only German.

b What is the probability that a student picked at random

   i studies French and not German

   ii only studies one language?

To work out the probabilities, you need to know the total number of students.

Total number of students = $15 + 5 + 25 = 45$

i P(French and not German) = $\frac{15}{45} = \frac{1}{3}$

You don't need to simplify the fraction for probability, but you can if you want to.

ii $15 + 25 = 40$

P(only one language) = $\frac{40}{45} = \frac{8}{9}$

40 study French or German, but not both

6 In a class of 30 students, 23 study Spanish and 11 study Mandarin.

6 students study both Spanish and Mandarin.

a Draw a Venn diagram to show this information.

b What is the probability that a student picked at random

   i studies Spanish only

   ii studies Spanish and Mandarin

   iii studies only one language?

c **Reasoning** 23 students study Spanish and 11 study Mandarin. Why aren't there 34 students in the class?

Q6a hint

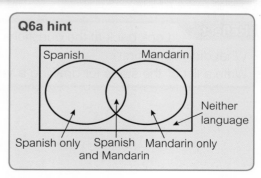

Spanish only   Spanish Mandarin only
and Mandarin

7 34 students play a sport. 24 students play an instrument.
8 students play a sport and an instrument.

   a Draw a Venn diagram to show this information.

   b What is the probability that a student picked at random plays an instrument but not a sport?

8 From a group of 80 students, 45 students study Art and 30 study Drama. 10 students study both.

   a Show this information in a Venn diagram.

   b What is the probability that a student picked at random

   i studies Art and Drama   **ii** studies Drama but not Art

   iii does not study Drama or Art?

9 The Venn diagram shows people's choices of starter (S), main course (M) and dessert (D) for a meal out.

   a How many people had

   i three courses

   ii only one course?

   b How many people went out for the meal?

   c What is the probability that one of these people, picked at random, had exactly two courses?

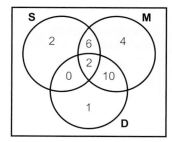

Challenge

1 **a** Copy and complete the Venn diagram to show the numbers of black cards (clubs or spades) and picture cards (jack, queen, king) in a normal pack of 52 cards.

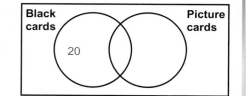

   b What is the probability that a card picked at random from a pack is

   i black   **ii** a picture card   **iii** a picture card from a black suit?

2 **a** Draw a Venn diagram to show the number of hearts in a pack of cards and the number of jacks.

   b What is the probability that a card picked at random from a pack is

   i a heart   **ii** the jack of hearts   **iii** a heart or a jack?

Reflect   Look back at the questions where you drew a Venn diagram.

What did you do first?

Write a list of the steps for drawing a Venn diagram.

9 Check up

Mutually exclusive events

1 The table shows the probabilities that trains arriving at a station are either early or late.

Arrival	early	late	on time
Probability	3%	9%	

   a Work out the probability that a train is on time.

   b 400 trains a week arrive at the station.
   How many of these trains would you expect to be late?

   c One week, 12 out of 450 trains are early.
   Does this mean that the probability of a train arriving early has changed?

2 A bag contains some sweets.
   A sweet is taken from the bag at random.

   a The probability of a toffee is $\frac{3}{8}$.
   What is the probability that it is not a toffee?

   b The probability of a chocolate is $\frac{1}{2}$.
   Which is more likely: a toffee or a chocolate?

   c What is the probability of choosing a toffee or a chocolate?

Probability from tables and diagrams

3 The two-way table shows the membership of a swimming club.

	Under 16	16–25	26–40	over 40	Totals
Male	9	23	5	7	44
Female	11	9	6	10	36
Totals	20	32	11	17	80

   A member of the club is picked at random.

   a What is the probability that this member is

     i male   **ii** aged 26–40
    iii a girl aged under 16   **iv** a man aged 16–40?

   b Which type of member is more likely to be picked: a man aged over 25 or a woman aged 25 or under?

   c All the female members' names are put into a hat and one is picked.
   What is the probability that the one picked is over 40?

4 Out of 30 customers in a café
    24 buy a drink
    23 buy a cake
    17 buy a drink and a cake.

   a Draw a Venn diagram to show this information.

   b One of these customers is picked at random.
   What is the probability they bought a drink but no cake?

5 Abi and Barry have these sets of number cards.
Chloë picks, at random, one of Abi's cards and one of Barry's cards.
   a Draw a sample space diagram to show all possible pairs of outcomes.
   b What is the probability that Chloë picks
      i two 4s
      ii at least one 3?

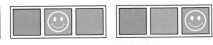

Experimental probability

6 Sandra buys scratch cards. There is always a red square, a blue square and a green square, with a smiley face in one of the squares. You win a prize if the smiley face is green. Sandra records the colour of the smiley face in this table.

Colour of smiley face	Frequency
red	47
blue	43
green	10

   a How many cards did she buy?
   b Work out the experimental probability of getting a green smiley face.
   c Sandra buys 20 more cards. How many more prizes is she likely to win?

7 Sam spins this spinner 100 times.
   a Do you think the spinner is unbiased? Explain.
   b In his next set of trials, the spinner lands on blue 72 times. How many trials do you think Sam carried out?

Score	Frequency
red	35
blue	36
green	29

8 In a game for two players, each player takes it in turn to spin these two spinners and add the scores together.
   • If the sum is odd, Player A gets a point.
   • If the sum is even, Player B gets a point.
   Is the game fair? Explain.

9 Alice spins this 5-colour spinner 200 times, and flips a coin each time. Here are the results.

	Red	Blue	Yellow	White	Black
Head	19	22	18	21	17
Tail	21	23	20	17	22

   a Use the results to estimate the experimental probability of getting blue and a head.
   b Do you think the coin is fair? Explain your answer.

Challenge   In a game you roll two dice and add them to get the total.
You win if the total is the same as the number of letters in your name.
   a Is this game fair? Explain your answer.
   b If you multiply the numbers instead of adding them, is the game fair?

Reflect   How sure are you of your answers? Were you mostly

   ☹ Just guessing   😐 Feeling doubtful   ☺ Confident

What next? Use your results to decide whether to strengthen or extend your learning.

9 Strengthen

Mutually exclusive events

1   **Reasoning**   Here is a set of cards.

Jamie picks one card at random.
Which of these pairs of events are mutually exclusive?

A   the card has a circle; the card has a 6

B   the card has an odd number; the card has a triangle

C   the card has a square number; the card has a square

D   the card has a factor of 10; the card has a circle

> **Q1 hint** If there is a card that fits both descriptions at once, the events are not mutually exclusive.

2   A bag contains red, yellow and pink counters. One counter is picked at random.

   a   Write down all the possible outcomes.

   b   Are all the possible outcomes mutually exclusive?

   c   What do the probabilities of all the mutually exclusive outcomes add up to?

   d   P(yellow) = 0.2 and P(red) = 0.5.
     Work out P(pink).

3   A game board has squares coloured red, white and black.
The probability of landing on

   •   a red square is $\frac{2}{9}$

   •   a black square is $\frac{4}{9}$.

What is the probability of landing on a white square?

4   There are 4 red, 3 yellow, 1 black and 2 orange sweets in a tin.
A sweet is picked at random.

   a   Which colour is most likely to be picked?

   b   Copy and complete the table to show the probability
     of each possible outcome.

Colour		
Probability		

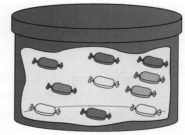
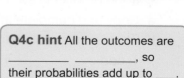

   c   What is the total of the probabilities in the table?
     Explain why.

   d   A sweet is picked at random.
     What is the probability that it is

     i   red or yellow or orange

     ii   not red, orange or yellow

     iii   black?

> **Q4c hint** All the outcomes are
> _____ _____, so
> their probabilities add up to ___.

   e   Why is the probability of picking a black sweet the same as the probability of picking a
     sweet that is not red, orange or yellow?

5 The table shows the probabilities that a bus is on time or late.

Q5 hint What percentage must the probabilities of all these outcomes add up to?

Arrival	on time	late	early
Probability	76%	9%	

What is the probability that a bus is early?

Probability from tables and diagrams

1 Angela spins these fair spinners.

a Copy and complete this sample space diagram for all the possible pairs of outcomes.

Spinner 1   Spinner 2

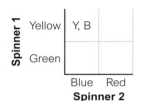

Spinner 1
Yellow | Y, B |
Green | |
  Blue   Red
Spinner 2

b What is the total number of possible outcomes?

c Work out the probability of getting green on spinner 1 and red on spinner 2.

Q1c hint The spinners are fair, so all the outcomes are equally likely.
$$P(G, R) = \frac{1}{\text{total number of possible outcomes}}$$

2 These tiles are placed face down. David picks one black tile and one white tile. He adds the numbers to find their sum.

a Copy and complete the sample space diagram to show all the possible equally likely outcomes.

Black tile
6 | | |
4 | | |
3 | | |
  3   4   7
White tile

b What is the probability that the sum will be

  i 10   **ii** 8   **iii** less than 9?

3 **Reasoning** In a game, Joe and Lisa roll two dice. They multiply the numbers together to find the product.

- If the product is odd, Joe scores a point.
- If the product is even, Lisa scores a point.

a Copy and complete the sample space diagram.

b Work out the probability that the product is

  i odd   **ii** even.

c Is the game fair?

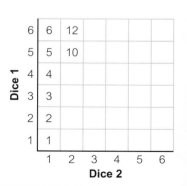

Dice 1
6 | 6 | 12 | | | | |
5 | 5 | 10 | | | | |
4 | 4 | | | | | |
3 | 3 | | | | | |
2 | 2 | | | | | |
1 | 1 | | | | | |
  1   2   3   4   5   6
Dice 2

Q3c hint For the game to be fair, P(odd) = P(even)

4 Tony spins both of these spinners.

   a Copy and complete the sample space diagram to show the possible outcomes.

Spinner 1

Spinner 2

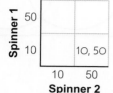

   b Work out the probability of

     i both spinners landing on 50   **ii** the spinners landing on different numbers.

5 The table shows data on the birth month of newborn babies.

	Jan–Mar	Apr–Jun	Jul–Sep	Oct–Dec	Totals
Female	36	25	41	29	131
Male	28	38	32	35	133
Totals	64	63	73	64	264

   a How many males were born in the months April to September?

   b What is the probability that a baby picked at random is

     i a male born in the months April to September

     ii a female born in the months October to December?

> **Q5b i hint** Use your answer to part **a** and the total number of babies born.

   c A male baby is picked.
     What is the probability that he was born in July, August or September?

> **Q5c hint** Use only the values for male babies.

   d A female baby is picked.
     What is the probability that she was born in the first half of the year?

6 In an athletics club
15 members train on Wednesdays
12 members train on Fridays
10 members train on Wednesdays and Fridays.

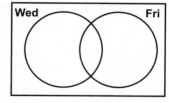

   a Copy the Venn diagram.

     i Write the number for 'Wednesdays and Fridays' in the section where the circles overlap.

     ii How many people need to go in the rest of the 'Wednesday' circle, so that the total in the whole 'Wednesday' circle is 15?

     iii How many people train on Fridays?
       Write in the number of people in the rest of the 'Friday' circle.

   b How many members are there altogether?

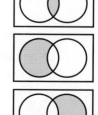

   c What is the probability that a member chosen at random trains

     i on Wednesdays and Fridays   **ii** only on Wednesdays?

7 16 people knit.
13 people sew.
9 people knit and sew.

a Copy the Venn diagram.
Write the number for 'knit and sew' in the section where the circles overlap.
The total in the whole 'knitting' circle needs to be 16.

b How many people need to go in the rest of the 'knitting' circle?
Write the number on your diagram.

c How many people need to go in the rest of the 'sewing' circle?
Write the number on your diagram.

d How many people are there altogether?

e What is the probability that a person picked at random
  i knits and sews   **ii** knits but does not sew?

Experimental probability

1 **a** What is the theoretical probability of 'tails' when you flip a fair coin?

b Dave flips a coin 80 times. Here are the results.
Work out the experimental probability of 'tails' for Dave's coin. $\frac{\square}{80}$

Heads	Tails
44	36

c Convert your fraction from part **b** to a decimal.

$\square \div 80 = \square$

d Do you think Dave's coin is fair? Explain.

> **Q1d hint** Is the experimental probability of a tail close to the theoretical probability?

2 **a** What is the theoretical probability of rolling a number greater than 4 on a fair dice?

b Lisa rolls a dice 150 times.
How many times would you expect her to roll a number greater than 4, if the dice is fair?

c Lisa gets a number greater than 4 on 26 rolls.
Do you think her dice is fair? Explain.

> **Q2c hint** Is the number of results greater than 4 close to the expected number?

3 These bags contain red and blue tiles numbered 1 to 3.
Rajiv picks a red tile and a blue tile.
He records the numbers and then replaces both tiles.

		Number on blue tile			
		1	**2**	**3**	**Total**
Number on red tile	**1**	5	4	3	
	2	6	5	4	
	3	3	4	2	
	Total				

a Copy and complete the two-way table. How many trials did Rajiv do?

b Work out the experimental probability of getting
  i 1 on the red tile and 3 on the blue tile
  ii 2 on the blue tile
  iii the same number on both tiles.

4 Reasoning In an experiment, Eric spins these two spinners 90 times.

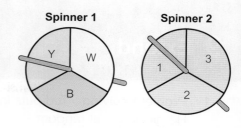

Spinner 1   Spinner 2

	Blue	Yellow	White
1	13	10	6
2	13	12	8
3	12	9	7

From these results, estimate the experimental probability of

a yellow and 3   **b** blue and 2   **c** white and 1.

> **Q4a hint** Calculate $\frac{\square}{90}$.

5 Reasoning Bella, Connie and Deepak all use the same dice in their experiments.

	Bella	Connie	Deepak
Number of rolls	30	120	240
Number of 6s	4	22	37

a What is the theoretical probability of rolling a 6?

b Work out the number of 6s Bella, Connie and Deepak should expect.

c Do you think the dice is fair? Explain your answer.

Challenge

The table shows the numbers of recorded offences in different cities and towns in 2011–12.

Town or city	Population (thousands)	Violence against the person	Robbery offences
Bristol	441.3	10 149	866
Hartlepool	91.3	1545	33
Carlisle and Penrith	156.4	2274	25
Derby	248.7	7280	412
Plymouth	258.7	5548	195

Source: ONS

a Where was the risk of violence against the person greatest?

b Where was the risk of robbery least?

Reflect   In these Strengthen lessons you have answered probability questions that use

- tables
- Venn diagrams
- sample space diagrams.

Which types of question were easiest? Why?

Which types of question were hardest? Why?

Write down one thing about probability that you think you need more practice on.

9 Extend

1 **Problem-solving** Ted puts these black and white sweets in a bag.
   He picks one at random.
   a What is the probability of picking a black sweet?
   He adds more black sweets to the bag.
   Ted says, 'The probability of picking black is now $\frac{2}{3}$.'
   b How many black sweets has he added?

2 **Problem-solving** Lily spins these two spinners and then
   adds the scores together.
   Is the total score more likely to be over 5 or under 5?
   Explain how you found your answer.

Spinner 1   Spinner 2

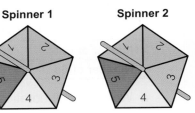

3 A spinner has sections labelled 1 to 5.

Number	1	2	3	4	5
Probability	$\frac{1}{12}$	$\frac{1}{4}$	$\frac{1}{6}$	$\frac{1}{3}$	

   What is the probability that it lands on 5?

4 The table shows the numbers of bicycle thefts in 2017–18.

	Number of car thefts	Population
Northamptonshire	1053	733 000
Suffolk	1439	757 000

Source: ONS

   Where is a car more likely to be stolen, Northamptonshire or Suffolk?
   Show your working.

5 **Problem-solving** Pip spins two spinners.
   This table shows her results.

		Spinner B		
		Blue	Red	Green
Spinner	Blue	14	16	28
A	Red	4	6	12

   a Work out the experimental probability of getting
      i blue with spinner A   **ii** blue with spinner B   **iii** green with spinner B.
   b Sketch a possible arrangement of the colours for each spinner.

6 Here is a summary table for a week's weather predictions last winter.

	Mon	Tue	Wed	Thu	Fri	Sat	Sun
Dry	45%	60%	80%		10%		60%
Rain		40%	20%	80%	80%	65%	
Snow/sleet/hail	0%		0%	5%		10%	30%

Work out the missing percentages.

7 Reasoning In a game, two players take turns to throw a piece of string onto this board.

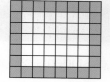 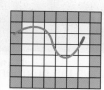 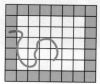

- Player A wins if the red end lands in a white square.
- Player B wins if the red end lands in a green square.

a What is the probability that
  i Player A wins   **ii** Player B wins?

b Explain why the game is unfair.   **c** Draw a board for a fair game.

8 In a game at a charity fête, players pay 50p to roll a dice and flip a coin. They win £1 if they roll an even number and flip a head.

a Copy and complete this sample space diagram to show all the possible outcomes.

b How many equally likely outcomes are there?

c What is the probability of winning?

d How much money can the stall expect to make when the game is played 200 times?

Coin						
T	T, 1					
H	H, 1	H, 2				
	1	2	3	4	5	6

Dice

9 Reasoning The table shows the earnings of a company's employees.

Earnings, e (per annum)	Number of employees
£0 < e ⩽ £10 000	5
£10 000 < e ⩽ £20 000	21
£20 000 < e ⩽ £30 000	30
£30 000 < e ⩽ £40 000	22
£40 000 < e ⩽ £50 000	3

a What is the probability that an employee picked at random earns
  i less than the median earnings   **ii** more than the mean?

b Explain why the probability you calculated in part **a ii** is an estimate.

> **Q9a i hint** Where is the median of a set of data?

Challenge   A Scrabble® set has 100 letter tiles. 42 are vowels, 56 are consonants and two are blanks.

At the start of a game you pick seven letters.

a Copy and complete the diagram to show the probabilities of picking seven vowels.

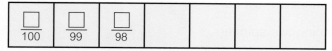

> **Hint** You pick the first vowel from 100 tiles. When you have picked a vowel the first time, for the second pick there are 41 vowels left and 99 to pick from, and so on.

b Convert the fractions to decimals. Are you more likely to pick a vowel on your first pick or your seventh pick, if all the letters picked already are vowels?

Reflect   Write two probability questions about a sports match, which each give the answer 0.4, for
  • mutually exclusive events   • experimental probability.

> **Hint** Look back at the lessons where you learned about these types of probability.

Compare your three questions with those of others in your class.

9 Unit test

1   The table shows the numbers of students choosing different team-building activities.

	Year 7	Year 8	Year 9	Totals
Rafting	32	33	38	103
Orienteering	35	33	29	97
Totals	67	66	67	200

A student is picked at random. What is the probability that it is

a   a Year 9 student

b   a Year 7 student who chose orienteering?

A student from each activity is picked at random.

c   Is a Year 8 student more likely to be selected from the rafting group or the orienteering group?

2   a   Draw a sample space diagram to show all the possible outcomes of picking one ball from each of these bags.

b   What is the probability of picking two balls of the same colour?

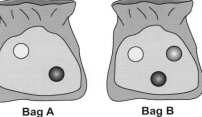

Bag A   **Bag B**

3   The Venn diagram shows the numbers of cat and dog owners at a pet show.

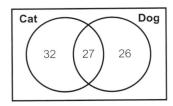

a   Write down the missing words.

   i   53 people own _____.

   ii   27 people own _____.

A pet food company chooses one of the people at the show at random to win a lifetime's supply of pet food.

b   What is the probability that the winner owns a cat?

4   Bernard records the results of spinning two spinners.

		Spinner A		
		Orange	Green	Yellow
Spinner B	Green	7	12	11
	Orange	23	19	18

a   Estimate the probability of getting orange with both spinners.

b   Estimate the probability of getting green with spinner A.

c   Do you think spinner A is divided into thirds? Explain.

5 A fair ordinary dice is rolled once.
   What is the probability of rolling
   a an even number   **b** a square number
   c an even number or a square number?

6 A bag contains a total of 24 red (R), yellow (Y) and green (G) marbles.
   $P(R) = \frac{3}{8}$ and $P(Y) = \frac{1}{4}$
   Work out
   a the probability of picking a green marble
   b the number of yellow marbles in the bag.

7 These two spinners are spun and the two numbers added
   together to give the score.
   What is the probability that the total is
   a less than 7   **b** more than 7   **c** exactly 7?
   Show your working to explain your answers.
   Jenn and Kane spin both spinners.
   Jenn wins if the score is more than 8.
   Kane wins if the score is less than 8.
   d Is the game fair? Explain your answer.

Spinner 1  **Spinner 2**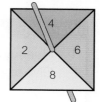

8 In a fairground game, this spinner is spun.
   You win if it lands on 'win'.
   In 200 spins, it lands on 'win' 17 times.
   Do you think this spinner is fair? Explain.

9 The table shows the results of dropping a
   drawing pin.
   Ted drops the drawing pin 50 times.
   How many times would you expect it to land
   point up?

Point down	Point up
264	36

Challenge   Draw a sample space diagram for the possible outcomes of spinning the two
spinners in Q7 and multiplying the scores.
Design a game using these two spinners.
Your game could be fair or one player could be more likely to win.
Ask someone to play your game with you.
Can they work out if the game is fair or not?

Reflect   Look back at the questions you answered in this test.
a Which one are you most confident that you have answered correctly?
   What makes you feel confident?
b Which one are you least confident that you have answered
   correctly?
   What makes you least confident?
c Discuss the question you feel least confident about with a classmate.
   How does discussing it make you feel?

Part c hint
Comment on your
understanding of
the question and
your confidence.

10 Comparing shapes

10.1 Congruent and similar shapes

Active Learn
Homework

• Use congruent shapes to solve problems about triangles and other polygons
• Work out whether shapes are similar, congruent or neither

Warm up

1 Fluency What is the size of each missing angle? Give reasons.

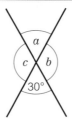

2 Copy this object onto a coordinate grid.
   a Translate the object 3 right, 4 down. Label the image A.
   b Rotate the object 180° about the origin. Label the image B.
   c Reflect the object in the y-axis. Label the image C.
   d Enlarge the object by scale factor 2 about the point $(-3, 6)$. Label the image D.
   e Which shapes are congruent? Explain.

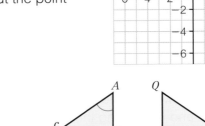

3 These two triangles are congruent. Copy and complete these sentences.
   a Side a and side ☐ are corresponding sides.
   b Side ☐ and side r are corresponding sides.
   c Angle ABC and angle ☐ are corresponding angles.

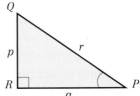

4 a Plot the points $(3, 2)$, $(5, 2)$ and $(4, 4)$ on a coordinate grid and join them to form a triangle.
   b Enlarge the triangle
      i by scale factor 2 with centre of enlargement $(4, 4)$
      ii by scale factor 3 with centre of enlargement $(4, 4)$.
   c What scale factor would result in a congruent image?

5 Reasoning The diagram shows four congruent scalene triangles.

a Draw a sketch of the diagram. Mark all angles with arcs.

b Mark equal angles with the same letter. Use your sketch to show that angles in a triangle add up to 180°.

Q5b hint Equal angles are marked with arcs.

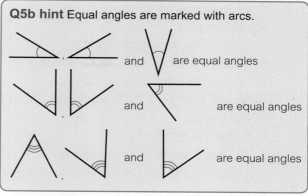

and are equal angles

and are equal angles

and are equal angles

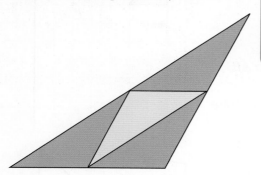

Key point   Shapes are **similar** if one is an enlargement of the other.
The enlarged image may be a reflection or rotation (or both) of the object.

---

6 Which shapes are similar to each other?

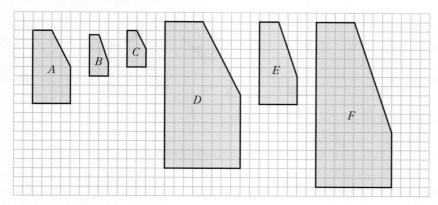

---

7 Reasoning For each shape, decide whether it is
- congruent to shape A
- similar to shape A
- neither of these.

Explain how you know.

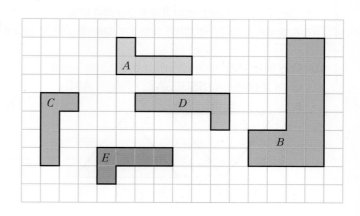

8 Copy the diagram onto squared paper.

Carry out the transformations.

For each transformation, state whether the image is congruent or similar to the object.

a Rotate triangle T 270° clockwise about P. Draw the image.
Label the image T_1.

b Reflect triangle T_1 in the line AB.
Draw the image. Label the new image T_2.

c Translate triangle T_2 5 units up parallel to AB.
Draw the image. Label this image T_3.

d Enlarge triangle T_3 with scale factor 2 and centre of enlargement at P. Label this image T_4.

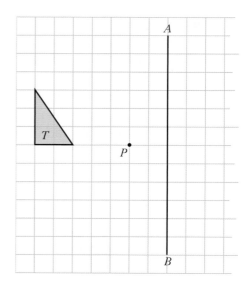

9 **Problem-solving**

a Trace these triangles.
Sort them into congruent pairs.

b Which triangles are left over?
Which ones can you sort into similar pairs?

c Look at your pairs. What can you say about

   i triangles with three sides the same

   ii triangles with two sides and the angle between them the same

   iii triangles with two angles and one side the same

   iv triangles with all angles the same?

d Does having two sides and an angle the same always give congruent triangles?

> **Key point**   Triangles are congruent if they have equivalent
> - SSS (all three sides)
> - SAS (two sides and the included angle)
> - ASA (two angles and the included side)
> - AAS (two angles and another side)
>
> Triangles where all angles are the same (AAA) are similar, but might not be congruent.

10 The triangles in each pair are congruent.
Give a reason (SSS, SAS, ASA or AAS).

a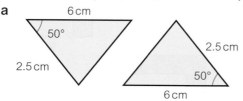

b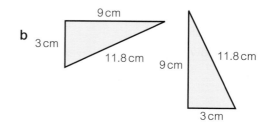

243

c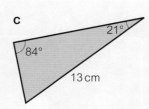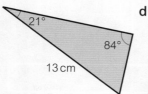

d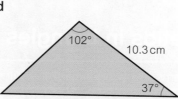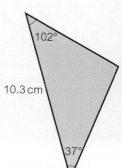

e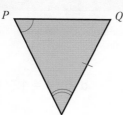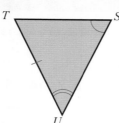

$\angle P = \angle S$
$\angle R = \angle U$
$QR = TU$

11 Reasoning Kamal says, 'These two triangles are congruent because they have an equal side and two equal angles, ASA.'
Is he correct? Explain.

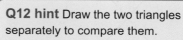 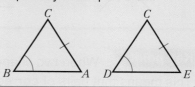

12 Reasoning In this diagram, equal sides and angles are marked.

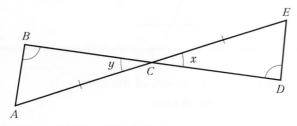

> **Q12 hint** Draw the two triangles separately to compare them.

a What can you say about angles x and y?
b Show that triangles ABC and EDC are congruent.
Give the reason for congruency (SSS, SAS, ASA or AAS).

13 Reasoning These triangles are all congruent.
Work out the missing sides and angles.

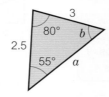 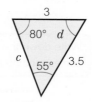 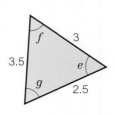

Challenge Are all right-angled triangles with one side 5 cm and hypotenuse 10 cm congruent? Sketch at least two triangles to check.

Reflect Write one fact that is always true about
- congruent shapes *and* similar shapes
- congruent shapes but *not* similar shapes.

10.2 Ratios in triangles

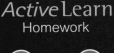
*Active*Learn
Homework

- Solve problems involving similar triangles

Warm up

1 Fluency What are the missing numbers?

a $2 : 4 = 3 : \square$　　**b** $20 : 4 = 30 : \square$　　**c** $7 : 14 = 5 : \square$　　**d** $6 : 4 = 12 : \square$

2 Are these triangles similar?
Explain.

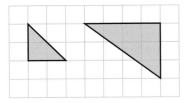

3 For each diagram, give the reason why the marked angles are equal.

a　　　　　　　　　**b**　　　　　　　　　**c**

Key point

When two shapes are similar, one is an enlargement of the other.
This means that pairs of **corresponding** sides are in the same ratio.

Worked example

Triangles A and B are similar.
Work out the height of triangle B.

$A : B$
$6 : 12$　　　　— Write down the ratios of corresponding sides.

$2 : x$

$2 \times 2 = x$ so $x = 4$ — Work out x.

Check your answer.

The arrows show the corresponding sides.

2 cm A　　6 cm　　　B　　x　　12 cm

4 Triangles P and Q, in each pair, are similar.
Work out the length l in each triangle Q.

a

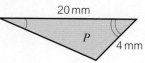

20 mm

4 mm

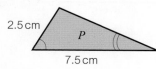

30 mm

l

b

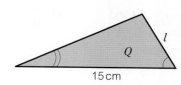

2.5 cm

7.5 cm

l

15 cm

5 **Reasoning** Jesse and Lucy are working out length l.

Jesse uses this working:

$$P \; : \; Q$$

$\times \square$

$$2 \qquad 6$$

$$2.2 \qquad l$$

$\times \square$

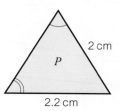

2 cm

2.2 cm

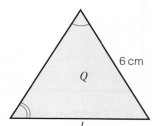

6 cm

l

Lucy uses this working:

$$P \; : \; Q$$

$\times \square$ $\quad 2 \qquad 6 \quad$ $\times \square$

$ \quad 2.2 \qquad l$

a Whose working do you prefer? Explain.

b What is length l?

6 Each set of right-angled triangles, A, B, C and D, are similar.
Work out the lengths labelled with letters.

a

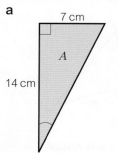

7 cm

14 cm

A

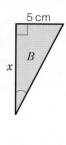

5 cm

x

B

2 cm

y C

4 cm

z

D

b

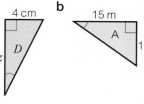

15 m

A

10 m

5 m

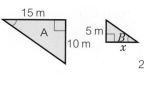

B

x

y

21 m

C

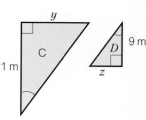

D

9 m

z

7 **Problem-solving** Are these triangles similar?
Show working to explain.

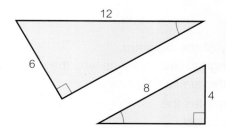

12

6

8

4

Q7 hint Write
down the ratios of
corresponding sides.

Key point When two triangles are similar, their angles are the same (AAA).

Worked example

a Show that triangles ABE and ACD are similar.

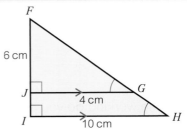

Triangle ABE	Triangle ACD
$\angle EAB$	$\angle EAB$
$\angle AEB = 90°$	$\angle ADC = 90°$

$\angle ABE = \angle ACD$ (corresponding angles)
The triangles have the same angles (AAA).

b Work out length ED.

Triangle ABE ×1.25 Triangle ACD

$$8 : 10$$
$$6 : AD$$

×1.25

Write down the ratio of corresponding sides.

$AD = 6 × 1.25 = 7.5$ cm

Work out AD.

$ED = AD - 6 = 1.5$ cm

Work out ED.

8 **Problem-solving**
   a Show that triangles FGJ and FHI are similar.
   b Work out length IJ.

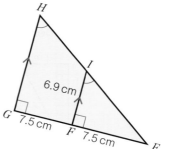

9 **Problem-solving**
   a Show that triangles EFI and EGH are similar.
   b Work out length GH.

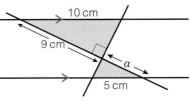

Key point When two triangles are similar, their corresponding angles are equal.

10 **Reasoning**
   a Sketch a copy of the diagram.
      Mark equal angles. Give reasons why they are equal.
   b Are the triangles similar? Explain.
   c Sketch the triangles the
      same way up. Label
      the sides you know
      and the equal angles.
   d Work out the length of a.

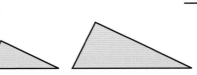

11 Reasoning Work out the lengths labelled with letters.

Q11 hint Use the method in Q10.

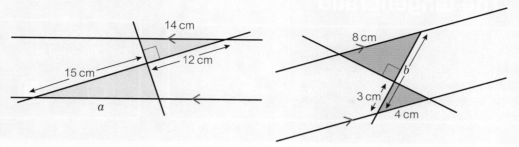

12 Problem-solving Work out the lengths labelled with letters.

Q12 hint
First show that
the triangles
are similar.

a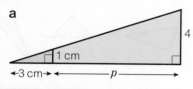

b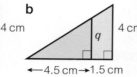

c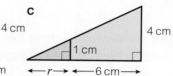

Challenge

A street lamp shines light on a circular
patch of ground.
When the top of the street lamp is
3 metres above the ground the diameter
of the circle of light is 4 metres.

a How far above the ground must the
top of the lamp be to throw light on a
circle of diameter 10 metres?

b A street is being fitted with lamp
posts that are 4.5 metres high. The
street is 120 metres long.
How many lamp posts will be needed to light the
length of the street?

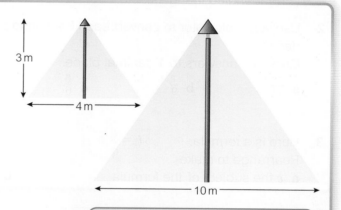

Hint The light shines at the same
angles, so the two triangles are similar.

Reflect Look back at Q12. To answer this question you had to
  • show that triangles are similar
  • identify corresponding lengths
  • solve equations.
Which of these tasks was easiest? Explain why.
Which of these tasks was hardest? Explain why.

10.3 The tangent ratio

- Use conventions for naming the sides of a right-angled triangle
- Work out the tangent ratio of any angle
- Use the tangent ratio to work out an unknown side of a right-angled triangle

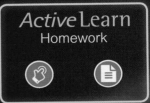

Active Learn
Homework

Warm up

1 Fluency
a How do you know which side is the hypotenuse in a right-angled triangle?
b Which side is the hypotenuse in each of these right-angled triangles?

2 Use your calculator to convert each fraction to a decimal.
Give your answers to 1 decimal place.

a $\frac{3}{11}$ **b** $\frac{7}{9}$ **c** $\frac{5}{6}$ **d** $\frac{2}{13}$ **e** $\frac{1}{17}$

3 Here is a formula. $b = \dfrac{c}{a}$
Rearrange to make
a c the subject of the formula
b a the subject of the formula.

Key point

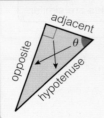

Theta (θ) is a letter in the Greek alphabet. It is often used in maths to label an angle that is unknown.
The side opposite to a chosen angle (angle θ in this diagram) is called the **opposite** side.
The side between the chosen angle and the right angle is called the **adjacent** side.

4 In each triangle, which side is
  i the opposite side to angle θ **ii** the adjacent side to angle θ
  iii the hypotenuse?

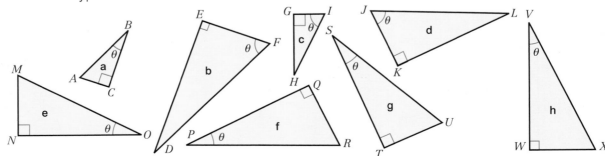

5 Reasoning

a Draw these triangles accurately using a ruler and protractor.

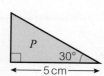

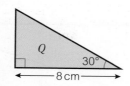

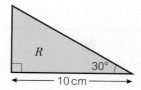

b Explain why all the triangles are similar.

c i Label the opposite side to 30° 'opp' and the adjacent side to 30° 'adj'.

   ii Measure the opposite sides and the adjacent sides.

d Copy and complete this table.

Triangle	Opposite length	Adjacent length	$\dfrac{\text{opposite}}{\text{adjacent}}$ (1 d.p.)
P			
Q			
R			

e i What patterns do you notice in your table?

   ii What do you think will happen for other right-angled triangles with an angle of 30°?

   iii Test your hypothesis by drawing some more right-angled triangles with an angle of 30°.

6 Repeat Q5 with an angle of 50° instead of 30°.

7 Reasoning Look back at your answers to Q5 and Q6. What do they tell you about the ratio of the sides of similar right-angled triangles?

> **Key point**   The ratio of the opposite side to the adjacent side in a right-angled triangle is called the **tangent** of the angle.
> The tangent of angle θ is written as **tan θ**.
>
> $\tan\theta = \dfrac{\text{opposite}}{\text{adjacent}}$
>
> You can use the tan key on a calculator to find the tangent of an angle.

8 Check your answers to Q5 and Q6 by using your calculator to find, correct to 1 decimal place

a tan 30°   **b** tan 50°

> **Q8a hint** On your calculator, enter tan   3   0   =

9 Use your calculator to find, correct to 1 decimal place.

a tan 32°   **b** tan 58°   **c** tan 60°   **d** tan 10°

10 Write tan θ as $\dfrac{\text{opposite}}{\text{adjacent}}$ for each triangle.

a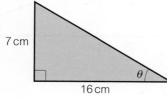

b

c

Key point You can use the tangent ratio to find the length of one of the shorter sides in a right-angled triangle.

Worked example

Use the tangent ratio to work out x, correct to 1 decimal place.

$\tan\theta = \dfrac{\text{opposite}}{\text{adjacent}}$ — Write the tangent ratio.

opposite = x

adjacent = 13 — Identify the opposite and adjacent sides.

$\theta = 26°$ — Substitute the sides and angle into the tangent ratio.

$\tan 26° = \dfrac{x}{13}$

$13 \times \tan 26° = x$ — Rearrange to make x the subject.

$x = 6.3\,\text{cm}$ (to 1 d.p.) — Use your calculator to work out x.

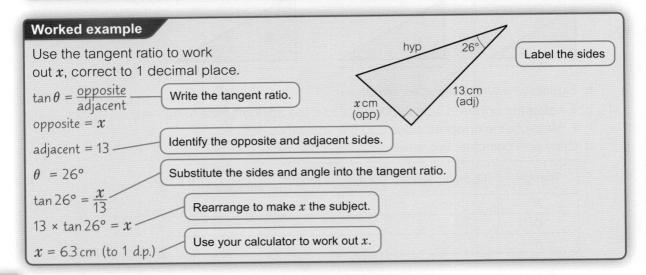

Label the sides

hyp, 26°, 13 cm (adj), x cm (opp)

11 Work out x for each triangle, correct to 1 decimal place.

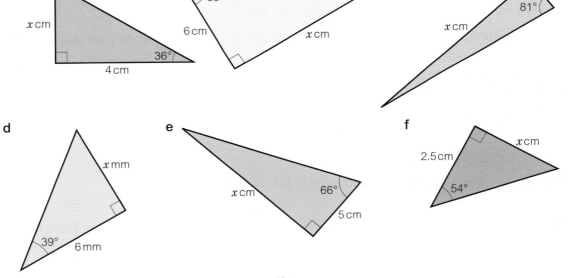

a x cm, 4 cm, 36°

b 60°, 6 cm, x cm

c 2.2 cm, 81°, x cm

d x mm, 39°, 6 mm

e x cm, 66°, 5 cm

f 2.5 cm, 54°, x cm

12 **Problem-solving** A gardener needs to know the height of a tree.
The gardener measures 20 metres from the bottom of the tree to a point on the ground.
The angle to the top of the tree is 21°.
What is the height of the tree? Give your answer to the nearest centimetre.

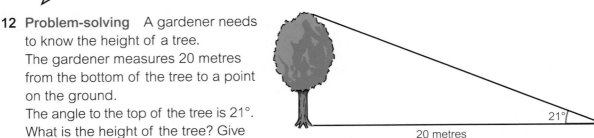

20 metres, 21°

13 Work out the value of x, correct to 1 decimal place.
The first one is started for you.

a

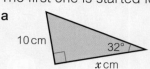

10 cm
32°
x cm

$$\tan\theta = \frac{\text{opposite}}{\text{adjacent}}$$
opposite = 10
adjacent = x
$\theta = 32°$

$$\tan 32° = \frac{10}{x}$$

> **Q13 hint** Rearrange to make x the subject.
> Use your calculator to work out x.

b

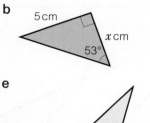

5 cm
x cm
53°

c

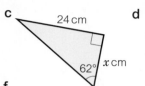

24 cm
62° x cm

d

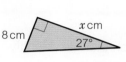

8 cm
x cm
27°

e

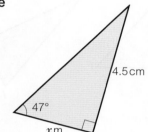

4.5 cm
47°
x m

f

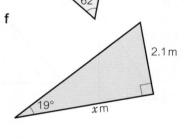

2.1 m
19°
x m

14 **Problem-solving** A ladder rests against a wall.
The top of the ladder reaches 2 metres up the wall.
The ladder makes an angle of 55° with the horizontal ground.
How far is the ladder from the bottom of the wall?

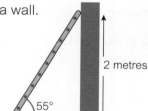

2 metres
55°

> **Q14 hint** Sketch the diagram. Label the opposite and adjacent.

15 **Problem-solving** An aircraft is landing.
Its descent makes an angle of 10° with the ground and its horizontal distance from landing is 4000 m.
Calculate the vertical height of the aircraft above the ground.

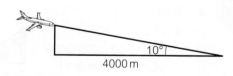

10°
4000 m

Challenge

a Sketch a right-angled isosceles triangle.

b Write on your triangle the sizes of the two angles that are not right angles.

c Use your calculator to work out the tangents of these angles.

d Explain why you get your answer to part **c**.

Reflect   Given an angle (other than the right angle) in a right-angled triangle, and the opposite side, list all the other information about the triangle you can work out.
State what maths knowledge you would use to work out each piece of information in your list.

10.4 The sine ratio

*Active*Learn
Homework

- Work out the sine ratio of any angle
- Use the sine ratio to work out an unknown side of a right-angled triangle

Warm up

1 **Fluency** For each triangle, identify
   i the opposite side to angle θ
   ii the adjacent side to angle θ
   iii the hypotenuse.

a

b

c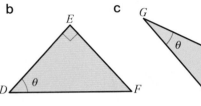

2 Here is a formula. $f = \dfrac{g}{h}$
   Rearrange to make
   a g the subject of the formula
   b h the subject of the formula.

3 Use the tangent ratio to work out x, correct to 1 decimal place.

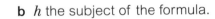

4 **Reasoning**
   a Draw these triangles accurately using a ruler and protractor.

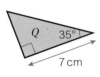

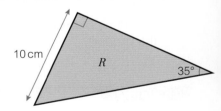

   b i Label the hypotenuse.
   ii Label the opposite side to 35° 'opp' and the adjacent side to 35° 'adj'.
   iii Measure the opposite sides and the hypotenuse.
   c Copy and complete this table.

Triangle	Opposite length	Hypotenuse length	$\dfrac{\text{opposite}}{\text{hypotenuse}}$ (1 d.p.)
P			
Q			
R			

d i What patterns do you notice in your table?

   ii What do you think will happen for other right-angled triangles with an angle of 35°?

   iii Test your hypothesis by drawing some more right-angled triangles with an angle of 35°.

5 Repeat Q4 with an angle of 70° rather than 35°.

6 Reasoning Look back at your answers to Q4 and Q5. What do they tell you about the ratio of the sides of similar triangles?

Key point The ratio of the opposite side to the hypotenuse in a right-angled triangle is called the **sine** of the angle. The sine of angle θ is written as $\sin\theta$.

$$\sin\theta = \frac{\text{opposite}}{\text{hypotenuse}}$$

You can use the $\boxed{\sin}$ key on a calculator to find the sine of an angle.

---

7 Check your answers to Q4 and Q5 by using your calculator to find, correct to 1 decimal place,

  a $\sin 35°$ **b** $\sin 70°$

> **Q7a hint** On your calculator, enter $\boxed{\sin}$ $\boxed{3}$ $\boxed{5}$ $\boxed{=}$

8 Use your calculator to find, correct to 1 decimal place

  a $\sin 45°$ **b** $\sin 75°$ **c** $\sin 60°$ **d** $\sin 15°$

9 Write $\sin\theta$ as a fraction for each triangle.

a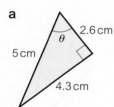

b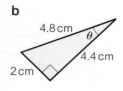

c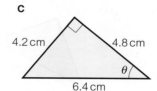

Key point You can use the sine ratio to find the length of the opposite side or hypotenuse in a right-angled triangle.

Worked example

Use the sine ratio to work out x, correct to 1 decimal place.

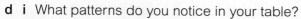

$\sin\theta = \dfrac{\text{opposite}}{\text{hypotenuse}}$ — Write the sine ratio.

opposite $= x$

hypotenuse $= 20$ — Identify the opposite and hypotenuse sides.

$\theta = 32°$

$\sin 32° = \dfrac{x}{20}$ — Substitute the sides and angle into the sine ratio.

$20 \times \sin 32° = x$ — Rearrange to make x the subject.

$x = 10.6\,\text{cm}$ (to 1 d.p.) — Use your calculator to work out x.

20 cm (hyp)   32°

x cm (opp)   Label the sides

10 Use the sine ratio to work out x for each triangle, correct to 1 decimal place.

a 12 cm, 38°, x cm

b 22°, 15 cm, x cm

c 10 cm, 64°, x cm

d x cm, 18°, 35 cm

e 53°, 5 m, x m

11 **Problem-solving** A kite flies on the end of a string that is tied to a stone on the ground.
The string is 100 metres long and makes an angle of 45° with the ground.
Use the sine ratio to work out how high the kite is flying.
Give your answer to the nearest centimetre.

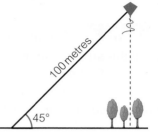

12 Work out the value of x, correct to 1 decimal place.
The first one is started for you.

a

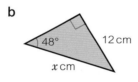

x cm
10 cm 18°

$\sin\theta = \dfrac{\text{opposite}}{\text{hypotenuse}}$

opposite = 10
hypotenuse = x
$\theta = 18°$

$\sin 18° = \dfrac{10}{x}$

> **Q12 hint** Rearrange to make x the subject. Use your calculator to work out x.

b 48°, 12 cm, x cm

c 15 cm, 54°, x cm

d 19 cm, 62°, x cm

e 32°, 14 m, x m

13 **Problem-solving** A skateboard ramp is 50 cm long and makes an angle of 35° with the ground. Calculate the height of the ramp.

50 cm, 35°

14 **Problem-solving / Reasoning** For each triangle
　i decide whether you need to use the tangent or the sine ratio
　ii work out the value of y.

a 15 cm, 20°, y

b 12 cm, 52°, y

c y, 15°, 9 cm

Challenge A 10-metre ladder rests against the side of a house at an angle of 75° to the ground. Will it reach a window sill that is 8 metres above the ground?

Reflect List all the maths skills and knowledge you used to answer these questions about the sine ratio.

10.5 The cosine ratio

- Work out the cosine ratio of any angle
- Use the cosine ratio to work out an unknown side of a right-angled triangle

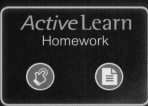

*Active*Learn
Homework

Warm up

1 Fluency In each of these right-angled triangles, identify
  i the hypotenuse
  ii the adjacent side for the marked angle.

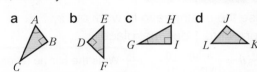

2 Copy and complete.
  a $\tan\theta = \dfrac{\square}{\square}$ **b** $\sin\theta = \dfrac{\square}{\square}$

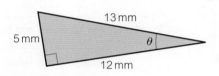

3 Here is a formula. $c = \dfrac{a}{h}$
  Rearrange to make
  a a the subject of the formula   **b** h the subject of the formula.

4 Reasoning Look at the triangles you drew in Q4 in lesson 10.4.
  a Copy and complete this table.

Triangle	Adjacent length	Hypotenuse length	$\dfrac{\text{adjacent}}{\text{hypotenuse}}$ (1 d.p.)
P			
Q			
R			

  b What patterns do you notice in your table?

5 Repeat Q4 for triangles with a 40° angle.

6 Reasoning Look back at your answers to Q4 and Q5. What do they tell you about the ratio of the sides of similar triangles?

Key point
The ratio of the adjacent side to the hypotenuse in a right-angled triangle is called the **cosine** of the angle.
The cosine of θ is written as **cos θ**.
  $\cos\theta = \dfrac{\text{adjacent}}{\text{hypotenuse}}$
You can use the $\boxed{\cos}$ key on a calculator to find the cosine of an angle.

7 Use your calculator to find, correct to 1 decimal place
  a cos 45°   **b** cos 65°   **c** cos 30°   **d** cos 25°

8 Write $\cos\theta$ as a fraction for each triangle.

a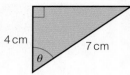

b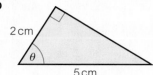

c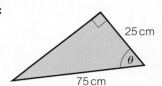

> **Key point** You can use the cosine ratio to find the length of the adjacent side or hypotenuse in a right-angled triangle.

Worked example

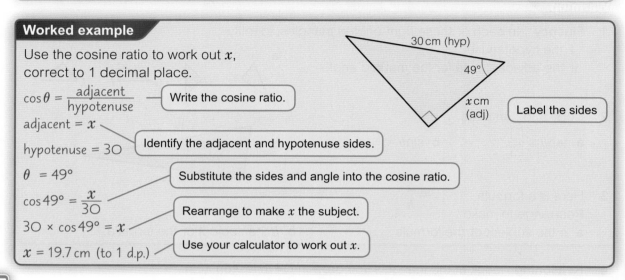

Use the cosine ratio to work out x, correct to 1 decimal place.

$\cos\theta = \dfrac{\text{adjacent}}{\text{hypotenuse}}$ ⟶ Write the cosine ratio.

adjacent = x

hypotenuse = 30 — Identify the adjacent and hypotenuse sides.

$\theta = 49°$

$\cos 49° = \dfrac{x}{30}$ — Substitute the sides and angle into the cosine ratio.

$30 \times \cos 49° = x$ — Rearrange to make x the subject.

$x = 19.7$ cm (to 1 d.p.) — Use your calculator to work out x.

9 Use the cosine ratio to work out x for each triangle, correct to 1 decimal place.

a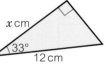

b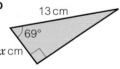

c

d

e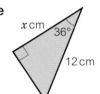

f

10 Problem-solving A tent is an isosceles triangular prism, and the sloping side length is 150 cm.
The side makes an angle of 50° with the horizontal.
Use the cosine ratio to find the width of the tent.
Give your answer to the nearest centimetre.

> **Q10 hint** Divide into two right-angled triangles.
>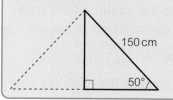

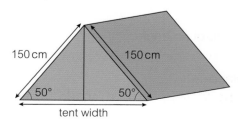

11 Work out the value of x, correct to 1 decimal place. The first one is started for you.

a

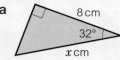

$$\cos\theta = \frac{\text{adjacent}}{\text{hypotenuse}}$$

adjacent = 8

hypotenuse = x

$\theta = 32°$

$$\cos 32° = \frac{8}{x}$$

Q11 hint Rearrange to make x the subject. Use your calculator to work out x.

b 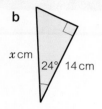   **c** 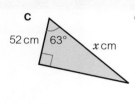   **d**   **e**   **f**

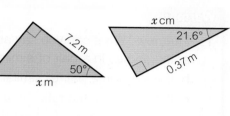

12 Problem-solving A flagpole, AB, is supported by two ropes, BC and BD.

a BC is secured 16.1 m away from the base of the flagpole at an angle of 38° to the ground.
How long is rope BC, correct to the nearest centimetre?

b BD is secured 13.1 m away from the base of the flagpole at an angle of 50° to the ground.
How long is rope BD, correct to the nearest centimetre?

c What can you say about the lengths of ropes BC and BD?

> **Key point** $\tan\theta$, $\sin\theta$ and $\cos\theta$ are called **trigonometric ratios**. They are part of a maths topic called **trigonometry**.

13 Problem-solving For each triangle, decide whether you need to use the tangent, sine or cosine ratio. Then work out the value of p.

a   **b**   **c**

> **Challenge**   The length of the diagonal of this rectangle is 15 cm.
>
> Use trigonometric ratios to work out the width and height of the rectangle.

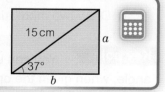

> **Reflect**
> $$\sin\theta = \frac{\text{opposite}}{\text{hypotenuse}} \qquad \cos\theta = \frac{\text{adjacent}}{\text{hypotenuse}} \qquad \tan\theta = \frac{\text{opposite}}{\text{adjacent}}$$
> Mathematicians remember these trigonometric ratios in different ways.
> Some remember SOH – CAH – TOA (pronounced 'soak a toe uh'!)
> Others remember Some Old Horses Chew Apples Happily Throughout Old Age.
> How will you remember them?

10.6 Using trigonometry to find angles

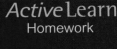

*Active*Learn
Homework

• Use the trigonometric ratios to work out an unknown angle in a right-angled triangle

Warm up

1 Fluency What can you say about
  a the angles in a pair of similar triangles
  b the sides in a pair of similar triangles
  c the trigonometric ratios in a pair of similar right-angled triangles?

2 For this triangle, write each of these trigonometric ratios as a fraction.
  a $\tan\theta$
  b $\sin\theta$
  c $\cos\theta$

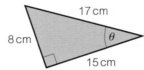

3 a Use the tangent ratio to work out the value of s.

  b Use the sine ratio to work out the value of x.

  c Use the cosine ratio to work out the value of y.

4 Problem-solving / Reasoning In this triangle, $\tan\theta = \frac{4}{5}$.
  a Write down possible values for a and b.
  b Make an accurate drawing of the triangle using these values.
  c Measure the angle θ to the nearest degree.
  d Draw two more triangles where $\tan\theta = \frac{4}{5}$, and use them to measure θ.

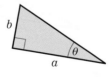

Key point

You can use the **inverse tangent function** ($\tan^{-1}$) to work out an unknown angle, when given the opposite and adjacent sides of a right-angled triangle.

$$\tan\theta = \frac{\text{opposite}}{\text{adjacent}} \quad \text{so} \quad \theta = \tan^{-1}\frac{\text{opposite}}{\text{adjacent}}$$

You can usually find the inverse tangent function on a calculator by pressing $\boxed{\text{inv}}$ or $\boxed{\text{SHIFT}}$ or $\boxed{\text{2nd}}$ and looking for $\boxed{\tan^{-1}}$.

5 Check your answer to part **c** in Q4 by using the inverse tangent function on your calculator to find θ.

6 Use the $\tan^{-1}$ function on your calculator to find θ.

  a $\tan\theta = \frac{1}{2}$ **b** $\tan\theta = \frac{5}{8}$ **c** $\tan\theta = 0.74$

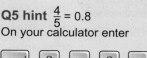

Q5 hint $\frac{4}{5} = 0.8$
On your calculator enter

Worked example

Use the tangent ratio to find the missing angle, θ, in this right-angled triangle, correct to 1 decimal place.

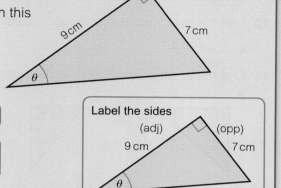

$\tan\theta = \dfrac{\text{opposite}}{\text{adjacent}}$ — Write the tangent ratio.

$\tan\theta = \dfrac{7}{9}$ — Substitute the sides into the tangent ratio.

$\theta = \tan^{-1}\dfrac{7}{9}$ — Use the inverse tangent function on your calculator to work out θ.

$\theta = 37.9°$

Label the sides
(adj)   (opp)
9 cm   7 cm

---

7 Use the tangent ratio to find the missing angles.

  a 12 cm, 7 cm, θ

  b θ, 10 cm, 7 cm

  c 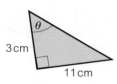 θ, 3 cm, 11 cm

---

Key point   You can use the **inverse sine function** ($\sin^{-1}$) to work out an unknown angle, when given the opposite side and the hypotenuse in a right-angled triangle.

$\sin\theta = \dfrac{\text{opposite}}{\text{hypotenuse}}$ so $\theta = \sin^{-1}\dfrac{\text{opposite}}{\text{hypotenuse}}$

You can usually find the inverse sine function on a calculator by pressing $\boxed{\text{inv}}$ or $\boxed{\text{SHIFT}}$ or $\boxed{\text{2nd}}$ and looking for $\boxed{\sin^{-1}}$.

---

8 Use the $\sin^{-1}$ function on your calculator to find θ.

  a $\sin\theta = \frac{7}{10}$ **b** $\sin\theta = \frac{3}{4}$ **c** $\sin\theta = 0.12$

9 Use the sine ratio to work out the missing angles.

  a 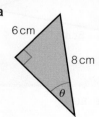 6 cm, 8 cm, θ

  b 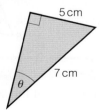 5 cm, 7 cm, θ

  c 13 cm, θ, 5 cm

Q9 hint Substitute the sides into the sine ratio. Use the inverse sine function on your calculator to work out θ.

  d Reasoning What do you notice about your answers to Q8 part **b** and Q9 part **a**? Explain.

10 Use the $\cos^{-1}$ function on your calculator to find θ.

    a $\cos\theta = \frac{3}{10}$ **b** $\cos\theta = \frac{3}{7}$ **c** $\cos\theta = 0.42$

 11 Use the cosine ratio to work out the missing angles.

    a   **b**   **c**

12 Sketch each triangle and label the sides: opposite, adjacent or hypotenuse.
Then use the correct inverse trigonometric function to work out the unknown angle.

    a   **b** 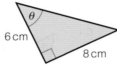   **c**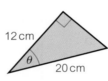

    d 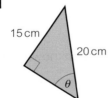   **e**   **f**

13 Problem-solving Jamie builds a skate ramp with 2 metres of wood. He wants the vertical height of the ramp to be 1 metre. What angle does the wood need to make with the ground?

Challenge

a Work out the sizes of the angles in this right-angled triangle.

b How many different ways can you work out each angle? Explain.

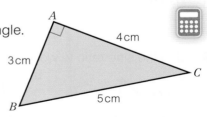

Reflect List any other maths topics where you have met the word 'inverse'.
What does 'inverse' mean in maths?

10 Check up

Congruence and similarity

1 Which rectangles are similar to rectangle A?

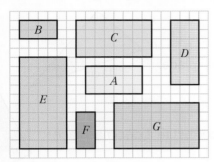

2 This pair of triangles are similar.
Find the value of x.

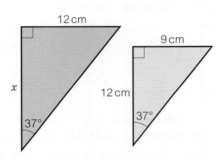

3 Decide whether these pairs of triangles are congruent.
Give a reason for each answer.

a

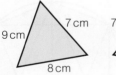

b

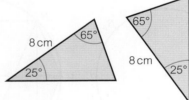

4 **a** Show that triangles PQT and PRS are similar.
    b Work out the value of p.

Unknown sides

a

5 In each triangle which side is
    i the opposite side to
       angle θ
    ii the adjacent side to
       angle θ
    iii the hypotenuse?

b

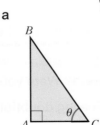
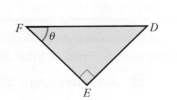

c

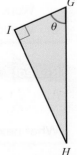

6 Use the tangent ratio to work out x, correct to 1 decimal place.

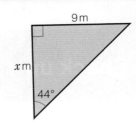

7 Use the sine ratio to work out x, correct to 1 decimal place.

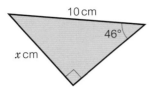

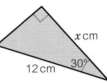

8 Use the cosine ratio to work out x, correct to 1 decimal place.

Unknown angles

9 Use the tangent ratio to work out the missing angle, correct to 1 decimal place.

10 Work out the missing angle, correct to 1 decimal place.

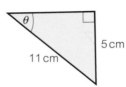

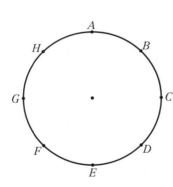

Challenge Eight points, labelled A to H, are spaced equally round a circle.
You can make different designs by joining different pairs of these points.
Here are three examples.

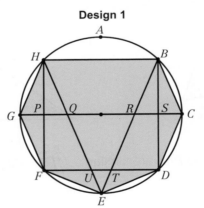

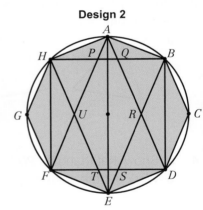

Design 1

Design 2

a In each of the designs 1 and 2, find similar and congruent shapes.
b Make your own different design on a blank copy of the circle.
  Look for similar shapes and congruent shapes in your own design.
  Work out as many angles as you can.
c Would the shapes still be similar if the points were not equally spaced? Why?

Reflect How sure are you of your answers? Were you mostly

😞 Just guessing 😐 Feeling doubtful 🙂 Confident

What next? Use your results to decide whether to strengthen or extend your learning.

10 Strengthen

Congruence and similarity

1 Reasoning Six congruent triangles are arranged like this.

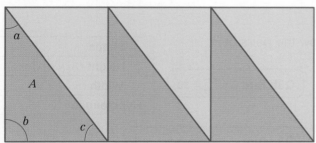

a Draw a sketch of the diagram.

b Label all the angles a, b or c so that equal angles have the same letter.

> **Q1 hint** Trace triangle A. Place it over the other triangles to help you find the equal angles. You will need to rotate your tracing for the yellow triangles.

2 Three groups of similar shapes have been mixed up.

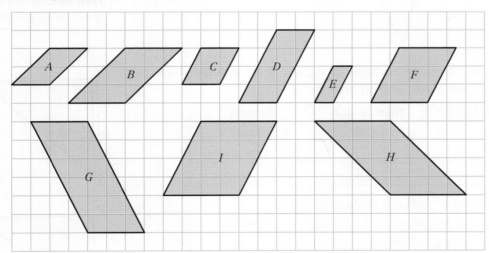

a Look at shapes A and B.
   i Are all the angles the same size?
   ii Are shapes A and B similar?

b Look at shapes C and D.
   i Are all the angles the same size?
   ii Are shapes C and D similar?

c Sort the rest of the shapes into the three groups of similar shapes.

> **Q2 hint** You could use tracing paper to check whether the angles are the same size.

3 Triangles P and Q are similar.

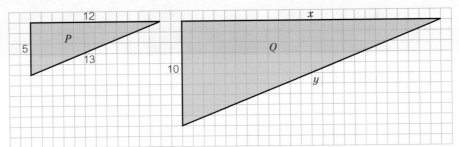

a Copy and complete the table. Show the pairs of corresponding sides.

b Use a pair of corresponding sides to work out the scale factor from P to Q.

> **Q3b hint** $5 \times \square = 10$

c Use the scale factor to work out x and y.

> **Q3c hint** $P \times$ scale factor $= Q$

Shape	P	Q
Height	5	10
Width		x
Hypotenuse	13	

4 For each pair of similar triangles, work out x and y.

a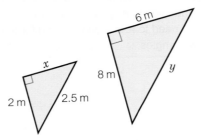

b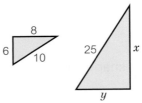

> **Q4 hint** Use the method in Q3.

> **Q4b hint** Identify the corresponding sides.

5 a Copy and complete the table to show that the triangles have the same angles (AAA) and so are similar.

Triangle ABE		Triangle ACD	Reason
$\angle BAE$	$=$	$\angle CAD$	Shared angle
$\angle ABE$	$=$	$\angle\square$	Both right angles
$\angle BEA$	$=$	$\angle\square$	_____ angles

Use the diagram and your table in part **a** to

b copy and complete the pair of triangles ABE and ACD with all the information you know about the sides and angles

c work out the length of CD.

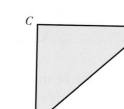

6 Reasoning The diagram shows two triangles.

a Give reasons why

   i $a = b$ **ii** $c = d$ **iii** $e = f$

b The three pairs of angles are equal.
What does this tell you about the two triangles?

c i Trace the triangles and then sketch them the same way up.

   ii Label the measurements you know.

   iii Use the method in Q3 to find the missing lengths.

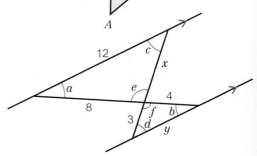

7 Reasoning

a Copy each pair of diagrams accurately.
Then draw, or continue, the lines to make two triangles.

i

ii

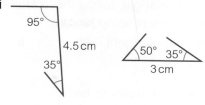

b Use the diagrams to help you decide whether two triangles are congruent if
   i two corresponding angles and the length of the side between them are equal (ASA)
   ii three angles are equal (AAA)
   iii the lengths of two corresponding sides and the angle between them are equal (SAS).

Unknown sides

1 Sketch each triangle and label
   a 'opp' on the side opposite to ∠θ
   b 'adj' on the adjacent side
   c 'hyp' on the hypotenuse.

Q1 hint

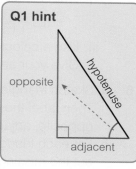

2 i

ii

iii

iv

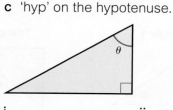

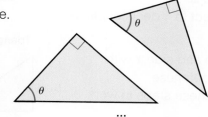

a Write the tangent ratio for each triangle.

Q2a hint $\tan\theta = \dfrac{\text{opposite}}{\text{adjacent}}$

b Write the sine ratio for each triangle.

Q2b hint $\sin\theta = \dfrac{\text{opposite}}{\text{hypotenuse}}$

c Write the cosine ratio for each triangle.

Q2c hint $\cos\theta = \dfrac{\text{adjacent}}{\text{hypotenuse}}$

3 a Sketch triangles 1 and 2.
      Then label the given side and
      side x with opposite, adjacent
      or hypotenuse.
   b For each triangle, follow these
      steps to work out the missing
      length.

Triangle 1   **Triangle 2**

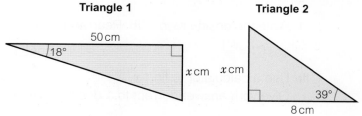

   i Write the tangent ratio.   ii Rearrange.

$$\tan\square = \frac{\square}{\square}$$ $$x = \square \times \tan\square$$

iii Use a calculator to find x. Give your answer correct to 1 decimal place.

4 **a** Sketch triangles 1 and 2.
Then label the given side and side x with opposite, adjacent or hypotenuse.

Triangle 1 **Triangle 2**

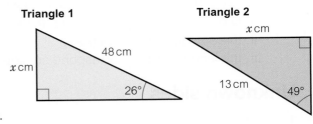

b For each triangle, follow these steps to work out the missing length.

i Write the tangent ratio.

$$\tan\square = \frac{\square}{\square}$$

ii Rearrange.

$$x = \frac{\square}{\tan\square}$$

iii Use a calculator to find x.
Give your answer correct to 1 decimal place.

5 **a** Sketch triangles 1 and 2.
Then label the given side and side x with opposite, adjacent or hypotenuse.

Triangle 1 **Triangle 2**

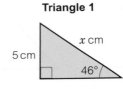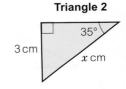

b For each triangle, follow these steps to work out the missing length.

i Write the sine ratio.

$$\sin\square = \frac{\square}{\square}$$

ii Rearrange.

$$x = \square \times \sin\square$$

iii Use a calculator to find x.
Give your answer correct to 1 decimal place.

6 **a** Sketch triangles 1 and 2.
Then label the given side and side x with opposite, adjacent or hypotenuse.

Triangle 1 **Triangle 2**

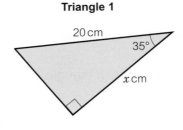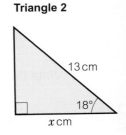

b For each triangle, follow these steps to work out the missing length.

i Write the sine ratio.

$$\sin\square = \frac{\square}{\square}$$

ii Rearrange.

$$x = \frac{\square}{\sin\square}$$

iii Use a calculator to find x.
Give your answer correct to 1 decimal place.

7 **a** Sketch triangles 1 and 2.
Then label the given side and side x with opposite, adjacent or hypotenuse.

Triangle 1 **Triangle 2**

b For each triangle, follow these steps to work out the missing length.

i Write the cosine ratio.

$$\cos\square = \frac{\square}{\square}$$

ii Rearrange.

$$x = \square \times \cos\square$$

iii Use a calculator to find x.
Give your answer correct to 1 decimal place.

8 a Sketch triangles 1 and 2.
Then label the given side and side x with opposite, adjacent or hypotenuse.

b For each triangle, follow these steps to work out the missing length.

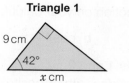

Triangle 1

9 cm
42°
x cm

Triangle 2

cm
4 cm
52°

i Write the cosine ratio.

$$\cos\square = \frac{\square}{\square}$$

ii Rearrange.

$$x = \frac{\square}{\cos\square}$$

iii Use a calculator to find x.
Give your answer correct to 1 decimal place.

Unknown angles

1 Use the $\tan^{-1}$ function on your calculator to work out θ.

a $\tan\theta = 0.3$ **b** $\tan\theta = \frac{3}{5}$

2 a Sketch triangles 1 and 2.
Then label the sides with opposite, adjacent and hypotenuse.

Triangle 1

6
7
θ

Triangle 2

θ
4
5

Q1a hint Rearrange to make θ the subject.
The inverse of tan is $\tan^{-1}$.
$\theta = \tan^{-1}0.3$

You may use [inv] or [2nd] on your calculator instead of [SHIFT].

b For each triangle, follow these steps to work out the missing angle.

i Write the tangent ratio.

$$\tan\theta = \frac{\square}{\square}$$

ii Rearrange.

$$\theta = \tan^{-1}\frac{\square}{\square}$$

iii Use a calculator to find θ.
Give your answer correct to 1 decimal place.

Q3 hint Press [SHIFT]
(or [inv] or [2nd]) [sin].

3 Use the $\sin^{-1}$ function on your calculator to work out θ.
a $\sin\theta = 0.2$
b $\sin\theta = \frac{2}{5}$

4 a Sketch triangles 1 and 2.
Then label the sides with opposite, adjacent and hypotenuse.

b For each triangle, follow these steps to work out the missing angle.

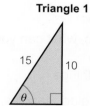

Triangle 1

15
10
θ

Triangle 2

θ
3
16

i Write the sine ratio.

$$\sin\theta = \frac{\square}{\square}$$

ii Rearrange.

$$\theta = \sin^{-1}\frac{\square}{\square}$$

iii Use a calculator to find θ.
Give your answer correct to 1 decimal place.

5 Use the $\cos^{-1}$ function on your calculator to work out θ.

  a $\cos\theta = 0.9$ **b** $\cos\theta = \frac{3}{8}$

6 a Sketch triangles 1 and 2.
Then label the sides with opposite, adjacent and
hypotenuse.

  b For each triangle, follow these steps to work out the
missing angle.

    i Write the cosine ratio.   **ii** Rearrange.

$$\cos\theta = \frac{\square}{\square}$$ $$\theta = \cos^{-1}\frac{\square}{\square}$$

    iii Use a calculator to find θ.
Give your answer correct to 1 decimal place.

Triangle 1   **Triangle 2**

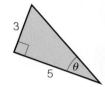

7 Follow these steps to work out the size of angle θ.

  a Copy the triangle and label the sides that you have been given or need
to find.

  b Choose the trigonometric ratio you are going to use.

  c Write the ratio.

  d Rearrange to make θ the subject.

  e Use your calculator to work out the missing angle.

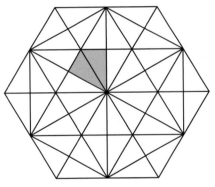

Challenge   This pattern is part of a tessellation of small
right-angled triangles.

a Trace the pattern. Draw round a shape that is
congruent with the pink kite.

b Draw round a shape that is similar to the pink kite.

c How many shapes can you find that are similar to the
pink kite?

d Make another copy of the pattern. Choose another
shape that you can see in the pattern. Draw round,
or shade in your shape.

e How many shapes can you find that are similar to your shape?

Reflect

1 When looking at triangles, what can you tell from just
the angles?
Write down at least four things.

> **Q1 hint** Think about what you
> can tell just by looking at the
> angles of one triangle. What about
> when comparing two triangles?

2 When looking at right-angled triangles, what can you
work out just from one other angle and the included side?
Write down at least four things.

> **Q2 hint**

10 Extend

1 This rectangle is made up of four congruent right-angled triangles.
   a Construct the diagram accurately.
   b **Reasoning** What kind of triangle is triangle *BFD*? Explain how you know.

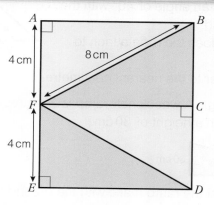

> **Q1a hint** Start with the triangle you know most about.

2 The four right-angled triangles in this diagram are all similar to each other. Work out *x*, *y* and *z*.

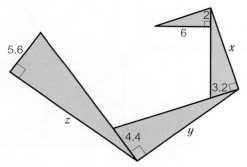

3 For each triangle, work out the value of *x*.

   a
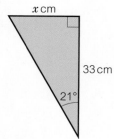

   b
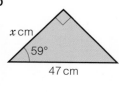

> **Q3 hint** Identify the labelled sides and choose the correct ratio.

4 A crane lifts a container onto a ship.
   The crane arm is 40 metres long and makes an angle of 20° with the vertical. The bottom of the container is level with the bottom of the crane arm.
   Use the cosine ratio to find the vertical distance, to the nearest cm, from the top of the crane arm to the bottom of the container.

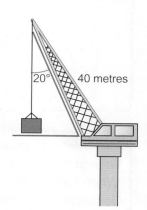

5 **Problem-solving** A flagpole is held in place
by three wire ropes.
Each rope is attached to the ground
2 metres from the bottom of the flagpole.
The rope makes an angle of 40° with the
horizontal ground.
At what height does the rope attach to
the flagpole?
Give your answer to the nearest centimetre.

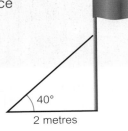

40°

2 metres

Q5 hint Sketch the
triangle and label the
height x. Label opposite,
adjacent and hypotenuse.

6 **Problem-solving** A wheelchair ramp is 2 metres long.
It needs to reach a height of 30 cm.

Q6 hint You must
have all measurements
in the same units.

2 m

30 cm

What angle must the ramp make with the ground?

7 **Problem-solving** A ladder is 6 m long and is leaning against a vertical wall.
In order for it to be safe, the ladder must be placed between 1.8 m and
2.4 m from the base of the wall.
  a What is the largest angle the ladder can make with the wall?
  b What is the smallest angle the ladder can make with the wall?

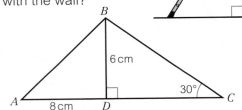

8 **a** Work out the length AB.
  b Work out the length BC.
  c Work out the length CD.
  d **Reasoning** Is ABC a right-angled triangle?
    Explain your answer.

B

6 cm

30°

C

A

8 cm

D

Challenge The square and the isosceles triangle have the same area.
Find tan θ.

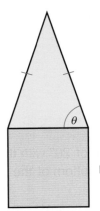

θ

Not to scale

Reflect Copy and complete this paragraph.
Write at least three sentences.
'When I am given a mathematics problem to solve, this is what I do...'
Compare your paragraph with others in your class.

10 Unit test

1 Which shapes are similar to shape A?

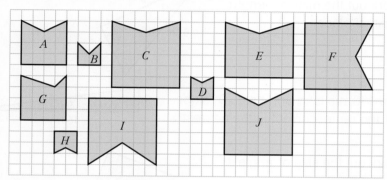

2 For each pair of triangles, decide whether the triangles are congruent, similar or neither. Give reasons for your answers.

a $PQ = AB$, $QR = BC$, $\angle PQR = \angle ABC$

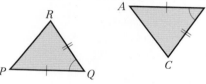

b $\angle GHK = \angle XYZ$, $\angle HGK = \angle YZX$

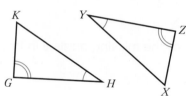

3 These triangles are all congruent. Work out the missing sides and angles.

a

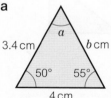

b

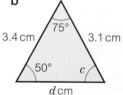

c

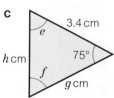

4 Triangles P and Q are similar.
Work out the missing length, x cm.

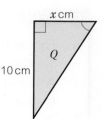

5 Use the tangent ratio to work out the missing length.
Give your answer to 1 decimal place.

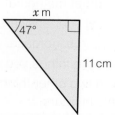

6 Use the sine ratio to work out the missing length. Give your answer to 1 decimal place.

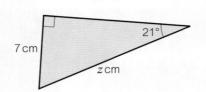

7 cm

21°

z cm

7 Use the cosine ratio to work out the missing length. Give your answer to 1 decimal place.

y cm

27°

0.6 cm

8 A portable wedge ramp is 450 mm long and has a 9° slope. Work out the height (*h*) of the ramp, correct to the nearest mm.

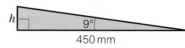

h

9°

450 mm

9 Use the cosine ratio to work out the size of angle *θ*.

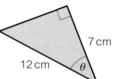

7 cm

12 cm

θ

10 Use the correct trigonometric ratio to work out side *s*.

s

44°

8 cm

11 Find the size of the missing angle *θ* in this triangle.

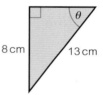

θ

8 cm

13 cm

Challenge

a Calculate the value of *x* and *y* when

  i $\sin x = 0.3$ $\cos y = 0.3$

  ii $\sin x = 0.6$ $\cos y = 0.6$

  iii $\sin x = 0.8$ $\cos y = 0.8$

  iv $\sin x = 0.9$ $\cos y = 0.9$

y

x

b Write down any patterns that you notice. Explain.

Reflect

a For each statement **A**, **B** and **C**, choose a score:

  1 – strongly disagree   2 – disagree   3 – agree   4 – strongly agree

  A I always try hard in mathematics.

  B Doing mathematics never makes me worried.

  C I am good at mathematics.

b Look back at your answers to the reflect task in lesson 1.1.

c Did your scores increase, decrease or stay the same? Why do you think this was?

d Did you do the things you wrote down in lesson 1.1?

e Write down two other things you could do so that you agree more strongly with these statements in future.

Answers

UNIT 1 Indices and standard form

1.1 Indices

1 8^2 and 5^3

2 a 1 **b** 27 **c** 125 **d** 1000
e 3 **f** 2 **g** 3 **h** 2

3 a 16 **b** 27 **c** 90 **d** 9000

4 a 16 **b** −64

5 a 67 **b** 18 **c** 20 **d** 100

6 a 15 **b** −3 **c** 20 **d** −10
e 0 **f** 130

7 a i 32 **ii** 32
  b They are the same.
  c The index in part **a i** is the sum of the indices in part **a ii**
  d $2^3 \times 2^4 = 2^7$

8

×	3^4	3^5	3^6
3^2	3^6	3^7	3^8
3^3	3^7	3^8	3^9
3^4	3^8	3^9	3^{10}

9 a 2^8 **b** 4^6 **c** 3^5 **d** 5^5
e 7^6 **f** 2^9 **g** $(-3)^5$ **h** $(-2)^3$
i $(-8)^8$

10 a 2^7 **b** 3^5 **c** 4^5 **d** 3^4
e 5^5 **f** 2^9

11 a 2^3 **b** 2^{15} **c** 32 768

12 a 25 **b** 7 **c** 27

13 a 8 **b** 2^3
  c $\dfrac{2 \times 2 \times 2 \times 2 \times 2 \times 2 \times 2}{2 \times 2 \times 2 \times 2} = \dfrac{2^7}{2^4} = 2^3$
  d $2^5 \div 2^3 = \dfrac{2^5}{2^3} = \dfrac{2 \times 2 \times 2 \times 2 \times 2}{2 \times 2 \times 2} = 2^2$
  e To divide two powers of the same number, subtract the indices.

14 a 5^3 **b** 4^5 **c** 3^3 **d** 2^1 or 2
e 5^2 **f** 6^3 **g** $(-2)^2$ **h** $(-3)^1$ or −3

15 a 2^2 **b** 2^3 **c** 3^1 or 3

16 2^{12} or 4096

17 a 3^3 **b** 4^4 **c** 5^4 **d** 2^5

18 a $2^7 \div (2^2 \times 2^3) = 2^7 \div 2^5 = 2^2$
  $2^7 \div 2^2 \times 2^3 = 2^5 \times 2^3 = 2^8$
  Different answers, so brackets were necessary.
  b $4^8 \div (4^2 \times 4^3) = 4^8 \div 4^5 = 4^3$
  $4^8 \div 4^2 \times 4^3 = 4^6 \times 4^3 = 4^9$
  Different answers, so brackets were necessary.
  c $2^8 \div (2^7 \div 2^5) = 2^8 \div 2^2 = 2^6$
  $2^8 \div 2^7 \div 2^5 = 2 \div 2^5 = 2^{-4}$
  Different answers, so brackets were necessary.
  d $(2^8 \div 2^7) \div 2^5 = 2 \div 2^5 = 2^{-4}$
  $2^8 \div 2^7 \div 2^5 = 2 \div 2^5 = 2^{-4}$
  Same answer, so brackets were unnecessary.

19 a 36 **b** 64 **c** 125 **d** 256
e 9 **f** 25 **g** 81 **h** 1

Challenge

C $3^2 + 2 \times 5^2$

1.2 Calculations and estimates

1 a 70 cm **b** £3 **c** 16 **d** 64

2 £180

3 a 240 **b** −27 **c** 54 **d** 5
e 48 **f** 40 **g** 8 **h** 4

4 a $\frac{16}{25}$ **b** 40 **c** $\frac{3}{2}$ **d** 8

5 a −2 **b** −3 **c** −5 **d** −10

6 a 4 **b** 5 **c** 11 **d** 2
e −4 **f** −1

7 a £53.00
  b Overestimate, because both prices were rounded up.

8 a Students' own answers, e.g.
  i $5 \times 2 \times £4 = £40$
  ii $4 \times 4 \times £4 = £64$
  iii $8 \times 10 \times £4 = £320$
  b i £39.90 **ii** £63.84 **iii** £319.20
  c better to overestimate

9 a Students' own answers, e.g.
  i $4 \times 1.2 \times £9 = 4.8 \times £9 \approx 5 \times £9 = £45$
  ii $4.5 \times 4 \times £9 = 18 \times £9 \approx 20 \times £9 = £180$
  iii $2 \times 4 \times 8 \times £9 = 64 \times £9 \approx 60 \times £9 = £540$
  b i £43.10 **ii** £167.03 **iii** £585.50

10 a $40 \times 60 = 2400$
  b overestimate
  c $30 \times 50 = 1500$
  d underestimate
  e $30 \times 60 = 1800$
  f $40 \times 50 = 2000$
  g 40×50 is closest to actual answer (1938)

11 a, b Students' own answers, e.g.
  i Sally's rule (round one up, one down): $12 \times 12 = 144$
  Round both to nearest whole number: $12 \times 12 = 144$
  Calculator answer: 142.68
  ii Sally's rule (round both up): $60 \div 12 = 5$
  Round both to nearest ten: $60 \div 10 = 6$
  Calculator answer: 5.05 (2 d.p.)
  iii Sally's rule (round both down): $70 - 50 = 20$
  Round both to nearest whole number: $71 - 52 = 19$
  Calculator answer: 18.9
  iv Sally's rule (round one up, one down):
  $2800 + 1200 = 4000$
  Round both to nearest ten: $2780 + 1220 = 4000$
  Calculator answer: 3995
  v Sally's rule (round one up, one down): $10 \times 10^2 = 1000$
  Round both to nearest whole number: $10 \times 11^2 = 1210$
  Calculator answer: 1118.36 (2 d.p.)
  vi Sally's rule (round both up): $600 \div 200 = 3$
  Round one up, one down: $600 \div 150 = 4$
  Calculator answer: 3.37 (3 d.p.)
  c Students' own answers
  d Students' own conclusions, e.g.
  Sally's rule gives answers close to the exact answers, and you can often choose 'nice numbers'.

12 a Students' own answers, e.g.
  i $(15 - 5) \times 2 = 10 \times 2 = 20$
  ii $5 \times (6 + 4) = 5 \times 10 = 50$
  iii $(3 - 2) \times 64 = 1 \times 64 = 64$
  iv $(22 - 2) \div 0.1 \approx 20 \times 10 = 200$
  b i 21.5 (1 d.p.) **ii** 48.8 (1 d.p.)
  iii 67.7 (1 d.p.) **iv** 227.9 (1 d.p.)

13 The mistake Pam made is that she estimated using −6 for $\sqrt{36}$ instead of the principal square root, which is +6.

14 a Students' own answers, e.g.
  i $\dfrac{83 - 63}{\sqrt{16}} = \dfrac{20}{4} = 5$
  ii $\dfrac{440}{2} = 22$
  iii $\dfrac{\sqrt{64}}{4} = \dfrac{8}{4} = 2$
  iv $\dfrac{\sqrt{16} \times \sqrt{100}}{5 \div 1} = \dfrac{4 \times 10}{5} = 8$
  b i 4.9 (1 d.p.) **ii** 20.2 (1 d.p.)
  iii 1.8 (1 d.p.) **iv** 7.9 (1 d.p.)

15 a i $\sqrt{16} = 4$ **ii** $\frac{8}{2} = 4$
  b The answers are the same.
  c i 5 **ii** 3
  d Students' own answers, e.g.
  No; $\sqrt{25} = 5$ and $\dfrac{\sqrt{144}}{\sqrt{16}} = \dfrac{12}{4} = 3$

e   i $\frac{1}{\sqrt{9}} = \frac{1}{3}$ ii $\frac{\sqrt{9}}{\sqrt{25}} = \frac{3}{5}$

16 a   i $\frac{4}{9}$ ii $\frac{4}{9}$
   iii The answers are the same.
   b   i $\frac{8}{27}$ ii $\frac{8}{27}$
   iii The answers are the same.
   c   To find a power of a fraction, work out the same power for both the numerator and the denominator.

17 a   i $\frac{9}{25}$ ii $\frac{49}{81}$ iii $\frac{64}{125}$ iv $\frac{27}{64}$
   b   The square or cube of a proper fraction is always smaller than the original fraction.

18 a   36   b $12\frac{1}{4}$ c $4\frac{21}{25}$ d $1\frac{11}{25}$
   e $5\frac{4}{9}$

19 a $\sqrt{\frac{25}{36}} = \frac{5}{6}$
   b $\left(\frac{1}{2}\right)^3 = \frac{1}{8}$
   c $\left(\frac{2}{7}\right)^2 = \frac{4}{49}$

20 a   36   b   16   c   8   d   12
   e   24   f   20

Challenge

Students' own answers, e.g.

a $\dfrac{\sqrt[3]{8} + 15.8}{9} \approx \dfrac{2 + 16}{9} = \dfrac{18}{9} = 2$

b $\dfrac{\sqrt[3]{125} + 15.8}{7} \approx \dfrac{5 + 16}{7} = \dfrac{21}{7} = 3$

c $\dfrac{\sqrt[3]{64} + 15.8}{-4} \approx \dfrac{4 + 16}{-4} = \dfrac{20}{-4} = -5$

1.3 More indices

1 a   10 000   b $\frac{1}{100}$ c   0.001   d $\frac{1}{2}, \frac{1}{7}, 5$
2 a 4^2 b 3^5 c 5^4 d 9^5
   e 10^7 f 2^3 g 10^2 h 2^5
3 a   0.045 km   b   0.25 m
4 a

Expression	Number in index form raised to a power	Single power
$4^3 \times 4^3$	$(4^3)^2$	4^6
$7^3 \times 7^3 \times 7^3$	$(7^3)^3$	7^9
$3^2 \times 3^2 \times 3^2 \times 3^2$	$(3^2)^4$	3^8

   b   To find a power of a number written in index form, multiply the powers.
5 a 2^{12} b 11^{12} c 10^{24} d 2^{28}
   e 6^{28}
6 a 2^{12} b 4^{10} c 5^{12}
7 a $10^3 = 1000$
      $10^2 = 100$
      $10^1 = 10$
      $10^0 = 1$
      $10^{-1} = 0.1$
      $10^{-2} = 0.01$
      $10^{-3} = 0.001$
      $10^{-4} = 0.000\,1$
      $10^{-5} = 0.000\,01$
   b $10^{-6} = 0.000\,001$

8 a $\frac{1}{10^2}$

   b   i $\frac{1}{10^3}$ ii $\frac{1}{10}$ iii 10^{-6}
      iv 10^{-9} v 10^{-4}
   c $10^{-n} = \frac{1}{10^n}$

9

Prefix	Letter	Power	Number
tera	T	10^{12}	1 000 000 000 000
giga	G	10^{9}	1 000 000 000
mega	M	10^{6}	1 000 000
kilo	k	10^{3}	1000
deci	d	10^{-1}	0.1
centi	c	10^{-2}	0.01
milli	m	10^{-3}	0.001
micro	μ	10^{-6}	0.000 001
nano	n	10^{-9}	0.000 000 001
pico	p	10^{-12}	0.000 000 000 001

10 a 10^6, M   b 10^{-2}, c   c 10^9, G
   d 10^{-1}, d   e 10^{-4}, no prefix
   f 10^{12}, T   g 10^{-5}, no prefix
   h 10^{-9}, n   i 10^{-3}, m

11 a   1000 m   b   0.000001 s or $\frac{1}{1\,000\,000}$ s
   c   1 000 000 t
   d   0.000 000 000 001 g or $\frac{1}{1\,000\,000\,000\,000}$ g
   e   1 000 000 000 000 Hz
   f   0.000 000 001 m or $\frac{1}{1\,000\,000\,000}$ m

12 a   1 000 000   b   1 000 000 000 000
   c   10   d   1 000 000 000
13 a   5 000 000 μm   b   2500 mg
   c   4 000 000 000 W   d   1 900 000 000 ns
   e   4 230 000 000 000 pg   f   0.005 g
14   2500
15   $2^3 = 8$
     $2^2 = 4$
     $2^1 = 2$
     $2^0 = 1$
     $2^{-1} = \frac{1}{2}$
     $2^{-2} = \frac{1}{4}$
     $2^{-3} = \frac{1}{8}$
     $2^{-4} = \frac{1}{16}$
     $2^{-5} = \frac{1}{32}$

16 a $10^0 = 1$ and $2^0 = 1$
   b $n^0 = 1$ for all values of n.
17 a   The negative powers of 10 and 2 are all less than 1.
   b   When $n > 1$, $n^{-\square}$ is less than 1. When $n < 1$, $n^{-\square}$ is greater than 1.

18   $\frac{1}{8}$

19 a $2^{-3} = \frac{1}{2^3}$
   b $2^{-4} = \frac{1}{2^4}$ c $2^{-1} = \frac{1}{2^1}$ or $\frac{1}{2}$
   d $\frac{1}{2^2} = 2^{-2}$ e $\frac{1}{2^6} = 2^{-6}$
   f   The reciprocal of 2^5 is 2^{-5}.
   g $2^{-n} = \frac{1}{2^n}$

20 a $\frac{1}{9}$ b $\frac{1}{125}$ c $\frac{1}{6}$ d   1
21 a 10^3 b 4^{-2} c 2^{-7} d 10^{-5}
   e 10^{-2} f 2^{-3} g 5^{-5} h 3^7
22 a $\frac{1}{4}$ b $\frac{1}{4}$ c $\frac{1}{2}$ d   1
   e   8   f   27   g $\frac{1}{32}$ h   64

Challenge

1 a i $\frac{1}{9}$ ii $\frac{1}{9}$ iii 4 iv 4

  b The square of a fraction is the same as the reciprocal of the fraction raised to the power -2.

2 a i $\frac{1}{27}$ ii $\frac{1}{27}$ iii 8 iv 8

  b The cube of a fraction is the same as the reciprocal of the fraction raised to the power -3.

3 A negative power of a fraction is the same as the reciprocal of the fraction raised to the same positive power.

4 Students' own answers

1.4 Standard form

1 a 1000 b 5000 c 7 000 000 000

2 a 3^5 b 1 000 000 c 10^{-3}
  d 6×1000 e $2.5 \times 10 000$ f $3.1 \times 10 000 000$
  g 2.3 million h 8.44 million

3 a 2000 b 6 000 000 c 71 000 000
  e 3 900 000 000

4 a i 0.07 ii 0.005
    iii 0.000038 iv 0.000 000 007 1
    v 0.000 12 vi 0.000003
    vii 0.4 viii 0.000 000 001
  b smaller

5 A, C, E, I, J, K, L

6 a 4.2×10^3 b 9×10^6 c 2.7×10^1
  d 6.4×10^{-3} e 2.19×10^{-2} f 7×10^{-7}
  g 3×10^{-1} h 9.9×10^{-11}

7 a Jacqui has confused millions and billions.
  b 6.4×10^9

8 a 2.4×10^{26} m b 1.8×10^{-15} m
  c 1.5×10^7 °C d 7.5×10^{-8} g

9 a i 11 000 000 g ii 1.1×10^7 g
  b i 149 600 000 km ii 1.496×10^8 km
  c i 1 350 000 000 000 m ii 1.35×10^{12} m
  d i 0.000025 m ii 2.5×10^{-5} m
  e i 0.0014 g ii 1.4×10^{-3} g

10 a 36 000 b 9 270 000
  c 0.018 d 0.000 000 75
  e 5.4 f 0.000 000 75; 0.018; 5.4; 36 000; 9 270 000

11 a 5.5×10^{12} b 7.32×10^7
  c 1.02×10^{-7} d 4.5×10^{-17}

12 a i yes ii 7 380 000 000 000
    iii Students' own calculator answers, e.g. 7.38^{12}, 7.38E12
  b i 0.000 000 125 m
    ii Students' own calculator answers, e.g. 1.25^{-7}, 1.25E-7

13 Vega

14 GPS satellite, Mercury, Alpha Centauri, Pole star, Horsehead nebula, Pisces galaxy

15 a blood cell, amoeba, grain of salt b yes
  c water molecule, DNA, virus, blood cell, amoeba, grain of salt

Challenge

  $0.0005 \text{ m} \div 100 000 = 5 \times 10^{-9}$ m

1 Check up

1 a 5^5 b 3^3 c 7^8 d $(-6)^1$ or -6
  e 4^5 f 2^{10} g 3^9 h 7^{15}

2 a 3 800 000 000 W b 0.007 g

3 a 10^{-5} b 2^{15} c 3^2

4 a $\frac{1}{25}$ b 1

5 A and C

6 -4

7 a -5 b 1

8 a $\frac{9}{25}$ b 144 c $\frac{1}{4}$

9 Students' own answers, e.g.
  a $(\sqrt{64} - 3) \times 3 = (8 - 3) \times 3 = 5 \times 3 = 15$
  b $(10 - 15) \times (8 + 10) = -5 \times 18 \approx -5 \times 20 = -100$
  c $\frac{56 + 3}{8 \times 4} \approx \frac{60}{30} = 2$

10 a 45 000 b 0.0012

11 B and C

12 a 7.5×10^5 b 2×10^{-8} c 8.3×10^9

13 3.71×10^{-2}

14 a 14 Tl (next best is 14 000 Gl)
  b 1.4×10^{13} litres

15 iodine

Challenge

1 $\frac{(-4)^2 + 8 \times 3}{10} = \frac{16 + 24}{10} = \frac{40}{10} = 4$

2 a $4 + 2^2 = 8$
    $4 + 2^2 + 2^3 = 16$
    $4 + 2^2 + 2^3 + 2^4 = 32$
  b increasing powers of 2
  c i 64 ii 62
  d $2^{n+1} - 2$

3 Students' own answers, e.g.
  a $10^3 \times 10^{-6} = 10^{-3}$
  b $2^4 \times 2^1 \times 2^{-1} = 2^4$
  c $5^8 \div 5^4 \div 5^4 \div 5^8 = 5^{-8}$
  d $10^5 \times 10^6 \times 10^{-11} \times 10^{-5} \times 10^{10} \div 10^5 = 10^5$

1 Strengthen: Indices and powers of 10

1 a 3^6 b 5^5 c 2^6 d 7^4
  e 5^9 f 10^8

2 a 6^3 b 5^2 c 2^4 d 7^2

3 a She has multiplied the powers instead of adding them. The correct answer is 2^7.
  b He has divided the powers instead of subtracting them. The correct answer is 10^6.

4 a $2^{4+3-5} = 2^{7-5} = 2^2$ b $10^{7+2-4} = 10^{9-4} = 10^5$
  c $8^3 \times 8^3 = 8^6$ d 4^6
  e 3^1 or 3

5 a 6×6 b 6^8
  c $6 \times 6 \times 6$ d 6^{12}
  e $7^3 \times 7^3 = 7^6$ f $7^5 \times 7^5 \times 7^5 = 7^{15}$

6 a 34 mm
  b 250 000 000 km c 0.8 nm

7 a 4.5 m b 0.08 mm c 3.5 Mm

8 a 460 MHz b 0.53 mg c 7 W
  d 270 000 000 ml

9 a 1 b $4^{2-2} = 4^0$ c 1
  d i $5^2 \div 5^2 = \frac{5^2}{5^2} = \frac{25}{25} = 1$
      $5^2 \div 5^2 = 5^{2-2} = 5^0$
    ii 1
  e When you write a number to the power 0, the answer is **1**.

10 a i 4^{-2} ii $\frac{1}{4^2}$ iii $4^{-2} = \frac{1}{4^2}$
  b i 10^{-3} ii $\frac{1}{10^3}$ iii $10^{-3} = \frac{1}{10^3}$
  c i $\frac{1}{2^3}$ ii $\frac{1}{10^4}$ iii 10^{-2} iv 10^{-1}

11 Sandhu

12 a 10^2 b 10^{-6} c 2^{-3} d 10^{-3}
  e 10^{-6} f 10^{-4}

13 a 2^3
  b i 2^8 ii 2^9 iii 2^6

1 Strengthen: Powers and roots

1 a $4 \times 9 = 36$ b $25 \times 16 = 400$
  c $16 \times 100 = 1600$

2 a $6^2 = 36$ b $20^2 = 400$ c $40^2 = 1600$

3 a The answers are the same.
  b $5^2 \times 6^2$

4 a -16 and 16
  b The square of a negative number is positive.
  c i 36 ii 36 iii 0
    iv -32 v 1 vi 11
    vii 16 viii -34

5 a -8 b -2 c -27 d -3
  e -4 f -5

6 a i 4   **ii** 49   **iii** $\frac{4}{49}$

  b i 25   **ii** 81   **iii** $\frac{25}{81}$

7 a $\frac{4 \times 4 \times 1 \times 5 \times 5}{2} = \frac{400}{2} = 200$

  b $\frac{4 \times 5 \times 4 \times 5}{10} = \frac{400}{10} = 40$

8 a To make an easy division

  b Students' own answers, e.g. $\frac{18}{6} - 1.5 = 3 - 1.5 = 1.5$

  c Students' own answers, e.g.
    i 9   **ii** $9 + 30 = 39$
    iii 7   **iv** $\frac{7 - 5}{2} = 1$

1 Strengthen: Standard form

1 a 23   **b** 230   **c** 2300
  d 160   **e** 16000
  f 39000   **g** 390000   **h** 3900000

2 15000000 °C

3 a 0.17   **b** 0.017   **c** 0.0017
  d 0.0082   **e** 0.00082
  f 0.00094   **g** 0.000094   **h** 0.0000094

4 B

5 a 5.3×10^3 **b** 4.9×10^4 **c** 6.3×10^7
  d 7×10^5 **e** 9×10^6 **f** 5.6×10^{10}

6 a 2.9×10^{-3} **b** 5.7×10^{-2} **c** 6.3×10^{-5}
  d 7×10^{-7} **e** 9×10^{-9} **f** 5.6×10^{-13}

7 a 4×10^7 m   **b** 1.4×10^{-9} m

8 a 9×10^{-6}, 2.7×10^{-4}, 7.3×10^2, 4.3×10^7
  b 1.2×10^6, 7.3×10^6, 3.5×10^7, 5×10^7

Challenge

1 a, b Students' own answers

2 a 5*2+3^2   **b** (5−2)^3   **c** SQRT(4+12)
  d 20/2^2   **e** 4^2/SQRT(16)
  f 3^2/(2*9) or (3^2)/(2*9)

1 Extend

1 a 2^{10} **b** 0.3 cm   **c** 1.024×10^5

2 $1200 \times 1800 \div (60 \times 30) = 1200$, underestimate
  $1200 \times 1800 \div (50 \times 25) = 1728$, overestimate
  $1200 \times 1800 \div (50 \times 30) = 1440$, best estimate
  $1200 \times 1800 \div (60 \times 25) = 1440$, best estimate

3 a i 2^{-2} **ii** 2^{-3} **iii** 2^{-6}
  b 0.03125

4 Students' own answers, e.g.

$$51.52 \times \frac{3000 \times \sqrt[3]{8.5}}{4} \approx 50 \times \frac{3000 \times \sqrt[3]{8}}{4}$$

$$= 50 \times \frac{6000}{4} = 50 \times 1500 = 75000$$

5 a between 7.1×10^{12} and 7.3×10^{12}
  b between $7000000000000 and $7500000000000
  c between $11400000 million and $11600000 million

6 9.3×10^5 hours (approximately 106 years)

7 a $10^2 = 100$ **b** $4 \times 25 = 100$
  c $10^3 = 1000$ **d** $8 \times 125 = 1000$

8 a To find a power of a product, work out the same power for both numbers in the product, then multiply.
  b i $10^4 = 10000$, $16 \times 625 = 10000$
    ii $30^2 = 900$, $4 \times 25 \times 9 = 900$

9 a $2^2 = 4$ **b** $36 \div 9 = 4$

10 a To find a power of a division, work out the same power for both the numerator and the denominator, then divide.
  b Students' own answers

11 a 3.64×10^9
  b i 8×10^{-14}
    ii Students' own answers, e.g.
    The possible values of N predicted by the equation vary too much to be able to say.

c Students' own answers, e.g.
The lowest value of N predicted by the equation is 0.008, but it is unlikely that *all* of the variables will take the minimum value from the range of possible values. So the equation suggests that there probably are other intelligent civilisations in space.

Challenge

a $\left(1\frac{1}{4}\right)^2 = 1\frac{9}{16}$

b $\left(6\frac{2}{3}\right)^2 = 44\frac{4}{9}$

c $\left(2\frac{2}{3}\right)^2 = 7\frac{1}{9}$

1 Unit test

1 a 10^7 **b** 4^2

2 a 4300 mm   **b** 3160000000 W

3 a 2^4 **b** 3^6

4 a 1   **b** $\frac{1}{125}$

5 C

6 a −10   **b** 33

7 Students' own answers, e.g.
  a $\frac{14 + 11}{5} = \frac{25}{5} = 5$
  b $(6 - 2) \times 12 = 4 \times 12 = 48$

8 Students' own answers, e.g.
  $4 \times 2 \times £20 = £160$

9 a 3200000000 W   **b** 3200000 kW

10 a 5^{-3} **b** 3^{12}

11 a 270000   **b** 0.0006

12 a 16   **b** 8   **c** 2

13 a 150 Gm or 150000000 km
  b 1.5×10^{11} m

14 5^{42}

15 a 4.7×10^{-8} **b** 1.2×10^{10}

16 The virus is bigger.

Challenge

1 $\frac{9}{4}$

2 Students' own answers

UNIT 2 Expressions and formulae

2.1 Solving equations

1 a 100° (alternate angles)
  b 70° (corresponding angles)

2 a $2x + 14$ **b** $5y$

3 a $x = 22$ **b** $y = 6$ **c** $z = 18$
  d $w = -8$ **e** $a = 3$ **f** $b = -2$
  g $c = 4.5$ **h** $d = 11$

4 a $x = 6$ **b** $x = 8$ **c** $x = 18$
  d $x = -6$

5 a $y = \frac{2}{5}$ **b** $y = \frac{7}{3}$ or $2\frac{1}{3}$ **c** $y = \frac{3}{4}$
  d $y = \frac{2}{3}$ **e** $y = -\frac{1}{2}$ **f** $y = \frac{5}{4}$ or $1\frac{1}{4}$

6 a $x = 0.9$ **b** $x = 0.6$ **c** $x = -0.75$
  d $x = 0.5$ **e** $x = 1.5$ **f** $x = 1.6$

7 a $x = 10$ **b** $y = 6$ **c** $a = 15$
  d $b = -8$ **e** $c = 36$ **f** $d = 1$

8 a $x = 13$ **b** $x = 10$ **c** $x = 14$
  d $x = -17$

9 $\frac{x}{2} + 5 = 8$; $x = 6$

10 $\frac{x + 17}{5} = 4$; $x = 3$

11 $x = 7$

12 a $x = 4$ **b** $x = 7$ **c** $x = -2$
  d $x = 2$ **e** $x = 10$ **f** $y = 8$
  g $y = 8$ **h** $y = -6$ **i** $x = 4$

13 a $x = 50°$, angle = 50°   **b** $x = 40°$, angle = 110°

14 $2(x + 1) = x + 16$; $x = 14$

15 a $d = 2$ **b** $s = 5$ **c** $t = 4$
  d $x = -5$ **e** $n = 3$ **f** $v = 8$

16 $x = 7$

Challenge

a $4a = 2a + 14$
b i $a = 7$ **ii** 3 and 11
c The value of a is always the sum of the two numbers.

2.2 Substituting into expressions

1 a 9   **b** 8   **c** 4   **d** 3

2 a 27   **b** 32   **c** 18   **d** 28
  e 3   **f** 6

3 a 13   **b** 3   **c** 40   **d** 240
  e $\frac{8}{5}$ or $1\frac{3}{5}$ **f** 31   **g** 89   **h** 39

4 a 9   **b** −25   **c** 14   **d** −15
  e 9   **f** 25   **g** 34   **h** −16
  i 27   **j** −125

5 a 0.16   **b** 0.36

6 a 13   **b** 17   **c** 36   **d** 24
  e 29   **f** 27   **g** −6   **h** 9

7 a 36   **b** 48   **c** 96   **d** 288

8 a 100   **b** 100   **c** 49   **d** 144
  e 117   **f** 176   **g** 17   **h** 11
  i 12

9 a $2(A + 4) = 14$ kg
  $2.5A + 8 = 15.5$ kg

b

Age	$2(A + 4)$	$2.5A + 8$
1	10 kg	10.5 kg
2	12 kg	13 kg
3	14 kg	15.5 kg
4	16 kg	18 kg
5	18 kg	20.5 kg

c $2(A + 4)$: add 2
  $2.5A + 8$: add 2.5
d the increase in weight each year

10 a 240   **b** 10   **c** 6   **d** 6.4
  e 5.5   **f** 0.04

11 a 4   **b** 5   **c** 3   **d** 24
  e 4   **f** 10

12 a C   **b** C   **c** B   **d** A
  e A

13 a 198   **b** −12   **c** 236   **d** 130
  e 146   **f** −62   **g** 4   **h** 27
  i 6

Challenge

Students' own answers, e.g.

a $\dfrac{xy}{2}, \dfrac{-u\sqrt{xy}}{2}, \dfrac{-xy}{v}$

b $2uv, -ux, xy - uv$

c $uv, \dfrac{xy}{3}, xy - 2uv$

d $xy + x, -5vx, -5(u + v)$

2.3 Writing and using formulae

1 A4, B5, C6, D1, E3, F2

2 a £54   **b** $9h$ **c** $E = 9h$

3 a £75   **b** $C = 35 + 20h$

4 a $C = 80 + 10p$ **b** £580

5 a $M = 40x + 30$
  b 182 minutes (3 hours 2 minutes)
  c 130 minutes (2 hours 10 minutes)

6 a i £60   **ii** £120
  b £40
  c $C = 40 + 20h$
  d £95

7 $C = 4 + 8d$

8 a £114   **b** $T = 32A + 25C$

9 a $T = 8a + 5c$ **b** £62

10 a 0.12 mm   **b** 0.12×3, $0.12 \times t$
  c $L = 10\,000 + 0.12t$ **d** 10 001.8 mm

11 a 30 N   **b** −8 N   **c** −5.88 N

12 a 0 m   **b** 6.4 m

13 1.8×10^{18} J

14 a −16   **b** −6   **c** −18   **d** 5

Challenge

$E = 76.8$

2.4 Using and rearranging formulae

1 a $A = bh$
  b $A = \frac{1}{2}bh$
  c $A = \frac{1}{2}(a + b)h$

2 a 15   **b** 0   **c** −2

3 a $x = 13$ **b** $x = 5$ **c** $x = 24$

4 a 20 cm²
  b 6 cm²
  c 15 cm²

5 a $m = 2.4$ **b** $a = 4.5$

6 a $12 = \frac{1}{2} \times b \times 3$ **b** $b = 8$ cm

7 a 2 hours
  b $3\frac{5}{6}$ hours (3 hours 50 minutes)

8 a $C = 10 + 5r$ **b** $50   **c** 15 rides

9 a $u = 19$ **b** $t = 6$ **c** $a = 2$

10 $a = 0.72$

11 $n = 0.4$

12 $N = 20$

13 a $x = \dfrac{P}{h}$ **b** $x = \dfrac{V}{r}$ **c** $x = A - y$
  d $x = F + r$ **e** $x = 2r$ **f** $x = Mn$
  g $x = t + 2v$ **h** $x = Y - np$ **i** $x = \dfrac{R - 4}{2}$

14 a $T = \dfrac{D}{S}$ **b** $S = \dfrac{D}{T}$ **c** $T = F - R$

    d $m = h + n$ **e** $n = k - 2l$ **f** $u = v - at$

    g $a = \dfrac{v - u}{t}$ **h** $T = F + mg$ **i** $m = Kt$

    j $t = \dfrac{m}{K}$ **k** $M = DV$ **l** $V = \dfrac{M}{D}$

Challenge

a $A = 4$, $G = 20$, $H = 3$, $I = 12$, $K = 8$, $N = 15$, $W = 5$

b HAWKING

2.5 Index laws and brackets

1 a 2^5 **b** 3^4 **c** 3^2

2 a x^4 **b** $y \times y \times y \times y \times y$

3 a $x^2 z^3$ **b** $6n^2$

4 a $3a + 7b - 3b$ **b** $7x + 3$

5 a p^7 **b** k^5 **c** a^6 **d** $3m^5$

    e $4a^3$ **f** $4b^4$ **g** $4c^4$ **h** $4d^5$

    i $10e^5$ **j** $18s^3$ **k** $10g^2$ **l** $12p^5$

6 a e^5 **b** a^5 **c** b^3 **d** c^3

    e $3c^3$ **f** $5b$ **g** $4a^5$ **h** $3d^3$

    i $8m$ **j** $4t^3$ **k** 6 **l** 7

7 a $4a^2$ **b** $25x^2$ **c** $64y^3$

    d $\dfrac{a^3}{27}$ **e** $\dfrac{x^2}{36}$ **f** $\dfrac{y^3}{8}$

8 a F   **b** T   **c** F   **d** T

9 a 3 **b** 6 **c** 1.5

    d 2 **e** $\dfrac{4}{5}$ or 0.8 **f** $\dfrac{4}{5}$ or 0.8

10 a $\dfrac{1}{6^2}$ **b** $\dfrac{1}{3^3}$ **c** $\dfrac{1}{5^1}$ or $\dfrac{1}{5}$

    d $\dfrac{1}{x^2}$ **e** $\dfrac{1}{y^4}$ **f** $\dfrac{1}{z^1}$ or $\dfrac{1}{z}$

11 a $x^{-5} = \dfrac{1}{x^5}$ **b** $y^{-4} = \dfrac{1}{y^4}$ **c** $z^{-6} = \dfrac{1}{z^6}$

    d $w^{-7} = \dfrac{1}{w^7}$ **e** $v^{-2} = \dfrac{1}{v^2}$ **f** $t^{-6} = \dfrac{1}{t^6}$

    g $m^{-2} = \dfrac{1}{m^2}$ **h** $n^{-1} = \dfrac{1}{n}$

12 a $3a^2$ **b** $5m^3$ **c** $2a^2 + 3b^2$

    d $2e^2 + e^4$ **e** $2y^5 + 2y^3$ **f** $3a^3$

    g $9p + 8p^2$ **h** $8h^2 + 6b^3$

13 a $y^3 + 5y$ **b** $y^3 + 5y^2$ **c** $x^3 - 2x^2$

    d $x^3 - 2x^3$ **e** $x^5 + 2x^3$ **f** $3n^3 - 6n$

    g $3n^3 - 6n^2$ **h** $15n^3 - 6n^2$

14 $x \times x \times (x + 7) = x^2(x + 7) = x^3 + 7x^2$

15 a $3m^2 + m$ **b** $11d^2 - 12d$ **c** $2s^2 + 14s - 6$

    d $3x^3 + 11x^2$ **e** $3b^3 + 19b^2$ **f** $3d^4 - 6d$

16 a $4(x + 2)$ **b** $4(x^2 + 2)$ **c** $4x(x + 2)$

    d $4x^2(x + 2)$ **e** $y^2(1 - 5y)$ **f** $3y^3(3y^2 - 1)$

    g $5y^2(2y^2 - 1)$ **h** $3y^5(4y^2 + 3)$

17 a $y(x + 1)$ **b** $y(x - 1)$ **c** $xy(x - 1)$

    d $xy(y + 1)$ **e** $2xy(y + 1)$ **f** $2xy(y + 2)$

    g $2xy(2y - 1)$ **h** $2xy(2y - 3)$

Challenge

LHS $= 3x^3 + 4x^3 + 9x^2 = 7x^3 + 9x^2$

RHS $= 7x^3 + 21x^2 - 12x^2 = 7x^3 + 9x^2 =$ LHS

2.6 Expanding double brackets

1 a -12 **b** 6 **c** -35 **d** 32

2 a a^2 **b** x^2 **c** $4a$ **d** $-2x$

    e $2a$ **f** $5x$ **g** $x^2 + 11x + 1$

    h $x^2 + 2x + 12$ **i** $a^2 - 3a - 7$

3 a $4x + 8$ **b** $8y - 8$ **c** $z^2 + 4z$ **d** $m^2 - 4m$

4 a $(x + 5)(x + 3)$

    b $3x$ and 15

    c $x^2 + 5x + 3x + 15 = x^2 + 8x + 15$

    d $(x + 5)(x + 3) = x^2 + 8x + 15$

5 a $(y + 1)(y + 2) = y^2 + 2y + y + 2 = y^2 + 3y + 2$

    b $(z + 4)(z + 8) = z^2 + 8z + 4z + 32 = z^2 + 12z + 32$

    c $(v + 4)(v + 2) = v^2 + 2v + 4v + 8 = v^2 + 6v + 8$

6 $x^2 + 15x + 54$ or $(x + 6)(9 + x)$ or $(x + 9)(6 + x)$ or $(x + 6)(x + 9)$

    or $(x + 9)(x + 6)$ or $(6 + x)(9 + x)$ or $(9 + x)(6 + x)$

7 a $x^2 + 10x + 21$ **b** $y^2 + 10y + 9$

    c $m^2 + 10m + 24$ **d** $p^2 + 19p + 88$

    e $q^2 + 18q + 45$ **f** $n^2 + 17n + 60$

8 a $x^2 - 2x - 15$ **b** $y^2 + 2y - 15$

    c $p^2 + 5p - 84$ **d** $q^2 - q - 72$

    e $s^2 - 3s - 10$ **f** $t^2 + 3t - 10$

9 a $m^2 - 6m + 8$ **b** $n^2 - 6n + 5$

10 Pawel is correct; the mistake Kaira made is that she simplified $3x - 4x$ to $1x$ instead of $-1x$.

11 a $x^2 + 6x + 9$ **b** $x^2 + 10x + 25$

    c $x^2 - 8x + 16$ **d** $x^2 - 16x + 64$

12 a $(x + 3)(x + 3) - x^2 = x^2 + 3x + 3x + 9 - x^2$

      $= 6x + 9$

    b $(x + 4)(x + 3) - x(x + 2) = x^2 + 3x + 4x + 12 - (x^2 + 2x)$

      $= x^2 + 7x + 12 - x^2 - 2x = 5x + 12$

    c $(x + 4)(x + 3) - (x + 1)(x + 2)$

      $= x^2 + 3x + 4x + 12 - (x^2 + 2x + x + 2)$

      $= x^2 + 7x + 12 - x^2 - 3x - 2$

      $= 4x + 10$

13 a $(x + 6)(x - 3) + x(2x - 5)$

      $= x^2 - 3x + 6x - 18 + 2x^2 - 5x$

      $= 3x^2 - 2x - 18$

    b $(n - 5)(n - 8) - 12(n - 2)$

      $= n^2 - 8n - 5n + 40 - 12n + 24$

      $= n^2 - 25n + 64$

Challenge

1 a $8 \times 15 - 7 \times 16 = 120 - 112 = 8$

    b $30 \times 37 - 29 \times 38 = 1110 - 1102 = 8$

2 All the answers are 8.

3

n	$n + 1$
$n + 8$	$n + 9$

4 $(n + 1)(n + 8) - n(n + 9)$

   $= n^2 + 8n + n + 8 - (n^2 + 9n)$

   $= n^2 + 9n + 8 - n^2 - 9n$

   $= 8$

5 The expression simplifies to 8.

6 Students' own answers.

7 The answer is always the number of columns in the grid.

2 Check up

1 a $x = 21$ **b** $n = 16$ **c** $r = 5$ **d** $c = 4$

    e $x = 17$

2 a 90 **b** 24 **c** 59 **d** 5

3 a 5 **b** 180 **c** 83

4 a 200 **b** -117.6

5 a £160   **b** $T = dx + f$ **c** £245

6 $t = 20$

7 $a = 3$

8 a $x = \dfrac{y}{k}$ **b** $x = an$ **c** $x = t + v$ **d** $x = \dfrac{u - d}{2}$

9 a $y^4 + 7y^2$ **b** $6x^4 + 3x^2$

10 $4x^2 + 32x$

11 a $49y^2$ **b** $\dfrac{x^3}{125}$

12 a w^5 **b** $12g^5$ **c** v^2

    d y^{-1} or $\dfrac{1}{y^1}$ or $\dfrac{1}{y}$ **e** 5 **f** $4a$

13 a $3x(3 - x^2)$ **b** $5y^4(4y^2 + 3)$

14 a $x^2 + 12x + 32$ **b** $x^2 + 6x - 27$

    c $m^2 - 9m + 20$ **d** $x^2 + 4x + 4$

Challenge

1 Students' own expressions

2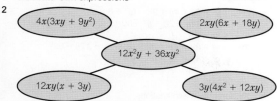

4x(3xy + 9y²)   2xy(6x + 18y)

12x²y + 36xy²

12xy(x + 3y)   3y(4x² + 12xy)

2 Strengthen: Solving equations

1 a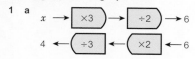

$x \rightarrow \boxed{\times 3} \rightarrow \boxed{\div 2} \rightarrow 6$

$4 \leftarrow \boxed{\div 3} \leftarrow \boxed{\times 2} \leftarrow 6$

b

$x \rightarrow \boxed{\times 3} \rightarrow \boxed{\div 5} \rightarrow 6$

$10 \leftarrow \boxed{\div 3} \leftarrow \boxed{\times 5} \leftarrow 6$

c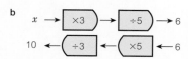

$x \rightarrow \boxed{\times 5} \rightarrow \boxed{\div 3} \rightarrow 10$

$6 \leftarrow \boxed{\div 5} \leftarrow \boxed{\times 3} \leftarrow 10$

d

$x \rightarrow \boxed{\div 3} \rightarrow \boxed{+7} \rightarrow 8$

$3 \leftarrow \boxed{\times 3} \leftarrow \boxed{-7} \leftarrow 8$

e

$x \rightarrow \boxed{\div 2} \rightarrow \boxed{+3} \rightarrow 7$

$8 \leftarrow \boxed{\times 2} \leftarrow \boxed{-3} \leftarrow 7$

f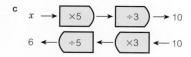

$x \rightarrow \boxed{\div 2} \rightarrow \boxed{-3} \rightarrow 7$

$20 \leftarrow \boxed{\times 2} \leftarrow \boxed{+3} \leftarrow 7$

g

$x \rightarrow \boxed{+7} \rightarrow \boxed{\div 3} \rightarrow 10$

$23 \leftarrow \boxed{-7} \leftarrow \boxed{\times 3} \leftarrow 10$

h

$x \rightarrow \boxed{-7} \rightarrow \boxed{\div 3} \rightarrow 10$

$37 \leftarrow \boxed{+7} \leftarrow \boxed{\times 3} \leftarrow 10$

2 25g

3 a $r = 3$ b $s = 4$ c $p = 2$ d $f = 2$

4 a $g = 2$ b $v = 3$ c $n = 10$ d $h = 0$

2 Strengthen: Substituting into expressions

1 a 17   b 22   c 29   d 1

2 a $2^2 + 1 = 4 + 1 = 5$ b $3^2 - 4 = 9 - 4 = 5$
c $2^2 + 3 = 4 + 3 = 7$ d $3^2 - 2 = 9 - 2 = 7$

3 a 18   b 45   c 72   d 36

4 a 25   b 4   c $2 \times 5^2 = 2 \times 25 = 50$
d $4 \times 2^2 = 4 \times 4 = 16$ e $5^2 \times 2^2 = 25 \times 4 = 100$
f $2 \times 5^2 \times 2 = 2 \times 25 \times 2 = 100$
g $3 \times 5 \times 2^2 = 15 \times 4 = 60$

5 a 24   b 21   c 20   d 25

6 a 14   b 33   c 24   d 20
e 65   f 75   g 14   h 2
i 2   j 5   k 6   l 2

7 a 3   b −3   c −6   d −30
e 15   f 1

8 a $2a + b = 2 \times 2 + -1 = 4 - 1 = 3$
b $6a - 4b = 6 \times 2 - 4 \times -1 = 12 + 4 = 16$
c $a^2 - b = 2^2 - -1 = 4 + 1 = 5$
d $3b^2 = 3 \times (-1)^2 = 3 \times 1 = 3$
e $4(b - a) = 4(-1 - 2) = 4 \times -3 = -12$
f $6(b^3 + 2a) = 6((-1)^3 + 2 \times 2) = 6(-1 + 4) = 6 \times 3 = 18$

9 a 14   b 69   c 95   d 282
e 12   f 1

2 Strengthen: Writing and using formulae

1 a

Number of days	Cost at £8 per day
1	$1 \times 8 = £8$
2	$2 \times 8 = £16$
3	$3 \times 8 = £24$
n	$n \times 8 = 8n$

b $C = 8n$ c £80

2 a

Number of days	Cost at £5 per day + one-off fee
1	$1 \times 5 + 30 = 5 + 30$
2	$2 \times 5 + 30 = 10 + 30$
n	$n \times 5 + 30 = 5n + 30$

b $T = 5n + 30$ c £55

3 a £30   b $6h + w$ c $hx + w$
d $T = hx + w$ e £38

4 a 72   b 75   c 1.7

5 a 3   b 38   c −15

6 a $b = 4$ b $b = 0.4$

7 a $p = 12$ b $p = 11$ c $m = 3$
d $m = 4$ e $u = 2$ f $u = 9$

8 $b = 12$

9 $b = \dfrac{A}{h}$

10 a $a = \dfrac{v}{t}$ b $n = Kt$

Strengthen: Indices, expanding and factorising

1 a i $m \times m \times m \times m \times m = m^5$
  ii $m^2 \times m^3 = m^{2+3} = m^5$
 b i $b \times b \times b \times b = b^4$
  ii $b^3 \times b = b^{3+1} = b^4$

2 a a^4 b c^4 c b^3 d g^5
e d^5

3 a $4d^8$ b $3p^3$ c $-10n^4$ d $6g^2n^2$

4 a $m^4 \times m^3 = m^7$ b $m^7 \div m^4 = m^3$
c $h^2 \times h^4 = h^6$ d $h^6 \div h^2 = h^4$
e $s \times s^4 = s^5$ f $s^5 \div s = s^4$
g $7m^3 \times m^2 = 7m^5$ h $7m^5 \div m^2 = 7m^3$

5 a $a^2 + 5a$ b $a^2 + 3a$ c $a^2 - 3a$ d $2a^2 - a$

6 a $d^2 + 4d$ b $d^2 + 5d$ c $d^2 + d$ d $2d^2 + 7d$
e $2d^2 + 11d$ f $7d^2 + 6d$

7 a $\dfrac{1}{2^2}$ b $\dfrac{1}{x^2}$ c $\dfrac{1}{2^3}$ d $\dfrac{1}{y^3}$

8 a x^{-1} or $\dfrac{1}{x^1}$ or $\dfrac{1}{x}$ b y^{-2} or $\dfrac{1}{y^2}$
c z^{-5} or $\dfrac{1}{z^5}$ d w^{-6} or $\dfrac{1}{w^6}$

9 a i 3   ii $4x$ iii $5x^2$
 b i $5(2x + 1)$ ii $5x(2x + 1)$
  iii $3x(4 - 3x)$ iv $5y^2(5y^3 + 2)$
  v $2a(7a^2 - 5)$ vi $b^2(1 + 3b^2)$
  vii $6c^2(2 + 3c)$

10 $a^2 + 7a + 10$

11 a $a^2 + 8a + 15$
 b $b^2 + 13b + 36$
 c $c^2 + 3c + 2$

12 a $a^2 + 6a - 16$ b $b^2 - b - 20$
 c $c^2 - 10c + 21$

Challenge

Students' own answers, e.g.

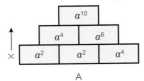

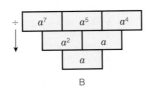

A

B

2 Extend

1 a $n = 20$ **b** $x = 8$ **c** $u = 9$ **d** $n = 1000$

2 a $m = 13$ **b** $b = 8$ **c** $k = 4$

3 a 4 **b** -6.25

4 8

5 a £920

   b $C = 35lw + 4(2l + 2w)$ or
     $C = 35lw + 8(l + w)$ or
     $C = 35lw + 8l + 8w$

   c £680.50

6 $\dfrac{3V}{40} = 6$, $V = 80$

7 $24 = \dfrac{60x}{15}$, $x = 6\,\text{m}$

8 a 324 **b** 56 **c** $12\,500$ **d** 2304

9 a 5 **b** 15

10 a $3x + 5(x + 2) = 8x + 10$

   b $8x + 10 = 30$, $x = 2.5$

   c $(4x + 14)\,\text{cm}$ or $24\,\text{cm}$

11 a $m = \dfrac{x}{2h}$ **b** $m = \dfrac{P}{gh}$ **c** $m = 2lr$

   d $m = \dfrac{4xy}{3}$ **e** $m = \pm\sqrt{y}$ **f** $m = \pm\sqrt{x - 2n}$

12 a $-30t^4$ **b** $6a^3$ **c** m **d** c^4

   e u^5 **f** p^4 **g** r^6 **h** s^6

   i $8w^4$ **j** $-d^{10}$ **k** $24b^{10}$ **l** $60x^7$

13 a $125m^3$ **b** $100a^2$ **c** $16c^4$ **d** $9p^2q^2$

14 a $x^4 + 3x^2 + 7x$ **b** $a^3 - 8a^2 + a$

   c $b^4 + 5b^3 - 6b$ **d** $8p + 10p^2 + 2p^3$

   e $6z^4 - 24z^3 + 54z$ **f** $2a^4 + 3a^3 - 4a^2$

   g $3k^4 - 18k^2 - 21k$

15 Hannah is correct. It is $2x^{-2}$ which can be written as $\dfrac{2}{x^2}$ not $\dfrac{1}{2x^2}$

16 a She hasn't factorised fully as the highest common
     factor is $4xy^2$.

   b $4xy^2(2x - z)$

17 a area of red square – area of square hole

   b $(x + 9)^2 - (x + 4)^2 = 10x + 65$

2 Unit test

1 a 54 **b** 7

2 -9

3 a 14 **b** 5 **c** 44 **d** 6

4 a £2700   **b** $px + hy$ **c** $T = px + hy$ **d** £3740

5 $9x^3 + 3x^2$

6 a $27x^3$ **b** $\dfrac{y^2}{16}$

7 a 16 **b** 80 **c** 2

8 $R = 6$

9 a x^{-2} or $\dfrac{1}{x^2}$ **b** y^{-6} or $\dfrac{1}{y^6}$ **c** z^{-2} or $\dfrac{1}{z^2}$

10 a $3x^4 - 4x^5$ **b** $10y^5 + 2y^3$

11 a $8x(3 + x)$ **b** $3x^3(4 - 3x^2)$

12 a $x = 14$ **b** $g = 15$ **c** $b = 15$ **d** $x = 7$

13 a $h = 7$ **b** $b = 2.5$

14 $m = 4$

15 a $x^2 + 13x + 42$ **b** $x^2 + 3x - 108$

   c $m^2 - 18m + 77$

16 a $x = F - p$ **b** $x = \dfrac{M}{R}$ **c** $x = \dfrac{d - h}{5}$

---

17 $x^2 + 12x + 36$

Challenge

a   LHS $= y^2 + 7y + 4y + 28 - (y^2 + 8y)$
       $= y^2 + 11y + 28 - y^2 - 8y$
       $= 3y + 28$
    RHS $= y^2 - 8y + 4y - 32 - (y^2 + 5y - 12y - 60)$
        $= y^2 - 4y - 32 - y^2 + 7y + 60$
        $= 3y + 28$
        $=$ LHS

b   Students' own explanations.

UNIT 3 Dealing with data

3.1 Planning a survey

1 **a** 70 **b** 200 **c** 18.5%

2 **a** 200 **b** 28 **c** 21%

 d 6–18; most people in this age group would be at school on a Monday morning in November.

3 100 times

4 B, D and E

5 B and C

6 **a** primary **b** secondary

7 **a** B (100) **b** B (70)

8 **a** **i** e.g. how many children in the school, how many children walk to school

 ii e.g. how many households in the country, how many TVs households have

 iii e.g. how many people in the country, how many eat at least five portions of fruit and vegetables a day

 b **i** e.g. a survey of children in the school (primary data)

 ii e.g. a survey of a sample of the population (primary data) or online data (secondary data)

 iii e.g. a survey of a sample of the population (primary data)

9 **a** B (survey) **b** C (questionnaire)

 c A (experiment)

10 **a** B (nearest mm)

 b B (nearest second)

 c C (nearest hundredth of a second)

 d B (nearest 0.1 kg)

11 **a** **i** 100 students **ii** e.g. nearest 5 minutes

 b A, D and E

12 Callum's sample is limited as he only asks his friends, who may have the same interests and like the same programmes.

13 **a** Method 2 because it ensures a random sample.

 b Method 1 – only students surveyed

 Method 3 – only customers of one shop surveyed

 Method 4 – only people Paul knows surveyed

 All three are unlikely to be representative of the whole population.

 c e.g. Rudi should also carry out the survey on other days of the week.

14 C and D

Challenge

Students' own answers

3.2 Collecting data

1 **a** $0.5 \leqslant l < 1$ **b** $0 < l \leqslant 0.5$

2 **a**

Age	Tally	Frequency
0–10	III	3
11–20	IIII	5
21–30	IIII IIII	10
31–40	IIII I	6

 b 30%

3 **a**

Car colour	Tally	Frequency
red	IIII II	7
blue	IIII	5
black	IIII	5
white	I	1
silver	II	2
green	IIII	4

 b Students' own answers, e.g.

 Yes, in order to record cars that are yellow or brown, for example.

4 **a**

Number of emails	Tally	Frequency
0–4		0
5–9	III	3
10–14	III	3
15–19	IIII	4
20–24	IIII I	6

 b 16 **c** 20–24

5 **a** discrete

 b Students' grouped frequency tables with 4 to 5 equal width classes, e.g.

Number of customers	Frequency
50–99	2
100–149	5
150–199	16
200–249	7

 c Answers will depend on table drawn in part **b**. For table above, answer is 150–199.

6 **a** continuous

 b Students' grouped frequency tables with 4 to 5 equal width classes, e.g.

Mass of parcel	Frequency
$0 \leqslant m < 2$	2
$2 \leqslant m < 4$	3
$4 \leqslant m < 6$	4
$6 \leqslant m < 8$	4
$8 \leqslant m < 10$	2

 c Answers will depend on table drawn in part **b**. For table above, answer is $4 \leqslant m < 6$ and $6 \leqslant m < 8$.

7 **a** continuous

 b **i**

		Age (years)		
		10–29	30–49	50+
Mass, m (kg)	$50 \leqslant m < 70$	2	2	2
	$70 \leqslant m < 90$	0	5	5
	90+	0	3	1

 ii 2 **iii** $\frac{1}{10}$ or 10% **iv** $\frac{1}{2}$ or 50%

8

	Year	
	8	9
French		
Spanish		
Mandarin		

9

		Dice	
		Even	Odd
Coin	Heads		
	Tails		

10 **a** Most people will agree.

 b Students' own answers

11 **a** **i** e.g. There are gaps between the groups and no option for more than 8 portions.

 Change groups to

 ☐ 0–2 ☐ 3–5 ☐ 6–8 ☐ 9+

 ii e.g. Most people will answer 'Yes'. You need to define 'enough fruit' as this is subjective.

 Change to:

 How many pieces of fruit have you eaten today?

 iii e.g. Most people will agree.

 Change to: Are fruit and vegetables good for you?

 ☐ Yes ☐ No

b Students' own answers, which could include questions like:
How many pieces of fruit do you eat a day?
☐ 0–2 ☐ 3–5 ☐ 6–8 ☐ 9+
How many portions of vegetables do you eat a day?
☐ 0–2 ☐ 3–5 ☐ 6–8 ☐ 9+
What do you consider a healthy diet?
What have you eaten today?

12 Students' own answers

Challenge

Students' own answers

3.3 Calculating averages

1 the 8th value

2 **a** 1 goal **b** 20 matches
c 1.75 goals **d** 5

3 2 cars

4 1 goal

5 **a**

Length, l (cm)	Frequency	Midpoint of class	Midpoint × Frequency
$0 \leq l < 6$	8	3	24
$6 \leq l < 12$	7	9	63
$12 \leq l < 18$	2	15	30
$18 \leq l < 24$	3	21	63
Total	20		180

b $6 \leq l < 12$ **c** 9 cm

6 **a** £10 000 < e ≤ £20 000 **b** £50 000
c £20 000 < e ≤ £30 000 **d** £23 190

7 **a** **i** $4 \leq a < 6$ **ii** $1 < b \leq 1.5$ **iii** $0 \leq l < 0.4$
b **i** 8 **ii** 2 **iii** 1.6
c **i** $4 \leq a < 6$ **ii** $1 < b \leq 1.5$ **iii** $0 \leq l < 0.4$
d **i** 4 **ii** 1 **iii** 0.584

8 **a** 21–30 marks **b** 21–30 marks **c** 27.5 marks

9 **a**

Distance, d (m)	Frequency
$10 \leq d < 20$	4
$20 \leq d < 30$	7
$30 \leq d < 40$	7
$40 \leq d < 50$	2

b $20 \leq d < 30$, and $30 \leq d < 40$
c 28.5 m **d** 30.0 m (1 d.p.)

10 **a** $6 < l \leq 7$ **b** 6.0 mm **c** 5.89 mm
d No

Challenge

Students' own answers

3.4 Displaying and analysing data

1 **a** 5 **b** 5 **c** 25 000

2 **a, c**

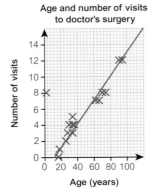

Age and number of visits to doctor's surgery

b positive
d all the people registered at the doctor's surgery

3 **a** 4 or 5 times, depending on the line of best fit
b 75 to 85 years old, depending on the line of best fit
c (1, 8)
Students' own explanation, e.g.
The outlier might have been caused by a very unwell child.

4 **a, b**

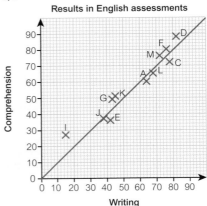

Results in English assessments

c Positive correlation: students with higher writing marks tend to get higher comprehension marks.
d **i** approximately 60, depending on the line of best fit
ii approximately 83, depending on the line of best fit

5 **a, d**

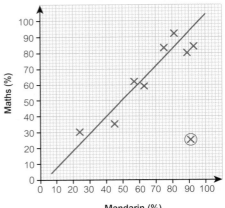

Mandarin and maths results

b **i** approximately 27% **ii** approximately 50%
iii approximately 95%
c **i** approximately 60% **ii** approximately 40%
iii approximately 70%
d outlier 91% Mandarin, 25% maths

6 **a** The data does seem to support the hypothesis.
b No; the sample should include about 500 patients.
c Students' own answers, e.g.
You would need to check the records of patients at the surgery generally, not simply those who have attended the surgery recently (otherwise the sample is biased). The best source of information would be secondary data (the patients' records) because patients themselves may not remember or may be reluctant to share the information with you directly.

7 **a** Students' own answers identifying the peak areas on the graph, e.g.,
10.45 – 11.30 am, 12 – 2 pm and 4.30 – 5.30 pm
b These might be times when people are not at work.
c Students' own answers, e.g.
i Likely to be the same
ii Likely to be different
d Students' own answers, e.g.
She should carry out the same survey on other days of the week.

8 a She has not plotted the points at the midpoints of the classes; and she has not included a title.

b

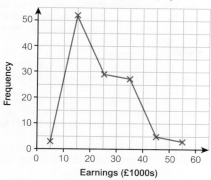

Annual earnings of employees

9 a, b

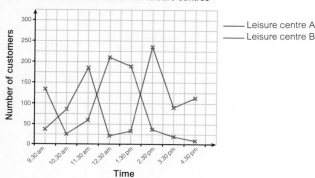

Number of customers in leisure centres

— Leisure centre A
— Leisure centre B

c Students' own answers, e.g.
Leisure centre B is busier over lunchtime, but leisure centre A is busier mid-morning and mid-afternoon.

d Students' own answers, e.g.
The leisure centres should also carry out the survey in the evenings and on other days of the week.

10 a 3 minutes
Students' own answers, e.g.
A time of 30 minutes was recorded incorrectly.

b Students' own frequency table with 4 to 5 equal width classes, e.g.

Time spent on homework, t (minutes)	Frequency
$10 < t \leqslant 25$	3
$25 < t \leqslant 40$	8
$40 < t \leqslant 55$	6
$55 < t \leqslant 70$	2

c Students' own line graph using answer to part **b**, e.g.

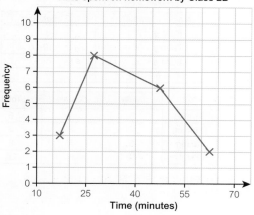

Time spent on homework by Class 2B

d the class with highest frequency from table in part **b**, e.g. $25 < t \leqslant 40$

e range = 43 minutes, mean = 38 minutes

f Students' own frequency tables with 4 to 5 equal width classes, e.g.

Time spent on homework, t (minutes)	Frequency
$10 < t \leqslant 25$	2
$25 < t \leqslant 40$	5
$40 < t \leqslant 55$	10
$55 < t \leqslant 70$	3

g Students' own line graph using answer to part **f**, e.g.

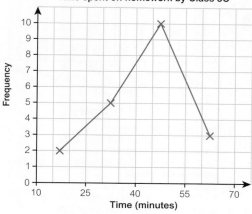

Time spent on homework by Class 3C

h the class with highest frequency from table in part **f**, e.g. $40 < t \leqslant 55$

i range = 42 minutes, mean = 43.35 minutes

j Students' own answers, e.g.
Using the mean, Class 3C spent longer on their homework than Class 2B.
The range of times was for higher for Class 2B.

k Students' own answers, e.g.
Ask more students from each class, over more days.

Challenge

Students' own answers

3.5 Presenting and comparing data

1 a 2.5   **b** 3   **c** 2   **d** 3.5

2 a

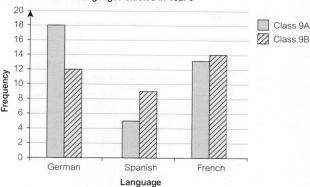

Languages studied in Year 9

☐ Class 9A
▨ Class 9B

b the mode

3 a i 0–5 years   **ii** 12–17

b

Age	Midpoint	Frequency
0–5	2.5	19 million
6–11	8.5	15 million
12–17	14.5	13 million

c 7.7 years   **d** 8.6 years

e Students' own answers, e.g.
The mean age of children in the USA in 2017 was higher than in 1950.

4 a

GDP per capita ($)

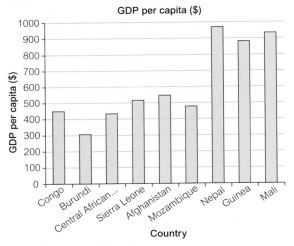

b Any two sensible sentences, e.g.
Nepal has the highest GDP per capita.
Burundi has the lowest GDP per capita.

c No; the number of countries is too small, and it is not a representative sample.

d Students' own answers, e.g.
Find the GDP per capita of more countries.

5 a Before video: median = 26, range = 36
After video: median = 37, range = 38

b Students' own answers, e.g.
The median has increased by 11.
The range has stayed about the same.

c The data does seem to support this hypothesis.

d 15 students

e Students' own answers, e.g.
Carry out a study with a larger sample size, different age groups.

6

a

Males		Females	Key: 5 | 12 means 12.5
8 4	11	9	12 | 2 means 12.2
5 5 0	12	0 2 8 8 9	
6 2	13	0 1	

b

	11 < t ≤ 12	12 < t ≤ 13	13 < t ≤ 14	Total
Male	3	2	2	7
Female	2	5	1	8
Total	5	7	3	15

c The data does seem to support the hypothesis.

7 a

Temperature of tea and coffee while cooling

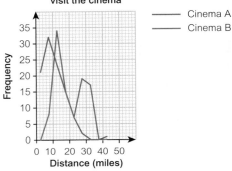

b Students' own answers, e.g.
The results suggest that tea cools more quickly than coffee.

However, it is important to consider whether the results are reliable. Were the conditions for both the tea and coffee kept the same (e.g. was the external temperature constant for both, were they both stirred for the same length of time, did they have the same volume, were they both in the same type of cup etc.)? More data would need to be collected to make this a reliable conclusion.

8 a Students' own answers
The report should include a graph. There should be some discussion about the best type to use; a line graph would work well here.
The report should comment on the outlier. The person travelling between 40 and 45 miles has come a very long way for the cinema. The report should suggest why this might have occurred, e.g. visiting friends.
The report should include an estimated mean 10.87 miles, modal class 5–10 miles and an estimated range 30 miles. (These figures exclude the outlier.)
The report should include suggestions on how to improve the investigation, e.g. the student could ask people at a neutral location. (They are asking people who are already at the cinema and it is possible that people will travel to other cinemas.) They could use a larger sample.

b

Distance travelled to visit the cinema

— Cinema A
— Cinema B

c i 19.8 miles   **ii** 30 miles   **iii** 10 < d ≤ 15

d People will generally travel further to Cinema B since the mean distance is greater for Cinema B.
The range is greater for Cinema B (35 miles).

e Students' own answers, e.g.
People are prepared to travel further to larger cinemas.

Challenge

Students' own answers

3 Check up

1 a A primary data, B secondary data

b 150 students

2 a overlapping groups

b leading question, as people are likely to agree

3 a cm   **b** mm   **c** m

4 a continuous

b, c Students' own frequency table with 4 to 5 equal width classes, e.g.

Mass, g (grams)	Frequency
60 ≤ g < 70	3
70 ≤ g < 80	10
80 ≤ g < 90	5
90 ≤ g < 100	2

5 a

	Male	Female	Total
Singing	5	1	6
Dancing	4	2	6
Acting	3	5	8
Total	12	8	20

b Singing   **c** Singing

6 D

7 **a** 12.2 days **b** $10 < w \le 15$
   c $10 < w \le 15$ **d** 20 days

8 **a**

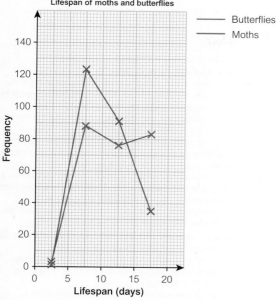

Lifespan of moths and butterflies

— Butterflies
— Moths

b On average, butterflies have a longer lifespan than moths
   (with an estimated mean of 12.3 days versus 10.7 days).

9 **a** (5, 1)
   b Students' own answers, e.g.
      This student might have driven off road before, or had a
      parent teach them.
   c 2 tests

Challenge

1, 23, 25, 25, 26   2, 21, 25, 25, 27
3, 19, 25, 25, 28   4, 17, 25, 25, 29
5, 15, 25, 25, 30   6, 13, 25, 25, 31
7, 11, 25, 25, 32   8, 9, 25, 25, 33

3 Strengthen: Surveys

1 **a** primary **b** secondary
2 **a** all the students in the school
   b 10% **c** B (nearest 10 minutes)
   d No; Year 11 students probably spend more time on
      homework than students in other years. He needs to ask
      students from all the years in the school.
3 80 people
4 A (nearest millimetre)
5 **a** both 0–10 and 10–20 **b** The groups overlap.
   c 0–9 cm, 10–19 cm, 20–29 cm

6

Time, t (minutes)	Tally	Frequency
$20 < t \le 30$	|	1
$30 < t \le 40$	|||	3
$40 < t \le 50$	||	2
$50 < t \le 60$	||	2
$60 < t \le 70$	||	2

7 Students' own frequency tables, e.g.

Time, t (minutes)	Tally	Frequency
$0 \le t < 20$		
$20 \le t < 40$		
$40 \le t < 60$		
$60 \le t < 90$		
$t \ge 90$		

8 **a, b**

	Beef	Chicken
Chips	20	35
Jacket potato	15	13
Mashed potato	13	17

9 **a, b**

	History	Geography
Spanish	2	1
German	3	2
Mandarin	2	0

   c German and History **d** Mandarin and Geography
10 **a** The survey only includes people whose pets are ill. It needs
      to include pet owners whose pets are well.
   b Most people will answer 'Yes'. The question doesn't
      tell you anything about whether people are likely to
      buy pet insurance.
   c C; the other questions are biased because they all suggest
      a point of view.

3 Strengthen: Calculating averages

1 **a** 25 **b** the 13th value **c** 20–29
2 10 minutes, because it is in the middle of 0–20.
3 **a**

Time, t (minutes)	Midpoint	Frequency	Midpoint × Frequency
$0 < t \le 20$	10	5	10 × 5 = 50
$20 < t \le 40$	30	12	30 × 12 = 360
$40 < t \le 60$	50	19	50 × 19 = 950
$60 < t \le 80$	70	8	70 × 8 = 560
$80 < t \le 100$	90	6	90 × 6 = 540
		Total 50	2460

   b 50 people **c** 2460 minutes **d** 49.2 minutes
4 **a** 'Midpoint' and 'Midpoint × Frequency'
   b

Number in audience, a	Frequency	Midpoint	Midpoint × Frequency
$100 < a \le 150$	5	125	5 × 125 = 625
$150 < a \le 200$	2	175	2 × 175 = 350
$200 < a \le 250$	2	225	2 × 225 = 450
$250 < a \le 300$	1	275	1 × 275 = 275
Total	10		1700

   c 170 people **d** $150 < a \le 200$
5 30–39

3 Strengthen: Displaying and analysing data

1 **a** (0.5, 1), (0.7, 6), (0.9, 2)
   b, c

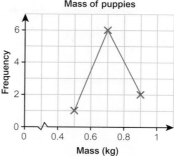

Mass of puppies

2 a, b

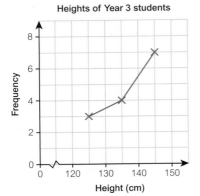

Heights of Year 3 students

3

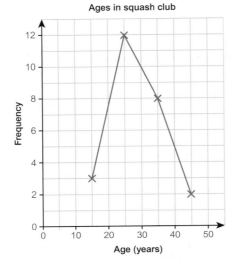

Ages in squash club

b

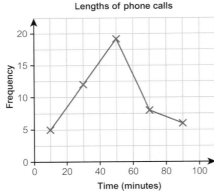

Lengths of phone calls

c

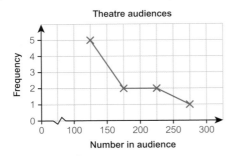

Theatre audiences

4 a, b 27.5 seconds
c i 29 seconds **ii** 28 seconds
d 20 seconds for 100 m, 25 seconds for 200 m

Challenge

a 72 passengers **b** 56 passengers
c 56, to support an argument that the train is not very popular.

3 Extend

1 Students' own answers, e.g.
Survey customers who come into the salon and refer to records to see who used to use the salon.

2 Should collect data for **B**, **C**, **D** and **E**:
B (age) should be recorded to show any trends in the data. (It would be best to use groups, since some people might be embarrassed about giving their age.)
C (level of satisfaction with the company) is what the company wants to find out so it should be included (with options).
D (number of years with the company) is relevant as people who are unhappy in their work do not stay with the company for long (with groups as people might not remember).
E (how their working conditions should be improved) should be included as it is relevant to the context of the survey (with space for a written answer and some suggestions).
Should not collect **A** (name) as it is better for a survey to be anonymous so that people will be honest.

3 a Students' own answers, e.g. information about accidents and deaths at work for different professions
b Students' own answers, e.g. life insurance companies (secondary), public records (secondary), companies' records (secondary)
c Students' own answers, e.g. insurance companies

4 a

	Revised	Didn't revise
Passed	75	23
Failed	20	2

b Students' own answers, e.g.
People may not be honest about how much revision they did.

5 a 11 **b** 6 **c** 3 or 18
6 10, 10, 12, 13 and 15
7 a

```
        English          Maths
      7 7 6 1 | 4 | 6 7 9
            0 | 5 | 5 7 7
            8 | 6 | 6
      9 8 3 3 2 | 7 | 3 5
        3 3 2 | 8 | 4 4 5 6
          2 0 | 9 | 0 0 4
```

Key: 7 | 4 means 47 and 4 | 9 means 49

b Students' own answers, e.g.
More students scored over 70% in English.
More students scored over 90% in Maths.

c

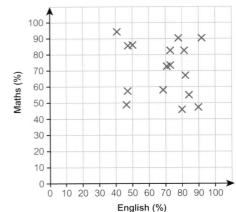

Year 10 exam results

8 People who phone in are more likely to have strong views on a subject.

9 **a** The question suggests an answer.
　b Students' own answers, e.g.
　　Which facilities do you use? Tick the most appropriate box.
　　☐ Play parks ☐ Library ☐ Sports centre ☐ Park
　　☐ Playing fields
　　Do any of these facilities need improvement?
　　Tick the most appropriate box.
　　☐ Play parks ☐ Library ☐ Sports centre ☐ Park
　　☐ Playing fields
　　Are there any further facilities you would like to see in this town?

10 a

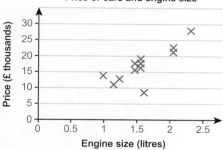

Price of cars and engine size

　b positive correlation
　c 1.6, 8.8; students' own answers, e.g. Car lacks other features so is cheaper.
　d approximately £15 000
　e The data does seem to support the hypothesis.
　f Students' own answers, e.g.
　　Carry out a study with a larger sample size, more than one manufacturer.

11 Older children took less time to complete the puzzle.

12 a

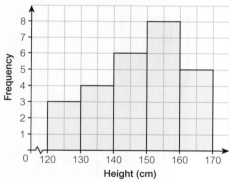

Heights of students

　b $150 \leq h < 160$　　**c** 13

3 Unit test

1 **B** (100 times)

2 **a** **A**: groups overlap
　　B: leading question
　b Students' own answers, e.g.
　　A: Change categories to
　　☐ 0–2 ☐ 3–5 ☐ 6–8 ☐ 9+
　　B: Change question to
　　Who has more accidents, men or women?

3 **B** is secondary data.

4 **a** Collect data on maths and English exam results from the maths and English departments.
　b 40 girls (or similar)

5 **a** **B** (nearest 1 mph)
　b Students' own data collection sheets with 4 to 5 equal width classes, e.g.

Speed, s (mph)	Frequency
$0 < s \leq 10$	
$10 < s \leq 20$	
$20 < s \leq 30$	
$30 < s \leq 40$	
$40 < s \leq 50$	

6

	Tennis	Badminton	Squash
Swimming			
Athletics			
Gymnastics			

7 **C**

8 **a** 5 goals　**b** 4 goals

9 **a** positive　**b** 26 °C
　c **i** approximately 26 °C
　　ii 27 or 28 ice creams

10 a **i** $80 \leq p < 120$　　**ii** $120 \leq p < 160$
　b Airline A: mean = 88.4
　　Airline B: mean = 111.6
　c Airline A: range = 160
　　Airline B: range = 120
　d Airline A: $80 \leq p < 120$
　　Airline B: $120 \leq p < 160$
　e

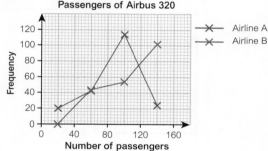

Passengers of Airbus 320

— Airline A
— Airline B

　f Students' own answers e.g.
　　Airline B has more passengers on average.
　　Airline A has a larger range.

Challenge

Students' own answers

UNIT 4 Multiplicative reasoning

4.1 Enlargement

1   **a**   3   **b**   2

2

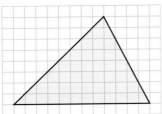

3   **a**   2 : 5   **b**   1 : 2.5

4   **a**

    b

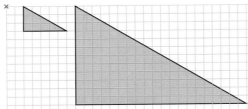

    c

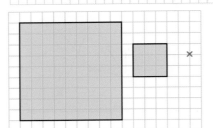

    d

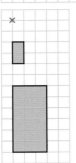

5

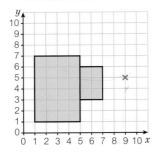

6   a, b, d

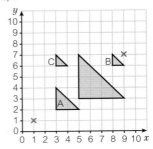

    c   same triangle

    e   No, as a scale factor of 3 will not give the same side lengths as the other triangle.

7   **a**

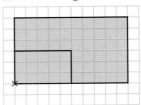

    b

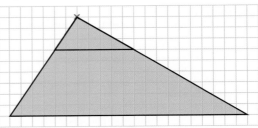

    c

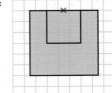

8

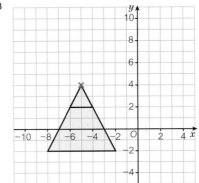

9 a

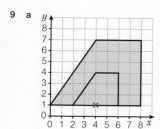

b same angles

c The lengths are all 2 times as big in the enlarged shape.

d Yes, enlargements are always similar to the original shape.

10 a

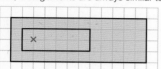

b

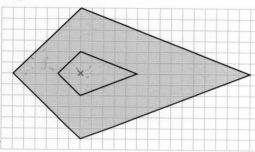

c

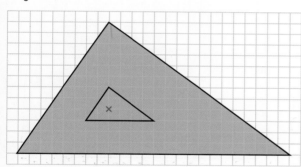

11

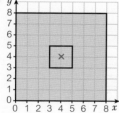

12 a 2

b

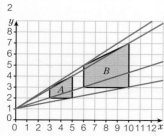

c (0, 1)

13 a scale factor 2, centre of enlargement (1, 1)

   b scale factor 3, centre of enlargement (3, 4)

14 a 2

   b **i** 1 : 2   **ii** 1 : 2

   c The scale factor (2) is the second number in the ratio (1 : 2).

   d **i** 1 : 3   **ii** 1 : 4   **iii** 1 : 7

15 a 12 : 480   **b** 1 : 40   **c** 40

16 a 35   **b** length 17.78 m, height 21.35 m

Challenge

Students' own enlargements and scale factors

4.2 Negative and fractional scale factors

1 a 2   **b** 1   **c** 3

2 a, b

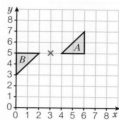

3 a

   b

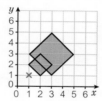

   c

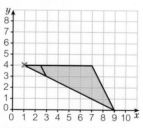

4 a

   b

   c

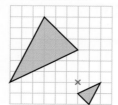

5 Corresponding side lengths and angles stay the same.

6 a, b

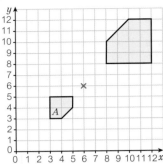

c The answers are the same. This means that enlarging by a negative scale factor is the same as enlarging by the same positive scale factor and then rotating 180° about the centre of enlargement.

7 a

b

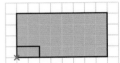

c

8 Corresponding side lengths in the image are smaller than in the original shape; the angles stay the same.

9 a i $\frac{1}{3}$ **ii** 3

   b i $\frac{1}{2}$ **ii** 2

   c i $\frac{1}{3}$ **ii** 3

10 a i

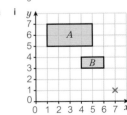

   ii 2 : 1
   iii scale factor 2, centre of enlargement (7, 1)

   b i

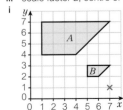

   ii 3 : 1
   iii scale factor 3, centre of enlargement (7, 1)

c i

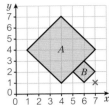

   ii 3 : 1
   iii scale factor 3, centre of enlargement (7, 1)

Challenge

   a i

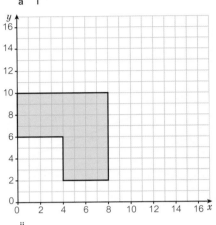

   ii

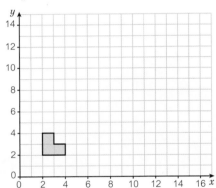

   iii

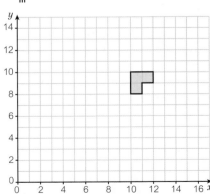

   b any combined transformation, e.g. rotate 90° clockwise about (4, 2) then translate 6 squares right and 6 squares up

4.3 Percentage change

1 a 17   **b** 16.9   **c** 17
   d 16.85   **e** 16.9   **f** 16.850
2 a 0.8   **b** 1.15   **c** 1.03

3 **a** 28.75 g   **b** 374.4 km   **c** £23.52

4 **a** 54%   **b** 64%

5 2 m

6 £47.50

7

	Original price
Item 1	£75
Item 2	£82
Item 3	£285

8 **a** £560
   b Sam saved more money.
     Jessica saved £560 − £420 = £140
     Sam saved £690 − £483 = £207

9 £1.5 million

10 14 kg

11 120 000

12 £498

13 actual change = £0.90
   percentage change = $\frac{0.9}{12} \times 100 = 7.5\%$

14 **a** £192   **b** 8%

15 2%

16 **a**

Item	Actual profit	Percentage profit
hoody	£9	75%
T-shirt	£3	60%
fleece	£15	50%
polo shirt	£10	125%

   b No, the item with the greatest actual profit is the fleece, but
     the item with the greatest percentage profit is the polo shirt.

17 12%

18 30%

Challenge

a **i** 2016 to 2017   **ii** 17.9%
b 41%

4.4 Compound measures

1 **a** 2.5   **b** 1000 m   **c** 1000 g
   d 75 minutes   **e** 36 minutes   **f** 3600 seconds

2 **a** $a = 125$ **b** $a = 5$

3 **a** 0.6 cm²   **b** 150 cm³

4 **a** 2 m²   **b** 0.0005 m²   **c** 0.002 53 m²

5 **a** 60 km/h   **b** 75 km/h
   c 5 mph   **d** 16 mph

6 **a** **i** 352 km   **ii** 54 km
   b **i** 3 hours   **ii** $1\frac{1}{2}$ hours

7 **a** 21.6 km/h   **b** 90 km/h
   c 20 m/s   **d** 45 m/s

8 **a** 1 hour 30 minutes   **b** 68.3 km/h

9 19.4 g/cm³

10 0.58 g/cm³

11 Diamond, as it has a greater mass per cm³.

12 9988 g

13 420 cm³

14 16 N/m²

15 0.6 N/cm²

16

Force	Area	Pressure
120 N	1.25 m²	96 N/m²
11.25 N	0.75 m²	15 N/m²
0.0072 N	3.6 cm²	20 N/m²
40 N	2.5 m²	16 N/m²

Challenge

a 36 cm²   **b** 14.5 N/cm²

4.5 Direct and inverse proportion

1 **a** 60p   **b** £1.50   **c** £1.04
   d 40 minutes

2 **a** 420 g   **b** £1.96
   c Yes; as the weight doubles, the cost doubles.

3 **a** £69
   b Yes; as the number of tickets is multiplied by 1.5,
     so is the cost.

4 **a** **i** 28p   **ii** 27p   **iii** 25p
   b Large multipack as the price per packet is the cheapest.
   c Students' own answer, e.g.
     Divide the number of packets by the price of the multipack;
     this would show how many packets for £1, so the highest
     number would indicate the best value for money.

5 **a** 18.5p, 7p, 8.5p
   b 250 g jar, as the price for 10 g is the cheapest.

6 Offer A: 18p per tablet or 5.56 tablets per £
   Offer B: 20p per tablet or 5 tablets per £
   Offer C: 18.75p per tablet or 5.33 tablets per £
   Offer A is the best value.

7 **a** Audrey's method is better as all the divisions are 'easy'.
   b Tip top compost (12 litres per £)
   c Green's compost (9 litres per £)

8 **a** Bob (£20 per hour)
   b Students' own answers, e.g.
     Approximate, because it is obvious that both £45 ÷ 2 and
     £65 ÷ 3 are more than £20.

9 $1\frac{1}{2}$ days

10 **a** 4 hours   **b** 8 hours   **c** 1 hour

11 **a** 40 minutes **b** 4 pumps

12 **a** 2 days   **b** $\frac{1}{2}$ day

13 **a** 25 minutes **b** directly proportional; more leaflets take
                      more time to print

14 **a** 3 more   **b** inversely proportional; more builders take
                     less time to build the house

Challenge

a A, C and F   **b** D and E   **c** B

4 Check up

1 **a**

   b

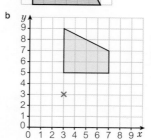

2 scale factor 2, centre of enlargement (0, 5)

3

4 4.75 m

5 10 m/s

6 **a** 57 mph   **b** 21 miles

7 0.67 g/cm³

8 46 N/m²

9 4 rolls: 48p each
   6 rolls: 42p each
   9 rolls: 43p each
   6-roll pack is the best value for money as the price per roll
   is the cheapest.

10 9 minutes

11 £40

12 a £384   **b** 12%

13 32%

Challenge

1 Students' own answers, e.g.
increase £400 by 20%
decrease £960 by 50%
decrease £600 by 20%

2 Students' own answers, e.g.
a 8 am (at a speed of 60 mph)
b 5.30 am (at a speed of 30 mph)

4 Strengthen: Enlargement

1 a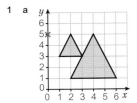

b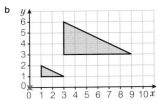

c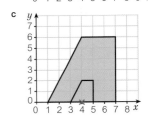

d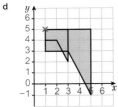

2 a (7, 1)   **b** 2
c The distance from the centre of enlargement to each point in B is twice the distance to the corresponding point in A.

3 Shape C is enlarged by scale factor 3, with centre of enlargement (3, 4).

4 a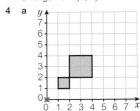

b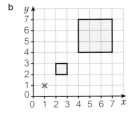

c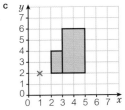

5 a right   **b** left   **c** down   **d** up

6 a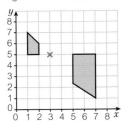

b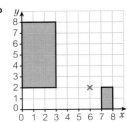

7 a 8 inches   **b** 12 inches

8 a 76
b i 6460 mm   **ii** 6.46 m

4 Strengthen: Compound measures and proportionality

1 a 9000 m/h   **b** 150 m/min   **c** 2.5 m/s
d 30 m/s

2

Distance (miles)	Time (hours)	Speed (mph)
165	3	55
102	$1\frac{1}{2}$	68
120	4	30
144	$2\frac{1}{4}$	64
70	2	35
180	$3\frac{3}{4}$	48

3

Metal	Mass (g)	Volume (cm³)	Density (g/cm³)
tin	731	100	7.31
iron	472.2	60	7.87
nickel	311.5	35	8.9

4

Force (N)	Area (cm²)	Pressure (N/cm²)
84	12	7
45	15	3
56	4	14

5 a 500 g: £1.52 for 1 kg
1 kg: £1.45 for 1 kg
3 kg: £1.42 for 1 kg
b 3 kg bag is the best value for money as the price per kg is the cheapest.

6 a 25p for one soap; £5 for 20 soaps
b Both packs are the same value for money.

7 a longer
b shorter
c **i**

| Number of gardeners | Time (minutes) | | **ii** | Number of gardeners | Time (minutes) |

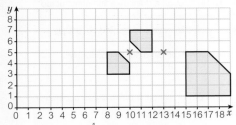

4 Strengthen: Percentage change

1 a 0.9   **b** £40
2 a 0.8   **b** 0.6   **c** 0.85   **d** 0.7
3 a £60   **b** £120   **c** £80   **d** £90
4 a 1.25   **b** 16
5 a 1.1   **b** 1.3   **c** 1.45   **d** 1.06
6 a 60   **b** 150   **c** 120   **d** 450
7 a 4%   **b** yes
8 a 25%   **b** 30%   **c** 85%
9 a 25%   **b** 15%   **c** 37%

Challenge

1 Tyler types faster.
(Lowri 39 words per minute, Tyler 44 words per minute)
2 a $70\,\text{cm}^2$
b any two measurements that multiply to give $70\,\text{cm}^2$, e.g. 7 cm and 10 cm

4 Extend

1 a scale factor −3, centre of enlargement (2, 5)
b scale factor −2, centre of enlargement (3, 3)
2 a 2 m   **b** 20 cm
c Raj is correct.
20 cm × 10 = 200 cm = 2 m and 2 m × 12 = 24 m
3 a 40   **b** 45
4 3 hours 46 minutes
5 a i 42 minutes   **ii** 52 minutes
b Average speed, as the train will not be travelling at the top speed for the entire journey.
6 a i 9%   **ii** 14%   **iii** 25%
b i is from 2008 to 2009 so uses 2008 as the denominator of the fraction, but **ii** is from 2009 to 2010 so it uses 2009 as the denominator of the fraction when working out the percentage increase. **iii** is from 2008 to 2010 so uses 2008 as the denominator of the fraction.
Percentage increases involve multiplication not addition. In this case, you have a multiplied by 1.09 (increased by 9%) and then multiplied by 1.14 (increased by 14%).
c i 14%   **ii** 8%
7 307 g
8 438 N
9 8.2 cm
10 2 hours 10 minutes
11 a, b

c scale factor $\frac{1}{2}$, centre of enlargement (1, 5)

4 Unit test

1

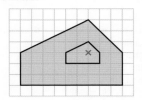

2 a scale factor 2, centre of enlargement (4, 4)
b scale factor 3, centre of enlargement (1, 6)
3

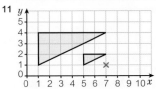

4 25
5 a £168   **b** 6%
6 22%
7 a 47 mph   **b** 26 km   **c** 48 minutes
8

Mass (g)	Volume (cm³)	Density (g/cm³)
322	280	1.15
846	450	1.88

9 $5.6\,\text{N/cm}^2$
10 Pack of 4: 29.5p per carton
Pack of 6: 28p per carton
Pack of 10: 28.5p per carton
Pack of 6 is the best value as it is the cheapest per carton.
11

12 a 16   **b** 1 : 16
13 40%

Challenge

Area of original triangle is $14\,\text{cm}^2$.
$2500\,\text{cm}^2$: scale factor 1 : 12 gives an enlarged triangle with the closest area ($2016\,\text{cm}^2$)
$1200\,\text{cm}^2$: scale factor 2 : 21 gives an enlarged triangle with the closest area ($1543.5\,\text{cm}^2$)
$600\,\text{cm}^2$: scale factor 2 : 11 gives an enlarged triangle with the closest area ($423.5\,\text{cm}^2$)
$300\,\text{cm}^2$: scale factor 2 : 11 gives an enlarged triangle with the closest area ($423.5\,\text{cm}^2$)

UNIT 5 Constructions

5.1 Using scales

1 a 2.5m b 25m c 250m d 2.5km
2 a 5cm line drawn accurately
   b 3.5 cm line drawn accurately
3 a 6cm, 1cm, 2cm, 2cm, 4cm, 3cm
   b 12m, 2m, 4m, 4m, 8m, 6m
4 a i 3cm ii 5cm
   b i 60m ii 100m
   c 60m
5 a 800m b 240m c 880m
   d Students' own answers, e.g.
      1mm on the map represents 20m in real life, and it
      is difficult to measure the map distances any more
      accurately than that.
6 a 1cm : 0.5m
   b i 2m ii 4m
      iii 2m^2 iv 0.75m^2
7 Floor plan drawn accurately using the scale of 1cm to 0.5m
8 a 1250m
   b i 2000m ii 2km
9 a i 500m ii 2000m
   b 3km
10 a 300m
   b i 2cm ii 20cm

Challenge

a 72.5km b 200km c Rhyl, 210km

5.2 Basic constructions

1 a At right angles
   b A line from the centre of a circle to the edge
2 a 6.5cm line drawn accurately
   b 10.6cm line drawn accurately
   c 27 mm line drawn accurately
3 40° angle drawn accurately
4 a Circle of radius 5cm drawn accurately
   b Circle of radius 8cm drawn accurately
5 a Perpendicular bisector of 7.5cm line constructed
   b Half the line should be 3.75cm
   c Angle should be 90°
6 a, b Perpendicular bisector of straight line constructed
7 a, b Angle bisector of 60° constructed and measured
8 Angle bisector of 75° constructed
9 Angle bisector of any obtuse angle constructed
10 a–d Perpendicular from a point to a 12cm line constructed
11 a, b Perpendicular from a point to a line constructed
12 a–c Perpendicular through a point on a line constructed
13 Perpendicular through a point on a line constructed

Challenge

a Perpendicular bisector of straight line constructed

b–d The distances from any point on the perpendicular bisector
     of a line segment to its two ends are equal.

5.3 Constructing triangles

1 2 triangles, 3 rectangles
2 Any working net of the square-based pyramid sketched
3 Perpendicular bisector of 9cm line constructed
4 a, b 5-6-7 triangle sketched then constructed accurately
5 7-4-10 triangle constructed accurately
6 a 8-8-4 triangle constructed
   b 29°
7 a–d Right-angled triangle constructed
8 a, b Right-angled triangle constructed
9 a Right-angled triangle constructed
   b 8cm
10 a, b Net of triangular prism drawn accurately
11 Any working net of the square-based pyramid drawn accurately
12 Any working net of the triangular prism drawn accurately

13 a Right-angled triangular prism
   b Any working net of the prism drawn accurately
   c 6cm

Challenge

a, b Wheel of Theodorus constructed
c 45°, 35.3°, 30°, 26.6°, 24.1°
   The angles get smaller and smaller.
d The angles are the same.

5.4 Using accurate scale diagrams

1 a 10m b 3cm
2 Perpendicular through point P on a line constructed
3 Triangle drawn accurately
4 a, b Triangle drawn accurately
   c 8.3cm
5 Accurate drawing of the ramp with height = 1cm and
   base length = 6.7cm
6 a Side view of ramp sketched and labelled
   b Side view of ramp drawn accurately using the scale 1:10
   c i about 572cm
      ii about 574cm
7 Scale drawing constructed
8 a $YA = 3.6$cm, $YB = 2.5$cm, $YC = 2.6$cm, $YD = 2.8$cm
   b YB
9 a Scale plan of drains constructed
   b About 4m
   c The new drain is at right angles to the main drain so its
      length is the perpendicular distance, which is the shortest
      possible distance.
10 a Scale plan of wind turbine, paths and road constructed
   b About 400m
11 a, b Right-angled triangle constructed
   c About 6.7km
12 a Scale drawing of roof truss constructed
   b i 90°
      ii Because the triangle is isosceles
13 a Any working net of the triangular prism drawn
      accurately to scale
   b 0.9m

Challenge

a, b Any working net of the square-based pyramid drawn
      accurately to scale and assembled

5 Check up

1 a 325cm b 100cm
2 Scale diagram drawn accurately
3 a 1500m b 1250m c 800m
4 Perpendicular bisector of 11cm line constructed
5 Angle bisector of 80° constructed
6 Perpendicular from a point to a line constructed
7 Perpendicular through a point on a line constructed
8 Triangle constructed accurately
9 a Right-angled triangle constructed accurately
   b 6.7cm
10 a Scale diagram of ramp drawn accurately
   b 2.02m c 8.5°

Challenge

Any working net of the triangular prism drawn accurately

5 Strengthen: Using scales

1 Logo drawn accurately
2 Board game drawn accurately
3 a 4m × 12m b 6m × 2m c 20m × 6m
4 a i 5cm ii 15m
   b i 2cm ii 6m
   c 12m × 9m

5 a

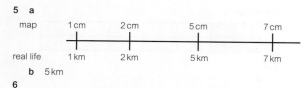

map	1 cm	2 cm	5 cm	7 cm
real life	1 km	2 km	5 km	7 km

b   5 km

6

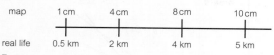

map	1 cm	4 cm	8 cm	10 cm
real life	0.5 km	2 km	4 km	5 km

7

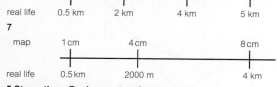

map	1 cm	4 cm	8 cm
real life	0.5 km	2000 m	4 km

5 Strengthen: Basic constructions

1   Perpendicular bisector of 6 cm line *AB* constructed
2   Perpendicular bisector of 14 cm line constructed
3   Angle bisector of 72° constructed
4   Angle bisector of 30° constructed
5   Angle bisector of 100° constructed
6   Perpendicular from a point to a line constructed
7   Perpendicular through a point on a line constructed

5 Strengthen: Constructing triangles

1   7-6-8 triangle constructed accurately
2   **a, b**   5-8-9 triangle sketched and then constructed accurately
3   **a–d**   Labelled net of the triangular prism sketched and then drawn accurately
4   Right-angled triangle constructed accurately
5   **a**   Right-angled triangle constructed accurately
    b   10.4 cm

5 Strengthen: Using scale diagrams

1   Scale drawing of triangle constructed accurately
2   Scale drawing of triangle constructed accurately
3   Scale drawing of diagram constructed accurately
4   Accurate plan constructed

Challenge

a   Plan of crop circle constructed
b   Students' own crop circle design constructed

5 Extend

1   5 cm
2   Any working net of 3 cm cube constructed accurately
3   Scale drawing of swing drawn accurately
4   No, she is wrong. If 1 cm represents 25 000 cm, then 10 cm represents 250 000 cm or 2.5 km.
5   1 cm : 0.5 km
6   **a**   Plan of the garden drawn accurately
    b   4.2 m   **c**   24 m²   **d**   9.36 m²
7   About 18 km
8   **a**   Triangle constructed   **b**   8.6 cm
9   **a**   135°
    b   Scale drawing of playground drawn accurately
    c   17.0 m
10   3.5 m
11   27 cm

Challenge

Students' own explanations

5 Unit test

1   **a**   45 cm   **b**   75 cm   **c**   30 cm by 22.5 cm
2   **a**   1060 m   **b**   380 m
3   Perpendicular bisector of 13 cm line constructed
4   Angle bisector of 42° constructed
5   Perpendicular from point to a line constructed
6   **a**   1250 m or 1.25 km   **b**   60 cm

7   10-12-8 triangle constructed accurately
8   Any working net of the triangular prism drawn accurately
9   **a**   Right-angled triangle constructed to scale
    b   3.8 m

Challenge

The red dots will form a spiral when joined.

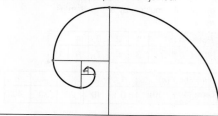

UNIT 6 Sequences, inequalities, equations and proportion

6.1 *n*th term of arithmetic sequences

1 a arithmetic, 4 **b** not arithmetic
  c arithmetic, −2 **d** arithmetic, 0.5

2 a 3, 6, 9, 12, 15 **b** 5, 6, 7, 8, 9

3 a i add 2 ii multiply by 8
  b i $n + 2$ ii $8n$

4 a

Position (*n*)	1	2	3	4	5
Term ($2n + 1$)	3	5	7	9	11

b

Position (*n*)	1	2	3	4	5
Term ($10n - 10$)	0	10	20	30	40

c

Position (*n*)	1	2	3	4	5
Term ($3n - 9$)	−6	−3	0	3	6

d

Position (*n*)	1	2	3	4	5
Term ($2n - 0.5$)	1.5	3.5	5.5	7.5	9.5

5 a 43, 403 **b** 68, 698 **c** 59, 509
  d 42, 582 **e** 28.5, 298.5 **f** 20.5, 200.5

6 a 4, 8, 12, 16, 20 **b** 3, 5, 7, 9, 11
  c 1, 4, 7, 10, 13 **d** $1\frac{1}{2}$, 2, $2\frac{1}{2}$, 3, $3\frac{1}{2}$
  e 15, 10, 5, 0, −5 **f** 1, −1, −3, −5, −7
  g The common difference is the same as the multiple of *n* in the *n*th term.

7 a 2, 4, 6, 8, 10, … $2n$
    4, 8, 12, 16, 20, … $4n$
    5, 10, 15, 20, 25, … $5n$
    6, 12, 18, 24, 30,… $6n$
    −2, −4, −6, −8, −10, … $-2n$
    −3, −6, −9, −12, −15, … $-3n$
  b $2n$: even numbers
    $5n$: multiples of 5

8 a $5n + 6$ **b** $3n - 1$ **c** $2n + 3$ **d** $4n - 3$
  e $-5n + 26$ **f** $-2n + 5$ **g** $-3n - 1$

9 a yes, $n = 15$ **b** yes, $n = 9$ **c** no
  d yes, $n = 4$ **e** no **f** no

10 a descending **b** −20 **c** 5

11 a
(dot pattern triangle)

b

Pattern number	1	2	3	4	5
Number of dots	4	7	10	13	16

  c $3n + 1$ **d** 121
  e $3n + 1 = 46$, $n = 15$, 15th pattern

12 a $2n - 1$ **b** 39
  c $2n - 1 = 50$, $n = 25.5$, 25th pattern

Challenge

a

n	1	2	3	4	5
$2n + 5$	7	9	11	13	15

b, c

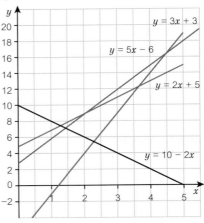

d Students' own answers, e.g.
The terms in each sequence form a straight line when plotted against the term number.

6.2 Non-linear sequences

1 a 2 **b** 10

2 a 50 **b** 12 **c** −36 **d** 18

3 a multiply by 2; 16, 32
  b multiply by $\frac{1}{2}$; 6.25, 3.125
  c multiply by 4; 256, 1024
  d multiply by 3; −162, −486
  e multiply by 0.5; 7.5, 3.75
  f multiply by 1.5; 10.125, 15.1875
  g multiply by $\frac{1}{3}$; $7\frac{11}{27}$, $2\frac{38}{81}$
  h multiply by 0.1; 0.1, 0.01
  i multiply by 5; −3125, −15625
  j multiply by −2; 48, −96
  k multiply by −1; 1, −1
  l multiply by $-\frac{1}{2}$; −1.5, 0.75

4 arithmetic sequences: **C, B**
  geometric sequences: **A, D, E, F**

5 a 0.3296 **b** 0.9765625 **c** 0.370…
  d 10^{-1}
  e No; all the first terms and all the multipliers are positive, and a positive multiplied by a positive always has a positive answer.

6 a Students' own sequences to match the descriptions
  b, c Students' own answers

7 a

Bounce number	1	2	3	4	5
Height of bounce (cm)	150	75	37.5	18.75	9.375

  b 9th, 0.6 cm (1 d.p.)

8 Yes; geometric progression with rule 'multiply by 3'.
  There will be 1215 on Saturday.

9 a 1, 4, 9, 16, 25 **b** 2, 8, 18, 32, 50
  c 4, 7, 12, 19, 28 **d** $\frac{1}{2}$, 2, $4\frac{1}{2}$, 8, $12\frac{1}{2}$

10 a Add 3, then add 5, then add 7, i.e. the odd numbers in order from 3
  b 37

11 a

Number of rows	2	3	4	5
Number of tins	3	6	10	15

  (+3, +4, +5)

  b 36

12 a i **A** 3, 6, 11, 18, 27
  B 6, 9, 14, 21, 30
  C −3, 0, 5, 12, 21
 ii 1st differences are in pattern +3, +5, +7, +9 for all three sequences.
 iii 2nd differences all +2
 b The 2nd difference is 2.
 c i 3, 9, 19, 33, 51
  1st differences +6, +10, +14, + 18
  2nd differences +4
 ii 3, 12, 27, 48, 75
  1st differences +9, +15, +21, +27
  2nd differences +6
 iii 3, 15, 35, 63, 99
  1st differences +12, +20 +28, +36
  2nd differences +8
 d The 2nd difference equals 2 × the multiple of n^2
  ($2 \times 2 = 4; 2 \times 3 = 6; 2 \times 4 = 8$).
 e 2nd differences are constant.
13 a 0, 6, 14, 24, 36
 b Quadratic because 1st differences are 6, 8, 10, 12 and 2nd differences are all 2.
 c Jenny is incorrect because nth term is
  $(n + 4)(n − 1) = n^2 + 3n − 4$, which does include n^2.

Challenge

a

Pattern 4

b 1, 3, 6, 10

c

Pattern number (n)	1	2	3	4
Rectangles	1	3	6	10

d 15, 21

Pattern 5   Pattern 6

e quadratic
f The sequence changes to 0, 1, 3, 6, 10, 15.

6.3 Inequalities

1 a a whole number, which can be positive, negative or 0
 b any three numbers less than 5, e.g. −3, 0, 2
 c any three numbers 2 or greater, e.g. 2, 3, 109
2 a $x = 8$ **b** $x = 9.6$ **c** $x = 3.5$
3 a $10 \leqslant x < 20$
 b 20, 21, 22, 23, 24, 25, 26, 27, 28, 29
4 a 6, 7, 8, 9
 b 7, 8, 9, 10, 11, 12, 13, 14
 c −5, −4, −3, −2, −1, 0, 1, 2, 3, 4
 d −7, −6, −5, −4, −3
5 a

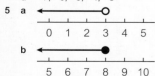

 b

 c

 d

 e

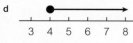

 f

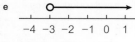

g

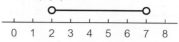

h

i

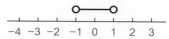

6 a $n > 4$ **b** $n < −4$ **c** $n \leqslant 14$
 d $n \geqslant −14$ **e** $8 < n \leqslant 12$ **f** $n > −3$
 g $−3 \leqslant n < 4$ **h** $8 \leqslant n \leqslant 12$
7 a 3, 4, 5, 6

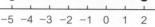

 b −2, −1, 0, 1, 2

 c 0

 d −5, −4, −3, −2, −1, 0, 1

 e −9, −8, −7, −6, −5, −4, −3, −2, −1

 f −4, −3, −2

8 a $4 < n$

 b $n < −5$

 c $n \geqslant −6$

 d $6 > n$

 e $−2 \leqslant n < 5$

 f $0 \leqslant n \leqslant 5$

 g $−7 < n \leqslant −2$

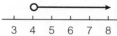

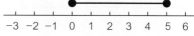

h $-5 \leqslant n < 2$

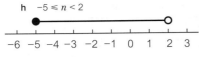

i $3 < n < 7$

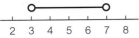

j $-5 \leqslant n \leqslant 0$

k $-5 \leqslant n < 0$

9 a $2n > 10$ **b** $3n > 15$
c $4n > 20$ **d** $2n + 1 > 11$

10 a $n + 7 < 12$ or $n < 5$ **b** 4

11 $2n + 7 < 15$ or $n < 4$
Possible solutions: any three numbers less than 4

12 a $-2 < 2x \leqslant 8$ **b** $-5 < 5x \leqslant 20$
c $-3 < 2x - 1 \leqslant 7$ **d** $-3 < 5x + 2 \leqslant 22$

13 4, 5, 6

Challenge

a $-2 < 2$ **b** $-7 < -3$
c $-18 < -6$ **d** $-3 < -1$
e Yes, these inequalities are all correct.
f $6 < 2$; multiplying both sides by -1 has made the inequality incorrect.

6.4 Solving equations

1 a $x = 4, x = -4$ **b** $x = 11, x = -11$
2 a $x = 9$ **b** $x = 4$ **c** $x = 15$ **d** $x = 19$
3 a $x = 6$ **b** $n = -3$ **c** $n = 5$ **d** $x = -3$
4 a $x = 6$ **b** $x = 8$ **c** $x = -1$ **d** $x = \frac{1}{2}$
5 8 m/s
6 a $x = 7$ **b** $a = 6$ **c** $b = 7$ **d** $y = 9$
7 a $n = -2$ **b** $d = -2$ **c** $n = -4$ **d** $p = -7$
8 3 (They both get the answer 6.)
9 a $y = \frac{7}{17}$ **b** $y = \frac{11}{18}$ **c** $x = -\frac{2}{5}$ **d** $x = -\frac{13}{14}$
10 a $x = 4, x = -4$ **b** $x = 7, x = -7$
c $x = 10, x = -10$ **d** $x = 8, x = -8$
e $x = 5, x = -5$ **f** $x = 13, x = -13$
11 a i $x = 15$ **ii** $y = 14$ **iii** $z = 16$
iv $y^2 - 11^2 = 203; y = 18$
b x, y and z all represent lengths, and a length cannot be negative.
12 a $x = 5.3$ **b** $y = 4.8$ **c** $z = 6.2$ **d** $a = 199.6$

13

Circuit	Power (watts)	Voltage (volts)	Resistance (ohms)
Circuit 1	2.5	5	10
Circuit 2	51.2	32	20
Circuit 3	36	24	16
Circuit 4	72	24	8
Circuit 5	31.25	25	20

Challenge

a $\dfrac{2(x + 3) - 2}{2} - x$

b Students' own answers

c $\dfrac{2(x + 3) - 2}{2} - x = \dfrac{(x + 3) - 1}{1} - x = x + 3 - 1 - x = 2$

d, e Students' own answers

6.5 Proportion

1 a £4.50 **b** £0.75 or 75p
2 a 2 hours **b** 4500
3 a gradient = 1 **b** $y = x$
4 a i gradient $= \frac{1}{2}$ **ii** $y = \frac{1}{2}x$
b i gradient = 1 **ii** $y = x$
c i gradient = 4 **ii** $y = 4x$
d i gradient = 5 **ii** $y = 5x$
5 a When m doubles, e doubles, and so on.
b The value is always 1.2
c

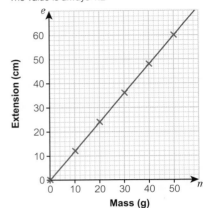

d gradient = 1.2
e The gradient is the same as the value of $\frac{e}{m}$
f $e = 1.2m$
g i 42 cm **ii** 15 g
6 A i $k = 2$ **ii** $e = 2m$
B i $k = 0.8$ **ii** $e = 0.80m$
C i $k = 1.25$ **ii** $e = 1.25m$
D i $k = 0.75$ **ii** $e = 0.75m$
E i $k = 1.75$ **ii** $e = 1.75m$
7 a yes ; the further you travel, the more time it takes
b 3
c $d = 3t$ **d** 250 seconds
8 a not direct proportion
b direct proportion, $C = £8n$
c not direct proportion
9 1200 lev

10 a

Number of painters, n	1	2	4	8
Hours to paint building, h	56	28	14	7

b nh is constant, 56.
c $nh = 56$ **d** $h = \frac{56}{n}$

11 a i $k = 12$ **ii** $y = \frac{12}{x}$
b i $k = 20$ **ii** $y = \frac{20}{x}$
c i $k = 18$ **ii** $y = \frac{18}{x}$

12 a $C = \frac{£448}{n}$
b i £32 **ii** £17.92
13 50 seconds
14 $y = 6.44$
15 1.04 cm (2 d.p.)

Challenge

a The length is always 1.414 times the width (3 d.p.).
b Students' own results

6 Check up

1 a 4, 8, 12 **b** 4, 7, 10 **c** 7, 4, 1
d 3, 6, 11 **e** 3, 12, 27 **f** 0, 6, 16
2 a 506 **b** -197

3 a 6n b −5n c n + 7
  d 4n − 2 e 13 − 2n f 3 − n
4 a 24, 29 b 112, 224 c 14, 19
  d 50, 25 e 17, 26 g 8.1, 24.3
5 a Arithmetic: a
  b Geometric: b, d, f
6 No, because 6n + 2 = 52 gives n = 8.33... which is not a position number (positive integer).
7 a x = 1 b x = 11
8 a x = 8 or x = −8 b x = 10 or x = −10
9 a all integers greater than but not including 7

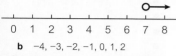

  b −4, −3, −2, −1, 0, 1, 2

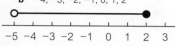

10 a x < 2 b −1 ≤ x < 2

11 Yes, because $\frac{\text{mass}}{\text{length}}$ = 17 for each pair of values.

12 a 72 minutes b 66.67 miles (2 d.p.)
13 a P = 0.26n
  b £25.48
14 a $t = \frac{120}{n}$ b 30 minutes

Challenge

Students' own answers

6 Strengthen: Sequences

1 a i

Position (n)	1	2	3	4	5
6n	6	12	18	24	30
−2	−2	−2	−2	−2	−2
Term (6n − 2)	4	10	16	22	28

  ii

Position (n)	1	2	3	4	5
4n	4	8	12	16	20
−10	−10	−10	−10	−10	−10
Term (4n − 10)	−6	−2	2	6	10

  b i 58 ii 30

2 a

Position (n)	1	2	3	4	5
− 3n	−3	−6	−9	−12	−15
+12	+12	+12	+12	+12	+12
Term (−3n + 12)	9	6	3	0	−3

  b −18

3 a  Sequence 6 11 16 21
  Differences +5 +5 +5
  The sequence goes up in 5s.
  b The 5 times table is 5, 10, 15, 20, ..., 5n
  c Each term in the sequence is 1 more than 5n.
  d The nth term is 5n + 1
  e When n = 1, 5n + 1 = 5 + 1 = 6 = 1st term

4 a 3n + 8 b 5n + 3 c 2n + 2
  d 6n − 5 e 2n − 5 f 10 − 2n
  g 8 − 3n h 3n − 10

5 a

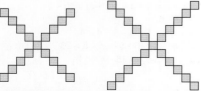

  b

Pattern number (n)	1	2	3	4	5
Number of squares	5	9	13	17	21

c +4 d 4n + 1 e 41
6 a

Position (n)	1	2	3	4	5
Term (5n − 1)	4	9	14	19	24

  b 16 lies between two adjacent terms, 14 and 19
  c i and ii 5n − 1 = 16 gives n = 3.4, which is not a positive integer (position number)

7 a 8 b 11 c 23
8 a ×3 b ×3 c $\times \frac{1}{3}$ d $\times \frac{1}{3}$
9 a +6, +6, +6 b +1, +2, +3
  c ×2, ×2, ×2 d −3, −3, −3
  e ÷10, ÷10, ÷10 f +3, +5, +7
10 a i Arithmetic: a, d ii +6, −3
   b i Geometric: c, e ii ×2, ÷10
   c Neither: b, f

6 Strengthen: Inequalities

1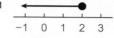

2 a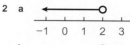

  b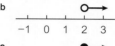

  c

3 a x < 1 b x ≥ −2 c x > 0 d x ≤ 2

4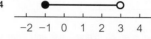

5 a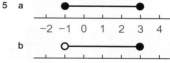

  b

  c

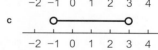

6 a −2 < x ≤ 1 b 0 ≤ x < 3

6 Strengthen: Solving equations

1 a $\frac{2x}{3} = 4$, 2x = 12, x = 6

  b $\frac{2x + 3}{2} = 5$, 2x + 3 = 10, 2x = 7, x = 3.5

  c $\frac{2x + 1}{5} = 1$, 2x + 1 = 5, 2x = 4, x = 2

  d $\frac{3x − 1}{4} = 5$, 3x − 1 = 20, 3x = 21, x = 7

2 a x = 7 b $x = \frac{1}{9}$ c $y = -\frac{1}{3}$

  e $x = -\frac{6}{11}$ e $a = -1\frac{4}{13}$ f $x = -1\frac{12}{13}$

3 a i 25 ii 49
  b i x = 9, x = −9 ii x = 4, x = −4
   iii x = 8, x = −8 iv x = 10, x = −10
   v x = 5, x = −5 vi x = 6, x = −6
4 a 12(x + 2) = 48; x = 2
  b 10x − 4x = 30; x = 5
  c x² − 48 = 208; x = 16

6 Strengthen: Proportion

1 a £15 per hour, the same for both pairs
  b yes
2 a no b no
3 a y = 2x b t = 1.5h c q = 6p

4 $B = \frac{5}{3}A$

5 a 13 HKD b $h = 13p$ c 1950 HKD

6 14 400 kroner

7 a 36, the same for all three pairs
  b yes

8 a $xy = 6, y = \frac{6}{x}$ b $sv = 48, v = \frac{48}{s}$

Challenge

Rachel 20 tracks, Anita 8 tracks, Peter 10 tracks

6 Extend

1 a i 4, 7 ii $3n - 2$ iii 58
  b i 6, 10 ii $4n - 2$ iii 78
  c i 10 ii $-2n + 14$ or $14 - 2n$
    iii -26
  d i 3, 7 ii $2n + 1$ iii 41

2 a $-2, -1, 0, 1$

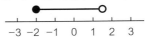

  b 1, 2, 3, 4, 5

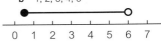

  c 0, 1, 2, 3

  d $-2, -1, 0, 1, 2, 3, 4$

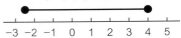

3 There are no integers between $x = 5$ and $x = 6$, and those two values are excluded.

4 a 2 b 6
  c

Number of chairs	2	3	4	5
Number of ways to sit	2	6	12	20

  d 90

5 a i $5n - 2$ ii $20 - 4n$ or $-4n + 20$
  b i 98 ii -60

6 b $p = 6k$ c $E = 37y$ d $c = 5x$ e $m = 3.5y$

7 b the perimeter of a regular octagon with sides of length s
  c the wage received for h hours' work at a rate of £9 per hour
  d weekly earnings for 30 hours' work at £w per hour
  e the number of miles travelled at a speed of 60 mph for h hours

8 a $\dfrac{4(x + 3)}{5} = \dfrac{3(2x + 2)}{6}$ b $x = 7$

9 a

Shape	Length (l)	Width (w)	Area (A)
A	4	2	8
B	6	3	18
C	8	4	32

  b $l = 2w$ c $A = 2w^2$

10 a $x = -2$ b $x = 30$ c $x = -\frac{1}{2}$
   d $x = -6$ e $x = 1$ f $x = -3$

11 a $a = 9$ b $p = 3$ c $x = -5$ d $t = 6$

12 a 64
   b i 64 players ii 32 matches
   c follows sequence 64, 32, 16, 8, 4, 2, 1, so 7 rounds of matches
   d one in each round, i.e. 7 matches
   e $64 + 32 + 16 + 8 + 4 + 2 + 1 = 127$

13 14, 6, 15

14 $\dfrac{4x + 1}{3} = 5x - 18; x = 5$

15 a any three numbers less than 8
   b any three numbers greater than -8
   c $x > -8$

16 $x \geq -2$

Challenge

Students' own answers

6 Unit test

1 $6n - 1$

2 a 5, 13, 21 b 4, 2, 0
  c 6, 9, 14 d 3, 12, 27

3 a

Pattern 4   Pattern 5

  b

Pattern number, n	1	2	3	4	5
Number of dots	4	6	8	10	12

  c $2n + 2$ d 22 e 49th pattern

4 a

Pattern number	1	2	3	4	5
White counters	4	8	12	16	20
Black counters	5	8	13	20	29

  b $4n$
  c arithmetic sequence, common difference is 4
  d 40
  e Yes; 68 is in the 4 times table, $4n = 68$ gives $n = 17$
  f quadratic
  g $n^2 + 4$

5 $-5, -4, -3, -2, -1, 0, 1, 2$

6 $3x > 12$

7 a $x = 1.25$ b $x = 7.5$

8 a $x = 4$ or -4 b $x = 6$ or -6

9 20 m/s

10 a $d = 4.5t$ b 12 seconds

11 $A = 3.705$

12 a i inverse ii $y = \dfrac{4.6}{x}$
   b i direct ii $y = 3.8x$

Challenge

Students' own answers, e.g.

A $bc - (a + b) = 5 \times 4 - (3 + 5) = 20 - 8 = 12$

B $2a + b + c = 2 \times 3 + 5 + 4 = 6 + 9 = 15$

C $a + c + \dfrac{a + b}{c} = 3 + 4 + \dfrac{3 + 5}{4} = 7 + \dfrac{8}{4} = 7 + 2 = 9$

D $\dfrac{a + b}{c} = \dfrac{3 + 5}{4} = \dfrac{8}{4} = 2$

E $2abc + b = 2 \times 3 \times 5 \times 4 + 5 = 120 + 5 = 125$

F $bc - 2(a + c) = 5 \times 4 - 2(3 + 4) = 20 - 2 \times 7$
  $= 20 - 14 = 6$

G $a + b - c = 3 + 5 - 4 = 8 - 4 = 4$

H $a^2 + c^2 - b = 9 + 16 - 5 = 25 - 5 = 20$

I $ab - c = 3 \times 5 - 4 = 15 - 4 = 11$

UNIT 7 Circles, Pythagoras and prisms

7.1 Circumference of a circle

1 **a** **i** 2.7   **ii** 2.66
   b **i** 9   **ii** 9.5
2 **a** 351 cm or 3.51 m   **b** 3505 mm
3 **a** 18 cm   **b** 5 cm   **c** 33 cm   **d** 4 cm
4 **a** Circle of radius 6 cm drawn accurately
   b, c e.g.

5 **a** 14 mm   **b** 25.4 cm
6 **a** 21 cm   **b** 0.95 m
7 No; the radius is $36 \div 2 = 9$ inches.
8 **a** $d = 2r$ **b** $r = \dfrac{d}{2}$
9 25 mm
10 **a**

Diameter, d (mm)	Circumference, C (mm)	$\dfrac{C}{d}$
51	160	3.14
57	179	3.14
65	204	3.14
71	223	3.14

   b C is directly proportional to d
   c $C = 3.14 \times d$ **d** 242 mm
11 **a** 25.8 cm   **b** 1477 mm   **c** 2.83 m
12 **a** 12.10 mm   **b** 176 cm   **c** 126 795 km
13 No; the circumference is $2 \times \pi \times 80 \approx 2 \times 250 = 500$ cm
14 24 819 miles
15 26 cm
16 421 cm
17 **a** $3 \times 9\text{m} = 27\text{m}$
   b Underestimate because both numbers were rounded down.
   c Overestimate, e.g. $3.5 \times 10\text{m} = 35\text{m}$
18 **a** $2 \times 3 \times 200 = 1200\text{m}$
   b $350\pi\text{m}$ **c** 1100 m
19 e.g. $3 \times 1\,500\,000 = 4\,500\,000$ km
20 **a** **i** 6.4 cm **ii** 0.80 m
   b **i** 24 mm **ii** 640 km
21 18 cm
22 **a** **i** 3.0 m **ii** 5 times
   b 64 cm

Challenge

1 **a** $L = 25\pi d$ **b** 325π mm
   c It is an approximation because the windings gradually increase the diameter.
2 Students' own experimental results

7.2 Area of a circle

1 **a** Multiply the radius by 2   **b** $\pi \approx 3$
2 **a** 64   **b** 900   **c** 0.25
   d 6   **e** 2.5 m   **f** 10 000 cm²
   g 7.5×10^{-2}
3 **a** 48   **b** 1412.64   **c** 3.74
4 0.75 m²
5 **a** 162.9 m²   **b** 2.0 m²   **c** 49 100 cm²
6 **a** **i** $3 \times 3^2\text{mm}^2 = 27\text{mm}^2$
     ii $3 \times 20^2\text{cm}^2 = 1200\text{cm}^2$
     iii $3 \times 100^2\text{km}^2 = 30\,000\text{km}^2$
   b **i** 25 mm²   **ii** 1400 cm²   **iii** 25 000 km²
   c $25\,000\,000\,000\text{m} = 2.5 \times 10^{10}\text{m}^2$
7 298 cm²
8 12.5π cm²
9 1230 m²

10 Area = 7.1 cm², perimeter = 10.7 cm
11 $\dfrac{25}{\pi} = r^2$, $7.957\ldots = r^2$, $2.82\ldots = r$, $r = 2.8$ cm (1 d.p.)
12 **a** 4.4 cm   **b** 0.28 m   **c** 13 mm   **d** 84.6 km
13 12 cm

Challenge

a 16 km
b Unless the value being square rooted is a perfect square, then it will always give a decimal answer. In such cases, the answer would be more accurate given to a number of decimal places.

7.3 Pythagoras' theorem

1 **a** 9   **b** 11   **c** 25   **d** 21
2 **a** 63 cm²   **b** 24 cm²
3 **a** 245   **b** 23.89   **c** 9.43   **d** 2.65
4 **a** 6.71   **b** 34.1   **c** 7.81   **d** 2
   e 5
5 **b** **i** $a = 20\,\text{mm}$, $b = 30\,\text{mm}$, $c = 36\,\text{mm}$
     ii 36 mm
   c **i** $A = 34°$, $B = 56°$, $C = 90°$
     ii The larger the angle, the longer the side.
6 **a** 13 cm   **b** 100 mm   **c** 7.3 cm   **d** 2.2 cm
7 No; the order does not matter because $a^2 + b^2 = b^2 + a^2$.
8 **a** 9.4 cm   **b** 37 cm   **c** 7.4 cm   **d** 17.5 cm
   e 6.4 cm
9 No, because a length can never be negative.
10 **a**

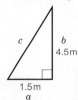

   b 4.74 m
11 11.5 inches
12 **a** 21.9 cm   **b** 63 mm   **c** 1.10 m   **d** 6245 mm
13 57.6 m
14 19.2 cm² (1 d.p.)
15 **a** 50 cm   **b** 74.8 cm   **c** 1.4967 m²

Challenge

1 **a** $\sqrt{15649}$ m   **b** 125 m   **c** 125.1 m
   d 125.095 96 m
2 **a** 125.095 96; it has the most decimal places or the surd as it has not been rounded at all.
   b 125 m; it is close to the accurate answer and is easy to measure.

7.4 Prisms and cylinders

1 **a** 50 000   **b** 250   **c** 0.001
   d 6 cm   **e** 6 cm²   **f** 2.5 litres
2 **a** 5 cm²   **b** 40 cm²   **c** 18 cm²
3 **a** 5 cm   **b** 31.42 cm   **c** 78.5 cm²
4 **a** **i** 64 cm³   **ii** 120 000 cm³
     iii 168 000 mm²
   b **i** 96 cm² **ii** 15 800 cm²
5 **a** 1 cm³   **b** 1000 mm³
   c 1 m³   **d** 1 000 000 cm³
   e **i** 1000 mm³   **ii** 1 000 000 cm³
     iii 1000 litres
6 **a** 64 000 mm³   **b** 0.12 m³   **c** 168 cm³
7 **a** Yes, rectangle   **b** Yes, triangle
   c Yes, hexagon   **d** No
   e No   **f** Yes, trapezium
8 Students' own answers, e.g.
It depends on the direction of the cut: two right prisms are produced if the cut is parallel to the end faces or to the length, but not if the cut is at an angle.

9 a i 1500 cm² ii 16 cm² iii 1400 mm²
  b i 120 000 cm³ ii 64 cm³ iii 168 000 mm³
  c The answers are the same.
10 a i 12 000 cm³ ii 4510 cm² (3 s.f.)
   b i 8 cm³ ii 31.4 cm²
   c i 235.2 cm³ ii 302 cm²
11 a i 360 m³ ii 360 000 litres
   b 20 hours
12 a πr^2 b $\pi r^2 h$ c $V = \pi r^2 h$
13 491 cm³
14 20.36 cm³
15 115 cm²
16 a

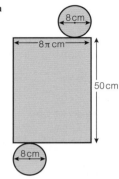

  b 25.1 cm or 251 mm c 1400 cm³

Challenge

Students' own sketches, e.g.

7.5 Errors and bounds

1 a i 18 cm ii 20 cm
  b i 430 g ii 430 g iii 400 g
  c 7 g
2 a i 44 cm² ii 42 cm² iii 40.4 cm²
  b i 1620 g ii 1764 g iii 1791 g
3 a 25.1 cm b 50.3 cm² c 754 cm³
4 a 4.5 cm b 5.5 cm
5 a 14.5 cm ≤ l < 15.5 cm
  b 3.5 kg ≤ m < 4.5 kg
  c 55 cm ≤ x < 65 cm
  d 110 cm ≤ n < 130 cm
  e 375 g ≤ m < 425 g
  f 2.95 cm ≤ l < 3.05 cm
6 a 29.5 cm, 30.5 cm b 89 cm, 91 cm
  c 2630 cm² ≤ A < 2780 cm²
7 a 175 cm ≤ r < 185 cm b 1100 cm ≤ C < 1160 cm
8 731 cm² ≤ A < 841 cm²
9 a 45 cm ≤ l < 55 cm b 2.7 m ≤ h ≤ 3.3 m
  c 38 litres ≤ c ≤ 42 litres d 99.5 kg ≤ m ≤ 100.5 kg
  e 235.2 ≤ n ≤ 244.8
10 a 190 g ≤ m ≤ 210 g b 276 ≤ n ≤ 324
11 970 ≤ n ≤ 1030
12 400 000 g

Challenge

a i 59 600 mm² ii 69 200 mm²
b 96.6 mm by 48.3 mm by 231 mm
c Students' own answers

7 Check up

1 23.6 cm
2 40π cm

3 177 mm²
4 a 57 cm² b 30.8 cm
5 9.5 cm or 95 mm
6 7.98 m or 798 cm
7 21.6 cm or 216 mm
8 a 18 mm b 30 mm
9 0.701 m²
10 a 144 cm³ b 231 cm²
11 6.91 cm³
12 603 cm² (nearest cm²)
13 640 litres
14 a 19.5 cm, 20.5 cm
   b 380.25 cm², 420.25 cm²
15 190 ≤ n ≤ 210

Challenge

1 Students' own answers
2 a 1 complete revolution (1.74 revolutions)
  b 11.9 cm

7 Strengthen: Circles

1 a 3.141 592 654 b 6.283 185 307
  c 78.539 816 34 d 12.566 370 61
  e 12.566 370 61
2 a 3 cm b $C = \pi \times 3$ cm c 9.4 cm
3 a 37.7 cm b 62.8 mm
4 a 25.1 mm b 39.3 cm
5 5π cm
6 a 6 cm b $C = \pi \times 6$ cm c 18.8 cm
7 a 31.4 cm b 40.8 cm
8 a 16 cm b $C = 16\pi$ cm
9 a 3.8 mm b 2.5 cm c 8.0 m
  d 0.6 m e 95.5 km f 0.2 mm
10 a 4 cm b $A = \pi \times 4^2$ c 50.3 cm²
11 a 78.5 cm² (1 d.p.)
   b 1521 cm² (nearest cm)
   c 28.3 m² (1 d.p.)
   d 177 m² (nearest metre)
12 121π cm²
13 a 3.1 cm b 2.0 cm c 5.6 cm
   d 0.9 m e 12.6 mm f 0.4 m
14 a 15 cm
   b $\frac{1}{2} \times \pi \times 15^2$ = 353.4... = 353 cm² (nearest cm²)
   c $\frac{1}{2} \times \pi \times 30$ = 47.1... = 47 cm (nearest cm)
   d 47 + 30 = 77 cm (nearest cm)

7 Strengthen: Pythagoras' theorem

1 i
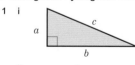
  ii

  iii

  iv
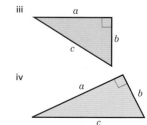

2 **a** 8.9 cm   **b** 5.4 cm   **c** 4.2 cm
3 **a** 6 cm   **b** 4.9 cm   **c** 5 cm
4 **a** **i** 11.3 cm   **ii** 22.6 cm²
    b **i** 22.4 mm   **ii** 447.2 mm²
    c **i** 9.2 cm   **ii** 36.7 cm²
    d **i** 7.1 cm   **ii** 60.7 cm²

7 Strengthen: Prisms and cylinders

1 **a** 1000 mm³
    b

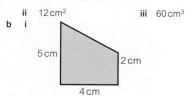

1 cm, 1 cm, 1 cm

    c 1 cm³   **d** 1000 mm³ = 1 cm³
    e **i** 2 cm³   **ii** 0.5 cm³
       iii 2.5 cm³   **iv** 3500 mm³
2 **a** **i** shaded area = 4 cm²; volume = 4 cm³
       ii shaded area = 4 cm²; volume = 8 cm³
       iii shaded area = 4 cm²; volume = 12 cm³
       iv shaded area = 4 cm²; volume = 16 cm³
    b Volume of prism = area of cross-section × length
3 **a** **i**

4 cm, 2 cm, 8 cm (trapezium)

       ii 12 cm²   **iii** 60 cm³
    b **i**

5 cm, 2 cm, 4 cm (quadrilateral)

       ii 14 cm²   **iii** 42 cm³
4 36 cm³
5 **a** 5
    b

6 cm, 5 cm, 4 cm, 3 cm, Rectangle 1, 5 cm, 3 cm, 3 cm, Rectangle 2, 5 cm, Rectangle 3

    c Area of each triangular face: 6 cm²
       Area of rectangle 1 = 6 × 4 = 24 cm²
       Area of rectangle 2 = 6 × 3 = 18 cm²
       Area of rectangle 3 = 6 × 5 = 30 cm²
    d 84 cm²
6 **a** 660 cm²   **b** 960 m²
7 **a** **i**

3 cm (circle)

       ii 28.27 cm² (2 d.p.)   **iii** 1696.5 cm³

b **i**

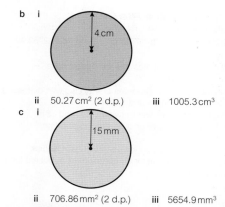

4 cm (circle)

       ii 50.27 cm² (2 d.p.)   **iii** 1005.3 cm³
    c **i**

15 mm (circle)

       ii 706.86 mm² (2 d.p.)   **iii** 5654.9 mm³

7 Strengthen: Errors and bounds

1 E, F, G and H
2 **a**

8 cm   8.5 cm   9 cm   9.5 cm   10 cm

    b lower bound 8.5 cm, upper bound 9.5 cm
3 **a** lower bound 7.5 cm, upper bound 8.5 cm
    b lower bound 75 g, upper bound 85 g
    c lower bound 57.5 cm, upper bound 62.5 cm
    d lower bound 250 cm², upper bound 350 cm²
    e lower bound 975, upper bound 1025

4

Lower bound	Upper bound	Inequality
10 cm	20 cm	10 cm ≤ x < 20 cm
6.5 g	7.5 g	6.5 g ≤ x < 7.5 g
30 km	34 km	30 km ≤ x < 34 km

5 **a** Length: lower bound 14 cm, upper bound 16 cm
       Width: lower bound 9 cm, upper bound 11 cm
    b

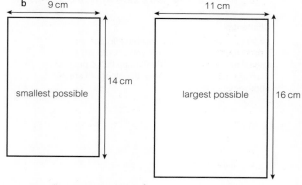

9 cm, 14 cm, smallest possible, 11 cm, 16 cm, largest possible

    c smaller rectangle: 126 cm²
       larger rectangle 176 cm²
    d 126 cm² ≤ A < 176 cm²
6 **a** 27 cm ≤ x ≤ 33 cm   **b** 95 cm ≤ x ≤ 105 cm
    c 196 g ≤ w ≤ 204 g   **d** 495 ≤ n ≤ 505

Challenge

Students' own answers based on Pythagorean triples, e.g.
3, 4, 5   5, 12, 13,   8, 15, 17   7, 24, 25,   ...
and/or multiples of them, e.g.
6, 8, 10   9, 12, 15,   10, 24, 26   15, 36, 39,   ...

7 Extend

1 Area = 57.1 cm², perimeter = 28.6 cm
2 314 cm²
3 **a** 420 ml
    b **i** 10.2 ml   **ii** 409.8 ml
    c 1.67 cm
4 **a** 65.25 mm²
    b 30.65 mm   **c** 613 layers
    d 1226 seconds or 20 minutes 26 seconds
5 17.7 m (1 d.p.)

6 AB = 3.6 cm, DE = 2.8 cm, FG = 4.1 cm,
   HJ = 6.4 cm, KL = 6.1 cm

7 **a** 749 250 mm³   **b** 7867 g   **c** £2753.49

8 **a** 1.8 g, 2.4 g
   b The calculation assumes that the sweets have
          identical masses.

9 **a** Calculate the circumferences of 4 circles with diameters
          40 cm, 80 cm, 120 cm and 160 cm.
          An approximate answer between 10 m and 15 m.
   b The length of the python is in direct proportion
          to its thickness.
          Yes, it would be half as long if it was half as thick.
   c This method is useful for an approximation, but not for an
          accurate answer.

Challenge

a 63.66 m
b 31.4 m
c **i** 62.8 m   **ii** 118 m

7 Unit test

1 **a** 8.4 cm   **b** 26.4 cm

2 **a** 14.3 m   **b** 7.2 m   **c** 161.1 m²

3 **a** 5.8 cm or 58 mm   **b** 11.3 cm or 113 mm

4 **a** 0.80 m   **b** 5.01 m or 510 cm

5 **a** 48 000 cm³ **b** 48 000 000 mm³

6 **a** 35 cm ≤ d < 45 cm
   b 110.0 cm ≤ c < 141.3 cm

7 11.25 m² ≤ A < 19.25 m²

8 **a** Minimum = 18, maximum = 22
   b 18 ≤ n ≤ 22

9 **a** 1.08 m²   **b** 1.5 m   **c** 14.16 m²

10 **a** 942 cm³   **b** 534 cm²

11 **a** 60 319 cm³ **b** 1164 kg
   c The value of the gold is $51 804 611, which is much more
          than $1 million.

Challenge

£2.20 tub: volume 785 cm³, price 0.28p per cm³
£14.10 tub: volume 5027 cm³, price 0.28p per cm³
£36.00 tub: volume 16 965 cm³, price 0.21p per cm³
The large tub is the best value; the other two are
approximately the same.

UNIT 8 Graphs

8.1 Using $y = mx + c$

1 a Graph B has positive gradient, graph A has negative gradient.

  b Graph A: x-intercept $(7, 0)$, y-intercept $(0, 8)$
    Graph B: x-intercept $(-2, 0)$, y-intercept $(0, 3)$

2 A **a** 1   **b** $(0, -4)$ **c** $y = x - 4$
  B **a** -2 **b** $(0, 3)$ **c** $y = -2x + 3$
  C **a** 3   **b** $(0, 0)$ **c** $y = 3x$
  D **a** -2 **b** $(0, -3)$ **c** $y = -2x - 3$

3 a C $(y = 3x)$
  b The steeper graph has the larger x-coefficient.
  c The gradients are the same.

4 a 2   **b** $(0, 5)$

5 Students' graphs of
  a $y = x + 3$ (goes through $(0, 3)$ and $(2, 5)$)

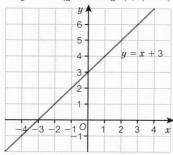

  b $y = 2x - 2$ (goes through $(0, -2)$ and $(2, 2)$)

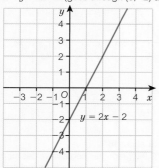

  c $y = 3x$ (goes through $(0, 0)$ and $(2, 6)$)

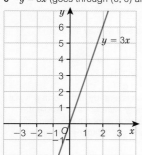

  d $y = 3x - 1$ (goes through $(0, -1)$ and $(2, 5)$)

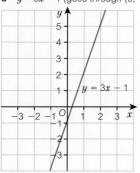

  e $y = \frac{1}{2}x$ (goes through $(0, 0)$ and $(2, 1)$)

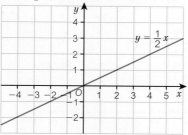

  f $y = \frac{1}{2}x - 3$ (goes through $(0, -3)$ and $(2, -2)$)

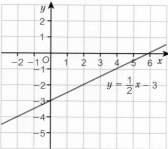

6 Students' graphs of
  a $y = -x + 2$ (goes through $(0, 2)$ and $(2, 0)$)

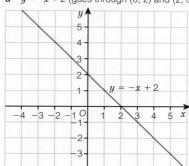

  b $y = -x - 2$ (goes through $(0, -2)$ and $(2, -4)$)

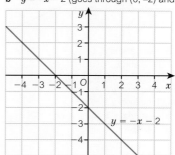

  c $y = -2x + 2$ (goes through $(0, 2)$ and $(2, -2)$)

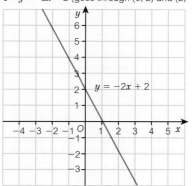

d $y = -3x + 1$ (goes through (0, 1) and (2, −5))

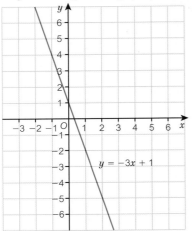

e $y = -\frac{1}{2}x + 3$ (goes through (0, 3) and (2, 2))

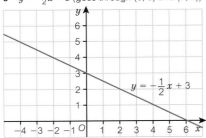

f $y = -\frac{1}{2}x - 3$ (goes through (0, −3) and (2, −4))

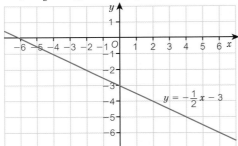

7 a No   **b** Axe, shield
8 a A and D, B and F, C and E
   b A, B and E at (0, 3); C and F at (0, −3)
9 a Any equation of the form $y = 3x + ...$
   b Any equation of the form $y = -2x + ...$
10 a $y = 3x - 2$ **b** $y = -4x + 3$ **c** $y = 2x$
11 a 4   **b** (4, 9)
12 (3, 11)
13 a (1, 5)   **b** (−4, −3)
14 a Students' graphs of $y = 25x + 1500$ (graph goes through
     (0, 1500) and (10, 1750))
   b £1500   **c** £25

Challenge

a Yes; their lines are not parallel so will intersect.
b No; their lines are parallel so will never meet.

8.2 More straight-line graphs

1 a $x = -3$ **b** $y = -5$ **c** $z = 3$
2 a $y = 3 - 2x$ **b** $y = 2x - 5$ **c** $y = \frac{1}{3}x + \frac{4}{3}$
3 a 0   **b** 0
   c **i** The y-intercept of a graph has x-coordinate 0.
      ii The x-intercept of a graph has y-coordinate 0.

4 Students' graphs of
  a $x + y = 3$ (goes through (0, 3) and (3, 0))
  b $2x + y = 1$ (goes through (0, 1) and ($\frac{1}{2}$, 0))
  c $3x + y = 3$ (goes through (0, 3) and (1, 0))
  d $3x + 2y = 3$ (goes through (0, $\frac{3}{2}$) and (1, 0))
  e $x + 3y = 6$ (goes through (0, 2) and (6, 0))
  f $2x + 3y = -12$ (goes through (0, −4) and (−6, 0))

5 Students' graphs of
  a $x - y = 3$ (goes through (0, −3) and (3, 0))
  b $2y - x = 2$ (goes through (0, 1) and (−2, 0))
  c $2x - y = -4$ (goes through (0, 4) and (−2, 0))

6 a

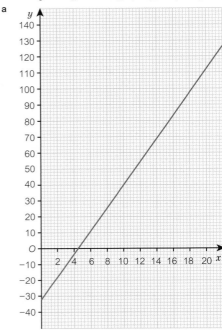

  b more
  c **i** about 110   **ii** about 16 °C
  d Below about 5°C the graph has negative values for the
     number of chirps per minute, which is not possible.

7 a $y = \frac{1}{2}x + 4$ **b** $\frac{1}{2}$
8 E ($2y - 7x = 8$)
9 None of the lines are parallel as they all have
   different gradients.
10 a $y = -\frac{1}{3}x + 2$ **b** $-\frac{1}{3}$
11 B ($2y - 3x = -4$) and E ($y = 3x - 2$)
12 Students' own answers, e.g.
  a 8.1 method; equation is already in the form $y = mx + c$ so it
     is easy to identify the y-intercept and gradient.
  b 8.2 method; it is easier to work out the intercepts by
     substituting $x = 0$ and $y = 0$ into the equation.

Challenge

Students' own answers, e.g.
A negative y-intercept
B passes through (0, 0)
C negative gradient
D decimal y-intercept

8.3 Simultaneous equations

1 B $(y = -\frac{3}{2}x)$

2 a

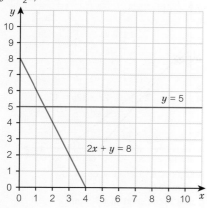

b $(1.5, 5)$

3 a $2x + 3y = 41$　　　b $3x + 2y = 40$

　c $5x + 3y = 12$, where x is the cost of an LED bulb and y is the cost of a halogen bulb

4 a i

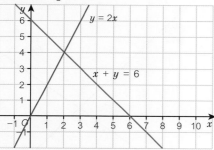

ii

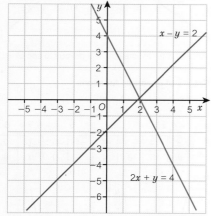

iii

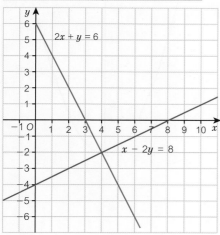

b i $(2, 4)$　　ii $(2, 0)$　　　iii $(4, -2)$

5 a $x = 6, y = 6$

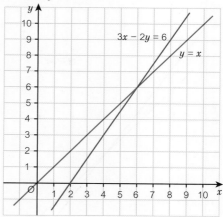

b $x = 5, y = -1$

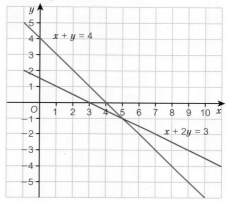

c $x = 1, y = 3$

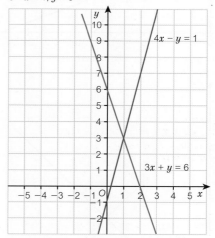

6 a $x + y = 12$ **b** $2x + 1.5y = 21$

c

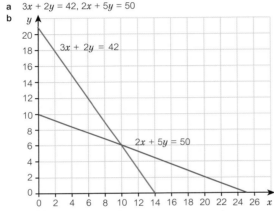

d 6 hardbacks, 6 paperbacks

7 a $3x + 2y = 42$, $2x + 5y = 50$

b

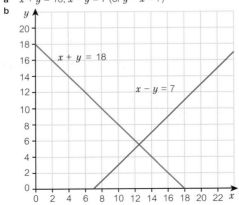

c Adult tickets cost £10, child tickets cost £6

8 a $x + y = 18$, $x - y = 7$ (or $y - x = 7$)

b

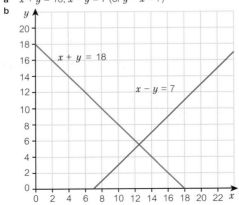

c $x = 12.5$, $y = 5.5$ (or vice versa)

9 a Mr Smith: $2x + 12y = 150$
Mrs Patel: $5x + 20y = 275$

b

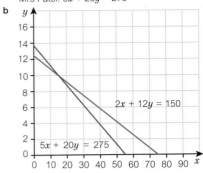

c Adults cost £15, children cost £10

10 At the point $(0, 6)$

11 Long stick 11 cm, short stick 7.5 cm

Challenge

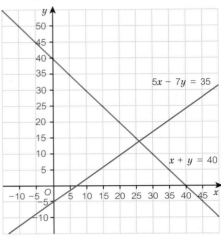

e.g. Answer is an estimate as it is difficult to see exactly where the two lines cross.

8.4 Graphs of quadratic functions

1 a $A = l^2$ **b** $A = \pi r^2$

2 a 3   **b** 48   **c** 3

3 a $x = 4$, $x = -4$ **b** $x = 6$, $x = -6$

4 a

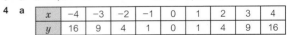

x	-4	-3	-2	-1	0	1	2	3	4
y	16	9	4	1	0	1	4	9	16

b–e

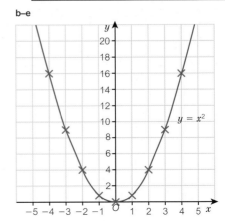

5 a

x	−2	−1	0	1	2
y	16	4	0	4	16

b

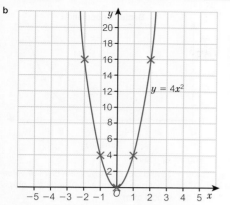

$y = 4x^2$

6 a Both pass through (0, 0) and are a parabola (U-shaped curve).

b Both are symmetrical about the y-axis (or line $x = 0$).

7 a $y = l^2$

b i about $30\,\text{cm}^2$ ii about $3.2\,\text{cm}$

c Calculator answers are

i $30.25\,\text{cm}^2$ ii $3.16\,\text{cm}$ (2 d.p.)

d The variable l represents a length, which cannot be negative.

8 a

r	0	1	2	3	4	5
A	0	3	12	27	48	75

b

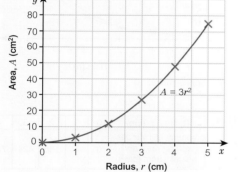

$A = 3r^2$

Area, A (cm^2)

Radius, r (cm)

c i about $19\,\text{cm}^2$ ii about $2.8\,\text{cm}$

d Calculator answers using π are

i $19.63\,\text{cm}^2$ (2 d.p.)   ii $3.78\,\text{cm}$ (2 d.p.)

9 a

x	−3	−2	−1	0	1	2	3
x^2	9	4	1	0	1	4	9
−1	−1	−1	−1	−1	−1	−1	−1
y	8	3	0	−1	0	3	8

b

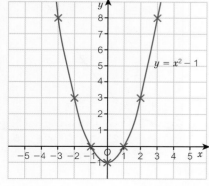

$y = x^2 - 1$

10

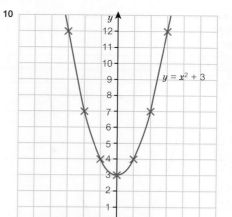

$y = x^2 + 3$

11 a They are all a parabola (U-shaped curve) and are symmetrical about the y-axis (or line $x = 0$). They are translations up or down of each other.

b They have different y-intercepts.

c A U-shaped curve which is symmetrical about the y-axis and passes through (0, 7)

12 a

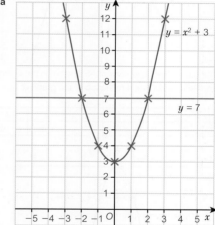

$y = x^2 + 3$

$y = 7$

b (−2, 7), (2, 7)

c i $x \approx 2.5$, $x \approx -2.5$

ii $x = 2.45$ (2 d.p.), $x = -2.45$ (2 d.p.)

iii e.g. answer from graph was 0.05 more/less than the actual values

d No, because there are no points of intersection between the line $y = 1$ and the parabola.

13 a about $19\,\text{m}$ **b** about $65\,\text{m}$

c The closer you are to the goalposts, the larger the angle of kick.

14 a

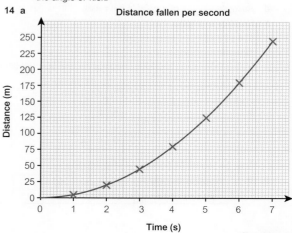

Distance fallen per second

Distance (m)

Time (s)

b quadratic   **c** between 6 s and 7 s

d about 6.3 s

Challenge

a

x	−4	−3	−2	−1	0	1	2	3	4
y	−16	−9	−4	−1	0	−1	−4	−9	−16

b i

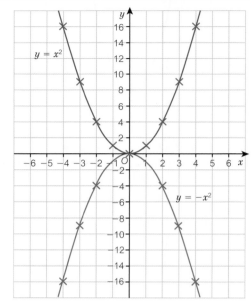

ii The curves are reflections of each other in the x-axis.

c i an ∩-shaped curve, a reflection of the graph of $y = 4x^2$ in the x-axis

ii

x	−2	−1	0	1	2
y	−16	−4	0	−4	−16

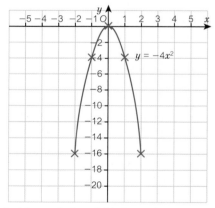

d Reflect the graph of $y = 2x^2$ in the x-axis.

8.5 Non-linear graphs

1 3, 4

2 339 cm³

3 Inverse proportion, because thatching the roof takes longer if there are fewer thatchers.

4 a i $k = 15$ **ii** $y = \frac{15}{x}$

    b i $k = 8$ **ii** $y = \frac{8}{x}$

5 a i 3 days   **ii** 2 days

    b 6   **c** 4   **d** $k = 6$

    e number of days = $\dfrac{6}{\text{number of workers}}$

6 a

Volume, V (cm³)	20	40	50	100
Pressure, P (bar)	5	2.5	2	1

b $k = 100$ **c** $P = \frac{100}{V}$

7 a 64

b, c, d

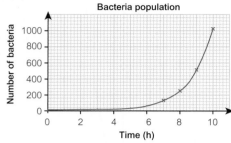

e i 100   **ii** 360

8 The graphs in Q5 and Q6; multiplying the pairs of values in the table in Q7 does not give a constant value (or the graph in Q7 intersects the vertical axis).

9 a 20–22 cps   **b** 17–18 minutes   **c** 25 minutes

    d No, because repeated dividing by 2 will always give a positive answer.

10 a, c

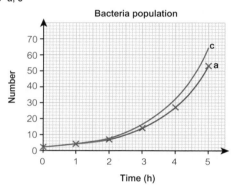

b approximately 10

d Model is good, particularly for shorter times, e.g. up to 3 hours.

11 a

Radius, r, (cm)	0	1	2	3	4	5
Volume of cylinder with radius r and height 15 cm (cm³)	0	47	188	424	754	1178

b

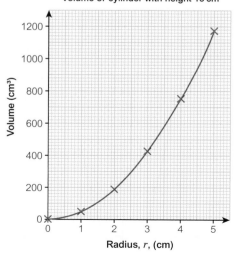

c 295 cm³

d 2.3 cm

12 a £8   **b** £18   **c** £2

   d The value is not included in the interval; for example, a stay of exactly 1 hour costs £2 not £4.

13 a £22

   b   **i** £27   **ii** £32

      iii £37   **iv** £32

   c £5

   d No; he could have used anything between 1.75 GB and 2 GB.

14 a He has used the wrong values on each axis, and the graph should have been a step graph not a line graph.

   b

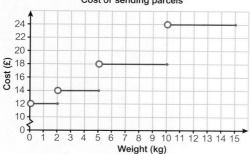

Cost of sending parcels

Challenge

a Students' own tables, e.g.

x	5	10	100	1000	10000	100000
$\frac{1}{x}$	0.2	0.1	0.01	0.001	0.0001	0.00001

b It gets smaller and smaller but will never reach zero.

c Students' own tables, e.g.

x	0.5	0.1	0.01	0.001	0.0001	0.00001
$\frac{1}{x}$	2	10	100	1000	10000	100000

It gets larger and larger.

d

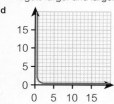

e No, the graph never touches either axis.

8 Check up

1 a, b

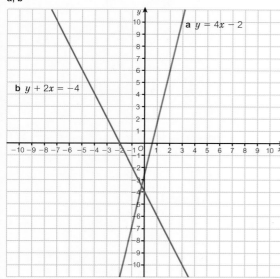

2 B and D

3 $y = -2x + 3$

4 $x = 2, y = 3$

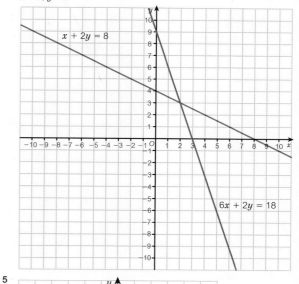

5

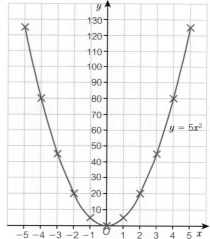

6 a   **i** 6 days   **ii** 4 days   **iii** about 4.8 days

   b 6   **c** $k = 12$

   d number of days $= \dfrac{12}{\text{number of volunteers}}$

   e The number of days is inversely proportional to the number of volunteers.

7 a   **i** £15   **ii** £30   **iii** £30

   b £7.50

Challenge

a, b Students' own answers, e.g.

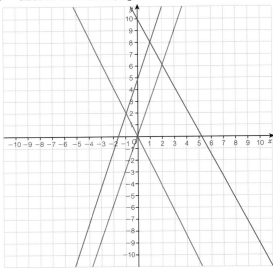

c Students' own answers, e.g.
$y = 3x$, $y = 3x + 5$, $y = -2x$, $y = -2x + 10$

d Many shapes can be made,
e.g. right-angled triangle using lines with gradient 1, −1 and 0
e.g. parallelogram using two lines with gradient 4 and two lines with gradient 0.

e Yes, by using two lines of gradient 1 and two lines of gradient −1.

8 Strengthen: Straight-line graphs

1 a

$y = mx + c$	Gradient m	y–intercept $(0, c)$
$y = 3x - 4$	3	$(0, -4)$
$y = 5x + 4$	5	$(0, 4)$
$y = -2x + 1$	−2	$(0, 1)$
$y = \frac{1}{2}x - 4$	$\frac{1}{2}$	$(0, -4)$
$y = 3x - 3$	3	$(0, -3)$

b $y = 3x - 4$ and $y = 3x - 3$

c $y = 3x - 4$ and $y = \frac{1}{2}x - 4$

d $y = -2x + 1$; the coefficient of x is negative.

2 a A, C have y-intercept $(0, 1)$

B, D have y-intercept $(0, -1)$

b $y = \frac{1}{2}x + 1$ gradient $= \frac{1}{2}$, positive
$y = 2x - 1$ gradient $= 2$, positive
$y = 2x + 1$ gradient $= 2$, positive
$y = -x - 1$ gradient $= -1$, negative

c i C **ii** B **iii** A **iv** D

3

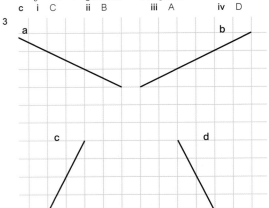

4 Students' graphs of

a $y = -\frac{1}{2}x + 1$ (goes through (0, 1) and (2, 0))

b $y = \frac{1}{2}x - 1$ (goes through (0, −1) and (2, 0))

c $y = 2x + 4$ (goes through (0, 4) and (2, 8))

d $y = -2x - 3$ (goes through (0, −3) and (2, −7))

5 a i same gradient **ii** different y-intercepts

b A and C **c** C **d** $y = 4x + 10$

e Any three equations of the form $y = 4x + ...$

6 a i (0, 3) **ii** (6, 0)

b

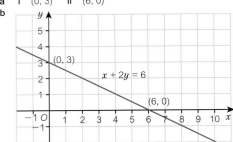

7 Students' graphs of

a $x + 3y = 6$ (goes through (0, 2) and (6, 0))

b $2x + y = 5$ (goes through (0, 5) and (2.5, 0))

8 a A $y = 3x + 4$
B $y = -3x + 2$
C $y = -3x - 1$

b A 3 **B** −3 **C** −3

c B and C

8 Strengthen: Simultaneous equations

1 a, b, c

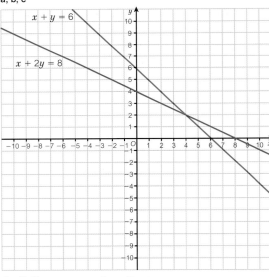

d (4, 2) **e** $x = 4$, $y = 2$

f i $x + y = 4 + 2 = 6$
ii $x + 2y = 4 + 2 \times 2 = 8$

2 a

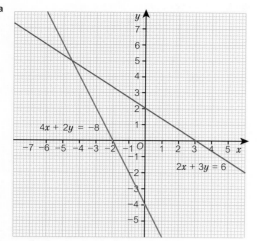

Lines labelled $4x + 2y = -8$ and $2x + 3y = 6$

b $(-4.5, 5)$ **c** $x = -4.5, y = 5$

d $2x + 3y = 2 \times -4.5 + 3 \times 5 = -9 + 15 = 6$
  $4x + 2y = 4 \times -4.5 + 2 \times 5 = -18 + 10 = -8$

8 Strengthen: Non-linear graphs

1 a $y = x^2$

x	−3	−2	−1	0	1	2	3
x^2	9	4	1	0	1	4	9

b $y = 2x^2$

x	−3	−2	−1	0	1	2	3
x^2	9	4	1	0	1	4	9
$2x^2$	18	8	2	0	2	8	18

c $y = 3x^2$

x	−3	−2	−1	0	1	2	3
x^2	9	4	1	0	1	4	9
$3x^2$	27	12	3	0	3	12	27

2 a, b, c

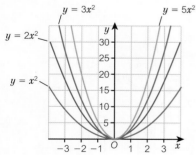

Curves labelled $y = 2x^2$, $y = 3x^2$, $y = 5x^2$, $y = x^2$

3 a $y = x^2 + 1$

x	−3	−2	−1	0	1	2	3
x^2	9	4	1	0	1	4	9
+1	+1	+1	+1	+1	+1	+1	+1
$x^2 + 1$	10	5	2	1	2	5	10

b $y = x^2 + 2$

x	−3	−2	−1	0	1	2	3
x^2	9	4	1	0	1	4	9
+2	+2	+2	+2	+2	+2	+2	+2
$x^2 + 2$	11	6	3	2	3	6	11

4 a, b, c

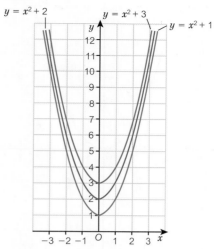

Curves labelled $y = x^2 + 2$, $y = x^2 + 3$, $y = x^2 + 1$

5 a i 10 days **ii** 5 days

  b i 5 **ii** 10

  c

Number of decorators (y)	2	4	5	10
Number of days (x)	10	5	4	2

  d $y = \dfrac{20}{x}$

  e $k = 20$

  f number of days $= \dfrac{20}{\text{number of decorators}}$

  g Inversely proportional, because painting the flat takes longer if there are fewer decorators.

6 a B **b** B **c** A

7 a i £150 **ii** £150 **iii** £100

  b £50 **c** The 8th day is free.

Challenge

a

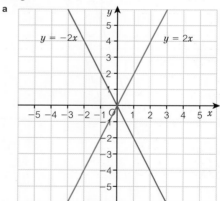

Lines labelled $y = -2x$ and $y = 2x$

b reflection in the y-axis (or the x-axis)

c reflection in the y-axis

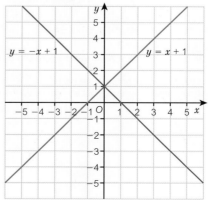

Lines labelled $y = -x + 1$ and $y = x + 1$

d reflection in the x-axis

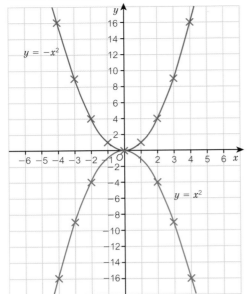

8 Extend

1 **a** $y = 3x + c$ **b** $4 = 3(-2) + c$
  c $c = 10$ **d** $y = 3x + 10$

2 $y = -2x + 5$

3 6

4 **a** (2, 60) and (5, 99)   **b** $P = 13h + 34$
  c cost per hour   **d** initial call-out fee

5 **a** $V = -1300a + 20\,500$ **b** £20 500

6 $-4x + 2y = 4$, $y - 2x = $ (any value), $3x - 1.5y = 8$

7 There are no points of intersection between the two lines

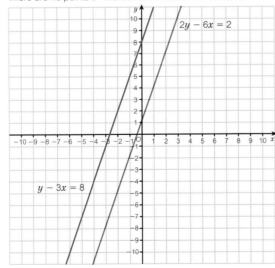

8 Students' own answers, e.g. $y = 1$, $y = x$, …

9 $y = 4x + 8$, or $y = \frac{1}{2}x + 5$

10 **a** Goes down by about 30 cm in 1st minute and by about 8 cm in 5th minute.
   b In the 1st minute; graph is steepest.
   c 10 cm, because water cannot flow out below this level.

11 **i** A   **ii** D   **iii** B
    iv E   **v** C

12 **a, b**

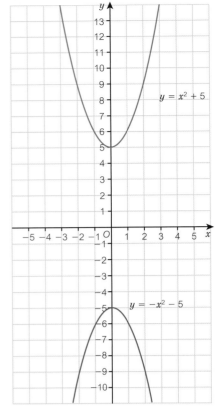

13 **a** about £6300   **b** after about 6 years
   c £5000   **d** £5400   **e** 8%

Challenge

a Point A is (5, 9)
   $2x - 1 = 2 \times 5 - 1 = 9$, so (5, 9) also lies on $y = 2x - 1$

b e.g. $y = 3x - 6$

8 Unit test

1 A, B and D

2 Students' graphs of
  a $y = 4x - 1$ (goes through (0, −1) and (2, 7))
  b $x + y = 2$ (goes through (0, 2) and (2, 0))

3 **a** A   **b** D   **c** A and C

4 **a, b** $x \approx 2.2$, $x \approx -2.2$

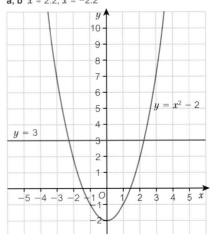

315

5 $x = 4, y = -1$

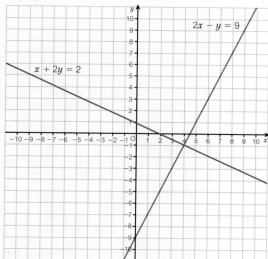

6 a   **i** £110   **ii** £110
       iii £170   **iv** £50
   b £30

7 a 75 counts per second   **b** 40 days   **c** 27 days

Challenge

a $P \approx 1.1$ units   **b** $d \approx 1.6\,\text{m}$ **c** 10 units
d $P = 1.111...$, which is close to the estimate of 1.1 in part **a**.

UNIT 9 Probability

9.1 Mutually exclusive events

1 a 1   **b** 0   **c** $\frac{1}{2}$

2 a $\frac{3}{8}$ **b** $\frac{4}{8}$ or $\frac{1}{2}$ **c** $\frac{7}{8}$

   d 0   **e** $\frac{7}{8}$ **f** $\frac{5}{8}$

3 a 20   **b** 5   **c** 20

4 a $\frac{2}{5}$ **b** $\frac{3}{5}$ **c** $\frac{3}{5}$

   d $\frac{2}{5}$ **e** $\frac{4}{5}$ **f** $\frac{4}{5}$

5 A and B

6 A, C and D

7 a Yes

   b i $\frac{1}{8}$ **ii** $\frac{1}{2}$ **iii** $\frac{3}{8}$

     iv $\frac{7}{8}$ **v** $\frac{5}{8}$ **vi** $\frac{1}{2}$

   c Yes; 1 red + 4 blue = 5 sections, so P(R or B) is $\frac{5}{8}$

8 a The canteen serves only one vegetable with every main meal choice, so you cannot have two different vegetables at the same time.

   b i 0.2   **ii** 0.8

     iii 0.4   **iv** 0.75

9 a Students' own tables

   b Yes; a counter cannot be two colours.

   c Students' own probabilities

   d 1

   e Students' own answers

   f The total is always 1.

10 a 0.1   **b** 6

11 14%

12 a Yes   **b** $\frac{2}{8}$ or $\frac{1}{4}$ **c** 5

13 a $\frac{7}{20}$ **b** chocolate   **c** 24

Challenge

0.3

9.2 Experimental and theoretical probability

1 a $\frac{29}{90}$ **b** $\frac{49}{200}$

2 a 50

   b i $\frac{11}{50}$ **ii** $\frac{13}{50}$

   c 56

3 a 27   **b** 100   **c** 1   **d** $\frac{27}{100}$

4 a 250   **b** 250

5 a $\frac{1}{6}$ **b** 58 or 59

6 a The statement is true for set 1, for which

     P(Red) = P(Blue) = P(Green) = $\frac{1}{3}$.

     But it is not true for set 2, for which

     P(Red) = $\frac{3}{14}$, P(Blue) = $\frac{4}{14}$ and P(Green) = $\frac{7}{14}$.

   b any set with equal numbers of each of three colours

   c any set with twice as many green pens as red

7 There could be more men than women, or vice versa. If there are 50 men and 60 women, each woman's chance of winning is $\frac{1}{60}$, which is less than each man's chance of winning.

8 a i 0.15   **ii** 0.17

   b i 0.167   **ii** 0.167

   c Yes

9 a Spinner P: $\frac{59}{120}$ Spinner Q: $\frac{30}{120}$ or $\frac{1}{4}$

     Spinner R: $\frac{32}{120}$ or $\frac{4}{15}$ Spinner S: $\frac{75}{120}$ or $\frac{5}{8}$

b Theoretical probabilities are

   Spinner P: $\frac{1}{2}$ Spinner Q: $\frac{1}{3}$

   Spinner R: $\frac{1}{4}$ Spinner S: $\frac{2}{3}$

c Spinner P: Experimental probability $\frac{59}{120}$ is very close to theoretical probability of $\frac{1}{2}$, so spinner is probably unbiased.

   Spinner Q: Experimental probability $\frac{30}{120}$ is not very close to theoretical probability of $\frac{1}{3}$ so spinner is probably biased.

   Spinner R: Experimental probability $\frac{32}{120}$ is very close to theoretical probability of $\frac{1}{4}$, so spinner is probably unbiased.

   Spinner S: Experimental probability $\frac{75}{120}$ is quite close to theoretical probability of $\frac{2}{3}$, so spinner is probably unbiased but we perhaps need more results to confirm.

   Conclusion: Students' own answers.

10 a Spinner P: 60   Spinner Q: 40

     Spinner R: 30   Spinner S: 80

   b Spinner P: 59 is close to 60, so probably unbiased

     Spinner Q: 30 is not close to 40, so probably biased

     Spinner R: 32 is close to 30, so probably unbiased

     Spinner S: 75 is fairly close to 80, so need more results to say.

   c Conclusion: Students' own answers.

11 Students' own answers, e.g.

No, because the frequencies would be roughly the same for all the scores if the dice was fair.

12 Students' own designs, roughly half red, one quarter blue and one quarter green

Challenge

1 Students' own results

2 a Students' own results, recorded in a table like this:

Score	2	3	4	5	6	7	8	9	10	11	12
Tally											
Frequency											

   b Students' own results (probably 7)

   c Students' own results (probably 2 or 12)

   d Students' own results (probably 7)

   e Player 2, because a score of 7 is more likely than 2 or 3.

   f Students' own explanations, e.g.

     Some totals (e.g. 7) can be made from several pairs of dice scores, but others can be made from only one pair, e.g. a score of 2 can only be made by rolling 1 and 1.

9.3 Sample space diagrams

1 a 1, 2, 3, 4, 5, 6

   b heads, tails

2 a 1, 2, 3, 4, 5, 6, 7, 8, 9

   b 1   **c** 4, 5, 6, 7

   d odd

3 a $\frac{1}{2}$ **b** $\frac{1}{2}$ **c** $\frac{2}{6}$ or $\frac{1}{3}$

   d $\frac{2}{6}$ or $\frac{1}{3}$ **e** $\frac{3}{6}$ or $\frac{1}{2}$ **f** $\frac{1}{2}$

4 a A green   B blue

     A green   B red

     A yellow   B blue

     A yellow   B red

   b $\frac{1}{4}$

5 H, 1   H, 2   H, 3   H, 4   H, 5   H, 6

   T, 1   T, 2   T, 3   T, 4   T, 5   T, 6

6

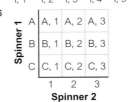

7 a

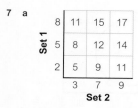

Set 1 \ Set 2	3	7	9
8	11	15	17
5	8	12	14
2	5	9	11

b 11

8 a

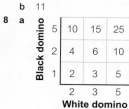

Black domino \ White domino	2	3	5
5	10	15	25
2	4	6	10
1	2	3	5

b i $\frac{1}{9}$ ii $\frac{2}{9}$

iii $\frac{1}{9}$ iv $\frac{5}{9}$

9 a

Dice 2 \ Dice 1	1	2	3	4	5	6
6	7	8	9	10	11	12
5	6	7	8	9	10	11
4	5	6	7	8	9	10
3	4	5	6	7	8	9
2	3	4	5	6	7	8
1	2	3	4	5	6	7

b i $\frac{1}{36}$ ii $\frac{2}{36}$ or $\frac{1}{18}$

iii $\frac{4}{36}$ or $\frac{1}{9}$ iv $\frac{3}{36}$ or $\frac{1}{6}$

c $\frac{11}{36}$ **d** $180 \times \frac{5}{36} = 25$

10 a $\frac{33}{100}$ **b** $\frac{6}{36}$ **c** 16 or 17

d No; the experiment produced roughly twice as many doubles as you would expect.

11 a

Dice 1 \ Dice 2	1	2	3	4	5	6
6	5	4	3	2	1	0
5	4	3	2	1	0	1
4	3	2	1	0	1	2
3	2	1	0	1	2	3
2	1	0	1	2	3	4
1	0	1	2	3	4	5

b i $\frac{12}{36}$ or $\frac{1}{3}$ ii $\frac{18}{36}$ or $\frac{1}{2}$

c No, the game is not fair as Gavin is more likely to win than Seema.

d Yes, this game is fair. (The sample space diagram is the same as for Q9.)

12 a P(J or A or M) = $\frac{7}{12}$; Greg is more likely to win

b She could win, but is less likely to.

c Any change that gives them both the same probability of winning a point, e.g. Greg has J, A, S and Amy has M, O, N, D, F.

Challenge

a Students' own results (probably about the same number of wins for both players)

b Students' own conclusions (probably yes)

c

Dice 1 \ Dice 2	1	2	3	4	5	6
6	5	4	3	2	1	0
5	4	3	2	1	0	1
4	3	2	1	0	1	2
3	2	1	0	1	2	3
2	1	0	1	2	3	4
1	0	1	2	3	4	5

d Player 1: $\frac{16}{36}$ or $\frac{4}{9}$ Player 2: $\frac{14}{36}$ or $\frac{7}{18}$

e No, because $\frac{16}{36}$ is greater than $\frac{14}{36}$ so Player 1 is more likely to win.

9.4 Two-way tables

1 $\frac{1}{25}$

2 a School A

b School A 82, School B 77

c 19 **d** 30 **e** $\frac{48}{159}$ or $\frac{16}{53}$

3 a

	Head (H)	Tail (T)
Head (H)	H, H	H, T
Tail (T)	T, H	T, T

b i $\frac{1}{4}$ ii $\frac{1}{2}$ iii $\frac{1}{2}$

4 a

		Silver coin		
		Heads	Tails	Total
Gold coin	Heads	23	30	53
	Tails	26	21	47
	Total	49	51	100

b 100 **c** 23 **d** $\frac{23}{100}$

e i $\frac{30}{100}$ or $\frac{3}{10}$ ii $\frac{47}{100}$

5 a $\frac{96}{200}$ or $\frac{12}{25}$ **b** $\frac{104}{200}$ or $\frac{13}{25}$ **c** $\frac{103}{200}$

d $\frac{97}{200}$ **e** $\frac{47}{200}$ **f** $\frac{48}{200}$ or $\frac{6}{25}$

6 a $\frac{76}{255}$

b Year 9 who learns French (probability $\frac{59}{255}$, compared with probability of $\frac{52}{255}$)

7 a i $\frac{10}{260}$ or $\frac{1}{26}$ ii $\frac{28}{260}$ or $\frac{7}{65}$

b $\frac{38}{78}$ or $\frac{19}{39}$

8 a $\frac{9}{72}$ or $\frac{1}{8}$ **b** $\frac{11}{72}$ **c** $\frac{22}{72}$ or $\frac{11}{36}$ **d** $\frac{19}{72}$

9 a

	0001–0600	0601–1200	1201–1800	1801–0000	Totals
Weekday	250	168	176	273	867
Weekend	42	28	30	33	133
Total	292	196	206	306	1000

b On a weekday, because there are more weekdays than weekend days.

c 0.20

d i 10404 ii 4824

10

	Numbers of 20s				
	0	1	2	3	Totals
George	0	2	0	6	8
Fiona	2	2	2	2	8
Anya	2	4	0	0	6

	Completely satisfied	Mostly satisfied	Dissatisfied
20–39	80	40	40
40–59	60	28	12
60 or over	100	12	28

9.5 Venn diagrams

1 a $\frac{1}{4}$ b $\frac{1}{2}$ c $\frac{3}{4}$

2 Yes, because the spinner cannot show red and blue at the same time.

3 a 6 b 1, 2 c 4

4 a Because the intersection is not empty: 1 is both a square number and is less than 4.
   b 5 and 6 are neither square numbers nor less than 4.
   c 2 d 6 e $\frac{2}{6}$ or $\frac{1}{3}$
   f $\frac{3}{6}$ or $\frac{1}{2}$ g $\frac{4}{6}$ or $\frac{2}{3}$ h $\frac{1}{6}$

5 a The intersection is empty: none of the numbers 1 to 6 is both a square number and a multiple of 3.
   b $\frac{2}{6}$ or $\frac{1}{3}$ c $\frac{2}{6}$ or $\frac{1}{3}$ d $\frac{4}{6}$ or $\frac{2}{3}$

6 a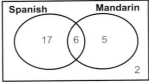
   b i $\frac{17}{30}$ ii $\frac{6}{30}$ or $\frac{1}{5}$ iii $\frac{22}{30}$ or $\frac{11}{15}$
   c 6 students study both Spanish and Mandarin, and these have been counted twice.

7 a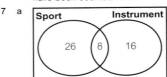
   b $\frac{16}{50}$ or $\frac{8}{25}$

8 a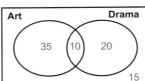
   b i $\frac{10}{80}$ or $\frac{1}{8}$ ii $\frac{20}{80}$ or $\frac{2}{8}$ iii $\frac{15}{80}$ or $\frac{3}{16}$

9 a i 2 ii 7
   b 25 c $\frac{16}{25}$

Challenge

1 a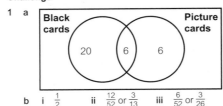
   b i $\frac{1}{2}$ ii $\frac{12}{52}$ or $\frac{3}{13}$ iii $\frac{6}{52}$ or $\frac{3}{26}$

2 a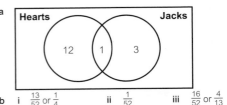
   b i $\frac{13}{52}$ or $\frac{1}{4}$ ii $\frac{1}{52}$ iii $\frac{16}{52}$ or $\frac{4}{13}$

9 Check up

1 a 88% b 36
   c No, it is 2.666…%, so not a great change in the probability.

2 a $\frac{5}{8}$ b chocolate c $\frac{7}{8}$

3 a i $\frac{44}{80}$ or $\frac{11}{20}$ ii $\frac{11}{80}$
     iii $\frac{11}{80}$ iv $\frac{28}{80}$ or $\frac{7}{20}$
   b woman under 25 c $\frac{10}{36}$ or $\frac{5}{18}$

4 a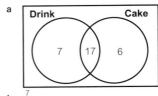
   b $\frac{7}{30}$

5 a

	2	3	4
4	4, 2	4, 3	4, 4
3	3, 2	3, 3	3, 4
2	2, 2	2, 3	2, 4

Abi's card (vertical) / Barry's card (horizontal)

   b i $\frac{1}{9}$ ii $\frac{5}{9}$

6 a 100 b $\frac{10}{100}$ or $\frac{1}{10}$ c 2

7 a Students own answers, e.g.
      No, because the frequencies would be roughly the same for all the scores if the spinner was unbiased, and 36 is quite a lot higher than 29; OR
      Yes, because the expected number for each score on an unbiased spinner is 33.333... and all the frequencies are quite close to this.
      The answer is a matter of opinion, and either answer Yes or No is acceptable as long as it is backed up by a reason.
   b 200

8 Yes, the game is fair.
   Students' own explanations, e.g.
   an ordered list of all possible sums or a sample space diagram

9 a $\frac{22}{200}$ or $\frac{11}{100}$ or 0.11
   b Yes, there are 97 heads out of 200 flips, which is 48.5%, close to the theoretical probability of 50%.

Challenge

Students' own answers

9 Strengthen: Mutually exclusive events

1 B and D

2 a red, yellow, pink
   b yes c 1 d 0.3

3 $\frac{3}{9}$ or $\frac{1}{3}$

4 a red

b

Colour	red	yellow	orange	black
Probability	$\frac{4}{10}$	$\frac{3}{10}$	$\frac{2}{10}$	$\frac{1}{10}$

c All the outcomes are mutually exclusive so their probabilities add up to 1.

d i $\frac{9}{10}$ **ii** $\frac{1}{10}$ **iii** $\frac{1}{10}$

e There are only four colours, so if a sweet is not red, orange or yellow, then it must be black.

5 15%

9 Strengthen: Probability from tables and diagrams

1 a

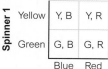

	Yellow	Y, B	Y, R
Spinner 1	Green	G, B	G, R
		Blue	Red

Spinner 2

b 4 **c** $\frac{1}{4}$

2 a

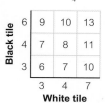

Black tile			
6	9	10	13
4	7	8	11
3	6	7	10
	3	4	7

White tile

b i $\frac{2}{9}$ **ii** $\frac{1}{9}$ **iii** $\frac{4}{9}$

3 a

Dice 1						
6	6	12	18	24	30	36
5	5	10	15	20	25	30
4	4	8	12	16	20	24
3	3	6	9	12	15	18
2	2	4	6	8	10	12
1	1	2	3	4	5	6
	1	2	3	4	5	6

Dice 2

b i $\frac{9}{36}$ or $\frac{1}{4}$ **ii** $\frac{27}{36}$ or $\frac{3}{4}$

c No, the game is not fair because the probability of getting an even product is greater than the probability of getting an odd product.

4 a

Spinner 1	50	50, 10	50, 50
	10	10, 10	10, 50
		10	50

Spinner 2

b i $\frac{1}{4}$ **ii** $\frac{2}{4}$ or $\frac{1}{2}$

5 a 70

b i $\frac{70}{264}$ **ii** $\frac{29}{264}$

c $\frac{32}{133}$ **d** $\frac{61}{131}$

6 a

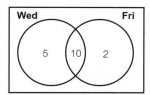

Wed / Fri: 5 | 10 | 2

b 17

c i $\frac{10}{17}$ **ii** $\frac{5}{17}$

7 a, b, c

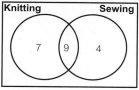

Knitting / Sewing: 7 | 9 | 4

d 20

e i $\frac{9}{20}$ **ii** $\frac{7}{20}$

9 Strengthen: Experimental probability

1 a $\frac{1}{2}$ **b** $\frac{36}{80}$ or $\frac{9}{20}$ **c** 0.45

d Students' own answers, e.g. Yes, because 0.45 is quite close to the theoretical probability, 0.5.

2 a $\frac{2}{6}$ or $\frac{1}{3}$ **b** 50

c No, because 26 is not close to 50.

3 a 36

		Number on blue tile			
		1	2	3	Total
Number on red tile	1	5	4	3	12
	2	6	5	4	15
	3	3	4	2	9
	Total	14	13	9	36

b i $\frac{3}{36}$ or $\frac{1}{12}$ **ii** $\frac{13}{36}$ **iii** $\frac{12}{36}$ or $\frac{1}{3}$

4 a $\frac{9}{90}$ or $\frac{1}{10}$ **b** $\frac{13}{90}$ **c** $\frac{6}{90}$ or $\frac{1}{15}$

5 a $\frac{1}{6}$

b Bella 5, Connie 20, Deepak 40

c Yes, all the experimental probabilities are close to the theoretical probability.

Challenge

a Derby **b** Carlisle and Penrith

9 Extend

1 a $\frac{2}{5}$ **b** 4

2 P(over 5) = $\frac{15}{25}$, P(under 5) = $\frac{6}{25}$
Score is more likely to be over 5.

3 $\frac{1}{6}$

4 Suffolk, probability 1.9×10^{-3}
(Northamptonshire 1.4×10^{-3})

5 a i $\frac{58}{80}$ or $\frac{29}{40}$ **ii** $\frac{18}{80}$ or $\frac{9}{40}$ **iii** $\frac{40}{80}$ or $\frac{1}{2}$

b Students' own spinner designs, e.g.

Spinner A   Spinner B

6 Thu, Dry 15%   Sat, Dry 25%
Mon, Rain 55%   Sun, Rain 10%
Tue, Snow 0%   Fri, Snow 10%

7 a i $\frac{30}{56}$ or $\frac{15}{28}$ **ii** $\frac{26}{56}$ or $\frac{13}{28}$

b The game is unfair because there is a higher probability of it landing in a white square.

c Students' own board designs, with an equal number of white and green squares.

8 a

Coin	T	T, 1	T, 2	T, 3	T, 4	T, 5	T, 6
	H	H, 1	H, 2	H, 3	H, 4	H, 5	H, 6
		1	2	3	4	5	6

Dice

b 12 **c** $\frac{3}{12}$ or $\frac{1}{4}$

d Income is £100, expected wins 50 so pay out £50. Expected profit for charity is £50.

9 a i 50% or $\frac{1}{2}$

ii The estimate for the mean is £24 629.63, which is £25 000 to the nearest 1000. It is reasonable to assume that approximately half the people in the £20 000 to £30 000 group earn more than this, so $\frac{40}{81}$, 49% or 50% would be good estimates for the number earning more than the mean.

b The mean is estimated. The number for those earning more than the estimated mean is itself an estimate.

Challenge

a

$\frac{42}{100}$	$\frac{41}{99}$	$\frac{40}{98}$	$\frac{39}{97}$	$\frac{38}{96}$	$\frac{37}{95}$	$\frac{36}{94}$

b 0.42, 0.414, 0.408, 0.402, 0.396, 0.389, 0.383 (all 3 d.p.) More likely to pick a vowel on your first pick

9 Unit test

1 a $\frac{67}{200}$ **b** $\frac{35}{200}$ or $\frac{7}{40}$

c The probabilities are the same

2 a

Bag A	W	W, B	W, W	W, R
	B	B, B	B, W	B, R
		B	W	R

Bag B

b $\frac{2}{6}$ or $\frac{1}{3}$

3 a i a dog **ii** a cat and a dog

b $\frac{59}{85}$

4 a $\frac{23}{90}$ **b** $\frac{31}{90}$

c Yes; spinner A landed on each colour approximately one third of the time.

5 a $\frac{3}{6}$ or $\frac{1}{2}$ **b** $\frac{2}{6}$ or $\frac{1}{3}$ **c** $\frac{4}{6}$ or $\frac{2}{3}$

6 a $\frac{3}{8}$ **b** 6

7 a $\frac{3}{12}$ or $\frac{1}{4}$ **b** $\frac{6}{12}$ or $\frac{1}{2}$ **c** $\frac{3}{12}$ or $\frac{1}{4}$

d Yes, P(more than 8) = P(less than 8) = $\frac{1}{2}$

8 Yes; the number of wins is the same as the expected number of wins (200 ÷ 12 = 16.67), to the nearest whole number.

9 6

Challenge

Spinner 1	5	10	20	30	40
	3	6	12	18	24
	1	2	4	6	8
		2	4	6	8

Spinner 2

Students' own answers

UNIT 10 Comparing shapes

10.1 Congruent and similar shapes

1 $a = 30°$ (vertically opposite angles)
    $b = 150°$ (angles on a straight line)
    $c = 150°$ (vertically opposite angles, angles on a straight line, or angles around a point)

2 **a–d**

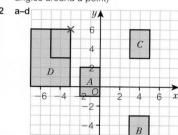

e The original object and images A, B and C are all congruent; when a shape is transformed by a translation, rotation or reflection, the original shape and the transformed shape are congruent, but in the enlargement all the lengths have increased by scale factor 2.

3 **a** Side a and side p are corresponding sides.
   b Side c and side r are corresponding sides.
   c Angle ABC and angle PQR are corresponding angles.

4 **a, b i**

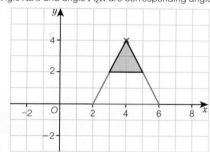

   b ii

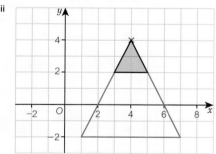

   c scale factor 1

5 **a** e.g.

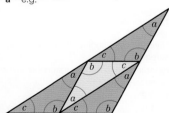

   b The angles of the triangle are a, b and c.
        a, b and c lie on a straight line. Angles on a straight line add to 180°, therefore angles in a triangle add up to 180°.

6 A, C, and D are similar to each other.
    B, E, and F are similar to each other.

7 B: neither similar nor congruent
    C: congruent
    D: neither similar nor congruent
    E: congruent

8 **a–d**

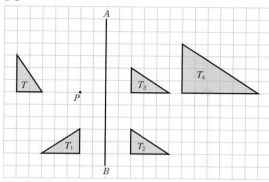

   a congruent   **b** congruent
   c congruent   **d** similar

9 **a** A and E, B and I, and D and H, are congruent pairs.
   b C, F, G, J, K, L are left over.
        C and G, and J and L, are similar pairs.
   c **i** congruent   **ii** congruent
        iii congruent   **iv** similar
   d Not necessarily: the triangles may be not congruent if the angle that is the same is not the one that is included between the two known sides.

10 **a** SAS   **b** SSS   **c** AAS
    d ASA   **e** AAS

11 Kamal is incorrect because the 8 cm side is between the two labelled angles in the first triangle (ASA) but not in the second triangle (AAS), so they are not corresponding sides.

12 **a** equal (vertically opposite angles)
    b $\angle BCA = \angle ECD$ (vertically opposite angles)
        $\angle ABC = \angle CDE$
        $AC = CE$
        Triangles ABC and EDC are congruent (AAS)

13 $a = 3.5$, $b = 45°$, $c = 2.5$, $d = 45°$, $e = 80°$, $f = 45°$, $g = 55°$

Challenge

Yes. Using Pythagoras' theorem, the third side is always 8.7 cm (1 d.p), so SSS.

10.2 Ratios in triangles

1 **a** 6   **b** 6   **c** 10   **d** 8

2 No. The ratio of the bases is not the same as the ratio of the heights.

3 **a** Vertically opposite angles are equal.
   b Alternate angles are equal.
   c Corresponding angles are equal.

4 **a** 6 mm   **b** 5 cm

5 **a** Students' own answers
   b 6.6 cm

6 **a** $x = 10$ cm, $y = 4$ cm, $z = 8$ cm
   b $x = 7.5$ m, $y = 14$ m, $z = 6$ m

7 Yes; the heights and hypotenuses are both in the ratio 3 : 2.

8 **a** Angles in triangle FGJ: $\angle JFG$,
        $\angle FJG = 90°$, $\angle FGJ$
        Angles in triangle FHI: $\angle IFH$,
        $\angle FIH = 90°$, $\angle FHI$
        $\angle JFG = \angle IFH$
        $\angle FJG = \angle FIH = 90°$
        $\angle FGJ = \angle FHI$ (corresponding angles)
        The triangles have the same angles (AAA)
   b $FI = 15$ cm, $IJ = 15$ cm − 6 cm = 9 cm

9 **a** Angles in triangle EGH: $\angle HEG$,
        $\angle EHG$, $\angle EGH = 90°$
        Angles in triangle EFI: $\angle IEF$,
        $\angle EIF$, $\angle EFI = 90°$
        $\angle HEG = \angle IEF$
        $\angle EGH = \angle EFI = 90°$
        $\angle EHG = \angle EIF$ (corresponding angles)
        The triangles have the same angles (AAA)
   b $GH = 13.8$ cm

10 a

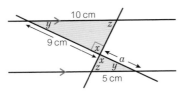

x vertically opposite angles, y alternate angles, z alternate angles

b Yes, the triangles are similar (AAA)

c

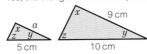

d 4.5 cm

11 a a = 17.5 cm **b** b = 9 cm

12 a p = 9 cm **b** q = 3 cm **c** r = 2 cm

Challenge

a 7.5 m **b** 20

10.3 The tangent ratio

1 a The longest side, the side opposite the right angle.
b AB, EF, GI

2 a 0.3 **b** 0.8 **c** 0.8 **d** 0.2
e 0.1

3 a $c = ab$ **b** $a = \frac{c}{b}$

4 a i AC **ii** BC **iii** AB
b i DE **ii** EF **iii** DF
c i GH **ii** GI **iii** HI
d i KL **ii** JK **iii** JL
e i MN **ii** NO **iii** MO
f i QR **ii** PQ **iii** PR
g i TU **ii** ST **iii** SU
h i WX **ii** VW **iii** VX

5 a 30° right-angled triangles drawn accurately
b Each triangle has angles of 90° and 30°; so the third angles are 60°: hence AAA.
c Triangles labelled and measured
d

Triangle	Opposite length	Adjacent length	$\frac{\text{opposite}}{\text{adjacent}}$ (1 d.p.)
P	2.9 cm	5 cm	0.6
Q	4.6 cm	8 cm	0.6
R	5.8 cm	10 cm	0.6

e i The ratio $\frac{\text{opposite}}{\text{adjacent}}$ is always 0.6.
ii The ratio will be 0.6.
iii Students' own 30° right-angled triangles and measurements

6 a 50° right-angled triangles drawn accurately
b Each triangle has angles of 90° and 50°; so the third angles are 40°: hence AAA.
c Triangles labelled and measured
d

Triangle	Opposite length	Adjacent length	$\frac{\text{opposite}}{\text{adjacent}}$ (1 d.p.)
P	6.0 cm	5 cm	1.2
Q	9.5 cm	8 cm	1.2
R	11.9 cm	10 cm	1.2

e i The ratio $\frac{\text{opposite}}{\text{adjacent}}$ is always 1.2.
ii The ratio will be 1.2.
iii Students' own 50° right-angled triangles and measurements

7 The ratio of the opposite and adjacent sides in similar right-angled triangles is the same.

8 a 0.6 **b** 1.2

9 a 0.6 **b** 1.6 **c** 1.7 **d** 0.2

10 a $\frac{7}{16}$ **b** $\frac{20}{9}$ **c** $\frac{11}{8}$

11 a x = 2.9 **b** x = 10.4 **c** x = 13.9
d x = 4.9 **e** x = 11.2 **f** x = 3.4

12 7 m 68 cm or 7.68 m

13 a x = 16.0 **b** x = 3.8 **c** x = 12.8
d x = 15.7 **e** x = 4.2 **f** x = 6.1

14 1.40 m (2 d.p.)

15 705 m

Challenge

a, b

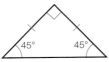

c tan 45° = 1

d Students' own answers, e.g.
The triangle can be bisected to give two right-angled isosceles triangles. The opposite sides to the 45° angles are equal to the adjacent sides:

So tan 45° = $\frac{\text{opposite}}{\text{adjacent}}$ = 1

10.4 The sine ratio

1 a i AC **ii** BC **iii** AB
b i EF **ii** DE **iii** DF
c i HI **ii** GH **iii** GI

2 a $g = fh$ **b** $h = \frac{g}{f}$

3 7.5 cm

4 a 35° right-angled triangles drawn accurately
b Triangles labelled and measured
c

Triangle	Opposite length	Hypotenuse length	$\frac{\text{opposite}}{\text{hypotenuse}}$ (1 d.p.)
P	3.5 cm	6.1 cm	0.6
Q	4.9 cm	8.5 cm	0.6
R	10 cm	17.4 cm	0.6

d i The ratio $\frac{\text{opposite}}{\text{hypotenuse}}$ is always 0.6.
ii The ratio will be 0.6.
iii Students' own 35° right-angled triangles and measurements

5 a 70° right-angled triangles drawn accurately
b Triangles labelled and measured
c

Triangle	Opposite length	Hypotenuse length	$\frac{\text{opposite}}{\text{hypotenuse}}$ (1 d.p.)
P	13.7 cm	14.6 cm	0.9
Q	19.2 cm	20.5 cm	0.9
R	10 cm	10.6 cm	0.9

d i The ratio $\frac{\text{opposite}}{\text{hypotenuse}}$ is always 0.9.
ii The ratio will be 0.9.
iii Students' own 70° right-angled triangles and measurements

6 The ratio of the opposite side to the hypotenuse in similar right-angled triangles is the same.

7 a 0.6 **b** 0.9

8 a 0.7 **b** 1.0 **c** 0.9 **d** 0.3

9 a $\frac{43}{50}$ **b** $\frac{20}{48} = \frac{5}{12}$ **c** $\frac{42}{64} = \frac{21}{32}$

10 a x = 7.4 **b** x = 5.6 **c** x = 9.0
d x = 10.8 **e** x = 4.0

11 70 m 71 cm or 70.71 m

12 a x = 32.4 **b** x = 16.1 **c** x = 18.5
d x = 21.5 **e** x = 26.4

13 28.7 cm

14 a i tangent **ii** 5.5 cm
   b i sine **ii** 15.2 cm
   c i tangent **ii** 2.4 cm

Challenge

Yes (it will reach 9.7 m up the wall)

10.5 The cosine ratio

1 a i AC **ii** AB
   b i EF **ii** DF
   c i GH **ii** GI
   d i KL **ii** JK

2 a $\frac{5}{12}$ **b** $\frac{5}{13}$

3 a $a = ch$ **b** $h = \frac{a}{c}$

4 a

Triangle	Adjacent length	Hypotenuse length	$\frac{\text{adjacent}}{\text{hypotenuse}}$ (1 d.p.)
P	5 cm	6.1 cm	0.8
Q	7 cm	8.5 cm	0.8
R	14.3 cm	17.5 cm	0.8

b The ratio $\frac{\text{adjacent}}{\text{hypotenuse}}$ is always 0.8.

5 a

Triangle	Adjacent length	Hypotenuse length	$\frac{\text{adjacent}}{\text{hypotenuse}}$ (1 d.p.)
P	5 cm	6.5 cm	0.8
Q	7 cm	9.1 cm	0.8
R	11.9 cm	15.6 cm	0.8

b The ratio $\frac{\text{adjacent}}{\text{hypotenuse}}$ is always 0.8.

6 The ratio of the adjacent side to the hypotenuse in similar right-angled triangles is the same.

7 a 0.7 **b** 0.4 **c** 0.9 **d** 0.9

8 a $\frac{4}{7}$ **b** $\frac{2}{5}$ **c** $\frac{25}{75} = \frac{1}{3}$

9 a $x = 10.1$ **b** $x = 4.7$ **c** $x = 36.0$
   d $x = 4.1$ **e** $x = 9.7$ **f** $x = 21.9$

10 193 cm

11 a $x = 9.4$ **b** $x = 15.3$ **c** $x = 114.5$
   d $x = 5.8$ **e** $x = 11.2$ **f** $x = 39.8$

12 a 20.43 m **b** 20.38 m
   c To the nearest 10 cm, the lengths are the same.

13 a cosine; 17.6 cm
   b sine; 7.1 cm
   c tangent; 10.9 cm

Challenge

$a = 9.0$ cm, $b = 12.0$ cm

10.6 Using trigonometry to find angles

1 a Corresponding angles are equal.
   b Corresponding sides are in the same ratio.
   c The trigonometric ratios for corresponding angles are the same.

2 a $\frac{8}{15}$ **b** $\frac{8}{17}$ **c** $\frac{15}{17}$

3 a $s = 13.3$ **b** $x = 11.4$ **c** $y = 31.8$

4 a Students' own suggested lengths, e.g.
   $a = 5$ cm, $b = 4$ cm
   b Right-angled triangle drawn accurately
   c 39°
   d Accurate drawings and angle measurements

5 38.7°

6 a 26.6° **b** 32.0° **c** 36.5°

7 a 59.7° **b** 35.0° **c** 74.7°

8 a 44.4° **b** 48.6° **c** 6.9°

9 a 48.6° **b** 45.6° **c** 22.6°
   d Answers are the same because the ratio $\frac{3}{4}$ is the same as the ratio $\frac{6}{8}$

10 a 72.5° **b** 64.6° **c** 65.2°

11 a 41.4° **b** 48.2° **c** 51.0°

12 a 23.6° **b** 53.1° **c** 53.1° **d** 48.6°
   e 61.9° **f** 39.7°

13 30°

Challenge

a $\angle CAB = 90°$, $\angle ABC = 53.1°$, $\angle ACB = 36.9°$

b $\angle CAB$ is given.

$$\angle ABC = \tan^{-1}\frac{4}{3} = \sin^{-1}\frac{4}{5} = \cos^{-1}\frac{3}{5}$$

$$\angle ACB = \tan^{-1}\frac{3}{4} = \sin^{-1}\frac{3}{5} = \cos^{-1}\frac{4}{5} = 90° - \angle ABC$$

10 Check up

1 B, C, E, F

2 16 cm

3 a Yes (SSS) **b** Yes (ASA)

4 a Angles in triangle PQT: angle P, angle $Q = 90°$, angle T
   Angles in triangle PRS: angle P, angle $R = 90°$, angle S
   Angle T = angle S (corresponding angles)
   The triangles have the same angles (AAA)
   b 4.5 m

5 a i AB **ii** AC **iii** BC
   b i DE **ii** EF **iii** DF
   c i HI **ii** GI **iii** GH

6 $x = 9.3$

7 $x = 7.2$

8 $x = 10.4$

9 66.0°

10 27.0°

Challenge

a Students' own similar and congruent shapes, e.g.
   HQP and BRS, HUF and BTD, and $PFUQ$ and $SDTR$, are congruent in the first design.
b Students' own designs
c No, because lengths and angles will no longer be equal.
   However, if the points are unequally spaced but with some sort of pattern (e.g. if H and B are closer to G and C, but the points on the circle still have a vertical line of symmetry), similar shapes can still be created.

10 Strengthen: Congruence and similarity

1 a, b

2 a i Yes **ii** Yes; A and B are similar
   b i Yes **ii** No; C and D are not similar
   c A, B and H; C, F and I; D, E and G

3 a

Shape	P	Q
Height	5	10
Width	12	x
Hypotenuse	13	y

b 2 **c** $x = 24$, $y = 26$

4 a $x = 1.5$ m, $y = 10$ m
   b $x = 20$, $y = 15$

5 a

Triangle *ABE*		Triangle *ACD*	Reason
∠*BAE*	=	∠*CAD*	Shared angle
∠*ABE*	=	∠*ACD*	Both right angles
∠*BEA*	=	∠*CDA*	Corresponding angles

b

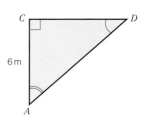

c 4.5 m

6 a i alternate angles
ii alternate angles
iii vertically opposite angles
b The triangles are similar.
c i, ii Students' own diagrams
iii $x = 6$, $y = 6$

7 a Students' own diagrams
b i Yes
ii Are similar, but not necessarily congruent
iii Yes

10 Strengthen: Unknown sides

1 Students' diagrams with opposite, adjacent and hypotenuse correctly labelled

2 a i $\frac{40}{75} = \frac{8}{15}$ **ii** $\frac{28}{45}$ **iii** $\frac{20}{21}$ **iv** $\frac{24}{7}$

 b i $\frac{40}{85} = \frac{8}{17}$ **ii** $\frac{28}{53}$ **iii** $\frac{20}{29}$ **iv** $\frac{24}{25}$

 c i $\frac{75}{85} = \frac{15}{17}$ **ii** $\frac{45}{53}$ **iii** $\frac{21}{29}$ **iv** $\frac{7}{25}$

3 a Students' labelled diagrams
b Triangle 1: 16.2 cm
Triangle 2: 6.5 cm

4 a Students' labelled diagrams
b Triangle 1: 22.4 cm
Triangle 2: 2.9 cm

5 a Students' labelled diagrams
b Triangle 1: 21.0 cm
Triangle 2: 9.8 cm

6 a Students' labelled diagrams
b Triangle 1: 7.0 cm
Triangle 2: 5.2 cm

7 a Students' labelled diagrams
b Triangle 1: 16.4 cm
Triangle 2: 12.4 cm

8 a Students' labelled diagrams
b Triangle 1: 12.1 cm
Triangle 2: 6.5 cm

10 Strengthen: Unknown angles

1 a 16.7° **b** 31.0°
2 a Students' labelled diagrams
b Triangle 1: 40.6°
Triangle 2: 51.3°
3 a 11.5° **b** 23.6°
4 a Students' labelled diagrams
b Triangle 1: 41.8°
Triangle 2: 10.8°
5 a 25.8° **b** 68.0°
6 a Students' labelled diagrams
b Triangle 1: 70.5°
Triangle 2: 58.6°

7 a

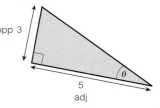

b tangent **c** $\tan\theta = \frac{3}{5}$
d $\theta = \tan^{-1}\frac{3}{5}$ **e** 31.0°

Challenge

a–e Students' own answers

10 Extend

1 a Students' own constructions
b equilateral ($BF = FD = DB$)
2 $x = 9.6$, $y = 13.2$, $z = 16.8$
3 a $x = 12.7$ **b** $x = 24.2$
4 37 m 59 cm or 37.59 m
5 1 m 68 cm or 1.68 m
6 8.6°
7 a 72.5° **b** 66.4°
8 a 10 cm **b** 12 cm **c** 10.4 cm
d No; $AB^2 + BC^2 \neq AC^2$

Challenge

Let h be height of triangle. Let x be the base of the triangle.

$x^2 = \frac{1}{2}xh$ so $h = 2x$

$\tan\theta = \dfrac{2x}{\frac{1}{2}x} = 4$

10 Unit test

1 D, F, H, J
2 a Congruent, SAS
b Similar but not necessarily congruent, AAA
3 a $a = 75°$, $b = 3.1$ cm
b $c = 55°$, $d = 4$ cm
c $e = 50°$, $f = 55°$, $g = 3.1$ cm, $h = 4$ cm
4 4 cm
5 10.3 cm
6 19.5 cm
7 0.5 cm
8 71 mm
9 54.3°
10 7.7 cm
11 38.0°

Challenge

a i 17.5° 72.5°
ii 36.9° 53.1°
iii 53.1° 36.9°
iv 64.2° 25.8°

b They add up to 90°. This is a right-angled triangle, and angles in a triangle add up to 180°, so the remaining two angles must add up to 90°.

Index